The
United States
as a
Debtor
Nation

Institute for International Economics
Center for Global Development

The
United States
as a
Debtor
Nation

William R. Cline

Washington, DC
September 2005

William R. Cline is a senior fellow jointly at the Institute for International Economics and the Center for Global Development. He has been a senior fellow at the Institute since its inception in 1981. During 1996–2001, while on leave from the Institute, he was deputy managing director and chief economist at the Institute of International Finance. He was a senior fellow at the Brookings Institution (1973–81); deputy director of development and trade research, office of the assistant secretary for international affairs, US Treasury Department (1971–73); Ford Foundation visiting professor in Brazil (1970–71); and lecturer and assistant professor of economics at Princeton University (1967–70). His publications include *International Debt: Systemic Risk and Policy Response* (1984), *Exports of Manufactures from Developing Countries* (1984), *The US-Japan Economic Problem* (1985), *Mobilizing Bank Lending to Debtor Countries* (1987), *The Future of World Trade in Textiles and Apparel* (1987), *United States External Adjustment and the World Economy* (1989), *The Economics of Global Warming* (1992), *International Economic Policy in the 1990s* (1994), *International Debt Reexamined* (1995), and *Trade and Income Distribution* (1997).

INSTITUTE FOR INTERNATIONAL ECONOMICS
1750 Massachusetts Avenue, NW
Washington, DC 20036-1903
(202) 328-9000 FAX: (202) 659-3225
www.iie.com

C. Fred Bergsten, *Director*
Valerie Norville, *Director of Publications and Web Development*
Edward Tureen, *Director of Marketing*

CENTER FOR GLOBAL DEVELOPMENT
1776 Massachusetts Avenue, NW
 Suite 301
Washington, DC 20036
(202) 416-0700 FAX: (202) 416-0750
www.cgdev.org

Nancy Birdsall, *President*

Typesetting and printing by Automated Graphic Systems, Inc.

Printed in the United States of America
07 06 05   5 4 3 2 1

Library of Congress Cataloging-in-Publication Data

Cline, William R.
  The United States as a debtor nation : risks and policy response / William R. Cline.
    p. cm.
  Includes bibliographical references and index.
  ISBN 0-88132-399-3 (alk. paper)
    1. Debts External—United States.
  2. Balance of trade—United States.
  3. United States—Commercial policy.
  4. Investments, American. I. Center for Global Development. II. Institute for International Economics (U.S.) III. Title.
  HJ8119.C55 2005
  336.3′4′0973—dc22   2005018957

The views expressed in this publication are those of the author. This publication is part of the overall program of the Institute and the Center, as endorsed by their Boards of Directors, but does not necessarily reflect the views of individual members of the Boards or the Advisory Committees.

Contents

Figures

Preface

The United States has swung from being the world's largest creditor to the largest debtor nation in accounting terms. Measured by the net international investment position (NIIP), the United States had net external liabilities of $2.5 trillion at the end of 2004, or 22 percent of GDP. The current account (goods and services, transfers, and capital income) was approximately in balance in 1991 but was massively in deficit last year, at about $670 billion (about 6 percent of GDP).

For some time the Institute for International Economics has been concerned about the financial and economic risks posed by this large deficit if capital inflows from the rest of the world were cut back because of a break in confidence and/or domestic politics shifted in a protectionist direction. To respond to these concerns, the Institute published *Is the U.S. Trade Deficit Sustainable?* by Catherine Mann in 1999 and the conference volumes *Dollar Overvaluation and the World Economy* in 2003 and *Dollar Adjustment: How Far? Against What?* in 2004, both edited by C. Fred Bergsten and John Williamson.

This is also an important subject for the Center for Global Development. This book is the first in the Center's nearly four-year history dealing with the effects of macroeconomic conditions in the United States on the developing world. Over decades the broad effects of the US economy have been strongly positive for the world's poor, with the notable exception of the interest-rate shock and severe recession in the early 1980s, which contributed to the Latin American debt crisis. A healthy US economy may matter more for the developing world than any particular aid or even trade policy. On the other hand, as the analysis in this book suggests, weaknesses in the US economy, and shortcomings in macro management in Washington, can also create serious (if unintended) risks not only for the United States's major trading and security partners but also for consumers and small producers in Africa, Asia, and Latin America.

William R. Cline is a joint senior fellow at the Center for Global Development and the Institute for International Economics. He wrote on the problem of US external imbalances in his 1989 Institute book, *United States External Adjustment and the World Economy*, which dealt with the 1980s episode of severe dollar overvaluation. But the previous record US deficit peaked in 1987 at 3.4 percent of GDP annually, suggesting that the risks this time around could be much larger. In this new study, Cline projects the current account deficit at about 7½ percent of GDP and the NIIP at −50 percent of GDP by 2010 in the absence of corrective measures. The gap and net liabilities would be even larger were it not for some corrective impact already in the pipeline from the decline of the dollar in 2002–04. This study confirms other recent Institute work suggesting that another 20 percent or so of foreign currency appreciation against the dollar will be needed, along with a reduction in the growth of domestic demand in the United States and some acceleration of foreign growth, to bring the current account deficit back down to a range of 3 percent of GDP, which is consistent with stabilizing net foreign liabilities at a long-term ceiling of about 50 percent of GDP.

This study breaks new ground, however, by examining the stock of international assets and liabilities as well as the annual flow of current account deficits. It finds that a surprising number of industrial countries are net debtors and that there tends to be a correlation between faster growth and rising net debt. This is contrary to the traditional debt cycle theory, which predicts that capital will flow from rich creditor countries to developing debtor countries. There would seem to be something fundamentally perverse about the present situation, in which a large number of developing countries are running current account surpluses and financing the deficit of the United States, meaning that capital is flowing from developing countries to the largest and richest economy instead of in the opposite direction. Moreover, today this capital is largely financing US private and public consumption rather than productive investment.

In a careful analysis of US net foreign liabilities, Cline finds that there are important favorable valuation effects for the United States. Unlike developing countries, the United States owes foreigners mainly in its own currency. Hence when the dollar depreciates, US liabilities do not rise but rather the dollar value of US direct investment and portfolio equity abroad increases. Without about $900 billion in gains from exchange rate valuation effects from a falling dollar in 2002–04, US net liabilities at the end of 2004 would have been about 30 percent of GDP instead of 22 percent. Perhaps even more important, systematically higher earnings on

US direct investment abroad than on foreign direct investment in the United States have kept the capital income balance positive despite the swing into sizable overall net liabilities. Cline suggests that the best measure of debt burden is in fact the capitalized value of net capital income; by this measure, the United States is not yet a net debtor though his projections show it soon will be.

Cline develops a simple general equilibrium model that shows the key role that adjustment of the US fiscal deficit will need to play in external adjustment, in combination with further correction of the dollar. On this issue he challenges some recent suggestions that fiscal adjustment would have only a minor impact on the trade deficit. He similarly challenges the hypothesis that America's trade deficit was imposed by a collapse of investment abroad and instead points to the huge swing of the United States itself from fiscal surplus to deficit, by 6 percent of GDP from 2000 to 2004. He then reviews the policy debate on the sustainability of the US external deficit, suggesting that chances for the classic "hard landing" for the dollar and the economy are probably still less than even but are rising with the current account deficit. He considers that the ultimate problem of the external imbalance may be not so much a pending crisis and recession but an inequitable distribution of consumption between the present decade and the one after this, when a sharp correction in the trade deficit and corresponding cut in consumption will have become almost inevitable.

The study emphasizes the challenge facing the rest of the world economy as the United States adjusts. The widening US trade deficit has boosted demand for exports from other countries, especially in the developing world, and they will need to shift away from reliance on exports toward domestic demand. A smooth international adjustment process is crucial to the health of developing economies because they would be severely affected by a US hard landing involving major recession and high interest rates. Cline shows that, even in the late 1980s adjustment, there was an uncanny mirror image between the narrowing US trade deficit and a reduction in growth rates of the non-G7 countries (from 5.2 percent in 1987 to 2.5 percent in 1992).

This time around the stakes are even higher. The rise in developing countries' trade balances with the United States from 1992 to 2002 boosted demand by 3.6 percent of developing-country GDP. A sudden, wrenching end to this episode of US imbalances could sharply depress demand for exports from developing countries and renew pressures on their external debt if accompanied by a surge in interest rates. Yet many of the developing countries, especially China and several other Asian economies, have become part of the adjustment problem because they have held their exchange rates against the dollar virtually unchanged, whereas most industrial countries have experienced sizable appreciations against the dollar since early 2002.

The study develops a model to examine the optimal allocation of further exchange rate appreciation across countries, depending on the state of their current account balances, that will be the necessary counterpart of US external adjustment. The currencies of several Asian developing countries will need to appreciate against the dollar by 30 percent or considerably more, although in a coordinated realignment the corresponding increases in their trade-weighted real effective exchange rates would be much smaller. The resulting reductions in their trade surpluses would be on a manageable scale, in contrast to much larger trade shocks that might occur with a hard landing for the US economy. Cline calls for an international Plaza or Smithsonian agreement, especially for Asian currencies, to carry out a coordinated appreciation of exchange rates against the dollar since each country fears loss of its own competitiveness if it appreciates in isolation. As part of an international adjustment package, he calls for the United States to adopt credible measures to eliminate its fiscal deficit by 2010. The study closes with consideration of less palatable measures of trade penalties (supported by IMF determination of inappropriate exchange rate policy) against countries deliberately preventing currency appreciation. It also considers the possibility that the United States may need to adopt some tax disincentive to capital inflows if private foreign investors continue to seek the US market so avidly that they push the US net foreign asset position ever deeper into debt even after foreign governments desist from piling up dollar reserves to keep their currencies weak.

This book is bound to have a long half-life. As Kenneth Rogoff, a reviewer, said, "Unlike the usual journalistic writings on the US current account that are passed off as serious research, Cline's analysis is solidly anchored in theory and data. The book contains a sober and careful summary of the main alternative points of view. Many people will use Cline's book to teach because it goes some way toward putting all the different approaches into a common framework." We hope it makes a difference—not only to the debate but also to the official decisions needed to correct the situation.

The Institute for International Economics is a private, nonprofit institution for the study and discussion of international economic policy. Its purpose is to analyze important issues in that area and to develop and communicate practical new approaches for dealing with them. The Institute is completely nonpartisan.

The Institute is funded by a highly diversified group of philanthropic foundations, private corporations, and interested individuals. Major institutional grants are now being received from the William M. Keck, Jr. Foundation and the Starr Foundation. About 33 percent of the Institute's resources in our latest fiscal year were provided by contributors outside the United States, including about 16 percent from Japan.

The Institute's Board of Directors bears overall responsibilities for the Institute and gives general guidance and approval to its research program, including the identification of topics that are likely to become important over the medium run (one to three years) and that should be addressed by the Institute. The director, working closely with the staff and outside Advisory Committee, is responsible for the development of particular projects and makes the final decision to publish an individual study.

The Center for Global Development is an independent, nonprofit policy research organization dedicated to reducing global poverty and inequality and to making globalization work for the poor. Through a combination of research and strategic outreach, the Center actively engages policymakers and the public to influence the policies of the United States, other rich countries, and such institutions as the World Bank, the IMF, and the World Trade Organization (WTO) to improve economic and social development prospects in poor countries. The Center's Board of Directors bears overall responsibility for the Center and includes distinguished leaders of nongovernmental organizations, former officials, business executives and some of the world's leading scholars of development. The Center receives advice on its research and policy programs from the Board and from an Advisory Committee that comprises respected development specialists and advocates.

The Center's president works with the Board, the Advisory Committee, and the Center's senior staff in setting the research and program priorities, and approves all formal publications. The Center is supported by an initial significant financial contribution from Edward W. Scott Jr. and by funding from philanthropic foundations and other organizations.

The Institute and Center hope that their studies and other activities will contribute to building a stronger foundation for international economic policy around the world. We invite readers of these publications to let us know how they think we can best accomplish this objective.

NANCY BIRDSALL	C. FRED BERGSTEN
President	Director
Center for Global Development	Institute for International Economics
August 2005	August 2005

Acknowledgments

I thank Rachel Block for excellent, painstaking research assistance. For comments on all or portions of an earlier draft, I thank, without implicating, the following individuals: Tamim Bayoumi, C. Fred Bergsten, Olivier Blanchard, Barry Bosworth, Christopher Erceg, Kristin Forbes, Joseph Gagnon, Pierre-Olivier Gourinchas, Edward Gramlich, Steven Kamin, Nicholas Lardy, Catherine Mann, Gian Maria Milesi-Ferretti, Michael Mussa, Jacques Polak, Kenneth Rogoff, Richard Sabot, Charles Siegman, Edwin Truman, Thomas Willett, and John Williamson.

Overview

The United States has once again entered into a period of large external imbalances. This time, the current account deficit, at nearly 6 percent of GDP in 2004, is much larger than during the last episode, when the deficit peaked at about 3.4 percent of GDP in 1987.[1] Indeed, the deficit is larger than at any other time in the 135 years for which data are available (figure 0.1). Moreover, the deficit is on track to become substantially larger over the next several years.

Policymakers and economists have been divided as to whether the large external deficit is a problem, and if so, what should be done about it. This study argues that the external imbalance is a serious problem, and that its correction requires both forceful US fiscal adjustment and further depreciation of the dollar. Resolving the problem will also require adjustment measures abroad, most notably exchange rate appreciation in China, East Asia, and to a lesser degree in other regions, as well as increased domestic demand abroad to sustain growth as the stimulus from trade surpluses with the United States grows smaller.

This study seeks to advance the debate by integrating analysis of the growing "stock" of external debt with the "flow" of current account deficits. In the long term, the stock issue determines whether there is a

---

1. The "current account" is the sum of the balance between exports and imports of goods and services ("trade balance"), net transfer payments, and net capital income. In 2004, the trade balance was -5.3 percent of GDP, the balance on transfers was -0.6 percent of GDP, and the balance on capital income was $+0.25$ percent of GDP (BEA 2005c).

Figure 0.1 US current account balance as a percent of GDP, 1869–2004

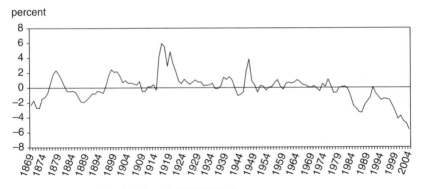

Sources: Jones and Obstfeld (2001); BEA (2005c).

problem. If the rest of the world were willing to finance the US current account deficit with outright grants-in-aid, then there would be no burden of future repayment, and no economic grounds for concern about the current account deficit (although there might still be political grounds, given potential protectionist pressures from large trade deficits). Instead, the United States incurs real debt obligations when it borrows abroad to finance the current account deficit, and building up this debt imposes a burden on future generations already beset by prospective increases in Social Security and Medicare-Medicaid obligations. Even though the true burden of the debt to date is much less than that implied by the accounting definition of US net foreign liabilities (see chapter 2), the trend implied by the growing current account deficit would mean a large future burden. This is especially the case because the resources coming from abroad are currently financing high levels of consumption and large fiscal deficits rather than high levels of investment.

In the near term, there is also a problem associated with potential crises of confidence. If foreign investors and central banks were to sharply curb their financing of the US current account deficit, there could be a wrenching impact on financial markets and the real economy. Although many (including in the official sector) have downplayed the likelihood of such a "disorderly adjustment" or "hard landing," the risk of such an outcome is high enough that it cannot be dismissed and should be taken into account in prudent policy formation.

Several factors have contributed to the widening of the current account deficit from a zero balance in 1991. The investment boom associated with the "new economy" in the late 1990s induced large capital inflows, whose counterpart was a large trade deficit. After the stock market bubble burst in 2000 and investment decelerated, the demand for outside resources was replaced by a decline in private saving and a large swing in the fiscal accounts from surplus to deficit (government dissaving). Higher prices for oil also contributed by 2004 and early 2005, and a slowdown in domestic investment and rising trade surpluses in East Asia and Latin America after the financial crises in 1997–98 also played a role. For US policy purposes, however, this study argues that it would be seriously mistaken to adopt the passive position that the deficit has largely been imposed by circumstances beyond US control, and on this basis, rationalize inaction on fiscal adjustment and indifference to needed exchange rate appreciation by important foreign economies not allowing their currencies to adjust.

This study begins by considering a potentially important dimension of US external imbalances: the transformation of the United States' net international investment position (NIIP) from large net-creditor to large net-debtor status. US external assets exceeded liabilities by about 11 percent of GDP in the early 1970s. By the late 1980s, the position was down to about zero. By 2004, the NIIP had reached net liabilities of about 22 percent of GDP.

The United States has had three major episodes of external imbalances and downward pressures on the dollar during recent decades. The first, in the early 1970s, led to the breakdown of the Bretton Woods regime of fixed exchange rates, which proved unsustainable because the rigidity of global pegging of exchange rates to the dollar imposed a straitjacket that prevented the United States from correcting balance of payments problems. The second episode was dollar overvaluation in the early 1980s, followed by large deficits and the need for coordinated action to correct the dollar through the Plaza Accord of 1985. The United States is now squarely in a third episode, which so far has been marked by a large rise and then major decline of the dollar against the euro and several other industrial-country currencies, and by the large external deficit. The cumulative effect of these rounds of imbalances has been to reduce the NIIP by about 33 percent of GDP, converting the United States from a creditor to a debtor nation by this measure.

This loss of net foreign assets, and the much larger current account deficit during the present episode compared with that of the 1980s, are two major reasons for concern that adjustment of the US external imbalance could prove more difficult this time around. In particular, even though the United States successfully avoided such "hard landings" as severe recession and a sharp decline in the dollar in the last episode of external adjustment, there is no assurance it will be able to do so this time in view of a deficit nearly twice as large and a weaker international asset position.

Chapter 1 approaches the problem from the standpoint of the international debt cycle, and asks whether the large US net debtor position can be understood in terms of theories about natural "stages" of creditor or debtor status as economies grow. The classical debt cycle theory holds that capital flows from creditor rich countries where capital is abundant to debtor developing countries where it is scarce and its rate of return is higher. The US position is an aberration in this framework, but chapter 1 finds that the United States is not unique. Several other industrial countries, notably Australia and Canada, have been net debtors and have run persistent current account deficits. The analysis finds that these countries have tended to have more rapid growth than the industrial countries fitting the traditional pattern of net creditor with current account surplus. This suggests that for debt cycle purposes, there has been a certain logic to departures from the expected pattern on grounds that some of the industrial countries are more aptly characterized as "developing" for purposes of relative return and directions of capital flows. This justification for US external deficits loses force, however, when large capital inflows are going primarily to finance fiscal deficits and to compensate for low levels of private saving, rather than to finance high investment. That is the case today, in contrast to the late 1990s, when there were large fiscal surpluses, but the private saving rate had not fallen as far as it has by now, and investment was high.

Chapter 2 examines the US NIIP more closely and finds a strong and persistent favorable difference between the rate of return on US direct investment abroad and foreign direct investment in the United States. This difference has meant that net capital earnings have remained positive even as the United States has become a large "net debtor nation" whose liabilities (including direct and portfolio equity capital) substantially exceed assets as measured by the accounting of the NIIP. Another advantageous feature of US external liabilities is that, unlike those of most other nations, they are denominated in the US home currency. This means that when the dollar depreciates, there is a windfall gain instead of a shock to the burden of external debt—the opposite of what happened in East Asia in 1997–98 and Argentina in 2002. The dollar value of liabilities remains unchanged, but the dollar values rise for equity assets owned abroad, which are typically denominated in foreign currency. These two features of US external assets and liabilities have helped curb the erosion of the NIIP to a slower pace than would otherwise have been expected from the cumulation of annual current account deficits.

Chapter 2 closes with an examination of the underlying concept of net external liabilities, in terms of long-term debt burden and short-term vulnerability. It suggests a measure of economically meaningful net foreign assets, based on the capitalized value of annual net capital income (CNCI). The discussion argues that the CNCI is a better gauge of long-term debt burden than the conventional accounting measure (NIIP). By the CNCI measure, US net external assets were still positive at the end of 2004 (at about 7 percent of GDP). The expected future trend of CNCI, however, is also strongly adverse.

Chapter 3 develops a simple model for forecasting the US current account deficit and net foreign assets (both economic CNCI and accounting NIIP). The baseline projections through 2010 indicate that the current account deficit would reach approximately 7½ percent of GDP by then in the absence of further exchange rate correction. Net external liabilities would reach about 52 percent of GDP as measured by the conventional NIIP, and about 22 percent even using the CNCI concept. The chapter also reviews other widely reported projections that show even more severe widening of the deficits. Those projections are less favorable because they tend not to incorporate either the dose of adjustment already in the pipeline from the decline of the dollar in 2003–04 or the favorable differential in the rate of return on foreign assets versus liabilities. Their qualitative implications are nonetheless the same as those in this study: The US external deficit is headed toward even larger magnitudes, strongly suggesting it eventually will be unsustainable.

Chapter 3 quantifies impact parameters indicating the extent of current account adjustment that can be expected from given amounts of dollar depreciation, accelerated foreign growth, or diminished domestic growth. Alternative simulations indicate that to reduce the US current account deficit to a more sustainable level of 3 to 3.5 percent of GDP by 2008–10, it will be necessary for foreign currencies to appreciate in real terms by about another 20 percent against the dollar from the level already attained in the January–May 2005 average, even with favorable assumptions about foreign growth. Foreign currencies had already risen in real terms by about 15 percent from the 2002 average to the average for the first five months of 2005 (using the Federal Reserve's broad real exchange rate index). This key finding indicates that the dollar has a considerable distance to fall further in order to restore a more sustainable current account balance, as also emphasized by Bergsten and Williamson (2004) and Mussa (2005).

Chapter 4 examines the fiscal imbalance that is part of the underlying problem of the US external imbalance. The US federal budget swung from a surplus of 2.4 percent of GDP in 2000 to a deficit of 3.6 percent of GDP in 2004. A decline in fiscal revenue by 4.7 percent of GDP was the driving force in the erosion, and by 2004, the bulk of this decline was attributable to the tax cuts of the first administration of President George W. Bush. The discussion considers the long-term fiscal problems posed by Social Security and, far worse, Medicare and Medicaid. The chapter's appendix develops a simple general equilibrium model designed to integrate the effects of fiscal adjustment and exchange rate adjustment in correcting the US external imbalance. The central message of the simulations of the model is that further depreciation of the dollar will have to be accompanied by a large fiscal correction if major external adjustment is to be achieved. Otherwise, the potential trade effects of a more competitive dollar will be dissipated by higher inflation and higher interest rates that partially bid the dollar back up, and real resources will not be sufficiently allocated away from government and private consumption toward use for increased exports.

Chapter 5 then examines the risks posed by the external deficit. The analysis first looks at whether foreign holdings of US assets have risen so fast that there is a risk of portfolio satiation, and hence reduced willingness of foreigners to accumulate even more assets by financing ongoing (and widening) deficits. US gross external liabilities rose from about 6 percent of the gross financial assets of the rest of the world (including domestic assets) in the early 1990s to about 14½ percent by 2004, and the baseline projections show this share rising to about 16 percent by 2010. This rapid increase suggests possible limits to future buildups, even allowing for some reduction in "home bias" in portfolios from traditional levels. The chapter gives special attention to the explosion of official foreign reserve holdings of US dollar assets, particularly by the central banks of Japan, China, and several other East Asian economies. Also noted are the signs that central banks want to diversify away from the dollar. In addition, the chapter examines the possibility of a surge in interest rates in the event that further accumulation of dollar reserves by foreign central banks comes to an end.

Chapter 5 also looks at the classic "hard landing" scenario of recession caused by higher interest rates provoked by a cutoff in foreign capital inflows. Although not the most likely outcome in the near term—in part because the Federal Reserve would likely only raise the policy interest rate if the economy were overheating—a hard landing for the economy becomes a more likely possibility as the current account deficit widens.

Traditional benchmarks for "dangerous" levels of the stock of external debt are then considered. Because these levels typically have been identified for developing countries, however, they are found to be inapplicable to the United States. Other statistical studies have shown that the debt difficulties of industrial countries do not show the same relationship to debt-to-GDP ratios as those of developing countries. The denomination of the United States' external liabilities in its own currency further reduces the relevance of developing-country debt benchmarks to the US economy. Nonetheless, chapter 5 suggests that flow problems—that is, a larger deficit than capital markets are willing to finance—can arise even if the debt stock problem is not acute. The chapter cites the international disagreement on the dollar and interest rates in 1987, which contributed to a run-up in US interest rates and a severe correction in the US stock market.

Chapter 5 closes with a review of the debate among economists over the sustainability of the current account deficit, and of the evolving perceptions of US policymakers toward greater concern about this issue, especially as the fiscal accounts have swung from surplus to deficit.

Chapter 6 examines the implications of US external adjustment for the rest of the world. It reviews what happened in the previous adjustment episode in the late 1980s, and finds that even though the United States avoided the feared hard landing, there were considerable signs of deceleration in foreign growth, especially for developing countries, as the United States curbed its external deficit. So far, during the present episode, the dominant influence of the widening US deficit has been to provide a strong source of demand stimulating growth in the rest of the world beyond levels that otherwise would have been attained. The potential negative spillover of higher interest rates spurred by the rising US demand on global capital has not proven to be significant, in part because of the sharp drop in US interest rates reflecting the phasing of the business cycle.

The discussion rejects the argument made by some that developing countries have been forced against their will by an inadequate international financial system to build up excessive and costly reserves. On the contrary, the large accumulations of reserves by such countries as China, Hong Kong, Taiwan, Malaysia, and even India have on balance been a part of the problem of international imbalances rather than a manifestation of damage inflicted by the financial system. Instead of building up excessive reserves, these economies should have been allowing their currencies to appreciate against the dollar, thereby participating in the global adjustment process that is needed to curb US external deficits. The chapter develops a simple model to identify the extent of exchange rate appreciation needed by individual major economies to be consistent with reduction of the US external deficit to a more sustainable level of about 3 percent of GDP. These currency adjustments are related to the size of current account surpluses. It is found that, whereas the euro and some other industrial-country currencies had already accomplished most of the needed appreciation by end-2004 (some of which was eroded by the dollar's subsequent rally through mid-2005), the Japanese yen had not done so, and the Chinese renminbi and several other Asian currencies in particular had carried out almost none of the needed real appreciation.

At the same time, the analysis indicates that, whereas the real appreciations needed against the dollar remain large, in trade-weighted terms they are much smaller, because a wide array of competing economies would be appreciating against the dollar at the same time and hence not losing competitiveness against each other. The chapter suggests that there is a "prisoners' dilemma" problem that discourages each country individually from being the first to allow its exchange rate to rise against the dollar, so that some form of international coordination may be required to facilitate the adjustments.

Chapter 7 concludes with an enumeration of the principal findings of this study in greater qualitative and quantitative detail than presented in this overview. The chapter then turns to policy implications, paramount among them the need for a large US fiscal adjustment. The other broad implication is the need for some means to obtain a widespread appreciation of currencies against the dollar, along the lines modeled in chapter 6. The discussion suggests some sort of agreement along the lines of the Plaza Accord (1985) or, more aptly, the Smithsonian Agreement of 1971, to coordinate such a realignment of exchange rates. Part of the problem is that today's monetary regime has in meaningful ways regressed to the fixed-rate regime of Bretton Woods. Not only have there been outright pegs of the Chinese renminbi, Hong Kong dollar, and Malaysian ringgit to the US dollar, but, in addition, the "fear of floating" in effect pegs numerous other developing-country currencies to the dollar. The overall effect is partially to recreate a straitjacket for the dollar (albeit this time through numerous bindings by smaller economies) similar to that at the end of the Bretton Woods system.

Although the optimal policy would likely be some form of coordinated appreciation against the dollar, chapter 7 also considers second-best alternatives if numerous countries with surpluses resist appreciation, an issue that so far has primarily been focused on China but applies more broadly. The United States might have a legitimate basis for imposing countervailing duties on imports from countries judged to be subsidizing exports by keeping their currencies artificially undervalued. A determination by the International Monetary Fund that certain countries were "manipulating" their exchange rates by heavy intervention could strengthen such a case. The possibility of such penalties might help prompt countries to allow their exchange rates to rise against the dollar. However, it would only be appropriate to consider such an approach after the United States had first placed its own house in order by adopting a credible plan to eliminate the fiscal deficit over a reasonable period. Finally, the chapter suggests that if large capital inflows into the United States continue to keep the dollar overvalued and provoke continued widening in the current account deficit, it could become desirable to impose a withholding tax on foreign earnings on assets held in the United States as a disincentive to these inflows.

The International Debt Cycle and the United States as an External Debtor

One of the greatest anomalies in the world economy today is that the United States has ceased being a net supplier of capital to developing countries and, after several years of large current account deficits, has itself become the world's largest debtor nation at least in accounting terms.[1] Neoclassical theory suggests the contrary—that rich countries with relatively abundant capital will tend to have a lower return on capital than poorer countries, and that capital will thus flow from rich to poor countries.

This chapter first reviews the "debt cycle" theory of the expected phases of capital flows and international asset position as a country grows, and considers the relevance of this theory to the US case. It then examines the empirical information on international creditor and debtor status for the principal industrial and developing economies. The United States is in fact only one of several industrial countries that are in a debtor phase of the debt cycle; conversely, several middle-income countries are "creditors." After considering the global data discrepancy between net-liability countries and net-asset countries, the analysis finds some empirical support for the idea that higher growth is the spur to capital inflows to those industrial countries that seem to be in the anomalous position of being net debtors.

International debt cycle theory helps provide a conceptual framework for judging whether the US external deficit is a problem. In short, the

---

1. "Debtor" or "creditor" status is used here in the broad sense as being in net-liability or net-asset status in terms of net international investment position, which includes direct investment, portfolio equities, and international reserves as well as debt.

diagnosis in this chapter is that the United States paradoxically is in the position of a "young debtor country" rather than being a "mature creditor" as might have been expected from its high levels of income and wealth. It is also found, however, that several other industrial countries are also in this paradoxical position, and, moreover, that the countries in this position have tended to experience more rapid growth, providing some confirmation to the notion that they may usefully be seen as still "developing." By implication, this chapter does not provide a basis for judging that the US current account deficit and external liabilities have already become too large for safety. It is only in the forward-looking analysis beginning in chapter 3 that the question of sustainability of the external imbalance going forward is addressed. The reader for whom a review of the debt cycle framework is secondary may wish to proceed directly to chapter 2, which examines key special advantageous factors slowing the buildup of US external debt, and then move to the projections and policy analyses beginning in chapter 3.

The Debt Cycle

International economists have for a long time both formally and informally understood international capital flows as being likely to follow a "debt cycle" linked to the stage of a country's development.[2] For example, Kindleberger (1958, 417) wrote that, traditionally, economists had identified four phases of the debt cycle—young debtor, mature debtor, young creditor, and mature creditor—based on net international asset position and on whether the external current account balance was positive or negative. The young debtor not only has net external debt, but is also building up this debt further by running annual current account deficits. The mature debtor, in contrast, runs current account surpluses and is in the process of repaying external debt. The young creditor has reached a position of positive net international assets and is continuing to build its creditor position by running current account surpluses. The mature creditor, like a senior citizen living on accumulated savings, is still in a net positive international asset position, but is running down its assets by running a current account deficit.

Figure 1.1 summarizes the cycle, which in principle involves clockwise advance from the northwest corner to the southwest corner. As the experience of the United States and some other industrial countries suggests, however, there may be more than one historical spin around this cycle.

---

2. The author would like to thank C. Fred Bergsten and Shafiqul Islam for their unpublished research in the late 1980s on the conceptual, empirical, and policy issues raised by the shift of the United States into net debtor status.

Figure 1.1 The debt cycle

	Current account < 0	Current account > 0
Foreign assets < liabilities	Young debtor	Mature debtor
Foreign assets > liabilities	Mature creditor	Young creditor

The optimal growth literature contains analyses seeking to confirm, qualify, or dispute the idea that there is a normal (clockwise) debt cycle in the process of economic growth. Fischer and Frenkel (1974) develop a simple two-sector model for a small economy facing fixed international terms of trade and interest rates to explore the optimal time path for external debt.[3] They show that under certain conditions, but not all, the optimal path will look like that in the traditional debt cycle, with the country moving from young to mature debtor and then from young to mature creditor. Their qualitative summation is as follows:

> Initially, since the levels of wealth and capital are relatively low, saving (the flow demand for securities) falls short of investment (the flow supply of securities); thus the economy becomes a net seller of securities, corresponding to a surplus in the capital account of the balance of payments and to an increase in the net debtor position. This process continues until the steady rise in wealth induces enough saving to match the flow supply of securities (which is declining through time as the capital stock is rising). At this point in time the capital account is balanced. As wealth continues to rise, saving exceeds the flow supply of securities and the economy becomes a net lender and thus reduces its net debtor position. (Fischer and Frenkel 1974, 513)

---

3. In the highly stylized model, there are two sectors: a consumption good and an investment good. Stability of the model (but not necessarily economic logic) requires that the consumption good be more capital-intensive than the investment good. Consumption is a function of real wealth and the international interest rate (permanent income hypothesis). Steady state per capita net ownership of foreign assets equals the excess of steady state per capita wealth over the per capita value of the domestic capital stock plus per capita human capital (wage rate divided by the international interest rate). Steady state equilibrium occurs when capital stock rises just enough to keep pace with population growth and investment equals saving. This means the country is no longer either accumulating external debt or external assets at the steady state. However, depending on the initial conditions, the country can "overshoot" from debtor to creditor before returning to zero net change in external assets (the debt stage tradition), or it can approach the steady state smoothly and asymptotically by running down large initial net external assets or reducing large initial net external debt.

In contrast, Bazdarich (1978, 426) applies optimal control theory to the same basic model and concludes instead that "the optimal growth plan of an economy will show no tendency to pass through such stages in its payments accounts. Rather, a developing economy will always be a net debtor and net borrower, with its net debt position monotonically approaching some long-term, steady-state level."[4] The economy accumulates net wealth only if the interest rate exceeds the discount rate (used in maximizing utility over time) plus the population growth rate. If instead the international interest rate is below the discount rate plus the population growth rate, the economy optimally depletes net wealth over time. Per capita capital rises, but an increasing fraction of capital and output is owned by foreigners (Bazdarich 1978, 435). Although this makes sense within the confines of Bazdarich's maximization problem, it does not take into account limits on foreign willingness to lend to the country as its net wealth declines.

Buiter (1981) develops a two-country model with trade and capital flows. This approach may be of special relevance to the United States, because it does not assume that the country is small relative to world markets with fixed terms of trade and fixed international interest rates. There is a single good, which can be used either for consumption or investment, and identical technology in both countries. The author demonstrates that the economy with the higher rate of pure time preference (the time discount rate applied to future consumption even in the absence of any expectation of rising income, or the discount rate for impatience) will run a current account deficit in the steady state, and the other country will run a current account surplus. Buiter (1981, 771) considers this outcome "hardly surprising" but emphasizes that the analysis demonstrates its "rigorous foundation in optimizing behavior."

If one considered the United States to have a higher pure time preference rate than other industrial economies, it might be tempting to expect the United States to be in permanent current account deficit. The recent US tendency toward high fiscal and external deficits is consistent with high pure time preference. However, observed real interest rate trends are not similarly consistent. The best measure of pure time preference is probably the real Treasury bill rate, because this is the rate at which households can transfer consumption over time with no credit or interest rate risk. The average real Treasury bill rate for the United States from 1949 through 2003 was 1.1 percent (IMF 2005a). This is not particularly high—the real Treasury bill rate for Germany from 1971 through 2003 was 2.2 percent,

---

4. In particular, Bazdarich finds that along the optimal path, the rate of growth in external debt per capita equals the price of the investment good relative to the consumption good multiplied by the rate of growth of the capital stock per capita. Assuming that for a developing country the initial per capita capital stock is below the steady state level, the implication is ever-positive growth in external debt.

and for Japan (for which the Treasury bill rate is not available), the average real money market rate was 1.5 percent. So if anything, the revealed pure time preference rate for the United States has historically been lower than that in Europe and Japan. Moreover, the recent US shift into fiscal and ever-widening external deficit has coincided with even lower (negative) real Treasury bill rates, so it is difficult to blame these trends on a higher rate of pure time preference. At a minimum, however, Buiter's analysis suggests that it is not axiomatic that all rich countries will necessarily be creditors, because the model shows at least one dimension in which otherwise identical countries can diverge into debtor or creditor status.

Measuring the Net International Investment Position

In recent years, the International Monetary Fund (IMF) has developed relatively comprehensive estimates for the international investment positions of member countries. In broad terms, a country with a net international investment position (NIIP) of less than zero can be considered a "debtor" country, while a country with a positive NIIP may be seen as a "creditor." This interpretation treats direct investment, portfolio equity, and reserves the same as it treats traditional "debt" instruments (primarily bank loans and bonds). Direct investment abroad (or inward foreign direct investment) creates an asset (liability) that generates earnings (payment obligations), just as lending (borrowing) abroad creates an asset (liability) generating interest income (payments). Inward direct investment will usually pose less of a potential vulnerability than borrowing abroad, for two reasons. First, profits and hence payments to the foreign owner will tend to be procyclical, so that when the domestic economy is weak the burden of profit remittances will also tend to be lower. Second, despite some potential for hedging through borrowing against the direct investment as collateral, in practice plant and equipment will tend to be "nailed down" and less subject to withdrawal during crisis periods than especially short-term debt obligations abroad. For its part, portfolio equity also provides some procyclicality and hence burden-sharing on the earnings side, but it is more "footloose" and hence a source of potential vulnerability in an external crisis.[5] More fundamentally, however, both equity and credit constitute the country's balance sheet vis-à-vis foreigners, and hence ultimately underpin its external creditworthiness.

---

5. In an attempt to address this vulnerability, Malaysia famously froze repatriations of funds from the sale of foreign holdings of domestic portfolio equities during the East Asian financial crisis of the late 1990s.

IMF estimates of the NIIP are available for at least a few recent years for most emerging-market economies and are typically available for the past three decades or so for the industrial countries. To fill in the years with missing data, this study starts from the earliest year available for the NIIP, and then works backward to prior years on a basis of subtracting each year's current account balance from that year's year-end estimate of the NIIP. This process is more fully described in appendix 1A.

An important feature of the NIIP is that, as a residual between assets and liabilities, it does not convey the extent to which the gross magnitudes of both assets and liabilities are large or small relative to GDP. For many countries, both sides of the balance sheet show large stock values, and the difference between them is modest in comparison. One implication is that there can be large proportionate changes in the NIIP from relatively moderate changes (including solely from valuation effects) in gross assets and/or gross liabilities.

Table 1.1 shows the importance of considering both the gross and net international investment positions. For the United States, gross external assets by 2003 were substantial at about 75 percent of GDP, but gross external liabilities were even higher at 97 percent, leaving an NIIP of −22 percent of GDP. Yet when valuation changes occur, and in particular when the dollar depreciates and as a result the dollar translation of direct investment and portfolio equity held abroad increases, the change in the NIIP can differ substantially from what would have been expected just on the basis of the year's current account outcome. Thus, despite a large current account deficit in 2003, the US NIIP as a percent of GDP *increased* (net debt declined) because of valuation effects, primarily from the decline in the dollar.[6] The role of valuation changes in the evolution of the US NIIP is discussed in chapter 2.

The larger the gross asset and liability positions relative to GDP, the greater is the potential for valuation changes to cause major swings in the NIIP as a percent of GDP that diverge from changes solely from the year's current account performance. Countries with exceptionally large gross positions relative to GDP include Ireland (average of gross assets and gross liabilities equal to 845 percent of GDP in 2003), Switzerland (477 percent), the Netherlands (382 percent), Belgium (388 percent), and the United Kingdom (358 percent). In comparison, the average of gross assets and liabilities for the United States stood at 86 percent of GDP, lower than any other industrial country except Japan (65 percent). The

---

6. The current account deficit in 2003 amounted to $520 billion, which was 4.7 percent of GDP (BEA 2005c). However, the favorable valuation change was even larger at $643 billion, composed of about $415 billion exchange rate valuation gain and $230 billion "other" change (including increased coverage; see table 2.1 in chapter 2). As a result, the NIIP improved from −$2.46 trillion at the end of 2002 to −$2.37 trillion at the end of 2003.

Table 1.1 External assets, liabilities, and net international investment position (NIIP), 1990 and 2003 (percent of GDP)

Country	Assets 1990	Assets 2003	Liabilities 1990	Liabilities 2003	NIIP 1990	NIIP 2003
Australia	26.5	72.9	72.3	141.4	−45.8	−68.6
Austria	66.9	174.6	71.1	191.4	−4.2	−16.8
Belgium	203.7	408.8	198.8	366.6	4.9	42.2
Canada	39.6	82.1	77.5	101.8	−37.9	−19.7
Denmark [a,c,d,e]	76.9	114.1	118.8	126.6	−43.4	−7.5
Finland	32.9	180.7	61.6	204.6	−28.7	−24.0
France	60.6	199.9	62.3	192.4	−1.8	7.5
Germany	65.0	164.9	44.9	157.9	20.1	7.1
Greece	n.a.	63.7	n.a.	132.6	−15.7	−68.9
Ireland	n.a.	834.4	n.a.	855.0	−72.3	−20.6
Italy	34.5	106.2	42.2	111.9	−7.7	−5.7
Japan	61.1	83.7	50.3	46.2	10.8	37.5
Netherlands	145.2	378.0	121.4	386.8	23.8	−8.8
New Zealand	19.9	67.0	107.6	153.6	−87.7	−86.7
Norway	42.8	n.a.	58.0	n.a.	−15.2	59.6
Portugal	n.a.	174.0	n.a.	231.1	−2.8	−57.0
Spain	26.2	119.0	38.3	162.3	−12.1	−43.3
Sweden	58.8	184.5	84.2	208.6	−25.4	−24.0
Switzerland	239.9	551.2	147.5	402.9	92.4	148.2
United Kingdom	175.7	356.3	178.1	358.7	−2.5	−2.4
United States	39.5	75.4	42.4	97.0	−2.8	−21.6
Argentina [a,d]	47.4	111.8	53.2	147.3	−5.4	−35.6
Korea	10.9	56.6	7.8	56.6	3.1	−14.2
South Africa [b]	19.1	63.0	31.4	69.2	−12.2	−6.2

n.a. = not available

a. 1991 assets.
b. 2002 assets.
c. 2001 assets.
d. 1991 liabilities.
e. 2001 liabilities.

Source: See appendix 1A.

relatively low ratios of the gross positions relative to GDP for both the United States and Japan reflect the greater size and resultingly lesser openness of the two economies compared with the other industrial countries.

Attention to the gross as well as net asset and liability positions also highlights the potential for divergence between expected and actual capital service burdens in the balance of payments. For the United States in particular, the balance on capital income has remained positive in recent years despite falling as a percent of GDP, even though the large net liability position of about $2.5 trillion (end-2004) might have been expected to generate a large net deficit on capital earnings.[7] This paradox stems

---

7. Thus, in 2004, US earnings on the end-2003 gross foreign assets of $8.3 trillion amounted to $376 billion, for an implicit overall return of 4.5 percent, whereas US payments on end-

from the persistent pattern of higher US earnings on foreign assets than foreign earnings on US liabilities. This paradox is also analyzed in chapter 2.

The Debt Cycle in Practice

Using the NIIP of each country over time, it is possible to conduct an informal review of how the debt cycle theory has tracked actual experience. At the simplest level, the theory has been contradicted by the facts— it has not been the case that industrial countries are systematically creditor countries, although it has been more common that developing countries are debtor countries. Even more surprising, a number of industrial countries, including the United States, have progressively shifted from being net creditor countries to being net debtor countries, and hence have embarked on a new circuit around the debt cycle.

Debt Cycle Patterns

Table 1.2 uses the combination of the average current account balance and the NIIP creditor or debtor position to classify 21 industrial and 24 developing countries into one of the four debt cycle categories of figure 1.1 in each of six subperiods since 1970. The table is based on annual data, assigning 1 to young debtor, 2 to mature debtor, 3 to young creditor, and 4 to mature creditor. The average status in each period is simply the numerical average for the years in question, and the numerical entry can appropriately be rounded off to arrive at the group in which the country belongs on average during that period. For example, in the period 1982–87, Austria is recorded at 1.67, which rounds to 2 and places the country as a mature debtor in that period.

Table 1.2 shades the country periods for creditors. A feature that immediately stands out is that only a minority of countries is in the creditor camp in most periods—that is, the table is mainly unshaded. For the 113 available industrial-country periods, only 46 (or 41 percent) show creditor status. This is perhaps the largest overall surprise, because according to the theory, industrial countries are supposed to be predominantly creditors rather than debtors. In contrast, for the developing countries, the expected debtor status dominates, accounting for 90 of the 106 country

2003 gross foreign liabilities of $10.67 trillion were only $340 billion, an implicit return of 3.2 percent (BEA 2005c, 2005e). Unusually low US interest rates associated with monetary stimulus following the 2001 recession have widened the chronic divergence between the higher rates of return on assets held abroad than on liabilities abroad, but the move toward monetary tightening beginning in mid-2004 is likely to narrow this gap, pushing the capital income account toward lower surplus or deficit.

Table 1.2 Country positions in the debt cycle, 1970–75 to 2000–03

Country	1970–75	1976–81	1982–87	1988–93	1994–99	2000–03
Industrial countries						
Australia	1.33	1.00	1.00	1.00	1.00	1.00
Austria	4.00	2.00	1.67	1.50	1.00	1.25
Belgium		3.83	3.50	3.00	3.00	3.00
Canada	1.17	1.00	1.17	1.00	1.33	2.00
Denmark			1.00	1.67	1.83	2.00
Finland		1.17	1.00	1.00	2.00	2.00
France		3.67	3.83	2.33	2.67	3.00
Germany	3.00	3.50	3.00	3.50	4.00	3.25
Greece		4.00	2.50	1.00	1.17	1.00
Ireland		1.00	1.00	1.50	2.00	1.00
Italy	3.00	3.50	2.50	1.17	2.33	2.50
Japan		3.33	3.00	3.00	3.00	3.00
Netherlands	3.00	3.33	3.00	3.00	2.00	2.00
New Zealand		1.00	1.00	1.00	1.00	1.00
Norway		1.33	1.67	1.83	2.67	3.00
Portugal		4.00	1.50	1.33	1.00	1.00
Spain		1.33	1.50	1.00	1.50	1.00
Sweden	1.50	1.00	1.33	1.00	2.00	2.00
Switzerland		3.33	3.00	3.00	3.00	3.00
United Kingdom	3.50	3.33	3.33	3.00	1.50	1.00
United States	3.33	3.50	4.00	1.67	1.00	1.00
Developing countries						
Argentina		3.50	2.00	1.17	1.00	1.50
Bangladesh		1.00	1.00	1.50	1.17	1.50
Brazil		1.00	1.17	1.67	1.00	1.25
Chile		1.17	1.00	1.00	1.17	1.00
China			2.67	1.83	2.50	3.00
Czech Republic					2.00	1.00
Hong Kong						3.00
Hungary			1.17	1.50	1.00	1.00
India		1.67	1.00	1.00	1.00	1.75
Israel	1.00	1.00	1.33	1.33	1.00	1.25
Korea		2.83	1.33	2.33	1.33	2.00
Malaysia		1.67	1.17	1.33	1.33	2.25
Mexico			1.67	1.00	1.00	1.00
Peru		1.33	1.17	1.00	1.00	1.00
Philippines		1.17	1.17	1.00	1.33	2.00
Poland		1.00	1.00	1.17	1.33	1.00
Russia					3.00	2.75
Singapore		1.00	1.17	2.00	2.33	3.00
South Africa	1.00	1.67	1.50	2.00	1.17	1.50
Taiwan			3.00	3.00	3.00	3.00
Thailand		4.00	2.67	1.00	1.33	2.00
Turkey		1.00	1.00	1.50	1.33	1.25
Ukraine					1.17	2.00
Venezuela	1.50	1.67	1.50	1.50	1.83	2.50

Notes: 1 = young debtor; 2 = mature debtor; 3 = young creditor; 4 = mature creditor. Creditor country-periods are shaded.

periods (85 percent). Nonetheless, as of 2000–03, fully half of the developing countries were in the "mature debtor" or higher stage, meaning that they were running current account surpluses rather than deficits.[8] The large incidence of current account surpluses among developing countries suggests a distortion in the recent pattern of international capital flows that is the flip side of the large current account deficits in the United States (along with current account deficits in Australia, Austria, Greece, Ireland, New Zealand, Portugal, Spain, and the United Kingdom).

Industrial-country debtors divide into two groups. The first includes countries persistently in debtor status during the past three decades: Australia, Canada, Denmark, Finland, Ireland, New Zealand, Spain, and Sweden. The second includes several countries that began as creditors but then shifted into debtor status: Austria, Greece, the Netherlands, Portugal, the United Kingdom, and the United States.[9] This second grouping shows that the United States is by no means unique among industrial countries in having shifted from creditor to (accounting) debtor status.

More generally, the progression from one stage of the cycle to the next is often not what one would expect. The debt cycle framework would predict that in each period, the country's status number in table 1.2 would be either the same as in the previous period or higher. The traditional theory does not envision backsliding. However, in 36 of the 113 industrial-country periods (32 percent), the debt cycle number is smaller than in the period before, violating one-way development. The figure is almost as high for developing countries (28 of 106 cases, or 26 percent).

Fitting the Mold: Industrial-Country Creditors

As suggested in table 1.2, only a handful of industrial countries have been persistent creditors in recent years. Switzerland has been in a league of its own, building a net creditor position that has consistently been several times as high as that of other industrial creditor countries and reaching an NIIP of about 140 percent of GDP by 2000–03 (figure 1.2). Japan has become the world's largest creditor country in absolute terms (at $1.61 trillion in 2003), but it ranks only fourth in NIIP relative to GDP (at an average of 33 percent in 2000–03), behind Switzerland, Belgium (50 per-

---

8. All developing countries shown with a score higher than 1.5.

9. This section will treat the "accounting" US NIIP as the basis for definition as creditor or debtor. However, as shown in chapter 2, because capital income services have remained positive, in meaningful economic terms the United States has moved from a large to a small net creditor but as of end-2004 had not yet become a net debtor. However, as discussed below, the United States is poised to move decisively into economic net debtor status by 2006.

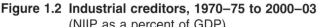

Figure 1.2 Industrial creditors, 1970–75 to 2000–03
         (NIIP as a percent of GDP)

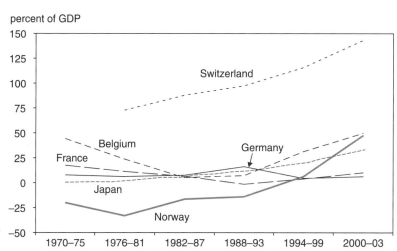

percent of GDP

NIIP = net international investment position

Source: See appendix 1A.

cent), and latecomer Norway (48 percent, after a meteoric rise from −33 percent in 1976–81).

Persistent Debtor Industrial Countries

Australia, New Zealand, and Canada are usually the industrial countries that are identified with the paradox of an industrial country with debtor status. As shown in figure 1.3, what is surprising for Australia and New Zealand is the intensification of their debtor status—their net debt increased from a range of 5 to 15 percent of GDP during 1970–75 to 60 to 80 percent by 2000–03. Canada, by contrast, eased its debtor position from about 40 percent of GDP in 1988–93 to less than 20 percent by 2000–03.

Some of the time paths for these debtor countries underscore the point made above about the sensitivity of the NIIP as a residual between two sometimes large numbers. Ireland had net international debt off the charts at about 250 percent of GDP in the early 1970s. Its net debt narrowed to about 150 percent of GDP in the mid-1980s, and rapidly declined to about 20 percent by 2000–03. Conversely, Finland experienced the steepest drop in its NIIP, from net debt of 33 percent of GDP in 1988–93 to 75 percent in 2000–03. In a single year, from 1998 to 1999, Finland's NIIP plunged from −77 percent of GDP to −169 percent, before rebounding to −41

Figure 1.3 Persistent industrial debtors, 1970–75 to 2000–03
(NIIP as a percent of GDP)

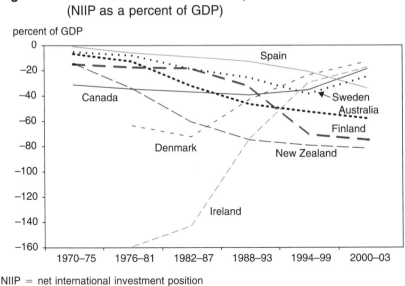

NIIP = net international investment position
Source: See appendix 1A.

percent by 2002. Finland's wide fluctuation was apparently driven by the bubble in high-tech stocks, combined with large foreign holdings.[10]

From Industrial Creditor to Debtor: Surprising Company

As shown in figure 1.4, the United States has been joined by Austria, Greece, the Netherlands, Portugal, and the United Kingdom in the creditor-to-debtor group. Italy is technically also a member of this group, but only marginally, and it is omitted from the figure as its changes are on a smaller scale.[11] Importantly, the magnitude of the swing for the United States has been broadly in the middle of the pack in this grouping. Thus, the NIIP swing of about 32 percent of GDP for the United States (from +11 percent to −21 percent) from the base in 1970–75 to the most recent period (2000–03) was small compared with the swing of about 115 percent of GDP (+70 percent to −45 percent) for Portugal, but about the same

10. Finland's portfolio equity liabilities to foreigners rose from $80 billion at the end of 1998 to $220 billion at the end of 1999, or from 62 to 171 percent of GDP (IMF 2005a). According to the *Wall Street Journal*, the market capitalization of Nokia alone rose from $71 billion to $225 billion over the same period before falling sharply by 2001–02 (http://online.wsj.com/home/US).

11. Italy's NIIP swung from an average of +2.1 percent of GDP in 1970–87 to −7 percent in 1988–93 and back to −1.2 percent in 2000–03.

Figure 1.4 Industrial creditors-to-debtors, 1970–75 to 2000–03
(NIIP as a percent of GDP)

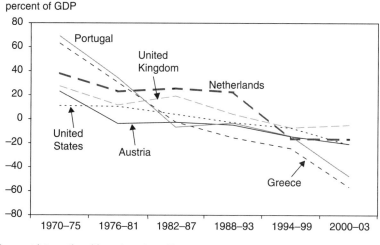

NIIP = net international investment position

Source: See appendix 1A.

as the downswing of about 30 percent for the United Kingdom, and much larger than that of only a percent or two for Italy. The Netherlands' downswing of about 55 percent of GDP is perhaps the most surprising of the group.

Storylines are generally not difficult to develop for the creditor-to-debtor group. For the key case of the United States, the optimistic interpretation is that more rapid labor force growth than in persistent creditor industrial countries, and, especially by the 1990s, higher rates of return on capital, have systematically attracted capital inflows. This interpretation can be augmented by the extra dose of capital inflows from China, Korea, and some other new-creditor countries, especially by the late 1990s and after, in part as a consequence of the dollar's reserve currency role. The pessimistic interpretation for the United States, of course, is that for a long time it has been living beyond its means, and has had nearly limitless access to credit to do so.

For Portugal and Greece, a reasonable interpretation of the steep swing from creditor to debtor status is that the process of European integration, and especially the move to a single currency, meant a narrowing of costs of capital among European countries and a corresponding increase in investment in what was formerly the periphery of the European Union. A similar interpretation, perhaps augmented by an oil shock diagnosis, can be made regarding the case of Austria, which experienced its NIIP downswing mainly during the 1970s. For the United Kingdom, the Thatcher period of privatizations, falling tax rates, and capital inflows coincides with the main downswing from net creditor to net debtor. The large downswing for the Netherlands beginning in the mid-1990s is much more difficult to explain, and appears to reflect a relatively extreme case of stock-flow discrepancies in the data or massive adverse valuation changes.[12] The Netherlands has unusually high gross foreign assets and gross foreign liabilities relative to GDP, so a moderate swing in valuation of existing stocks can yield an outsized swing in NIIP as a percent of GDP.[13]

For the purposes of this study, perhaps the salient pattern in figure 1.4 is that *the United States is not unique*. It lies squarely in the middle of this pack of six industrial countries that have steadily transited from initial creditor positions to debtor positions during the course of the past three decades. At least one implication of this pattern is that it is not necessarily the unique financial and economic position of the United States as the reserve-currency country and the largest economy in the world that has made it possible to pursue this apparently not-so-unusual round trip in the debt cycle from mature creditor back to young debtor. However, the company of five other industrial countries does not necessarily mean that the United States can indefinitely continue its downward NIIP path in the creditor-to-debtor group in a manner that is safe for itself or the world economy.

Creditor Developing Countries

Perhaps even more surprising than the record of persistent-debtor industrial countries and the creditor-to-debtor group is the advent of a few super-creditors among the developing countries. Four countries or regions alone accounted for a remarkable $980 billion net creditor position in 2003: Hong Kong ($394 billion), Taiwan ($308 billion), China ($202 billion), and Singapore ($76 billion).[14] Smaller creditor positions were held by Malaysia ($4 billion) and Venezuela ($10 billion). Russia, illustrating the volatility of the NIIP as a residual, swung from net assets of $27 billion in 2002 to net liabilities of $8 billion in 2003 before returning to net assets

---

12. Thus, from end-1993 to end-1998, the Netherlands' NIIP swung from + $63 billion to − $153 billion. This decline of $216 billion flatly contradicts the data for the cumulative current account balance during 1994–98, which amounted to + $103 billion. The cumulative stock-flow discrepancy in this period amounts to $319 billion, or 84 percent of the value of GDP in 1998.

13. In 2003, the Netherlands' gross international assets were 378 percent of GDP, and gross external liabilities were 387 percent of GDP (table 1.1). So, if valuation changes cause a 5 percent marking-up of liabilities and a 5 percent marking-down of assets, for example, this will cause the NIIP to fall by about 38 percent of GDP.

14. Singapore has experienced a dramatic upswing from large net external debt amounting to an extraordinary 2,100 percent of GDP average in 1970–75, 945 percent in 1976–81, and 480 percent in 1982–87. These observations are omitted from figure 1.5 to keep the scale of relevance for the other countries.

Figure 1.5 Developing creditors, 1970–75 to 2000–03 (NIIP as a percent of GDP)

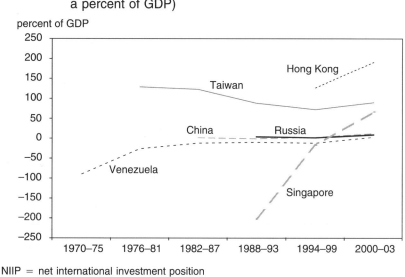

NIIP = net international investment position

Source: See appendix 1A.

of $50 billion at the end of 2004. Russia and Venezuela represent oil exporters that have built up a hoard of private flight capital from current account surpluses even as their governments have remained in debt.[15]

Relative to the size of the economy, the NIIP of Hong Kong is by far the highest, at an average of 190 percent in 2000–03 (figure 1.5). This means that Hong Kong outstrips even Switzerland as the premier creditor country or region. The NIIPs of Taiwan (90 percent of GDP) and Singapore (67 percent of GDP) also place them well ahead of their industrial-country counterparts in the creditor league (Belgium and Norway, both at about 50 percent). While it is ironic that the top three "developing-country" creditors surpass the top three industrial countries, they represent exceptions that prove the rule because their income levels have risen so much that they are now in the ranks of high-income countries.[16]

Trends for Debtor Developing Countries

Figures 1.6 through 1.8 show trends in NIIPs for debtor developing countries. Several patterns emerge. First and simplest, most developing coun-

---

15. At the end of 2002, the public sector had external debt greater than external reserves in both Russia ($100 billion versus $44 billion) and Venezuela ($23 billion versus $12 billion) (IMF 2004b, World Bank 2004b).

16. In 2003, purchasing power parity per capita GDP was $24,500 in Singapore and $27,000 in Hong Kong, compared with $29,500 for all high-income countries (World Bank 2005).

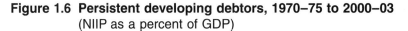

Figure 1.6 Persistent developing debtors, 1970–75 to 2000–03
(NIIP as a percent of GDP)

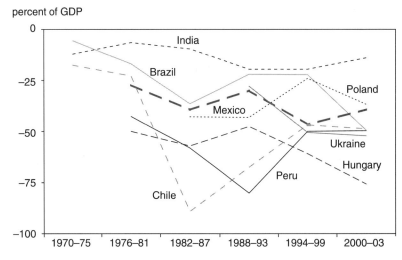

NIIP = net international investment position
Source: See appendix 1A.

Figure 1.7 Mature developing debtors, 1970–75 to 2000–03
(NIIP as a percent of GDP)

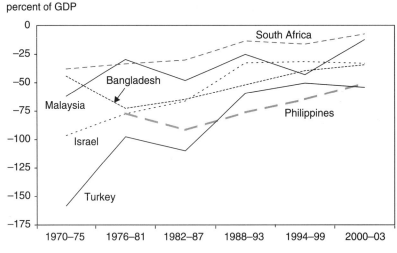

NIIP = net international investment position
Source: See appendix 1A.

**Figure 1.8 Developing creditors-to-debtors, 1970–75
to 2000–03** (NIIP as a percent of GDP)

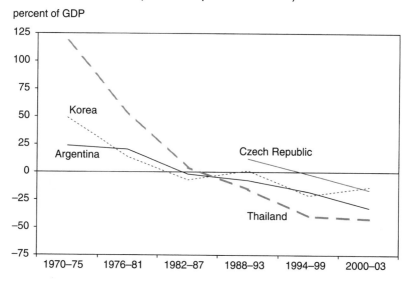

percent of GDP

NIIP = net international investment position
Source: See appendix 1A.

tries have been and remain net debtors. Second, the mean and median debt ratios were both approximately 35 percent of GDP for the 18 net debtor countries over 2000–03. Third, dispersion is high, with the standard deviation at 21 percentage points of GDP. Fourth, several well-known debtor countries started out as substantial creditors in the 1970s, including Argentina, Chile, Korea, and Thailand. Fifth, of the two largest Latin American debtors (Brazil and Mexico), debt ratios by 2000–03 were back to levels even higher than at the height of the region's debt crisis in the mid-1980s, a testimony to the vigor of the emerging bond market that arose in the 1990s following the Brady Plan restructuring of bank claims, and a reflection of the far lower interest rates (and hence higher debt-carrying capacity) in the 1990s than in the early 1980s. Sixth, several countries have systematically reduced their relative indebtedness and can be seen as mature debtors that have not yet transited to young creditors, including South Africa, Malaysia, Israel, and the Philippines. Seventh, among transition economies, Hungary stands out as persistently more heavily indebted, with net debt at about 75 percent of GDP in 2000–03.

The Global Balance Sheet Discrepancy

To recapitulate, in broad-brush terms, the principal aberration in global external balance sheet positions is that several industrial countries, espe-

Figure 1.9 External assets and liabilities of 45 industrial and developing nations, 1970–2003 (billions of dollars)

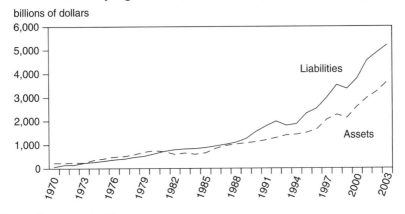

billions of dollars

Source: See appendix 1A.

cially the United States, are net liability countries rather than net creditors as traditional debt cycle theory predicts. At a second level of analysis, the question becomes whether characteristics of these countries would in fact make them good candidates for debtor status under the traditional theory. First, however, it is important to take note of a possible bias in the overall findings toward identifying countries as debtors rather than creditors.

It is well known that the world chronically has an aggregate current account deficit instead of the definitional balance, because of statistical problems (IMF 2003a). Thus, in 1990–92, the global current account showed a deficit averaging $118 billion (IMF 2005b). The global discrepancy eased to an average of − $59 billion during 1993–96 and dropped to − $4 billion in 1997, but then returned to an average of − $124 billion in 1998–2003 and stood at − $81 billion in 2004. Although the discrepancy fell from − 1.5 percent of world current account transactions in 1990 to − 1.1 percent in 2001 and − 0.4 percent in 2004, it remains substantial.

If the current account statistics are systematically biased toward deficits, then we should suspect that international investment positions will be systematically biased toward net liabilities. That is, the change in the NIIP of each country in principle equals the year's current account surplus or deficit (before valuation changes for currencies and asset prices), so systematic bias toward deficits will cause a systematic understatement of increases in assets or a systematic overstatement of increases in liabilities.

As it turns out, the NIIP data do indeed show a large discrepancy between global external assets and liabilities. Figure 1.9 shows that, for the 45 industrial and developing countries examined above (see appendix table 1A.1), the sum of NIIPs for creditor countries in 2003 was $3.64 trillion, whereas the sum for debtor countries was $5.2 trillion. The "world–45" global asset-liability discrepancy was thus − $1.55 trillion.

Figure 1.10 Global current account discrepancy and change in global asset discrepancy, 1990–2003 (billions of dollars)

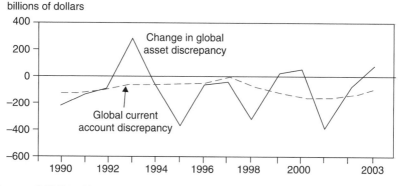

Sources: IMF (2005b); figure 1.9.

One place to look for the missing assets is in those members of the Organization of Petroleum Exporting Countries (OPEC) that are not included in the compilation. An extremely rough estimate would place the combined net international assets of five Middle Eastern oil economies at about $500 billion by 2003.[17] Taking these countries into account would thus still leave about $1 trillion in missing global external assets.

Figure 1.10 shows the annual change in the global asset discrepancy and compares it to the global current account discrepancy of the year in question. For the full period from 1990 to 2003, the sum of the current account discrepancies is surprisingly close to the change in the global asset discrepancy, at − $1.34 trillion and − $1.37 trillion respectively. Even though the time path of the current account discrepancy is much more stable than that for the change in the global asset discrepancy (which even swings to large reductions in the discrepancy—or increments in assets in excess of increments of liabilities—especially in 1993 but also in 2000 and 2003), the cumulative pattern suggests that the asset discrepancy is driven by the current account discrepancy. This diagnosis would further imply that valuation changes are not the main influence behind the global asset discrepancy, because valuation changes are applied independently to the asset and liability stocks and are thus not directly captured by the current account discrepancies.

In principle, the global asset discrepancy might help explain the paradox of the large number of debtors among the industrial countries. That is,

---

17. For 1999–2003, cumulative current account surpluses (or, for Qatar and the United Arab Emirates, trade surpluses) were as follows: United Arab Emirates, $166 billion; Kuwait, $153 billion; Qatar, $124 billion; Saudi Arabia, $50 billion; and Libya, $15 billion. Note that Saudi Arabia's cumulative current account peaked at $166 billion in 1982.

perhaps some of them would be recorded as net creditors if their external assets were corrected for understatement associated with the global asset discrepancy. It turns out, however, that an exercise allocating the global asset discrepancy across the net debtor countries does not transform any of them from net debtor to net creditor status, although it moderates the extent of their reported net debt.[18]

Debt Cycle Status and Growth Performance

For the United States, a popular argument justifying its paradoxical young-debtor status is that its economy more closely resembles that of a developing country with high return to capital than a mature industrial economy with ample capital and relatively low returns (Cooper 2001). The high-growth, high-return explanation of the paradox of industrial-country debtors suggests that we should find higher growth rates associated with those industrial countries that have been either persistent debtors (figure 1.3) or have transited from creditor to debtor status (figure 1.4). Similarly, even for persistent creditors, one might expect higher-growth economies to be building up net international assets relatively more slowly, or reducing them more rapidly, than lower-growth economies. The relationship is "reduced form" in the sense that it reflects various simultaneous influences. A high level of domestic growth boosts import demand rapidly and hence can widen the trade and current account deficits and build up liabilities. Similarly, high growth can be associated with high interest rates, attracting capital inflows, and with expectations of high returns, again attracting capital.

Figure 1.11 shows annual averages for real GDP growth and change in NIIP as a percent of GDP from 1976–90 and from 1991–2002 for 13 industrial countries, including the six persistent creditors (figure 1.2) and the seven creditors-to-debtors (figure 1.4). The data labels indicate 1 for the first period and 2 for the second period. The northwest and southeast extremes capture stylized-fact relationships between slow-growing creditors (Switzerland) and fast-growing new debtors (Portugal). Notable exceptions to the general downward-sloping relationship between growth and change in NIIP include Norway (especially NW2) and Japan (especially JP1). If a dummy variable is included for Norway, on grounds that its experience of asset accumulation in response to oil exports is essentially unique among the industrial countries, there is a statistically significant

---

18. When the estimated $1 trillion in "missing" external assets at the end of 2003 is allocated across the debtor-status countries, not a single industrial-country debtor is shifted into net asset status. For the United States, this exercise reduces the net debt from $2.4 trillion to $1.9 trillion, not enough to change the qualitative accounting diagnosis of net debtor.

Figure 1.11 Annual change in NIIP and growth rate (percent of GDP and percent)

average change NIIP/GDP

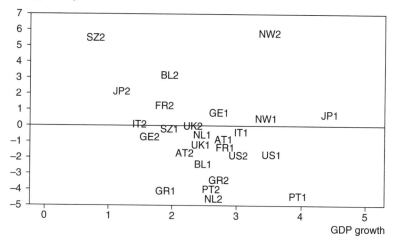

Sources: World Bank (2004a), author's calculations.

relationship between growth and the change in NIIP. Each percentage point of additional growth is associated with a 1.5 percentage point additional annual reduction in NIIP as a percent of GDP.[19]

For the United States in particular, average annual GDP growth over 1990–2000 was 3.4 percent, whereas the average for all high-income countries was 2.4 percent (World Bank 2002, 237). If the coefficient from the simple regression associated with figure 1.11 is applied, the NIIP over the decade 1990–2000 could have been expected to decline by 15 percentage points of GDP as a consequence of the faster growth in the United States than in other industrial countries. In fact, the US NIIP fell from −2.8 percent of GDP to −16.1 percent over this period, or by 13.3 percentage points of GDP. Thus, although these relationships should be seen as rough and the statistical estimates as more heuristic than rigorous, the implication is that the persistent escalation of net international liabilities for the United States over the past decade has been driven primarily by growth in the United States at rates higher than in other industrial countries.

19. The regression is: dNIIP%Y = 2.95 (1.9) − 1.55 g (−2.5) + 5.3 Dn (3.0); adj. R^2 = 0.29, where dNIIP%Y is the average annual change in NIIP as a percent of GDP, g is average annual real growth, Dn is the Norway dummy variable, and t-statistics are in parentheses.

Appendix 1A
Estimating the Net International Investment Position

In recent years, the International Monetary Fund (2005a) has published NIIP data for numerous industrial and developing countries. For many of these countries, however, there are extended periods for which data are not available. This study uses a combination of the directly reported NIIP data for the years with data available and an estimated NIIP for other years. To fill in the missing data for early years, the earliest reported NIIP is taken as the base, and each previous year's NIIP is estimated by working backward decumulating annual current account balances. Considering that the NIIP is an end-of-year stock, this means that if the earliest available NIIP is K_T, then the estimate for NIIP n years earlier is:

$$K_{T-n} = K_T - \sum_{t=T-n+1}^{T} CA_t \qquad (1A.1)$$

where CA_t is the current account balance in year t. Similarly, for those cases in which the most recent year is earlier than 2003 (the general end year), the current account of each year is cumulated to obtain the end-of-year NIIP.

Lane and Milesi-Ferretti (2000) have similarly used cumulative current accounts to develop more sophisticated series on estimated NIIPs from 1970 through 1998. They make adjustments for the composition of capital flows by type (direct investment, portfolio equity, debt) in order to arrive at valuation adjustments. These can be important, for example, because of increases in stock prices that make external liabilities on portfolio equity larger than the cumulated sum of past portfolio equity inflows. For purposes of the present study, however, approximation by simple summation of current accounts should provide a broadly accurate picture of changes in debt cycle status over time.

Table 1A.1 reports the years for which direct estimates of the NIIP are available and the years for which the NIIP is estimated by cumulating or decumulating the current account balance for each of the 45 countries considered.

For the special case of the United States, NIIP data are from the US Department of Commerce (BEA 2005e). They refer to the NIIP with direct foreign investment valued at market prices, from 1982 to 2003. For 1976–81, only the NIIP with direct investment at book value is available, and this series is used for that period. The market-valued NIIP was surprisingly lower than the book value in 1982–84, perhaps because of the 1982 recession. This suggests that use of the book value in the preceding five years will not significantly understate the NIIP. The Department of Commerce series does not cover 1970–75, and for this period, backward cumulation of the current account is applied starting from the 1976 book value of NIIP.

Table 1A.1 Data source by time period

Countries	Constructed from current account	NIIP from IFS
Developing countries		
Argentina	1975–90	1991–2003
Bangladesh	1975–99	2000–03
Brazil	1974–2000	2001–03
Chile	1974–96	1997–2003
China	1982–2003[a]	none
Czech Republic	1992	1993–2002
Hong Kong	1997–99	2000–03
Hungary	1981–96	1997–2003
India	1974–96, 2003	1997–2002
Israel	1970–88	1989–2003
Korea	1975–79, 1995–2000	1980–94, 2001–03
Malaysia	1973–79, 1995–2000, 2003	1980–94, 2001–02
Mexico	1978–2000, 2003	2001–02
Peru	1976–85	1986–2003
Philippines	1976–2000	2001–03
Poland	1975–93	1994–2003
Russia	none	1993–2003
Singapore	1971–2000	2001–03
South Africa	none	1970–2003
Taiwan	1980–99	2000–03
Thailand	1974–94	1995–2003
Turkey	1973–99	2000–03
Ukraine	1993–2000	2001–03
Venezuela	1970–82	1983–2003
Industrial countries		
Australia	1970–85	1986–2003
Austria	1970–79	1980–2003
Belgium	1974–80	1981–2003
Canada	none	1970–2003
Denmark	1980–90, 2002–03	1991–2001
Finland	1974	1975–2003
France	1974–88	1989–2003
Germany	1970–79	1980–2003
Greece	1975–97	1998–2003
Ireland	1973–2000	2001–03
Italy	none	1970–2003
Japan	1976–79	1980–2003
Netherlands	1970–79	1980–2003
New Zealand	1971–88	1989–2003
Norway	1974–79, 1994–2003	1980–93
Portugal	1974–95	1996–2003
Spain	1974–80	1981–2003
Sweden	1970–81	1982–2003
Switzerland	1976–82	1983–2003
United Kingdom	1970–79	1980–2003
United States	1970–75[b]	1976–2003[c]

IFS = *International Financial Statistics*, IMF (2005a).

a. Lane and Milesi-Ferretti (2000) for 1982 base.
b. BEA (2005c).
c. BEA (2005e).

2

Valuation Effects, Asymmetric Returns, and Economic Net Foreign Assets

US Valuation Effects

If the biggest paradox for the traditional debt cycle is that the largest and richest economy in the world is also the largest debtor economy, there are two additional smaller paradoxes that may help explain the larger one. The first is that valuation changes have predominantly tended to limit the extent of US external indebtedness to less than would have been expected solely from its chronic current account deficits. The second is that higher returns on US assets abroad than on foreign holdings of assets in the United States have similarly kept the net external debt position from being as much of a burden as would otherwise have been expected.[1] As quantified below, the United States has indeed remained an "economic" creditor despite becoming an "accounting" net debtor. To a considerable degree it has been true that the United States has enjoyed "debt without pain," or even "free debt." Both of these second-level paradoxes are driven by the fact, emphasized in chapter 1, that net external debt is the residual between large external assets and even larger external liabilities, such that influences on the large gross stocks have highly leveraged effects on net debt as the residual.

This chapter first examines the valuation effects, and then considers asymmetric returns on capital. It closes with an analysis of alternative concepts of net external liabilities, proposing an "economic" measure

---

1. Chapter 5 discusses the findings of an important recent study by Gourinchas and Rey (2005) that emphasizes these valuation effects.

of net foreign assets as opposed to the "accounting" net international investment position (NIIP), as well as other metrics of debt burden and vulnerability.

To foreshadow the key results of this chapter, it will first be shown that although favorable price and exchange rate valuation effects over time can be expected to provide some mitigation to the pace of buildup of net external liabilities for the United States, in the absence of major adjustment, the size of these effects is too small on an ongoing basis to provide a fundamental deflection of the US net position from the strongly negative trend imposed by large current account deficits. In a scenario of major external adjustment, exchange rate valuation gains could provide as much as one-third of the cutback in NIIP net liabilities by 2010 from the baseline level they would otherwise reach. For capital returns, the earnings rate on US direct investment abroad has systematically been much higher than that on foreign direct investment in the United States, and this phenomenon has kept the capital income account in surplus despite the swing of the US NIIP into deficit. Finally, when capitalized net capital income is used as a gauge of economically meaningful net international assets, the United States was found to still be a net creditor nation at about +7 percent of GDP at the end of 2004, rather than a debtor with net assets of about −22 percent of GDP in accounting terms.

Prices

The United States has enjoyed systematic accounting advantages in the sense that valuation effects have typically adjusted foreign assets relative to liabilities upward from what would have been expected solely from the path of the current account deficit. There are two principal reasons for this. First, US external assets tend to be more heavily in equities and US external liabilities more heavily in debt obligations. Equities appreciate in nominal terms with inflation and stock market booms; in contrast, the nominal value of existing debt is unaffected by either. Second, unlike developing countries (and to a greater degree than most other industrial countries), the external liabilities of the United States are denominated in its own currency, whereas external assets are much more heavily denominated in foreign currency. As a result, when the dollar depreciates against other major industrial-country currencies, the dollar value of US foreign assets has risen while that of US foreign liabilities has not been affected as much. What the US NIIP loses from annual current account deficits, it has thus tended to gain back at least partially through valuation effects from the slide in the dollar's value. In an extreme formulation, the United States could be said to have been able to devalue away a significant part of its external debt.

Table 2.1 reports the US current account balance and NIIP for 1991–2004. It also shows the "statistical discrepancy" in the balance of payments data. There are three "flow" concepts in the balance of payments: the current account (exports of goods, services, and income receipts, minus imports of goods, services, and income payments, minus net unilateral transfers abroad); the "capital account," which involves de minimus transactions for the United States and can basically be ignored;[2] and the "financial account," which is the flow concept for foreign acquisition of home-country assets minus US residents' acquisition of assets abroad. Because net financing from abroad must cover the deficit on goods, services, and transfers, the sum of the three accounts should be zero. Any difference from zero is the statistical discrepancy.

The change in the NIIP equals the amount contributed from the financial account *flows*, plus the change in dollar valuation of asset and liability *stocks* resulting from changes in their local currency prices and from exchange rate changes. Table 2.1 shows that from 1991 through 2004, the cumulative total current account outcome for the United States amounted to −$3.61 trillion. This deficit was financed by net financial inflows of $3.63 trillion (offset slightly by a cumulative "capital account" deficit of $25 billion). The $3.6 trillion in cumulative net financial account flows comprised $8.68 trillion in foreign financial inflows less US financial outflows of $5.05 trillion.

The actual increase in the US net international liability position from end-1990 to end-2004 was $2.38 trillion, or $1.26 trillion less than the cumulative total of the financial account flows (table 2.1). This difference represented gains for the NIIP from valuation changes.

The paradox of large current account deficits but small increases in net external liabilities was acute from 2002–04, during which the cumulative US current account deficit was $1.66 trillion. Yet net international liabilities increased by only $203 billion. Seven-eighths of the US imbalance in current transactions with the rest of the world in this period was in effect obtained for free because of huge favorable asset valuation changes. This is also why the US NIIP paradoxically improved relative to GDP from a trough of −23.4 percent of GDP at the end of 2002 to −21.7 percent at the end of 2004, despite current account deficits averaging 5 percent of GDP during that period.

This recent experience constitutes an extraordinary free ride that is highly unlikely to continue. There is a longer-term favorable valuation

---

2. Introduced into the International Monetary Fund's (IMF) balance of payments methodology in 1995, the "capital account" perhaps unfortunately appropriated—for what usually appear to be trivial transactions in fixed capital—a term traditionally used to refer to what is now called the financial account. The economic concept that goods and services deficits must be covered by "capital inflows" remains valid, but the IMF terminology must now be used with care.

Table 2.1 US balance of payments and net international investment position (NIIP), 1991–2004 (billions of dollars)

	1991	1992	1993	1994	1995	1996	1997	1998	1999	2000	2001	2002	2003	2004	Sum 1991–2004
Current account	2.9	−50.1	−84.8	−121.6	−113.7	−124.9	−140.9	−214.1	−300.1	−416.0	−389.5	−475.2	−519.7	−668.1	−3,615.6
Percent GDP	0.0	−0.8	−1.3	−1.7	−1.5	−1.6	−1.7	−2.4	−3.2	−4.2	−3.8	−4.5	−4.7	−5.7	
Statistical discrepancy	−44.8	−45.6	4.6	−3.7	28.3	−12.2	−79.4	145.0	68.8	−69.4	−9.6	−23.7	−37.8	85.1	5.6
Subtotal	−41.9	−95.7	−80.2	−125.3	−85.4	−137.1	−220.3	−69.0	−231.3	−485.4	−399.0	−499.0	−557.4	−582.9	−3,610.0
Capital account	−4.5	−0.6	−1.3	−1.7	−0.9	−0.6	−1.0	−0.7	−4.9	−0.9	−1.2	−1.4	−3.2	−1.6	−24.6
Financial account (FA)	46.4	96.3	81.5	127.1	86.3	137.7	221.3	69.7	236.1	486.4	400.2	500.3	560.6	584.6	3,634.6
Outflows	−64.4	−74.4	−200.6	−178.9	−352.3	−413.4	−485.5	−353.8	−504.1	−560.5	−382.6	−294.0	−328.4	−855.5	−5,048.4
Inflows	110.8	170.7	282.0	306.0	438.6	551.1	706.8	423.6	740.2	1,046.9	782.9	794.3	889.0	1,440.1	8,683.0
Subtotal	41.9	95.7	80.2	125.3	85.4	137.1	220.3	69.0	231.3	485.4	399.0	499.0	557.4	582.9	3,610.0
NIIP															
Begin year	−164.5	−260.8	−452.3	−144.3	−135.3	−305.8	−360.0	−822.7	−1,070.8	−1,037.4	−1,581.0	−2,339.4	−2,455.1	−2,372.4	
− FA	−46.4	−96.3	−81.5	−127.1	−86.3	−137.7	−221.3	−69.7	−236.1	−486.4	−400.2	−500.3	−560.6	−584.6	−3,634.6
+ Valuation change (VC)	−49.9	−95.2	389.5	136.1	−84.3	83.5	−241.4	−178.3	269.5	−57.2	−358.2	384.7	643.4	414.7	1,256.9
Price	−95.8	−75.6	292.7	23.2	−152.5	84.2	−92.1	−287.9	329.7	133.7	−224.2	−59.6	−1.7	146.5	20.8
Exchange rate	4.6	−22.0	−22.0	73.1	39.0	−66.1	−207.6	68.1	−126.0	−270.6	−151.7	231.3	415.5	272.3	185.0
Other	41.2	55.3	118.8	39.8	29.2	65.4	58.3	41.5	65.8	79.7	17.7	213.0	229.6	−4.1	1,051.1
End year	−260.8	−452.3	−144.3	−135.3	−305.8	−360.0	−822.7	−1,070.8	−1,037.4	−1,581.0	−2,339.4	−2,455.1	−2,372.4	−2,542.2	
Percent GDP	−4.3	−7.1	−2.2	−1.9	−4.1	−4.6	−9.9	−12.2	−11.2	−16.1	−23.1	−23.4	−21.6	−21.7	

Source: BEA (2005b, c, e).

Table 2.2 Composition of US international assets and liabilities,[a]
1990 and 2004 (in billions of dollars and in percent)

	1990		2004	
	Value	Share	Value	Share
Assets	2,294.1	100.0	9,972.8	100.0
Official reserves	174.7	7.6	189.6	1.9
Other US government	84.3	3.7	83.6	0.8
US private				
Direct investment abroad	731.8	31.9	3,287.4	33.0
Bonds	144.7	6.3	916.7	9.2
Corporate stocks	197.6	8.6	2,520.1	25.3
US nonbank claims	265.3	11.6	801.5	8.0
US bank claims	695.7	30.3	2,174	21.8
Liabilities	2,458.6	100.0	12,515.0	100.0
Foreign official assets	373.3	15.2	1,982.0	15.8
Foreign private assets				
Direct investment in US	539.6	21.9	2,686.9	21.5
US Treasury securities	152.5	6.2	639.7	5.1
Corporate and other bonds	238.9	9.7	2,059.2	16.5
Corporate stocks	221.7	9.0	1,928.5	15.4
US currency	85.9	3.5	332.7	2.7
US nonbank liabilities	213.4	8.7	581.3	4.6
US bank liabilities	633.3	25.8	2,304.6	18.4
Assets minus liabilities (NIIP)	−164.5		−2,542.2	

a. With direct investment valued at market prices.

Source: BEA (2005e).

drift, but it is likely to be much smaller, except in periods of sharp dollar depreciation. Some favorable trends can be expected because the composition of US foreign assets is more heavily weighted toward direct investment and portfolio equities than the composition of US liabilities to foreigners (table 2.2). At the end of 2004, 58.3 percent of US assets abroad were in direct investment and portfolio equities, compared with only 36.9 percent of foreign assets in the United States. Direct and portfolio equity prices tend to rise both with inflation and with real earnings growth. In contrast, nominal values of debt obligations typically remain unchanged. In principle, this should mean that the United States has a structural advantage in price valuation adjustments that tend to increase the value of assets held abroad by more than the corresponding valuation adjustment for foreign holdings in the United States. The greater proportion of direct and portfolio equity in US assets abroad than in liabilities to foreigners also means there should be sizable favorable exchange rate valuation changes when the dollar declines.

The big surprise in table 2.1, however, is that in sharp contrast to the experience of the most recent three years, the US Commerce Department's estimate of valuation change over 1991–2004 as a whole attributes the great bulk (five-sixths) of the windfall difference between cumulative current account deficits and the decline in the NIIP to "other" effects, rather than to either price or exchange rate effects.

The minimal cumulative price valuation effect over 1991–2004 reflects two influences. First, even though direct and portfolio equity constitute a larger share of US foreign assets than foreign holdings of assets in the United States, the absolute magnitudes for equity are relatively close on the two sides. Thus, in both 1990 and 2004, US equity holdings abroad exceeded foreign holdings in the United States by 22 percent (at $5.8 trillion external equity assets versus $4.6 trillion liabilities at end-2004). Second, the boom in equity prices was larger in the United States than abroad during this period, so foreigners' gains on holdings of US equities were about the same in absolute terms as US gains on foreign holdings, even though the foreign holders had a smaller base. Thus, from end-1990 to end-2004, the US S&P 500 index rose 267 percent, whereas the increases in major foreign stock indexes were smaller: 184 percent for the German DAX; 154 percent for the French CAC 40; 125 percent for the UK FTSE 100; and a decline of 52 percent for the Japanese Nikkei 225 (Bloomberg LP 2005).

The large favorable valuation effect ($1.05 trillion) from end-1990 to end-2004 in the category labeled "other" (table 2.1) unfortunately remains basically a puzzle. This category is defined by Commerce as comprising "changes in coverage, capital gains and losses of direct investment affiliates, and other statistical adjustments to the value of assets" (Abaroa 2004, table 1). It is not clear why capital gains and losses would not be already included in the price changes.[3] When the Commerce Department obtains new data on assets previously not recorded, the changes typically tend to be greater on the side of assets abroad than on the side of foreign-held assets in the United States. The "other" valuation changes averaged a relatively steady $60 billion annually over 1991–2000. The annual average rose to $114 billion during 2001–04, but there were much wider swings. In the absence of further information, it is useful to take note of the relatively persistent statistical "manna from heaven" on the order of perhaps about $60 billion annually or more, which acts to limit the buildup of net external liabilities beyond amounts otherwise expected.

Returning to price effects, and looking forward, it is possible to obtain a plausible magnitude for the annual valuation adjustment to the US NIIP that might be expected from the asymmetric weight of equity in US

---

3. A regression of the "other" valuation change on the price and exchange rate valuation change during 1991–2003 shows statistically significant coefficients on the price valuation component (a $1 price valuation change is associated with a 14-cent "other" valuation change) and the exchange rate valuation component (a $1 exchange rate valuation change is associated with a 24-cent "other" valuation change), but these relationships turn insignificant when the data for 2004 are added. That would suggest that prior to 2004, a modest part of the "other" change has been from interaction effects with the main price and exchange rate valuation impacts.

external assets versus liabilities. Portfolio equity prices would be expected to rise at the pace of nominal earnings per share. Earnings in turn can be expected to rise along with nominal profits in GDP. Nominal profits have risen relative to GDP in recent years, but as a longer-term pattern, the share of profits in GDP is likely to be relatively constant. This suggests that a reasonable assumption is that equity prices rise at the pace of nominal GDP. For the United States, this would mean perhaps a 6 percent price increase on average. For Japan and the European Union, the nominal pace would be slower, but for developing countries (and especially Asia) the pace would be faster. So a reasonable assumption is that equity prices rise by 6 percent in nominal terms for both external assets and liabilities. It is also reasonable to assume that the market value of direct investment rises at the same pace as portfolio equity prices.

The total (direct and portfolio) equity share in US foreign assets is approximately 58 percent; in US foreign liabilities, approximately 37 percent. A 6 percent price appreciation path might thus be expected to raise the valuation of total external assets by 3.48 percent annually (6 percent × 0.58) and the valuation of total external liabilities by 2.22 percent annually (6 percent × 0.37). Applied to the end-2004 external asset and liability bases of $10 trillion and $12.5 trillion respectively (table 2.2), these estimates imply total asset revaluation of about $350 billion annually, and total liability revaluation of about $280 billion annually. This means that the larger base of foreign liabilities largely offsets the higher weight of equity in foreign assets, leaving only a moderate natural favorable drift in the range of about $50 billion annually from price valuation effects of asymmetric portfolio composition between US external assets and liabilities. Moreover, even this prospective modest, positive secular contribution of price change to NIIP change assumes that US equity prices begin to rise at only the same rate as foreign equity prices, rather than outpace them as in the past 15 years. If instead US equity prices continue to rise faster than those abroad, the price valuation effect could be smaller or even negative. Thus, for 1991 to 2003, the annual average price valuation effect was − $9.7 billion (table 2.1).

Exchange Rates

The potential help from favorable valuation effects should be considerably greater for exchange rates if a large further decline is in store for the dollar.[4] US debts tend to be denominated in dollars, and equity assets

---

4. Tille (2003) provided an early analysis of the importance of exchange rate valuation effects in the NIIP. He attributed almost one-third of the deterioration of the US NIIP during 1999–2001 to the appreciation of the dollar. He inferred that the large downswing in the NIIP might thus be less of a cause for concern than at first appearance, because a likely subsequent depreciation of the dollar (already under way in 2002) could be expected to reverse some of the deterioration.

are priced in dollars, whereas US assets abroad (especially in industrial countries rather than emerging markets) are likely to be denominated in euros, yen, and other foreign currencies rather than dollars. When the dollar depreciates, the result is to balloon the dollar value of foreign assets without much impact on the dollar value of liabilities to foreigners. When this is combined with the likelihood of some degree of secular dollar decline—because of both the eventual need to restrain or reduce the size of the US current account deficit and at least some degree of "elasticity asymmetry" whereby US exports tend to respond less to foreign income growth than do US imports to US income growth—the result is some natural secular drift in valuation that boosts foreign assets more than foreign liabilities in dollar terms.[5]

The actual record for end-1990 to end-2004 instead shows only a minor positive exchange rate valuation effect, as noted above. This outcome reflects the fact that for much of this period, the dollar was rising rather than falling. The Federal Reserve's real index of the dollar against "major currencies" (with March 1973 = 100) was higher in December 2004 (at 85.1) than in December 1990 (80.7). So for the period as a whole, little exchange rate valuation effect would have been expected (and it might have been expected to be mildly negative rather than positive). It was only from the end of 2001 to the end of 2004 that a large decline of the dollar occurred, yielding massive exchange rate valuation gains in this more recent period.

In contrast to the experience of 1991–2004 as a whole, it is likely that this effect will make a sizable positive contribution to valuation change over the next few years. The reason is simply that the United States will almost certainly need to enter a period of at least stabilizing, and more likely reducing, the large current account deficit—just the opposite of the trend in the past 15 years. It will require substantial further depreciation of the dollar to arrest and especially to reverse the widening current account deficit.

It is possible to develop a parameter for the impact of dollar depreciation on the exchange rate valuation of the US NIIP by considering the currency composition of foreign assets and liabilities. As a first approximation, US external liabilities are heavily in dollars. All equity liabilities (direct and indirect) are dollar based, and so is practically all US debt. So examination of currency composition can appropriately focus on the asset side.

Table 2.3 shows the percentage composition of end-2001 US private external assets by currency of the country in question (or, for the euro, for all counties in the euro bloc). All equity is treated as being denominated in the host country's currency. As a memorandum item, the table also

---

5. The elasticity asymmetry is known as the "Houthakker-Magee effect," for the first econometric study that identified it.

Table 2.3 Estimated currency composition of US private external assets (percent)

Currency	Direct investment	Portfolio equity	Bonds	Bank claims	Nonbank claims	Weighted total
US dollar	0	0	70.40	100	100	37.3
Euro	30.4	29.1	14.90	0	0	19.3
Japanese yen	4.1	10.5	5.70	0	0	4.7
Canadian dollar	10.8	5.6	3.50	0	0	5.4
UK pound	15.2	21.7	2.90	0	0	11.1
Other	39.5	33.1	2.60	0	0	22.2
Norwegian krone	0.5	0.5	0.04	0	0	0.3
Swedish krona	1.6	1.5	0.12	0	0	0.9
Swiss franc	4.8	4.7	0.37	0	0	2.9
Australian dollar	2.3	2.3	0.18	0	0	1.4
New Zealand dollar	0.2	0.1	0.01	0	0	0.1
Singapore dollar	3.2	1.3	0.10	0	0	1.4
Chinese yuan	0.7	0.1	0.01	0	0	0.3
Hong Kong dollar	2.5	1.9	0.15	0	0	1.4
Taiwanese dollar	0.6	1.2	0.09	0	0	0.5
Korean won	0.7	1.8	0.14	0	0	0.7
Thai baht	0.4	0.1	0.01	0	0	0.2
Malaysian ringgit	0.4	0.2	0.02	0	0	0.2
Philippine peso	0.3	0.1	0.01	0	0	0.1
Indonesian rupiah	0.6	0.01	0.00	0	0	0.2
Argentine peso	0.6	0.04	0.00	0	0	0.2
Brazlian real	1.7	1.4	0.11	0	0	1.0
Chilean peso	0.6	0.01	0.00	0	0	0.2
Colombian peso	0.2	0	0.00	0	0	0.1
Mexican peso	3.4	1.6	0.13	0	0	1.6
Peruvian new sol	0.2	0	0.00	0	0	0.1
Venezuelan bolivar	0.6	0	0.00	0	0	0.2
Israeli sheqalim	0.3	0.8	0.06	0	0	0.3
Russian ruble	0.1	0.3	0.02	0	0	0.1
South African rand	0.2	0.4	0.03	0	0	0.2
Other	12.80	12.74	1.00	0	0	7.7
Memorandum:						
Billions of dollars (end 2004)	3,287.4	2,520.1	916.7	2,174	801.5	9,699.7

Sources: Table 2.2; BEA (2004d); US Treasury (2003, 2004a).

shows the value of the stock of assets for each category at the end of 2004.[6] Data from the US Commerce Department provide detail on direct investment abroad (BEA 2004d). Data compiled by the US Treasury (2003) are used for the country composition of portfolio equity and for the currency denomination of credit securities ("bonds" in the table).[7] It is

---

6. The modest amount of US official reserve and other foreign assets, totaling $273.2 billion at end-2004, is omitted.

7. The Treasury survey data are for 2001 and are part of the IMF's Coordinated Portfolio Investment Survey (CPIS) covering 67 countries. The credit securities currency composition is also summarized in Bertraut and Griever (2004, 25). Note that for credit securities the details are available only for the first five currencies in table 2.3. The country decomposition of the rest is assumed proportional to that of portfolio equity securities.

assumed that all bank and nonbank claims (i.e., all loans) are denominated in dollars. Although the Treasury Department's International Capital System (TIC) does show some bank claims in foreign currency, they are small at only 6 percent of the total at end-2003 (US Treasury 2004a). Moreover, banks typically balance foreign currency claims and liabilities, making the net impact on the NIIP from exchange valuation change close to zero for bank claims.

The estimates of table 2.3 indicate that 37 percent of US external assets are denominated in dollars. Because 63 percent of US external assets are in foreign currency, a uniform 1 percent depreciation of the dollar would be expected to raise the dollar value of US external assets by 0.63 percent, or by $61 billion (0.52 percent of GDP) when applied to the end-2004 gross external asset stock.[8]

To test this approach to estimating foreign exchange valuation effects, table 2.4 examines the rise of foreign currencies against the dollar from end-2001 to end-2003. The first column shows the share of each currency in total US foreign currency assets. (This share is the same as the final column of table 2.3, but expanded for the removal of dollar assets.) The second column shows the percent rise of the currency in question against the dollar over this period, and the third column indicates these increases after weighting by the share of the currency in question. (It is assumed that all currencies not shown individually kept unchanged exchange rates against the dollar.) The total external-asset-weighted rise in foreign currencies amounted to 24.2 percent.

It is useful to pause and consider the implications of table 2.4 for adjustment of the overvalued US dollar. The data graphically confirm that there has been a sharply differentiated process of exchange realignment, with three tiers of adjustment. The highest tier has been for Europe, Australia, and New Zealand. The euro, Norwegian krone, Swedish krona, Swiss franc, Australian dollar, and New Zealand dollar appreciated by an average of 44 percent from end-2001 to end-2003.[9] In the second tier, the Japanese yen, Canadian dollar, and UK pound sterling all appreciated by a virtually identical 23 percent against the dollar.

The third tier is, broadly, the developing countries as a group. Weighting by each developing country's share in non-dollar US external assets, table 2.4 shows that the developing countries depreciated against the dollar by 3.5 percent over this period. The best known case is that of the Chinese yuan (renminbi), which has been fixed against the dollar, but Hong Kong,

---

8. The projection model of chapter 3 simplifies by applying the exchange rate valuation effect only to US foreign equity assets (direct and portfolio). This omits a modest amount of US bond holdings denominated in foreign currency, and generates a valuation gain of 0.5 percent of GDP for 1 percent uniform foreign currency appreciation.

9. Note that table 2.4 includes the Danish krone in the euro bloc because of its narrow intervention band around the euro.

Table 2.4 Change in currencies against the dollar, weighted by US external assets from end–2001 to end–2003 (percent)

Currency	Weight in non-dollar external assets	Change against the dollar	Contribution to weighted change
Euro	30.75	43.0	13.2
Japanese yen	7.43	23.1	1.7
Canadian dollar	8.69	23.3	2.0
UK pound	17.65	22.8	4.0
Other			
Norwegian krone	0.48	34.9	0.2
Swedish krona	1.50	48.4	0.7
Swiss franc	4.60	35.5	1.6
Australian dollar	2.22	47.1	1.0
New Zealand dollar	0.15	57.1	0.1
Singapore dollar	2.28	8.8	0.2
Chinese yuan	0.42	0.0	0.0
Hong Kong dollar	2.16	0.5	0.0
Taiwanese dollar	0.84	1.8	0.0
Korean won	1.15	10.1	0.1
Thai baht	0.26	11.7	0.0
Malaysian ringgit	0.30	0.0	0.0
Philippine peso	0.20	−7.5	0.0
Indonesian rupiah	0.33	22.9	0.1
Argentine peso	0.34	−65.6	−0.2
Brazilian real	1.52	−19.7	−0.3
Chilean peso	0.33	9.5	0.0
Colombian peso	0.11	−17.2	0.0
Mexican peso	2.52	−18.7	−0.5
Peruvian new sol	0.11	−0.6	0.0
Venezuelan bolivar	0.32	−52.3	−0.2
Israeli sheqalim	0.50	0.9	0.0
Russian ruble	0.18	2.3	0.0
South African rand	0.28	82.7	0.2
Other	12.35	0.0	0.0
Total	100.00		24.2

Sources: Table 2.3; IMF (2004b).

Taiwan, and Malaysia have also kept their currencies unchanged against the dollar (with formal pegs for Hong Kong and Malaysia). Through the end of 2003, Singapore, Korea, and Thailand had appreciated against the dollar but only by a modest average of 10 percent. The exceptional appreciations of Indonesia (23 percent) and South Africa (83 percent) are more than offset by the large depreciations of Argentina (with the collapse of its dollar parity), Brazil, Colombia, and Mexico. In short, only the first tier of mainly European countries had moved exchange rates by the large amount likely to be needed to correct the dollar. The East Asian economies, in particular, have been laggards in the adjustment process relative to the strength of their external sectors. These patterns and developments through early 2005 are examined further in chapter 6.

Returning to the exchange rate valuation estimates for US external assets, the 24.2 percent increase in the weighted average exchange rate against the dollar can be applied to the estimated 63 percent of external assets in non-dollar assets to arrive at a magnitude for the expected valuation effect. With gross external private assets at $6.71 trillion at the end of 2001, the exchange rate valuation impact should have amounted to $1.02 trillion (= 0.63 × $6.71 trillion × 24.2 percent). Instead, the Commerce Department estimates that the gross exchange valuation effect on US external assets amounted to $231 billion in 2002 and $416 billion in 2003 (table 2.1).[10] The total of $647 billion is in the same order of magnitude as the estimate here of $1.02 trillion, but is nonetheless considerably smaller. This is partly due to the fact that Commerce Department estimates indicate that there is an offset from higher dollar valuation of foreign liabilities (ignored here) that amounts to about one-seventh of the valuation gain on external non-dollar assets (Abaroa 2004, 32).

If the Commerce Department's relationship of liability to asset adjustments is applied (an offset of one-seventh), then the summary parameter implied by the analysis of table 2.3 is the following: a 1 percent depreciation of the dollar increases the dollar valuation of external assets by 0.45 percent of GDP.[11] For its part, the International Monetary Fund (IMF) has estimated that a 20 percent decline in the nominal effective exchange rate of the dollar would increase the US net foreign asset position by 7 percent of GDP, gauged against the end-2001 asset position (IMF 2002, 73).[12] A 20 percent dollar depreciation is a 25 percent foreign currency appreciation, so the IMF estimate implies that each percentage point of foreign appreciation provides net exchange valuation gains on US external assets amounting to 0.28 percent of GDP (= 7/25).

If we focus on the 2002–03 Commerce Department estimates of exchange valuation effects, the parameter is almost the same. The net valuation effect for the two years is only $647 billion. Applying the 24.2 percent external-asset-weighted appreciation of other currencies against the dollar (table 2.4), the impact amounts to $26.8 billion per percentage point. Against GDP in 2001 (the proper comparison), this amounts to 0.26 percent of GDP. On this basis, and in light of the estimates here and the earlier IMF estimate, *each percentage point rise in foreign currencies against the dollar contributes an exchange valuation improvement in the US NIIP of 0.26 to 0.45 percent of GDP, with a preferred estimate of 0.33 percent of GDP.*[13]

---

10. The figure originally reported for 2003, $469 billion, was mainly from direct investment ($200 billion) and corporate stocks ($201.8 billion), tending to confirm the assumption here that other claims are largely in dollars (Abaroa 2004).

11. That is, six-sevenths of the 0.52 percent of GDP identified above.

12. The study also stated that there was a 25 percent effective appreciation of the dollar from end-1995 to end-2001, and that this had reduced the dollar value of US assets held abroad by 12 percent. The 20 percent depreciation indicated here is characterized by the IMF (2002) as a "reversal of the appreciation of the dollar. . . ."

13. The average for the three estimates. Note again that the projection model of chapter 3 directly applies the foreign appreciation to the stock of direct and portfolio assets abroad,

Figure 2.1 US real effective exchange rate, 1973–2004

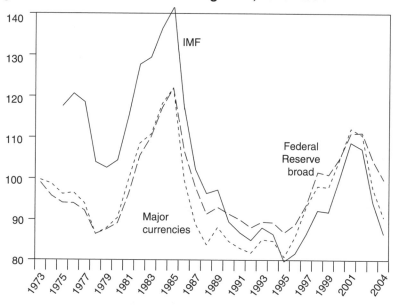

IMF = International Monetary Fund
Sources: IMF (2005a), 2000 = 100; Federal Reserve Board (2005d), March 1973 = 100.

Combined Valuation Drift

The earlier discussion of price valuation effects suggested a future favorable drift of about $50 billion annually for the US NIIP because of greater concentration of assets than liabilities in equities rather than fixed income obligations. In addition, some secular drift can be expected to the extent that the dollar follows a long-term downward trend. An even larger dollar valuation effect might arise in the medium term because of the likelihood of a substantial further depreciation of the dollar when and if capital markets decide the large and growing current account deficit is not sustainable.

The IMF's real effective exchange rate index for the dollar against 17 industrial countries, based on unit labor costs in manufacturing and 1989–91 trade weights for manufactured goods, shows a secular downward trend (figure 2.1). Based on a simple (log-linear) regression, the trend line shows a highly significant decrease of 0.48 percent annually during 1975–2004. In contrast, both the "broad" and "major currency" real effective exchange

---

which amounted to $5.81 trillion, or 49.5 percent of GDP at the end of 2004. The resulting coefficient of 0.50 percent GDP exchange valuation gain for each 1 percent foreign appreciation is modestly higher than the range estimated here. The projection model omits any secular "other" valuation changes (discussed above), however.

rate indexes for the dollar estimated by the Federal Reserve show no secular trend during 1973–2004. Part of the difference may be the use of consumer price indexes to deflate, in the Federal Reserve series, rather than unit labor costs as in the IMF index. All three series move generally together after about 1993. The drop from an initially higher level in the IMF index in the 1970s, absent in the Federal Reserve series, would be consistent with more rapidly rising real wages in other major industrial countries than in the United States in this period, and hence more rapidly rising unit labor costs than in the United States.

Taking a simple average between the IMF series trend and the zero trend in the Federal Reserve series, the secular decline of the dollar can be placed at about 0.25 percent per year. Applied to a coefficient of 0.33 percent of GDP NIIP improvement per 1 percent dollar depreciation, this implies an annual drift of 0.082 percent of GDP, or $10 billion, from the long-term downward trend in the dollar. When this is combined with a +$50 billion annual valuation trend from the asymmetric portfolio composition effect, it would appear that the US NIIP enjoys a positive valuation drift of about $60 billion annually, or about 0.5 percent of GDP.

The future favorable valuation drift is even larger if, in addition, the statistical "manna from heaven" ("other" valuation changes) continues at its seemingly persistent level of about $60 billion annually. This would boost the valuation drift to about 1 percent of GDP. However, it would seem imprudent to count on this large an effect, particularly because experience has shown that differential equity price appreciation has left the price effect less favorable than might otherwise be expected, in addition to the dubious comfort of relying on a persistent statistical discrepancy embodied in "other" valuation changes.

In short, whereas the sign of the valuation trend is favorable, the size of the effect—at about .5 percent to at most about 1 percent of GDP annually—is too small to provide much comfort about moderating the US net international liability position in the face of a current account deficit running at about 6 percent of GDP. These rough calculations establish an important point. Despite the experience of favorable valuation effects that have held the US net liability position below what otherwise might have been expected from the cumulative current account deficit, *the secular trend of valuation gains is simply too small compared with the large current account deficit to make much difference in the underlying trend in US net external indebtedness.*

Valuation Impact of a Major Dollar Adjustment

Potentially much larger is the boost to the US NIIP that would occur solely from exchange rate valuation in the event of a major depreciation of the dollar that constituted part of an external adjustment process. Various experts have suggested that the real value of the dollar needs to fall about 30 percent from its early 2002 peak if the US current account deficit is to be constrained to a level that is more comfortable from a sustainability standpoint, or perhaps to 2 percent of GDP.[14] This would amount to a foreign real appreciation of 43 percent. By end-2004, the real trade-weighted appreciation of foreign currencies against the dollar from the February 2002 dollar peak amounted to 19 percent (Federal Reserve Board 2005b), suggesting another 20 percent to go.

Based on a parameter of 0.33 percent of GDP NIIP valuation improvement from 1 percent depreciation, an additional foreign appreciation against the dollar by 20 percent would contribute a reduction of about 6.6 percent of GDP in the net international liability position (i.e., from about 22 to 15 percent). However, an ongoing current account deficit still at 2 to 3 percent of GDP would reverse this valuation effect in just two to three years.

The projections in chapter 3 provide a more specific estimate for the role of further dollar depreciation. In the favorable adjustment scenario set forth in table 3.4, foreign currencies appreciate by an additional 21 percent from their average level of the first five months of 2005. (In addition, foreign growth is temporarily modestly higher than in the baseline.) The NIIP for end-2010 improves from a baseline −$8.1 trillion to −$4.8 trillion as a result. The contribution from exchange rate valuation effects is $1.23 trillion, or 36 percent of the total improvement. On this basis, *in a successful US external adjustment scenario with 20 percent additional foreign appreciation against the dollar, exchange rate valuation effects can be expected to contribute about one-third of the total adjustment in the NIIP from the baseline level otherwise reached.*[15]

Nonetheless, even with a large further dollar depreciation, the effects from exchange rate valuation would be one-time gains, and an ongoing current account deficit of, say, 3 percent of GDP would continue to raise net external liabilities (albeit not relative to GDP). Moreover, the country composition of the next phase of foreign appreciation could mean a somewhat lower favorable exchange rate valuation effect. Roubini and Setser (2004) argue that the bulk of the exchange valuation gains that the United

---

14. For example, Mussa (2005) uses a rough parameter of 1 percent of GDP external adjustment for 10 percent real decline in the dollar, and calls for reducing the current account deficit from $500 billion to $200 billion annually.

15. As discussed in chapter 5, this fraction is about the same as that identified by Gourinchas and Rey (2005) for the role of exchange rate valuation effects in past US adjustments, even though their modeling approach is radically different. Note, however, that if the temporary acceleration in foreign growth is omitted, leaving only exchange rate change (scenario ER21 in figure 3.7 in chapter 3), the NIIP adjustment is smaller and the fraction contributed by the exchange rate valuation effect is even larger at 45 percent.

States can expect from dollar correction has already occurred. This is based on their view that these gains could has been expected mainly from the European and other industrial-country currency movements, and that these are the currencies that have already moved about as far as can be expected in the US external adjustment process.

This question can be examined by considering the optimal exchange realignment analysis set forth in chapter 6. The model there constrains overall foreign appreciation to reach a target level needed for US external adjustment, and then identifies which countries should appreciate and by how much in order to keep the resulting country changes in current accounts as close as possible to a desired profile of current account adjustments. The results do show much greater appreciation by countries that have not yet appreciated much against the dollar (e.g., a 45 percent appreciation against the dollar by the Chinese renminbi) than by those that have already appreciated sharply (e.g., only a 5 percent appreciation of the euro against the dollar from its March 2005 level). Even so, when the menu of "optimal" exchange realignments is weighted by the currency denomination shares in US external assets from table 2.3, the result is a weighted average foreign real appreciation that is three-fourths as large as when weighting by trade.[16] Moreover, in practice it seems highly likely that the US adjustment will involve some continuation of the pattern of relatively greater appreciation of the euro and other industrial-country currencies, compared to developing country-currencies, than would be recommended by the type of optimal realignment exercise conducted in chapter 6.[17] In short, considerable exchange rate valuation gains for the NIIP seem likely to play a role in US external adjustment, even after taking account of the fact that it has been the industrial-country currencies that have already appreciated the most.

US Asymmetric Capital Returns

The true economic meaning of US net external liabilities has been even more enigmatic because of differential returns on capital than because of secularly-ameliorating valuation effects. The implicit average rate of

---

16. Applying the Salomon Smith Barney (2001) trade weights normalized for the same country inclusion as for foreign assets in table 2.3, remaining appreciation against the dollar beyond March 2005 as identified in table 6.2 amounts to 17.2 percent. Weighting instead by the non-dollar weights in table 2.3, the weighted remaining foreign appreciation against the dollar is 12.9 percent.

17. For example, the optimal profile identified in chapter 6 calls for a depreciation of the Canadian dollar against the US dollar by 8.4 percent. Just setting this currency's change to zero would boost the foreign (equity) asset-weighted foreign appreciation to 13.9 percent, or 81 percent of the trade-weighted appreciation.

return on US foreign assets has systematically exceeded that on US foreign liabilities by enough to more than compensate for the excess of liabilities over assets, leaving net receipts on capital income positive rather than negative. To the extent that this differential return could be relied upon, the implication would seem to be considerably less of a real economic burden than would be expected based solely on the NIIP balance sheets, because they would not generate correspondingly higher net capital earnings payments to foreigners.

At the outset of this analysis, it is essential to recognize that there is a key structural reason why the rate of return on US foreign assets should be expected to exceed that on US foreign liabilities. The theory of portfolio balance (Markowitz 1952, Tobin 1958) holds that investors optimize their portfolios by holding a mixture of higher-risk, higher-return assets and lower-risk, lower-return assets.[18] The large and liquid US asset market, with its legal guarantees and (despite Enron) transparency, make the United States the natural place for foreign investors to place the lower-risk spectrum of their portfolios. Conversely, US investors will tend to seek foreign assets to obtain the higher-risk, higher-return spectrum of their portfolios. The result will be a systematic excess of observed rates of return on US assets abroad over those on foreign assets in the United States (even though the risk-adjusted rates of return might be equal).

As shown in figure 2.2, whatever the global interest rate environment—extremely high in the early 1980s, extremely low in the most recent three years—the rate of return on US foreign assets has exceeded that on foreign liabilities.[19] The excess annual return on assets averaged 1.2 percent in the period 1983–90, 1.3 percent in 1991–95, 0.9 percent in 1996–2000, and 1.3 percent in 2001–04. Average annual rates of return on external liabilities in these periods were 6.9 percent, 4.4 percent, 4.2 percent, and 2.9 percent, respectively.

As shown in the figure, US rates of return on foreign assets were higher than the rates of return earned by foreigners on assets in the United States in all 22 years considered. The probability of this outcome happening randomly is 1 in 4 million $(1/2^{22})$, so this record lends support to the portfolio-balance hypothesis as to why to expect an ongoing favorable differential in the rates of return.

Higher return on foreign assets than on liabilities is consistent with the greater concentration of foreign assets in equities, given the normal presence of a risk premium for equities over bonds. Moreover, the fraction

---

18. The optimal allocation depends on the degree of risk aversion and the correlation between returns on alternative assets.

19. The rates of return are obtained by dividing capital income received on foreign assets (or paid on liabilities to foreigners), as reported in the US balance of payments, by the gross external asset position (or liability position) at the end of the preceding year.

**Figure 2.2 Return on US external assets and liabilities,
1983–2004** (percent)

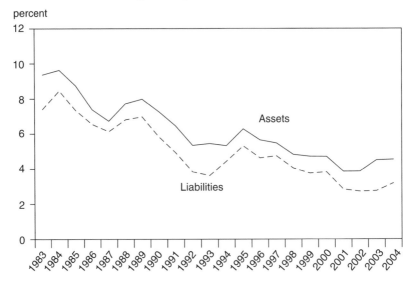

percent

Assets

Liabilities

Source: BEA (2005c, e).

of foreign official and private holdings in US government obligations (17.2 percent; see BEA 2005e) is much higher than the fraction of US foreign holdings even in all bonds (9.2 percent; see table 2.2), and foreign government bonds likely comprise a minority of this bond total. So even within the lower-return component of portfolios (bonds), there is an asymmetry showing a higher concentration of foreign holdings in the lower-return component (government obligations).

A somewhat surprising feature of the differential return is that its magnitude appears to have been much more stable than the underlying levels of the rates of return. Thus, the absolute differential in the 1980s was almost the same as in 2001–04. But this means that the ratio of the *level* of the rate of return on assets to that on liabilities has risen substantially. The ratio of the rate of return on foreign assets to that on liabilities to foreigners stood at 1.17 in the 1980s, rose to 1.26 in the 1990s, and reached 1.45 over 2001–04.

The relative stability of the differential return also suggests that the problem is not primarily one of poor data, because in contrast the statistical discrepancy in the balance of payments has been highly unstable. Thus, in 1998 there was a statistical discrepancy of +$145 billion; in contrast, in 2000, the discrepancy was −$69 billion. If there were a steady negative statistical discrepancy, approximately of the same size as the difference between reported capital service payments and a higher amount that would occur if the return on foreign liabilities were as high as that on

**Figure 2.3 US capital services exports, imports, and balance,
1983–2004** (billions of dollars)

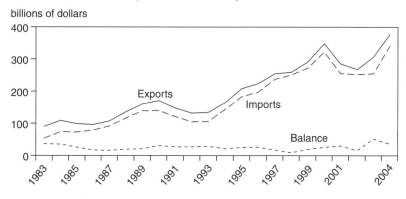

Source: BEA (2005c).

foreign assets, then it would be tempting to conclude that the differential
return is an illusion and the problem is one of poor data. An extra 1.2
percentage point return on foreign liabilities (i.e., closing the gap between
rates of return) would have amounted to an average statistical discrepancy
of about − $40 billion annually in the early 1990s, and about − $115 billion
annually during 2001–04. But the statistical discrepancy averaged + $4
billion in the period 2001–04 (with a large positive swing in 2004), and
+ $11 billion annually in 1996–2000. Not only has the size of the statistical
discrepancy been too small to make it the explanation of the missing
payments on external liabilities that would be required to eliminate the
capital return differential. In addition, and more dramatically, its wide
swings from positive to negative would have necessitated correspondingly wide swings in the opposite direction in capital earnings to provide
a strong clue about a persistent data bias of this sort. But these swings
have not occurred, as is evident in the nearly strictly parallel paths of the
two rates of return in figure 2.2.

The paradox of a persistent capital services surplus despite a large
swing from net international assets to net international liabilities reflects
the fact that, like the balance on stocks and hence the NIIP, the balance
on payments is a small differential between two large and growing aggregates. As shown in figure 2.3, both earnings on foreign assets (capital
service exports) and payments on foreign liabilities (capital service imports) have risen in close parallel, from around $50 billion to $90 billion
annually in 1983 to around $250 billion to $350 billion in 1999–2004. The
figure also shows the balance, which has remained positive in every year
and moreover was about the same in nominal dollar terms in 2003 and
2004 as in 1983.

Figure 2.4 shows the corresponding paths of the NIIP itself and the
capital services balance. If the rate of return were identical on both the

Figure 2.4 US NIIP and capital services, 1984–2004
(billions of dollars)

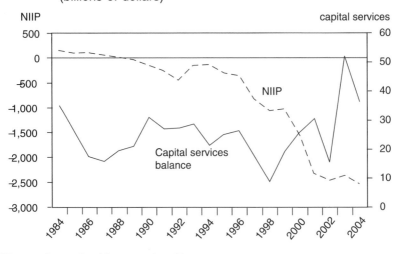

NIIP = net international investment position

Source: BEA (2005c, e).

asset and liability sides, there would be a lockstep decline in capital services earnings paralleling that in the NIIP. Moreover, capital services would have been negative in every year since 1990, when the NIIP turned negative. Instead, the capital services account remained in surplus and was essentially flat in nominal dollar magnitude, despite wide fluctuation over the past two decades. A simple statistical regression of the capital services balance against the NIIP shows no relationship whatsoever, whereas if there were a single rate of return applicable to both assets and liabilities, there would be a highly significant coefficient and its magnitude would be the rate of return.[20]

Disaggregation of the capital services accounts and rates of return provides a clearer picture of the main cause of the capital services puzzle: the behavior of income on direct foreign investment. Appendix table 2A.1 reports the stock and income flow data for the components of the NIIP and the capital services account for 1992–2004, as well as the implied rate of return for each category.[21] Figure 2.5 summarizes the data on rates of

---

20. The regression for 1983–2003 yields: ksb = 23.2 (11.2) -0.00059 $NIIP_{-1}$ (-0.3); adj. R^2 = -0.05, where ksb is the capital services balance in billions of current dollars, and $NIIP_{-1}$ is the net international investment position at the end of the previous year, also in billions of dollars, with t-statistics in parentheses. The regression coefficient has the wrong sign and is statistically insignificant. The inclusion of a time trend variable does not change this result, and the time trend is insignificant.

21. Calculated as the ratio of income in year t to the corresponding category of capital stock at the end of year $t-1$.

Figure 2.5 Rates of return on foreign assets and liabilities, 1992–2004 (percent)

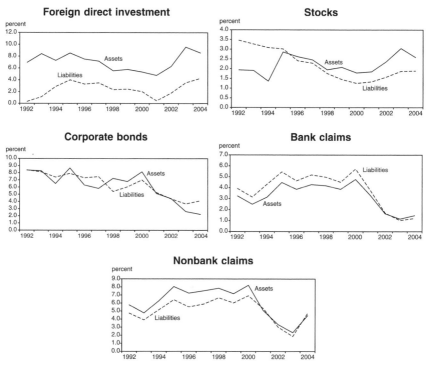

Source: See appendix table 2A.1.

return. (The return paid on US government liabilities is not shown, and US government assets abroad are negligible and can be ignored.)

It is immediately evident in figure 2.5 that the key source of advantageous differential return is in earnings on direct investment. Over the 13-year period 1992–2004, the rate of return on US direct investment abroad averaged 7.06 percent, while that on foreign direct investment in the United States averaged only 2.46 percent. During the early 1990s, this favorable differential was compounded by the fact that the stock of direct investment abroad exceeded that of foreign direct investment in the United States. Although by 1998–2000 the two stock magnitudes were virtually the same, by 2003–04 a favorable gap in the stock appeared again (see figure 2.6).[22] Even without the benefit of a larger asset stock, however, the differential return of about 4.6 percentage points on the average stock of about $3 trillion on both the asset and liability sides

---

22. End-2004 US direct investment assets abroad stood at $3.29 trillion, and liabilities stood at $2.69 trillion, a ratio of 1.22 to 1.

Figure 2.6 US direct investment assets and liabilities,
1991–2004 (trillions of dollars)

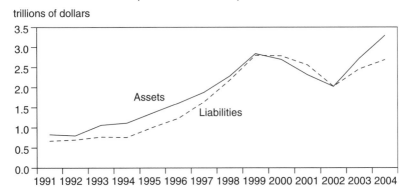

Source: BEA (2005e).

means that the balance on capital services for direct investment tends to be a large positive amount (about $140 billion annually). In a nutshell, the United States is not a net international debtor in terms of economic burden because the high return on its direct investment abroad more than offsets the deficit it runs on interest paid on debt.

It is equally striking in figure 2.5 that the rates of return on both the asset and liability sides are extremely close (and growing closer) for bank and nonbank claims, and (to a lesser extent) for corporate bonds. Here, however, there is a potential vulnerability to a rebound in international interest rates, because it is in fixed-income assets that the stock magnitude has grown much more rapidly for US external liabilities than for US foreign assets. Thus, figure 2.7 shows total bond, bank, and nonbank credit assets and liabilities for the US private sector (first panel) and the US government (second panel), and the now large and growing gap clearly shows the United States as a net debtor in fixed-income obligations.

Thus, whereas in 1991 the sum of non-equity (i.e., bond and other credit) US private and government foreign liabilities was only 31 percent larger than corresponding US foreign assets (at $1.79 trillion versus $1.36 trillion), by 2004 the excess of foreign liabilities was 90 percent ($7.9 trillion versus $4.16 trillion). The absolute buildup over this period in net credit liabilities was somewhat greater for the US government (an increase of $1.9 trillion) than for the US private sector (an increase of $1.5 trillion). The end-2004 position in net credit liabilities of $3.7 trillion (private plus US government, excluding US currency on the liability side and US official reserves—mainly gold—on the asset side) means that *each percentage point increase in US and foreign interest rates now raises net interest payments abroad by about $37 billion annually.* Considering that the capital services account stood in surplus at $36 billion in 2004, this means that it would take

Figure 2.7 Bonds and other credit foreign assets and liabilities, 1991–2004

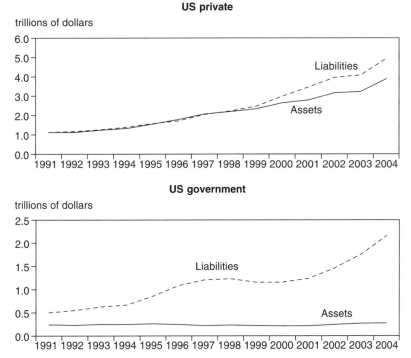

US private

trillions of dollars

US government

trillions of dollars

Source: BEA (2005e).

only about a 100 basis point rise in interest rates to eliminate the capital services surplus.

Finally, the rates of return in dividends on portfolio equities have shifted from being higher on US liabilities at the beginning of the 1990s to being higher on foreign equities since the late 1990s. The dividend rates are relatively low on both sides, however, reflecting the fact that the main return to stocks has been in price appreciation, an effect accounted for in balance sheet price valuation adjustments each year rather than in the earnings flows. The underlying portfolio equity stocks are about three-fourths as large as the direct investment amounts on both sides. With a somewhat larger absolute level as well as somewhat higher returns on the asset side, there were net positive earnings abroad for portfolio equities amounting to about $20 billion annually by 2003–04.

Table 2.5 recapitulates the overall effect of differential rates of return and underlying asset and liability stocks to show the recent trends in the components of the US capital services accounts. The table makes it clear that the capital services account has been kept positive by a chronic large surplus on direct foreign investment earnings, which has persistently more than offset the negative balance on all other capital service items.

Table 2.5 US capital services accounts, 1999–2004
(billions of dollars)

	1999	2000	2001	2002	2003	2004
Income receipts	291.2	348.1	285.4	267.8	306.9	376.5
Direct investment	131.6	151.8	128.7	145.6	193.3	233.1
Other private[a]	156.4	192.4	153.1	119.0	108.9	140.4
Bonds	40.3	44.6	29.3	24.6	18.4	19.4
Stocks	30.6	35.8	34.2	38.0	41.8	53.7
Nonbank claims	42.2	57.9	42.4	28.0	21.0	26.5
Bank claims	38.9	51.5	40.5	22.7	18.0	25.7
US government assets	3.2	3.8	3.6	3.3	4.7	3.0
Income payments	272.1	322.3	255.0	252.4	255.0	340.3
Direct investment	53.4	56.9	12.8	45.8	71.4	105.1
Other private[a]	138.1	180.9	159.8	129.9	110.1	145.4
Bonds	43.8	57.7	56.1	58.8	56.2	70.0
Stocks	17.1	19.1	20.7	23.2	23.3	32.1
Nonbank claims	29.3	40.0	39.4	24.1	16.6	21.5
Bank claims	45.6	61.0	43.7	22.5	15.7	23.1
US government liabilities	80.5	84.5	82.4	76.6	73.5	89.7
Net capital income	19.1	25.7	30.3	15.5	51.8	36.2
Of which:						
Direct investment	78.2	94.9	115.9	99.8	121.9	128.0
All other	−59.1	−69.2	−85.6	−84.3	−70.1	−91.8

a. Components are before latest data revisions and may not add up to total.

Sources: BEA (2005c); Survey of Current Business, various issues.

The data also show that the decline in interest rates has led to a relatively constant nominal level of US government interest payments despite the rapidly rising US government external debt.

Because the differential return on direct investment plays such an important role, it warrants a closer look, in particular to consider whether it can be expected to continue in the future. One strand of the relevant literature concerns the differential return on direct investment in the United States between foreign-held and domestic firms. Mataloni (2000) examines these returns (on a basis that includes interest paid on debt) and finds lower returns for foreign-held firms, but the differential is relatively modest and falling: from 2 percent in 1988 to 1 percent by 1997. Moreover, there is no difference in the rate of return for firms with a market share of 30 percent or higher, suggesting that a major source of the lower return for foreign firms in the US market is their lesser degree of oligopoly power than for the large US firms. Industry composition has little effect on the differential return, whereas age of establishment does matter: The differential declines as the firm's experience increases. Analysis of intensity of imported inputs from affiliates does not confirm profit shifting abroad through transfer pricing, tending to discount that possible source of the differential. Grubert (1997) also finds that profit shifting does not explain much of the differential, and that firm age is an important determinant of return.

The literature on the differential return between foreign direct investment in the United States and US direct investment abroad is even slimmer. In a now somewhat dated study, Landefeld, Lawson, and Weinberg (1992) suggested several possible reasons for this differential, although they did not empirically demonstrate them. They hypothesized that foreign firms might accept low profits to gain access to the large US market, including for imported inputs from home firms. They noted that foreign firms tended to buy distressed US firms, leading to low or negative initial returns. They emphasized that in the face of the decline of the dollar, many foreign firms saw direct investment in the United States as a bargain. The authors also suggested that expansion into the US market could permit economies of scale that primarily boosted profits in the home firm rather than in the US subsidiary. They noted that with US corporate taxes higher than those in most other industrial countries, foreign multinationals would have an incentive to channel profits out of the United States (although the more recent studies previously cited tend not to confirm this pattern).

Returning to figure 2.5, the extremely wide gap between the return on US direct investment abroad and that on foreign direct investment in the United States in 1992–93 is consistent with the "war stories" about disastrous foreign efforts to invest in the United States (most colorfully, perhaps, the Japanese investments in the Pebble Beach golf course in California and in Rockefeller Plaza in New York, both later sold at large losses). However, by 1994 and thereafter, the gap had settled down to a more moderate but persistent differential that averaged 4.2 percent in the period 1994–97, 3.3 percent in 1998–2000, and 4.8 percent in 2001–04. This would suggest that, for example, the "age" factor cannot be counted on to remove the large differential in the return on the two sides of the direct investment picture, because large differences persist even though foreign firms by now have had a long and growing presence in the United States.

Capital Services and Economic Versus Accounting Net Foreign Assets

Turning from rates of return to the actual outcome for the capital services balance, whether income on assets exceeds income payments on liabilities depends on whether the ratio of the rates of return for assets relative to liabilities exceeds or falls short of the ratio of the stock of assets to liabilities. When the product of these two ratios exceeds unity, there is a surplus on the capital income account; when the product is less than unity, there is a deficit. For the last two decades the return ratio has exceeded the stock ratio by enough to generate chronic, albeit falling, capital income

Table 2.6 Relative stocks and rates of return for US foreign assets and liabilities, 1983–2004 (in ratios and in billions of dollars)

	1983–90	1991–95	1996–2000	2001–04
Stock year	1986	1993	1998	2003
Foreign assets	1,595	3,091	6,179	8,297
Foreign liabilities	1,494	3,236	7,250	10,669
Assets/liabilities (RS)	1.07	0.96	0.85	0.78
Average return (percent) on:				
Assets	8.10	5.77	5.07	4.19
Liabilities	6.93	4.42	4.20	2.88
Ratio (RR)	1.17	1.31	1.21	1.45
Product of ratios (RS x RR)	1.25	1.26	1.03	1.13
Memorandum:				
Average capital				
services balance	25.2	25.8	19.4	33.5

Source: BEA (2005c, e).

surpluses (table 2.6). This is the crowning irony of the United States as an external debtor: Judged by capital earnings, it remains a net creditor rather than a net debtor. Thus, in 2004, there was a surplus of $36 billion on the capital income account, even with net liabilities at $2.37 trillion at end-2003.

Figure 2.8 shows the path of the NIIP as a percent of GDP for the United States over the past two decades, along with the corresponding path of the capital services balance as a percent of GDP (on a different scale, right hand side). The figure shows that there has been a sharp downward trend in both. However, net capital income has still not fallen below zero. Net capital earnings were about 1 percent of GDP in 1983 and fell as low as 0.1 percent in 1998 and 0.15 in 2002 before rebounding to 0.47 percent of GDP in 2003 and 0.31 percent in 2004.

The fact that the capital services balance has not yet turned negative despite the large move into net debtor status does not mean that there has been no cost from higher external debt. The United States has already lost nearly 1 percent of GDP in annual net capital income from abroad as a consequence of the deterioration in its international investment position. It is at least conceivable that the extra investment domestically made possible by borrowing from abroad has increased US domestic income by enough to offset this loss of foreign income. This is unlikely, however, because the average gross investment rate in the United States has fallen rather than increased during the period when the United States has shifted from net creditor to net debtor (figure 2.9). Instead, private consumption has steadily risen as a percent of GDP over the past three decades, albeit partly with an offset in falling government consumption, thanks to the "peace dividend."[23] The broad pattern is more consistent with the deple-

---

23. Government consumption fell from 17.2 percent of GDP on average over 1970–85 to 14.9 percent over 1991–2003 (IMF 2005a).

Figure 2.8 US NIIP (left) **and capital services balance** (right) **as percent of GDP, 1983–2004**

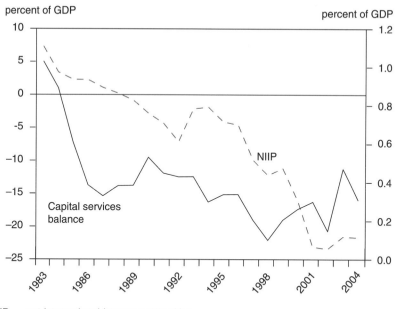

NIIP = net international investment position

Source: BEA (2005c, e).

tion of net foreign assets and erosion of net capital income from abroad as a means of paying for rising consumption rather than a shift toward investing for the future domestically.

The jury is still out, moreover, on how long the paradox of a large net external debt coinciding with positive net capital income can persist. As US monetary policy returns interest rates to more normal levels (following their reduction to the lowest level for the past 40 years in order to promote recovery from the 2001 recession), there will be a leveraged erosion in the "ratios product" (RS × RR) of table 2.6. The rise in US interest rates will tend to narrow the gap between the rate earned on foreign assets and the rate paid on external liabilities. Moreover, the rise in the base level will mean that the ratio of the absolute levels will shrink even more than if the same narrowing of the spread occurred with an unchanged domestic base rate.

Thus, suppose that the rates of return on foreign assets and liabilities revert to their averages in the 1990s. At 5.42 percent on assets and 4.31 percent on liabilities, the spread would narrow to 1.11 percent from the 2001–04 average of 1.31 percent, and the ratio would shrink from 1.45 to 1.26. Because the ratio of assets to liabilities at end-2004 was not much different from that at the end of 2003 (thanks to rescue by exchange rate valuation effects), the result would be that the ratios product would sink

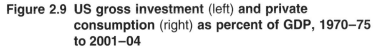

Figure 2.9 US gross investment (left) **and private consumption** (right) **as percent of GDP, 1970–75 to 2001–04**

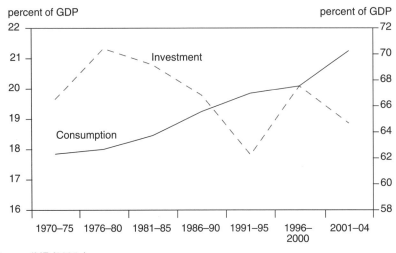

Source: IMF (2005a).

to unity, meaning that asset earnings would no longer exceed liability income payments. Thus, using the end-2004 ratio of assets to liabilities of 0.80 ($9.973 trillion/$12.515 trillion), the product of RS and RR would reach 0.80 × 1.26 = 1.008. The expected capital services balance would collapse to $1 billion. This would be a downswing of $35 billion from the outcome in 2004, or about 0.3 percent of GDP, and would represent an important milestone by marking the end of surpluses in the capital income account.

To summarize, the asymmetric return on foreign assets and liabilities for the United States is no panacea that removes any reason to be concerned about rising net external indebtedness. Although it means that the deterioration from capital service surpluses has been smaller than would have been expected just based on the NIIP, there has nonetheless been a downward trend relative to GDP that is now on the verge of reaching actual negative balances on capital income. Nevertheless, there is an underlying validity to the notion that the differential return makes the net debt less burdensome than would be indicated by face value. Indeed, one way to calculate the "quasi net debt" is to take the annual capital services flow and capitalize it at an appropriate interest rate.

Illusory external debt is present, of course, in other international contexts, most notably low interest rates on development assistance. Thus, at end-2002, sub-Saharan Africa had a face value of $210 billion in long-term external debt, yet its interest payable on this debt in 2003 was only $3.65 billion, for an average interest rate of 1.7 percent (World Bank 2004b).

If this interest is capitalized at 5 percent, the imputed debt stock is only $73 billion, or about one-third of the face value of the debt. US external debt is like that of sub-Saharan Africa in that the real burden is less than the face value because of a low effective interest rate. The difference is that for Africa the overstatement of the burden from looking at the accounting face value of debt stems from concessional interest rates, whereas for the United States it comes from the fact that net debt is a residual between assets and liabilities, and return is higher on assets than on liabilities.

This approach can be pushed to its logical conclusion by estimating a measure of economically meaningful net foreign assets based on the capitalization of annual net capital income flows (capitalized net capital income, CNCI). Capitalized value equals the year's net capital income divided by the long-term interest rate.[24] This measure shows that *the United States has remained a persistent "economic" net creditor throughout the past three decades* despite its transit into net debtor status in accounting face values 15 years ago.

The economic net foreign asset position as measured by the CNCI will be equal to the NIIP only if the rates of return on all assets and liabilities are equal, and if all are equal to the long-term bond rate. If all assets and liabilities in 2004 had earned exactly the long-term bond rate of 4.27 percent on the end-2003 principal amounts, then gross capital income would have been about $354 billion, gross capital income payments about $456 billion, net capital income about −$102 billion, and capitalized net capital income about −$2.4 trillion, the same as the NIIP.[25]

Figure 2.10 shows the results of such an exercise. It obtains the CNCI net foreign assets by capitalizing each year's net capital services income at the average US long-term bond rate (10-year US Treasury bond) for that year. By this method, US economic net assets held broadly steady at about 5 percent of GDP over almost the full period.[26] In 2004, the CNCI was +7.2 percent of GDP, whereas the NIIP was −21.7 percent of GDP. As examined in chapter 3, however, it is likely that the CNCI will turn negative and trend downward parallel to the NIIP in the coming years.

In terms of the debt cycle, using the "economic net asset" position suggested in figure 2.10, the United States was a mature creditor throughout the past two decades. Now, however, the United States is on the verge of beginning the cycle anew as a young debtor, as it shifts to the sizable quasi net debt (chapter 3).

---

24. The present value of an infinite stream of income x discounted at interest rate r is x/r.

25. Based on gross foreign assets of $8.3 trillion and liabilities of $10.7 trillion at the end of 2003.

26. The spike of CNCI to 11.7 percent of GDP in 2003 (figure 2.10) reflected high capital services income that year (figure 2.8) combined with the lowest bond rate for the past four decades (4.02 percent).

Figure 2.10 US net foreign assets: Accounting (NIIP) and economic (CNCI), 1980–2004 (percent of GDP)

percent of GDP

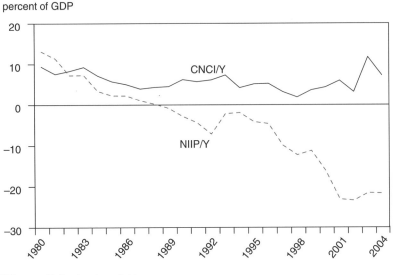

CNCI = capitalized net capital income
NIIP = net international investment position

Source: BEA (2005c, e).

Another perspective on the US position of asymmetric returns on assets and liabilities can be obtained by comparing the US returns with those of other industrial countries to determine whether the United States is unusual. Figure 2.11 examines average rates of return on the NIIP for each of the three groups of industrial countries by debt cycle stage as discussed in chapter 1. The rates of return are obtained by dividing the capital services balance for the year by the NIIP of the previous year, with the group averages weighted by the share of each member country in the total NIIP for the group. For the group of persistent creditors (Switzerland, Belgium, France, Germany, and Japan), the rate of return rises from about 3 percent in the late 1970s to 6 percent by 1988–93 and then plateaus at about 5 percent. For the group of persistent debtors (Australia, Canada, Denmark, Finland, Ireland, New Zealand, Spain, and Sweden), the rate of return is relatively stable over the full period, in the range of 9 to 10 percent. Calculation of a rate of return is ambiguous for the creditors-to-debtors group because at some point in time the NIIP base shifts from positive to negative. The figure only shows the rate of return for the initial period as creditors (Austria, Netherlands, and the United Kingdom), and for the final period for debtors (Austria, Greece, Netherlands, and Portugal).[27] For the initial and final periods, the creditor-to-debtor group shows a rate of return of about 5 percent.

---

27. The UK rates of return for the latter period fluctuate wildly as the NIIP turns to small negative values while capital services remain sizable and positive.

Figure 2.11 Industrial-country rates of return on NIIP by group, 1971–75 to 2000–02 (percent)

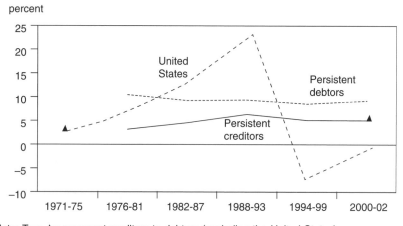

percent

Note: Two ▲s represent creditors-to-debtors (excluding the United States).
Sources: IMF (2005a); appendix table 1A.1.

Figure 2.11 shows that, whether the country is a net debtor or net creditor, the rate of return will be positive if the capital services balance has the same sign as net external assets. For all of the countries except the United States, the rate of return is reasonably stable. The time path for the United States, in contrast, shows a sharp increase in the rate of return as the net asset position fell toward zero, and then a plunge to negative returns by 1994–99, when net assets turned negative but the capital services balance was still positive. The swing into negative rates of return for the net asset position makes the United States unique, and the contrast with other countries suggests that other net debtors (based on NIIPs) do not enjoy a comparably favorable differential in rates of return on external assets versus liabilities.[28] This contrast underscores the importance of evaluating the "economic" net asset position of the United States because of its apparently unique, or nearly unique, large favorable differential in rates of return on assets as opposed to liabilities.

Alternative Measures: Cash Flow Versus Debt Burden

This chapter has argued that a country with positive net capital services earnings does not have a net external debt burden in a meaningful eco-

---

28. Martin Wolf has called my attention to the fact that the United Kingdom seems to be another important exception. Like the United States, it appears to be highly efficient in the intermediation of capital services, achieving positive net capital services income despite a negative NIIP. The UK NIIP averaged − $100 billion over 1995–2003, yet net capital income averaged $19 billion annually over 1996–2004 (IMF 2005a).

nomic sense. The CNCI measure of net investment position is the amount of the capital services surplus divided by the long-term bond rate. It captures the net international assets as gauged by an infinite ongoing stream of capital services continuing at the rate in the most recent year.

However, some would argue that it is instead the accounting NIIP that reflects the nation's vulnerability to an external sector crisis. Implicitly, the grounds for this argument are that it is not the long-term economic burden of the net external "debt" that matters, but the amount of demands that might be placed on the capital markets if the foreign holders of assets in the United States decided to sell them off for repatriation. This section further considers alternative measures of "debt" in terms of different approaches to measuring vulnerability.

Although the CNCI has not been used as a debt measure, the international official community has widely used the concept of net present value of debt (NPVD). This is the measure that is used to evaluate the debt burden of nations that qualify for relief under the Heavily Indebted Poor Countries (HIPC) initiative. Essentially, this concept differs from CNCI by including principal repayments along with interest payments before obtaining the present value by capitalizing at a market interest rate. The discussion above suggests that it is only interest (capital services income) that matters for the true burden of debt, because principal can be rolled over. However, it is useful to consider the NPVD concept as well, or its closest analogue as applied to the United States, by taking into account equity as well as debt.

It is possible to construct a multiyear schedule of plausible capital earnings and principal payments to arrive at an NPVD type of concept for the United States. Chapter 3 develops a projection model for the US current account and international assets and liabilities. The data and parameters of the model can be applied to evaluate what can be called the present value of net foreign assets (PVNFA) at a given point in time (end-2004, in the estimate here). This is the best analogue of NPVD for debt alone. The estimate assumes that all short-term debt is paid at the end of year 1; medium-term debt in year 5; and long-term debt in year 10. It applies the interest rates identified in chapter 3 for these categories.[29] All portfolio equity is treated as being repayable at the end of one year, because in effect it is "footloose." In contrast, the calculation here treats all direct investment as the equivalent of 20-year, single-repayment loans, but with annual increases for inflation in the stock of this loan-equivalent (set at the 1.8 percent US GDP deflator rate used in chapter 3).

The estimates in chapter 3 place the share of short-term debt at about one-third for US liabilities and two-thirds for US credit assets; medium-

---

29. The interest rate on short-term debt is set at 1.77 percent below the 10-year bond rate, and on medium-term debt at 0.79 percent below the 10-year rate.

term debt at 12 percent for liabilities and 19 percent for assets; and long-term debt at 54 percent for liabilities and 16 percent for assets. These "maturities" can be applied to the $7.9 trillion of end-2004 US debt liabilities and $4.2 trillion in credit assets to obtain principal payments due at the end of years 1, 5, and 10. The $1.9 trillion in portfolio equity liabilities and $2.5 trillion in portfolio equity assets are assumed to be "repaid" at the end of one year. The $2.7 trillion in direct foreign investment liabilities and $3.3 trillion in direct investment assets are "repaid" in year 20 (with the inflation adjustment noted). The rates of return on all of these categories are those reported in table 3.1 in chapter 3. The resulting streams of interest and principal "payments" on both the asset and liability sides are then consolidated to present value applying the US long-term bond rate of 2004 (4.27 percent; see IMF 2005a). *The result of this exercise is an estimated present value of net foreign assets of −$179 billion or −1.5 percent of GDP for 2004.*

This means that when the "principal" is taken into account, instead of just capital services income, the United States is found to have been a net international debtor at the end of 2004. However, the size of the net present value of debt is small, at 1.5 percent of GDP rather than about 22 percent as measured by the NIIP. The concept most widely used in official international deliberations for evaluating the "burden" of external debt thus generates only a small net liability position for the United States. The CNCI amounted to a positive $849 billion or 7.2 percent of GDP, indicating that by this measure *there was no economic burden yet of net external liabilities.*[30] The small negative PVNFA in turn indicates that at the end of 2004, there was still only a small economic burden of net liabilities, even after taking account the potential "principal repayments." The present value of the higher earnings on direct investment abroad than on foreign direct investment in the United States accounts for the much smaller PVNFA net debt than NIIP net debt.

To underscore the importance of direct investment (and to a much lesser degree portfolio equity) in enabling the United States to continue to have virtually no long-term debt "burden" in economic terms, it is useful to exclude these equity components from the PVNFA calculation. When this is done, the United States does show a net debt position that is even larger than the NIIP. The present value of non-equity net foreign assets (PVNFA-NE) turns out to have been −$3.7 trillion at end-2004, or about −32 percent of GDP. However, it would be highly misleading to exclude equity investment in determining the overall economic burden (or benefit) of the United States' foreign assets and liabilities.

---

30. Capital income in 2004 was $376.5 billion and capital income payments were $340.3 billion (table 2.5). The capital services net income of $36.2 billion has a capitalized value of $849 billion when the discount rate is 4.27 percent.

Table 2.7 Alternative concepts of US net external assets, 2004

Concept	Billions of dollars	Percent of GDP
Net international investment position	−2,542.2	−21.7
Capitalized net capital income	848.6	7.2
Present value of net foreign assets	−179.4	−1.5
Present value of net foreign assets excluding equity	−3,709.2	−31.6
Net receivable credit payments due within one year	−123.7	−1.1

Source: See text.

If the concern instead is vulnerability to cash flow problems, then presumably the best analogy is to "short-term debt," essentially the category of liability that got countries such as Korea into serious trouble during the East Asian debt crisis. The measure used for this concept here is short-term debt plus interest on short- and long-term debt. These "net receivable credit payments within one year" (NRCPOY) turn out to have been −$124 billion at the end of 2004, or −1.1 percent of GDP. Once again, although this figure suggests a net short-term debtor position, and hence cash-flow liability rather than an asset situation, its magnitude is small, at only about one-twentieth the size of the NIIP. On this basis, even the concern about cash-flow vulnerability would seem to fail as a basis for resurrecting the NIIP. Instead, the NIIP would appear to seriously overstate the economic burden of the debt, especially when gauged by the CNCI, but also when measured by present value including principal (PVNFA) as well as by a short-term cash flow measure (NRCPOY).

Table 2.7 summarizes the estimates for these various concepts of net foreign assets. It is essential to emphasize, however, that whereas the core of the argument here is that the NIIP overstates the present extent of the United States' net foreign liability position, all of the projection analysis of chapter 3 will show a serious negative trend in the US position going forward because of large (and in the baseline, growing) current account deficits. The point of the analysis of alternative measures is not to dismiss the problem of US external imbalances, but instead to clarify that their accumulated burden from the past remains minor and it is their unfavorable prospects for the future that warrant the true concern.

Appendix 2A

Table 2A.1 Stocks, earnings flows, and rates of return, 1992–2004 (in billions of dollars and in percent)

	1992	1993	1994	1995	1996	1997	1998	1999	2000	2001	2002	2003	2004	Average
Total external assets	**2,466.5**	**3,091.4**	**3,315.1**	**3,964.6**	**4,650.8**	**5,379.1**	**6,179.1**	**7,399.7**	**7,401.2**	**6,930.5**	**6,807.8**	**8,296.6**	**9,972.8**	
Private assets abroad														
Direct investment	798.6	1,061.3	1,114.6	1,363.8	1,608.3	1,879.3	2,279.6	2,839.6	2,694.0	2,314.9	2,022.6	2,718.2	3,287.4	
Income receipts	57.5	67.2	77.3	95.3	102.5	115.3	104.0	131.6	151.8	128.7	145.6	193.3	233.1	
Rate	7.0	8.4	7.3	8.5	7.5	7.2	5.5	5.8	5.3	4.8	6.3	9.6	8.6	7.1
Bonds	200.8	309.7	310.4	413.3	481.4	543.4	594.4	548.2	572.7	557.1	705.2	874.4	916.7	
Income receipts	14.8	16.6	20.1	26.9	26.0	28.0	39.2	40.3	44.6	29.3	24.6	18.4	19.4	
Rate	8.4	8.3	6.5	8.7	6.3	5.8	7.2	6.8	8.1	5.1	4.4	2.6	2.2	6.2
Corporate stocks	314.3	543.9	626.8	790.6	1,006.1	1,207.8	1,475.0	2,003.7	1,852.8	1,612.7	1,374.7	2,079.4	2,520.1	
Dividends	5.4	6.0	7.4	17.9	20.7	24.7	23.5	30.6	35.8	34.2	38.0	41.8	53.7	
Rate	1.9	1.9	1.4	2.9	2.6	2.5	1.9	2.1	1.8	1.8	2.4	3.0	2.6	2.2
Nonbank credits	254.3	242.0	323.0	367.6	450.6	545.5	588.3	704.5	836.6	839.3	902.0	597.0	801.5	
Income receipts	14.8	12.1	15.2	26.0	26.6	33.9	42.8	42.2	57.9	42.4	28.0	21.0	26.5	
Rate	5.8	4.8	6.3	8.1	7.2	7.5	7.8	7.2	8.2	5.1	3.3	2.3	4.4	6.0
Bank credits	668.0	686.2	693.1	768.1	857.5	982.1	1,009.0	1,082.9	1,231.5	1,390.9	1,559.5	1,759.3	2,174.0	
Income receipts	22.4	16.6	21.5	31.0	29.6	36.7	41.0	38.9	51.5	40.5	22.7	18.0	25.7	
Rate	3.2	2.5	3.1	4.5	3.9	4.3	4.2	3.9	4.8	3.3	1.6	1.2	1.5	3.2
Total external liabilities	**2,918.8**	**3,235.7**	**3,450.4**	**4,270.4**	**5,010.9**	**6,201.9**	**7,249.9**	**8,437.1**	**8,982.2**	**9,269.9**	**9,263.0**	**10,669.0**	**12,515.0**	
Government liabilities to foreigners														
Securities and other[a]	547.9	625.3	666.5	858.0	1,087.6	1,208.0	1,231.5	1,155.6	1,157.1	1,239.1	1,461.0	1,752.1	2,156.4	
Income payments	39.1	39.4	44.2	55.6	66.6	81.7	84.2	80.5	84.5	82.4	76.6	73.5	89.7	
Rate	7.8	7.2	7.1	8.3	7.8	7.5	7.0	6.5	7.3	7.1	6.2	5.0	5.1	6.9
Private liabilities to foreigners														
Direct investment	696.2	768.4	757.9	1,005.7	1,229.1	1,637.4	2,179.0	2,798.2	2,783.2	2,560.3	2,027.4	2,457.2	2,686.9	
Income payments	2.2	7.9	22.2	30.3	33.1	43.0	38.4	53.4	56.9	12.8	45.8	71.4	105.1	
Rate	0.3	1.1	2.9	4.0	3.5	3.5	2.5	2.0	0.5	1.8	3.5	4.3		2.5
Bonds	299.3	355.8	368.1	459.1	539.3	618.8	724.6	825.2	1,068.6	1,343.1	1,531.0	1,707.2	2,059.3	
Income payments	23.0	24.3	26.3	29.1	33.5	40.2	33.4	43.8	57.7	56.1	58.8	56.2	70.0	
Rate	8.4	8.1	7.4	7.9	7.3	7.5	5.4	6.0	7.0	5.3	4.4	3.7	4.1	6.3
Corporate stocks	300.2	340.6	371.6	510.8	625.8	893.9	1,178.8	1,526.1	1,554.4	1,478.3	1,248.1	1,700.9	1,928.5	
Dividends	9.4	9.8	10.5	11.2	12.3	14.3	15.7	17.1	19.1	20.7	23.2	23.3	32.1	
Rate	3.5	3.3	3.1	3.0	2.4	2.3	1.8	1.5	1.3	1.3	1.6	1.9	1.9	2.2
Nonbank liabilities	220.7	229.0	239.8	300.4	346.8	459.4	485.7	578.0	738.9	798.3	892.6	454.3	581.3	
Income payments	9.9	8.6	11.8	15.4	16.6	20.4	30.6	29.3	40.0	39.4	24.1	16.6	21.5	
Rate	4.7	3.9	5.2	6.4	5.5	5.9	6.7	6.0	6.9	5.3	3.0	1.9	4.7	5.1
Bank liabilities	652.7	677.1	784.9	815.0	828.2	968.8	1,014.0	1,067.2	1,168.7	1,326.1	1,538.2	1,921.1	2,304.6	
Income payments	25.0	20.5	29.2	42.7	37.7	42.8	48.0	45.6	61.0	43.7	22.5	15.7	23.1	
Rate	3.9	3.1	4.3	5.4	4.6	5.2	5.0	4.5	5.7	3.7	1.7	1.0	1.2	3.8

a. Excludes currency.

Sources: BEA (2005c, e); Survey of Current Business, various issues.

3

Projecting the US Current Account
Deficit and Net Foreign Assets

The degree of urgency for the United States to achieve external adjustment depends in part on the expected baseline for the current account deficit and net international liabilities in the absence of adjustment. The more explosive this baseline, the more critical it is that adjustment be early and decisive. This chapter presents results of a projection model developed to examine this question. The model builds on the traditional workhorse "elasticities" model, in which the growth of imports and exports depends on the real exchange rate, domestic and foreign growth, and the income and price elasticities for trade. The model incorporates the influence of capacity growth, however, and thereby importantly reduces the "Houthakker-Magee asymmetry" in which the income elasticity is much higher for imports than for exports (Houthakker and Magee 1969). The current account model projects changes in the levels of three categories of external assets and liabilities: direct investment, portfolio equity, and debt instruments (bonds, bank claims, and nonbank loans). A key feature of the model is its attention to the differential rates of return on direct investment assets abroad and direct investment liabilities to foreigners. Another important feature is the direct incorporation of valuation changes in direct and portfolio equity positions resulting from price increases and exchange rate changes.

A Simple Projection Model

Let X and M be, respectively, nominal exports and imports of goods and (nonfactor) services. Let P be price, with subscripts x and m for exports and imports respectively. Let the asterisk denote real quantities; R^* be the real exchange rate, measured in real dollars per real foreign currency (deflating by the consumer price index); L refer to the lagged value of the real exchange rate; the overdot refer to proportionate change from the previous year; g refer to real annual growth (in proportionate terms), with subscripts d for domestic and f for foreign; gc refer to trend annual output capacity growth; and $\hat{g}_d$ be average US growth and $\hat{g}_f$ average foreign growth over 1992–2003. The basic projection equations for trade in goods and services can then be written as:

$$X^*_t = X^*_{t-1}(1 + \beta\phi\dot{R}^*_L)(1 + \eta g_f)(1 + \varepsilon gc_d)(1 + \Omega\{g_f - \hat{g}_f\}) \qquad (3.1)$$

where β is the absolute value of the price elasticity of foreign demand for US exports, ϕ is the exchange rate pass-through ratio for exports, η is the income elasticity of foreign demand for US exports, ε is the elasticity of US exports with respect to trend growth in domestic production capacity, and Ω is the cyclical elasticity of export demand.[1] Gagnon (2003) suggests this incorporation of capacity growth, along with parallel inclusion of foreign capacity growth on the import side:

$$M^*_t = M^*_{t-1}(1 + \alpha\theta\dot{R}^*_L)(1 + \gamma g_d)(1 + \delta gc_f)(1 + \lambda\{g_d - \hat{g}_d\}) \qquad (3.2)$$

where α is the price elasticity of demand for US imports, θ is the exchange rate pass-through ratio for imports, γ is the income elasticity of demand for US imports, δ is the elasticity of US imports with respect to trend growth in foreign output capacity, and λ is the cyclical elasticity of imports.[2]

Gagnon (2003) has developed empirical estimates for this structure (except without the cyclical terms) for the United States, placing the price elasticities at unity on both exports and imports, the income elasticities at 1.5 on both the export and import sides, and the output capacity elasticities at 0.75 on both sides. This structure is appealing to those who consider that rapidly outward-shifting supply in developing countries in particular is a more reasonable explanation than Houthakker-Magee asymmetry for a greater difference between US import and export growth than would be expected from comparison of US and foreign income growth (Krugman 1989, Cline 1995a). In the capacity-enhanced equations,

---

1. The export pass-through ratio is $\phi = 1$ if exporters do not increase their dollar price in foreign markets when the dollar depreciates or appreciates, and $\phi = 0$ if they fully increase (decrease) their dollar price to offset dollar depreciation (appreciation).

2. The import pass-through ratio is $\theta = 1$ if foreign suppliers fully increase (decrease) the dollar price they charge in the US market when the dollar depreciates (appreciates), and $\theta = 0$ if they do not increase (decrease) dollar prices at all when the dollar depreciates (appreciates).

income "taste" parameters can be symmetrical, yet higher trend capacity growth abroad (because of such countries as China) than at home can drive US imports to grow more rapidly than exports.

With real exports and imports in hand, nominal values are obtained by applying expected export and import price levels. The set of price and nominal trade and income identities is

$$M_t = M^*_t P_{mt};$$
$$X_t = X^*_t P_{xt};$$
$$Y_t = Y_{t-1}(1 + g_{dt})(1 + \dot{P}_d); \tag{3.3}$$
$$P_{mt} = P_{m,t-1}(1 + \dot{P}_{mt});$$
$$P_{xt} = P_{x,t-1}(1 + \dot{P}_{xt})$$

where $\dot{P}$ equals the inflation rate (proportionate terms) for the variable in question, Y is nominal GDP, and P_d is the GDP deflator.

Import and export price inflation rates are predicted as follows:

$$\dot{P}_{mt} = a_m + b_m\dot{P}_{dt} + \theta\dot{R}^*_t;$$
$$\dot{P}_{xt} = a_x + b_x\dot{P}_{dt} + (1 - \phi)\dot{R}^*_t \tag{3.4}$$

The past several years have shown that import and export prices tend to lag behind domestic inflation. Also, there is some degree of pricing to market on both the export and, especially, import sides. Otherwise, export price inflation could simply be set at that for domestic production ($a_x = 0$, $b_x = 1$, $\theta = 0$), and import price inflation at domestic inflation plus the proportionate rise expected from real exchange rate depreciation ($a_m = 0$, $b_m = 1$, $\phi = 1$).

Transfers in the current account are simply projected at a fixed proportion of GDP based on recent experience, or

$$TR_t = \tau Y_t \tag{3.5}$$

The capital services account is then built up from projections of the main components of external assets and liabilities, and from application of expected corresponding rates of return. Direct investment flows abroad are projected at their average ratio to GDP in recent years, as are direct investment inflows from abroad. Stocks of direct investment then equal the previous year's stock, plus the annual flow, plus valuation changes for exchange rate change and price change. Price change is simply set at the US GDP deflator rate, for both sides. Thus:

$$FDIA_t = FDIA_{t-1}(1 + \dot{P}_{dt} + \dot{R}^*_t) + FDIAF_t = FDIA_{t-1}(1 + \dot{P}_{dt} + \dot{R}^*_t) + \pi_a Y_t;$$
$$FDIL_t = FDIL_{t-1}(1 + \dot{P}_{dt}) + FDILF_t = FDIL_{t-1}(1 + \dot{P}_{dt}) + \pi_L Y_t \tag{3.6}$$

where *FDIA* is the stock and *FDIAF* is the flow of direct investment abroad; *FDIL* is the stock and *FDILF* is the flow of foreign direct investment in the United States; π is the parameter expressing annual flow of direct investment as a proportion of GDP; and subscripts a and L refer to assets (outflows) and liabilities (inflow) respectively.

Portfolio equity stock valuation adjustments are similarly applied on the external asset side for dollar depreciation and inflation and on the liability side for inflation. Annual flows of portfolio equity investment are obtained by applying the current-year real GDP growth rate to the end of previous-year stock, with the effect of maintaining the real stock of portfolio investment. Portfolio investment stocks are thus:

$$PEA_t = PEA_{t-1}(1 + \dot{P}_{dt} + \dot{R}^*_t) + PEAF_t = PEA_{t-1}(1 + \dot{P}_{dt} + \dot{R}^*_t + g_{dt});$$

$$PEL_t = PEL_{t-1}(1 + \dot{P}_{dt}) + PELF_t = PEL_{t-1}(1 + \dot{P}_{dt} + g_{dt}) \qquad (3.7)$$

where *PEA* is the stock and *PEAF* is the flow of portfolio equity assets abroad; and *PEL* is the stock of portfolio equity liabilities abroad and *PELF* is the annual flow of foreign purchases of US portfolio equity.

All other external assets and liabilities are either bonds, bank claims, or nonbank claims, and are aggregated into assets abroad *(BBNA)* and liabilities abroad *(BBNL)*. It is this category of external liability that becomes the balancing category for accumulation of additional net debt abroad as a consequence of the current account deficit and net capital flow in other categories. For projection purposes, it is simply assumed that *BBNA* assets abroad remain unchanged. The balancing item is thus *BBNL* external liabilities, which increase each year by the amount of the current account deficit plus (or minus) additional financing requirements (or availability) from net outflows (inflows) of direct investment and portfolio equity. A key difference between these credit instruments and the equity (direct and portfolio) instruments is that credit claims have no valuation adjustments for inflation or for exchange rate change. It is assumed that all credit claims (on both sides) are denominated in nominal dollars.

The current account balance for each year must be calculated sequentially in order to obtain the balancing increment in credit liabilities abroad (change in *BBNL*). The current account balance equals the balance on goods and services, plus transfers, plus the balance on capital services *(KSV)*. The latter is obtained by applying rates of return to external assets and liabilities. Thus:

$$KSV_t = \rho_1^a FDIA_{t-1} + \rho_2^a PEA_{t-1} + \rho_3^a BBNA_{t-1} - \rho_1^L FDIL_{t-1}$$

$$- \rho_2^L PEL_{t-1} - \rho_3^L BBNL_{t-1} \qquad (3.8)$$

where ρ is the rate of return on the asset, superscript a refers to asset and L to liability, and subscripts 1, 2, and 3 refer to direct investment, portfolio equity, and the aggregate of bonds and credit claims, respectively.

The current account is then obtained as

$$CA_t = X_t - M_t + TR_t + KSV_t \qquad (3.9)$$

With non-equity liabilities abroad as the balancing item, non-equity liabilities and assets are then

$$BBNL_t = BBNL_{t-1} - CA_t + FDIAF_t - FDILF_t + PEAF_t - PELF_t;$$

$$BBNA_t = BBNA_0 \qquad (3.10)$$

where external non-equity assets *(BBNA)* remain unchanged at the base year value.

This system thus provides projections of the current account balance and the components of the net international investment position (NIIP), which is simply

$$NIIP_t = FDIA_t - FDIL_t + PEA_t - PEL_t + BBNA_t - BBNL_t \qquad (3.11)$$

Calibration and Data

Table 3.1 presents the parameter values applied to the model. This main version of the model may be designated "KGS," for a Krugman and Gagnon symmetrical elasticities structure. An alternative variant is also run based on the more traditional Houthakker-Magee asymmetrical (HMA) elasticities structure. In both models the price elasticity is set at unity for both import and export demand, a value Gagnon (2003) describes as "typical for the literature." The exchange rate pass-through ratio is set at 0.5 for imports and 0.8 for exports, again representative values from the literature (Hooper and Marquez 1995). In the KGS model, the income elasticity is set at 1.5 on both the import and export sides, and an elasticity on output capacity growth of 0.75 is applied on both sides as well. These income and capacity elasticity values are central estimates suggested by Gagnon (2003) for implementation of a Krugman-type model in which expansion of foreign capacity adds new "varieties" to imports and boosts import magnitudes independently of a rise in domestic income or an observed reduction in relative import price for the "old" varieties (i.e., the influence of the real exchange rate).[3] In this model, any secular slide

3. In a subsequent paper, Gagnon (2004) conducted estimates suggesting that the coefficient relating export growth to home GDP growth is higher—at or above unity—and that the theoretically expected value should be unity. However, this set of results finds export price elasticities that are considerably lower than usually encountered in empirical trade studies. In part for this reason, the implementation of the KGS model here uses the lower coefficient of exports on home GDP, 0.75, suggested by Gagnon in his 2003 paper. In part, this quantification can be thought of as treating the world as substantially but not entirely of the "different varieties" structure in the underlying model of Helpman and Krugman (1985) invoked by Gagnon.

Table 3.1 Projection model parameters

Parameter	Concept	Value
α	Import price elasticity	-1
β	Export price elasticity (absolute value)	1
γ	Import income elasticity	1.5 (1.7)
η	Export income elasticity	1.5 (1.0)
δ	Import foreign capacity elasticity	0.75 (0)
ε	Export US capacity elasticity	0.75 (0)
λ	Import cyclical income elasticity	2
Ω	Export cyclical income elasticity	2
θ	Import pass-through ratio	0.5
ϕ	Export pass-through ratio	0.8
$\hat{g}_d$	Trend US growth	0.035
a_m	Import inflation constant	-0.018
b_m	Import inflation coefficient on domestic inflation	1
a_x	Export inflation constant	-0.018
b_x	Export inflation coefficient on domestic inflation	1
τ	Transfers/GDP	0.0065
π_a	Annual FDI outflow/GDP	0.013
π_L	Annual FDI inflow/GDP	0.0123
$\dot{P}_d$	US GDP deflator inflation	0.018
g_d	US growth rate	0.035
g_f	Foreign growth (US X wts)	0.031
gc_f	Foreign capacity growth (US M wts)	0.035
ρ^a_1	Return on FDI assets	0.071
ρ^L_1	Return on FDI liabilities	0.025
ρ^a_2	Return on portfolio equity assets	0.022
ρ^L_2	Return on portfolio equity liabilities	0.022
ρ^a_3, ρ^L_3	Return on bonds, loans	Variable

FDI = foreign direct investment

Notes: Main values: Krugman-Gagnon symmetrical (KGS) model. Houthakker-Magee asymmetrical (HMA) model parameters are in parentheses.

toward trade deficit for the United States arises not from Houthakker-Magee income elasticity differences but from more rapid growth in foreign capacity (and hence imports) than domestic capacity (exports). In the alternative HMA model, the import income elasticity is set at 1.7 and the export foreign income elasticity at 1.0 (the values used by Mann 2004), while the capacity elasticities are set to zero on both sides.

The cyclical import and export elasticities are set at 2, which essentially boosts the income elasticity to 3.5 on both sides for the increment in the growth rate above the long-term trend rate. This term helps capture the decline of imports during US recession (because the difference term becomes negative), and the decline of US exports during recession abroad. Trend US growth is set at 3.5 percent annually, and trend foreign export-weighted growth is set at 3.1 percent.[4]

---

4. Real US GDP grew at a compound rate of 3.7 percent from 1992 to 2000, and at 3.2 percent from 1992 to 2003 (incorporating the 2001 recession). Foreign growth, weighting by US exports, averaged 3.18 percent during this period.

The parameters for the import and export price equations are based on trends estimated in simple regressions of annual proportionate growth in trade prices against the corresponding annual US GDP deflator inflation and the proportionate rise in the real exchange rate (dollars per foreign currency).[5] The estimated coefficients on domestic inflation are close to unity, so a value of 1 is applied on both sides. Also, the constant terms on both sides imply trade price deflation of close to 2 percent annually if domestic inflation reaches zero. The constant terms are both set at –0.018, for compatibility with the projections' assumption of annual domestic inflation (GDP deflator) of 1.8 percent. Finally, on the import side the estimated coefficient on the real exchange rate (0.44) is close enough to confirm the assumed pass-through parameter of 0.5. On the export side, the pass-through parameter of 0.8 is simply imposed, because the estimated coefficient has the wrong sign.

The term for net outflow of transfers is based on the average rate in 2002–04 (0.65 percent of GDP), which is significantly above the average of the previous decade (0.56 percent). The parameters for direct investment outflow and inflow as a fraction of GDP are set at their averages for 1993–2003. In the main forecast variants, the US GDP is projected to grow at 3.5 percent over 2005–10 (after rising 4.2 percent in 2004). Foreign growth is based on the average growth of the 36 economies in the Federal Reserve broad exchange rate index as weighted by shares in US exports. Foreign capacity growth weighted by US import shares is based on growth for the same countries. Both rates are set close to the actual rates for 1992–2003.[6] Higher growth weighting by imports reflects the fact that US import shares are higher than export shares for key rapidly growing economies such as China.

The rates of return on the various NIIP components are as follows. Equity returns are based on the 1992–2004 averages, which are 7.1 percent for direct investment assets abroad, 2.5 percent for foreign direct investment in the United States, and 2.2 percent for portfolio equity on both the asset and liability sides. Interest rates on both assets abroad and foreign holdings in the United States are set at rates reflecting the asset class. The Treasury bill rate is applied to official reserves and bank claims.

---

5. See footnote 10 below for derivation of the nonoil import price series. The regression equation estimated for nonoil import price inflation is
$\dot{P}_{mt} = -.0197 \ (-3.5) + 0.966 \ \dot{P}_{dt} \ (5.6) + 0.440 \ \dot{R}^*_t \ (8.17)$; adj. $R^2 = 0.77$; t-statistics in parentheses. For exports, the price inflation equation based on domestic inflation alone is
$\dot{P}_{xt} = -0.0176 \ (-2.3) + 0.82 \ \dot{P}_{dt} \ (3.8); R^2 = 0.37$; t-statistics in parentheses. Note, however, that the real exchange rate has the wrong sign in the export price equation, and is thus omitted.

6. The rates are set slightly higher to adjust for recession in 2001. The actual 1992–2003 average for foreign growth weighting by US export shares was 2.94 percent. Weighting by US import shares, it was 3.3 percent.

The medium-term (5-year) bond rate is applied to nonbank claims, and the long-term (10-year) rate is applied to corporate and government bonds. The yield curve is set to its average for the past decade.[7] Because bonds are more heavily represented in US liabilities (especially US government bonds) than in US claims abroad (e.g., bank credits), the weighted interest rate is higher on US debt liabilities *(BBNL)* than on its external credit assets *(BBNA)*.[8]

Identifying the Exchange Rate Lag

A crucial question is the appropriate lag to choose for the influence of the real exchange rate on trade. Often analysts and business persons suffer from "exchange rate fatigue" when they lament the failure of the trade balance to improve soon after a sizable depreciation. A lagged effect of up to two years suggests instead that improvement requires patience. Indeed, the J-curve effect will make matters worse due to higher import values in the first year, because the price rises immediately with the exchange rate depreciation while the quantity responds only with a year or two lag.

Past research has shown a lag of about two years (Cline 1989, 1995a). More recent data on the real exchange rate and trade performance continue to suggest that a lag of two years is relevant. Figure 3.1 shows a relatively close relationship between the current year's ratio of nonoil imports of goods and services as a percent of exports of goods and services (nonoilM/X) to the level of the Federal Reserve's broad real exchange rate index for two years earlier.[9]

To obtain a more accurate lag specification, simple statistical tests can be applied to estimates of real nonoil imports and real exports from the US national accounts (BEA 2004e) and the real exchange rate. Data on the real exchange rate are for the Federal Reserve's broad index against 36 industrial and developing countries (Federal Reserve Board 2005b, Leahy 1998). The index is in real terms, deflating by consumer prices. The tests indicate that both imports and exports are influenced by the real exchange rate with a one-year and two-year lag. Real nonoil imports

---

7. The medium-term bond rate is set at 0.79 percent below the 10-year bond rate, and the Treasury bill at 1.77 percent below the 10-year bond rate.

8. Based on end-2003 stocks, 64.7 percent of US credit assets are imputed at the bill rate, 19.4 percent at the medium-term bond rate, and 15.9 percent at the long-term bond rate. In comparison, US debt liabilities are 33.7 percent at the bill rate, 7.1 percent at the medium-term bond rate, and 59.2 percent at the long-term bond rate.

9. In the figure (and the underlying Fed index), the index indicates units of real foreign currency per real dollar, deflating by consumer prices, so an increase indicates real appreciation.

Figure 3.1 Ratio of nonoil imports to exports and lagged real exchange rate, 1980–2003 (percent and index)

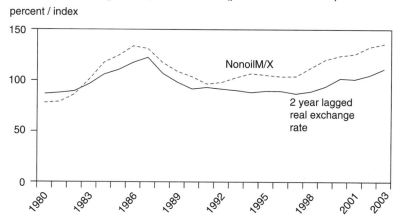

NonoilM/X = nonoil imports of goods and services as a percent of exports of goods and services.

Sources: Federal Reserve Board (2005b); BEA (2005c).

are obtained as follows. Nominal nonoil imports are deflated by a price index for nonoil imports of goods and services. This index is derived residually from the overall price deflator for goods and services imports after removing the contribution of the oil price deflator.[10] Real exports are simply the quantity index of exports of goods and services in the national accounts. When these two series are related to the relevant growth variables and lagged real exchange rates (this time inverted for consistency with equations 3.1 and 3.2), the following simple regressions are estimated, using annual data for 1979–2003:

$$\dot{M}^*_t = -0.273\dot{R}^*_{t-1} - 0.238\dot{R}^*_{t-2} + 2.45g_d; \quad \overline{R}^2 = 0.692$$
$$\quad (-1.9) \qquad\quad (-1.62) \qquad (12.2) \qquad\qquad\qquad (3.12)$$

$$\dot{X}^*_t = 0.387\dot{R}^*_{t-1} + 0.197\dot{R}^*_{t-2} + 1.97g_f; \quad \overline{R}^2 = 0.694$$
$$\quad (3.1) \qquad\quad (1.56) \qquad\quad (11.9) \qquad\qquad\qquad (3.13)$$

In these regressions, the dependent variable is the percent change of real nonoil imports or real exports in the current year. The independent variables are the percent change in the real exchange rate one or two years earlier, and the percent real growth rate for domestic GDP or foreign (export-weighted GDP). The t-statistics are shown in parentheses.

---

10. That is: $P_{nom} = (P_m - \phi_o P_o)/(1 - \phi_o)$, calculated on an annual chained basis, where P is the price index, "o" is for oil, "nom" is nonoil goods and services imports, and ϕ_o is the share of oil in total imports of goods and services.

These simple regressions confirm that both the one-year lagged real exchange rate and the two-year real exchange rate affect trade on both the import and export sides. Although the statistical significance for the two-year lag is low (at about the 12.5 percent level), the adjusted R^2 results show that inclusion of the two-year lag improves statistical explanation.[11] The results show highly significant influences of income on trade (t-statistics at about 12). The growth parameters confirm mild Houthakker-Magee asymmetry, with the import income elasticity at about 2.5 and the export income elasticity at about 2. Again, however, if capacity considerations were taken into account, this asymmetry would not necessarily persist. As for the exchange rate elasticities, they amount to a combined -0.51 on the import side and 0.58 on the export side. These are completely consistent on the import side with the assumed model parameters of 0.5 for exchange rate pass-through and -1 for price elasticity. On the export side, the coefficient is a bit lower than the assumed parameters would imply (pass-through of 0.8 times price elasticity of 1), but nonetheless confirm a strong relationship despite an extremely simple formulation for the test.

On the basis of equations 3.12 and 3.13, and weighting proportionally by the parameters estimated, on the import side, the weights are 0.53 for the prior year and 0.47 for two years before. On the export side, the corresponding weights are 0.66 and 0.34 respectively. Thus, for imports (e.g., equation 3.2), $R^*_L = 0.53\ R^*_{t-1} + 0.47\ R^*_{t-2}$. Similarly, for exports (equation 3.1), $R^*_L = 0.66\ R^*_{t-1} + 0.34\ R^*_{t-2}$.

Backcast Performance

Before turning to projections of the current account and NIIP, it is useful to consider how well the model would have performed in the past. For this purpose, a "backcast" is made, in which the actual values of the independent variables are applied (US and foreign growth, real exchange rate path, US bond rate, and actual price index series for GDP, for exports of goods and services, and for imports of goods and services) to the model to "predict" the trade and current account outcomes.[12] For any given year, there are several backcasts, one for each of several alternative prior base-year applications of the model. For example, if the base year is 1993, actual import and export values in that year provide the basis for application of

---

11. Note that because the regressions are in percent change form, stationarity is not an issue.

12. For the backcast, the capacity growth terms vary over time and are set at the average of actual growth in the current and two previous years. For import prices, actual values refer to all goods and services, including oil. By the 1990s, the share of oil in imports was sufficiently reduced that the nonoil import price index moved closely with the overall import price index, despite, for example, a large drop in oil prices in 1998 and a large increase in 2000.

Figure 3.2 Current account as a percent of GDP backcasts, KGS model, 1993–2003

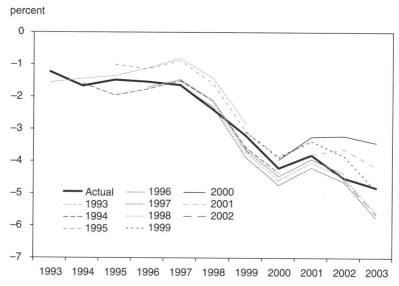

percent

Actual	—— 1996	—— 2000
---- 1993	········ 1997	– – 2001
– – – 1994	······ 1998	— — 2002
– – 1995	· · · · 1999	

KGS = Krugman-Gagnon symmetrical

the model. A 1993 base model generates predictions for 1993–98 (six years is the maximum horizon applied to each base year).[13]

Figure 3.2 shows the backcast outcomes for the US current account deficit for 1993–2003 for the main variant of the model, KGS. The field of backcasts broadly flanks the actual outcome. The base year for each backcast is identified in the key.

Figure 3.3 presents the corresponding backcasts using the HMA variant of the model. Although these also tend to flank the actual outcomes, inspection suggests that the HMA model performance is not as good as that of the KGS model.

A closer examination of the components of the backcasts shows that it is systematic underestimation of US exports as time progresses from the base year, in the HMA version, that leads to the greater divergence from actual outcomes (figure 3.4).

A summary measure for the current account deficit as a percentage of GDP confirms that the fit is better for the KGS model than for the HMA variant. This measure is the square root of the average squared residual of predicted from actual.[14] This weighted average deviation amounts to

---

13. Only exports and imports are set at actual levels in the base year, so there is some divergence of the model from the actual current account even in the base year.

14. With s as the summary measure and r_i as the residual of predicted from actual current account deficit/GDP for observation i, and with n observations: $s = (\Sigma_i\, r_i^2/n)^{0.5}$.

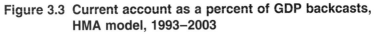

Figure 3.3 Current account as a percent of GDP backcasts, HMA model, 1993–2003

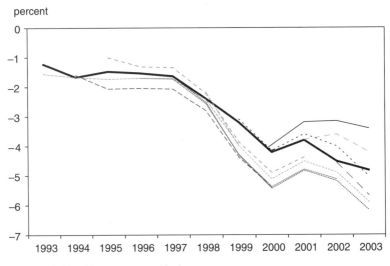

percent

HMA = Houthakker-Magee asymmetrical
Note: Key for figure 3.3 is the same as figure 3.2.

0.56 percent of GDP for the KGS model and 0.74 percent of GDP for the HMA variant. This suggests that the symmetrical elasticity approach of the KGS model, and its incorporation of capacity growth effects, provides a closer approximation of trade and current account performance for at least the past decade than does the more traditional asymmetric elasticity approach of the HMA version.

Baseline Projections

The projection model developed above can now be used to obtain alternative forecasts of the US current account deficit and accounting-based NIIP. The corresponding "economic" net foreign asset position based on capitalized net capital income (CNCI) flows can also be calculated.

The base year for the projections is 2004, with the adjustments discussed below. The projections for 2005–10 then apply the following baseline assumptions (also see table 3.1):

- The real exchange rate remains unchanged at the average level in the first five months of 2005.

- US domestic growth is a steady 3.5 percent annually.

- Growth of foreign capacity (weighted by US import shares) is a steady 3.5 percent annually.

Figure 3.4 Alternative export backcasts, 1993–2003
(billions of dollars)

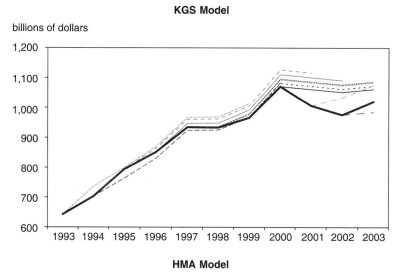

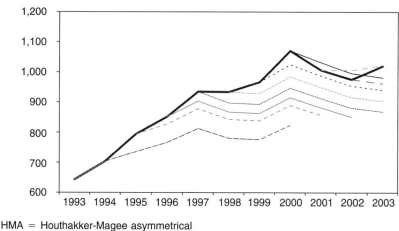

HMA = Houthakker-Magee asymmetrical
KGS = Krugman-Gagnon symmetrical

Note: Key for figure 3.4 is the same as figure 3.2.

■ Growth of foreign GDP weighted by US export shares is a steady 3.1 percent annually.

■ GDP deflator inflation is a steady 1.8 percent annually, while the equations relating import and export price inflation to the GDP deflator and real exchange rate generate zero trade price inflation (in the base case).

- The structure of returns on external assets and liabilities remains the same as described above, with rates for fixed income rising along with the bond rate.

- The long-term (10-year) bond rate rises from 4.3 percent in 2004 to 4.4 percent in 2005 and then 5.5 percent by 2006 and thereafter.[15]

- The price of oil remains at about $50 per barrel over the medium term.

Because the KGS and HMA models do not explicitly separate out oil trade, the projections are adjusted by adding a constant $35 billion (nominal) annually to the import bill otherwise predicted by the models to take account of the rise in oil prices from their 2004 base. Recent oil price futures show light sweet crude oil remaining at about $50 per barrel through end-2007 and still at $47 at end-2008. This $50 benchmark is about 20 percent above the average for 2004 (for West Texas Intermediate oil; IMF 2005a). The total oil import bill in 2004 stood at about $180 billion (BEA 2005a), so applying the 20 percent increment results in an additional $35 billion in total import value not otherwise captured by the models.

A second important adjustment seeks to take account of actual trade trends in the first four months of 2005. In this period, nonoil imports of goods and services were 13 percent higher than a year earlier, while exports were 11.5 percent higher (BEA 2005a). Direct application of the model instead calls for the value of imports to rise by 6.8 percent (before the special adjustment for oil). Export value is projected by the model to rise 12.6 percent in 2005, close to the pace in the first four months. To take account of the stronger-than-projected actual import trend, a special increase of 2.6 percent is imposed on the model estimates for 2005 (prior to the increment for oil).[16]

It is important to emphasize that the baseline already incorporates substantial real depreciation of the dollar. The calculation uses annual averages. The Federal Reserve's real broad exchange rate index for the dollar fell from its highest recent annual level of 111.15 in 2002 to an average of 104.41 in 2003, 99.78 in 2004, and an average of 96.6 in the period January–May 15, 2005. This base was slightly stronger than the December 2004 level (95.25). Calculations applying the Federal Reserve currency weights indicate that if the index had been calculated for December 31, 2004, it would have been even weaker, at 94.30.

---

15. The 5.5 percent rate is the same as that projected by the Congressional Budget Office (CBO 2005a) in early 2005. Note that for 2005, the average short-term rate is set at 3.15 percent, which places it at a smaller spread below the long-term rate (1.25 percentage point spread) than applied in 2006–10 (1.77 percentage points).

16. This increase is based on the assumption that nonoil import values rise 12 percent in the first half of 2005 from a year earlier, and that the pace then slows to the model-based 6.8 percent rate. The average rate of 9.4 percent is then 2.6 percent above the model-based rate.

The modest rebound of the dollar in the first five months of 2005—by about 2.4 percent in real trade-weighted terms from end-2004—was probably attributable to such factors as uncertainty about the euro in the run-up to the French referendum on the EU constitution; repatriation of retained earnings from abroad during the one-year window for special US tax advantages; and the rise in US interest rates. Nonetheless, the January–May base level used for 2005 stands 3.2 percent below the full-year average for 2004, indicating continuation of a broader downward trend for the dollar. More specifically, the real dollar fell by 13.1 percent from the 2002 annual average to the average for the first five months of 2005 (or, equivalently, foreign currencies appreciated in real terms against the dollar by 15.1 percent).[17]

Table 3.2 shows the baseline projections under the assumptions just enumerated, using the preferred KGS model. The first salient feature about these projections is that they show further erosion through 2010 in the current account deficit as a percent of GDP. The current account deficit widens by 0.3 percent of GDP in 2005, 0.1 percent annually in 2006–07, 0.4 percent annually in 2008–09, and another 0.3 percent in 2010. The deficit reaches 7.3 percent of GDP in 2010, and a sobering if not daunting absolute magnitude of $1.18 trillion.

The pace of the current account erosion is slower than in the recent past, as the average deterioration over the past six years was 0.55 percent of GDP. Essentially, the pipeline effects of the already sizable decline of the dollar should slow but not reverse the erosion of the current account. Overall, these projections indicate that the United States remains far from being on a path of correction of the external imbalance.

For its part, the net foreign asset position substantially deteriorates, in both accounting (NIIP) and (especially) economic (CNCI) terms. Capital services remain slightly positive in 2005, at 0.1 percent of GDP, but then turn negative for the first time in 2006, and by 2010 are contributing about $190 billion annually to the current account deficit. The accounting NIIP moves from about −22 percent of GDP at end-2004 to −27 percent at end-2005 and to −50 percent by end-2010. Capitalizing net capital services flows at the bond rate (as discussed in chapter 2), the economic net foreign asset position (CNCI) shifts from +7.2 percent of GDP in 2004 to −22 percent of GDP by 2010.

An important feature of the NIIP baseline projections is that there is a large deterioration in 2005, as the NIIP jumps from −$2.5 trillion to −$3.3

---

17. The Federal Reserve's real broad index stood at 99.13 for June 2005, or 2.6 percent stronger than the January–May 15 base used for the baseline projections of this chapter. The rejection of the EU constitution in the French and Dutch referendums pushed the euro down sharply against the dollar, from $1.36 at end-2004 to $1.21 at the end of June (for an increase in the dollar by 12.7 percent against the euro). However, the rise in US interest rates also boosted the dollar against other key currencies in the same period: by 6.4 percent against the Japanese yen, 7.8 percent against the pound sterling, and 2.1 percent against the Canadian dollar.

Table 3.2 Baseline projections, KGS model, 2004–10 (in billions of dollars, in percent, and in ratios)

	2004	2005	2006	2007	2008	2009	2010
Exports, GS	1,151.5	1,296.9	1,434.6	1,554.3	1,669.3	1,792.8	1,925.4
Imports, GS	1,769.0	1,938.4	2,052.7	2,200.2	2,376.5	2,567.0	2,772.6
Trade balance	−617.6	−676.5	−653.0	−680.9	−742.2	−809.2	−882.3
Transfers	−80.9	−80.4	−84.7	−89.2	−94.0	−99.0	−104.4
Capital services	36.2	12.6	−58.9	−87.1	−117.7	−152.3	−191.5
Current account	−668.1	−744.3	−796.6	−857.3	−953.9	−1,060.6	−1,178.1
CA/Y	−5.7	−6.0	−6.1	−6.2	−6.6	−7.0	−7.3
Net foreign assets							
Accounting: NIIP	−2,542.3	−3,346.4	−4,122.1	−4,957.5	−5,888.7	−6,925.4	−8,078.7
NIIP/Y (percent)	−21.7	−27.1	−31.6	−36.1	−40.7	−45.4	−50.3
Economic: CNCI	848.6	286.1	−1,070.8	−1,583.9	−2,139.7	−2,769.3	−3,481.0
CNCI/Y (percent)	7.2	2.3	−8.2	−11.5	−14.8	−18.2	−21.7
ERvaladj	272.3	−81.3	0.0	0.0	0.0	0.0	0.0
Real dollars/FC	0.968	1.0	1.0	1.0	1.0	1.0	1.0
Real dollars/FC (-2)	0.869	0.925	0.968	1.0	1.0	1.0	1.0
Bond rate (ppa)	4.3	4.4	5.5	5.5	5.5	5.5	5.5
FDI return difference (ppa)	4.3	4.6	4.6	4.6	4.6	4.6	4.6

CA/Y = current account balance as percent of GDP
CNCI = capitalized net capital income
ERvaladj = exchange rate valuation change
FC = foreign currency
FDI = foreign direct investment
GS = goods and services
KGS = Krugman-Gagnon symmetrical elasticities structure model
NIIP = net international investment position
ppa = percent per annum

trillion at end-2005 (and from -21.7 to -27.1 percent of GDP). A major reason is that the *appreciation* of the trade-weighted real dollar from end-2004 to the base used for 2005 (January–May 15) causes a modest exchange rate valuation *loss* by end-2005, rather than a large gain as in the past three years.

The baseline outlook is moderately worse if the asymmetric income elasticities variant (HMA) is applied, as shown in table 3.3. The current account deficit reaches 8.1 percent of GDP by 2010, or 0.8 percent of GDP higher than in the symmetrical elasticities (KGS) model.

The much lower income elasticity on the side of exports (1.0) in the HMA model, combined with the absence of a supply capacity elasticity on the export side, leads to a substantially lower path for US exports in this model variant. Although imports also grow somewhat more slowly (as the presence of the foreign capacity elasticity more than offsets the higher import income elasticity of 1.7 versus 1.5 in the KGS model), the trade deficit is wider by 2010 than in the KGS model (at 6.2 percent of GDP rather than 5.5 percent). This is the primary reason the current account deficit is wider by 0.8 percent of GDP in the asymmetrical elasticities structure. If anything, the surprise in this result is that the elasticity asymmetry does not make an even greater difference.

The difference between the paths of net foreign assets (both accounting NIIP and economic CNCI) in the two models is relatively small. NIIP reaches -53 percent of GDP in 2010 instead of -50 percent, while CNCI reaches -23.3 percent instead of -21.7 percent. On the basis of the trends in both the current account deficit and net external liabilities, in qualitative and policy terms the two models tell the same basic story: *The United States is not on an external adjustment path but instead is on a trajectory of a widening external imbalance and rising net external liabilities.*

Comparison with Other Projections

Recent similar long-term projections of the US current account and net external debt by Mann (2004) and Roubini and Setser (2004) warrant special attention for comparison with the projections here. The baseline current account deficit projected by Mann is far worse than the projections in this study, while that of Roubini and Setser is about halfway between those of Mann and the projections here.

As shown in figure 3.5, Mann projects that under unchanged exchange rates, the baseline US current account deficit would reach 12.7 percent of GDP by 2010. The differences between the Mann baseline and the KGS model baseline used in this study can be decomposed as follows. First, Mann uses asymmetric income elasticities. The HMA variant of the model here uses the same elasticities as Mann (1.7 on the import side and 1.0 on the export side). Second, Mann excludes any lagged exchange rate

Table 3.3 Baseline projections, HMA model, 2004–10 (in billions of dollars, in percent, and in ratios)

	2004	2005	2006	2007	2008	2009	2010
Exports, GS	1,151.5	1,245.0	1,322.1	1,375.1	1,417.7	1,461.7	1,507.0
Imports, GS	1,769.0	1,936.4	2,010.0	2,111.6	2,235.1	2,366.0	2,504.7
Trade balance	−617.6	−691.4	−687.9	−736.5	−817.4	−904.3	−997.7
Transfers	−80.9	−80.4	−84.7	−89.2	−94.0	−99.0	−104.4
Capital services	36.2	12.6	−59.6	−89.6	−122.9	−161.5	−205.7
Current account	−668.1	−759.1	−832.2	−915.2	−1,034.3	−1,164.9	−1,307.7
CA/Y	−5.7	−6.1	−6.4	−6.7	−7.2	−7.6	−8.1
Net foreign assets							
Accounting: NIIP	−2,542.3	−3,361.2	−4,172.5	−5,065.9	−6,077.5	−7,218.6	−8,501.5
NIIP/Y (percent)	−21.7	−27.2	−32.0	−36.9	−42.0	−47.4	−53.0
Economic: CNCI	848.6	286.1	−1,083.9	−1,628.3	−2,235.2	−2,935.8	−3,739.4
CNCI/Y (percent)	7.2	2.3	−8.3	−11.9	−15.5	−19.3	−23.3
ERvaladj	272.3	−81.3	0.0	0.0	0.0	0.0	0.0
Real dollars/FC	0.968	1.0	1.0	1.0	1.0	1.0	1.0
Real dollars/FC (−2)	0.869	0.925	0.968	1.0	1.0	1.0	1.0
Bond rate (ppa)	4.3	4.4	5.5	5.5	5.5	5.5	5.5
FDI return difference (ppa)	4.3	4.6	4.6	4.6	4.6	4.6	4.6

CA/Y = current account balance as percent of GDP
CNCI = capitalized net capital income
ERvaladj = exchange rate valuation change
FC = foreign currency
FDI = foreign direct investment
GS = goods and services
HMA = Houthakker-Magee asymmetrical elasticities structure model
NIIP = net international investment position
ppa = percent per annum

Figure 3.5 Alternative projections of the US current account deficit, 2004–10 (percent of GDP)

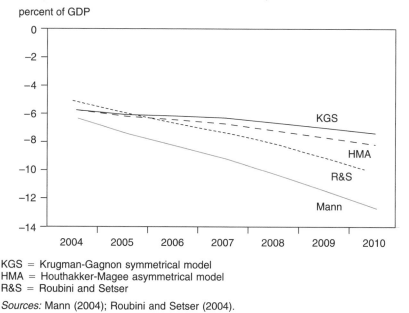

percent of GDP

KGS = Krugman-Gagnon symmetrical model
HMA = Houthakker-Magee asymmetrical model
R&S = Roubini and Setser

Sources: Mann (2004); Roubini and Setser (2004).

"pipeline" effects from the depreciation of the dollar after 2002. In contrast, the lag structure in the models developed here means that real trade in 2005 is affected by the change in the real exchange rate from 2002 to 2004, which was a total real foreign appreciation of 10.2 percent.[18] Third, Mann omits any rate of return differential on foreign direct investment assets and liabilities. Fourth, Mann's calculation directly applies the income elasticities to nominal income growth rather than real income growth. This overstates nominal import growth by 1.26 percent annually, or a cumulative 7.8 percent over six years.[19]

---

18. That is, for 2005 the percent change in real exports and real imports from the 2004 base depends on the change in the weighted 2003–04 exchange rate average from the corresponding 2002–03 weighted average.

19. It can be shown algebraically that applying the income elasticity to nominal rather than real income growth overstates nominal import growth by the rate of inflation multiplied by the excess of the elasticity over unity. For example, suppose inflation is 3 percent, real growth is 3 percent, and the import elasticity is 1.7. The standard calculation would then yield 3% × 1.7 = 5.1 percent real import growth. Adding inflation would yield 8.1 percent nominal import growth. If instead the income elasticity is directly applied to nominal GDP growth, and with nominal real GDP growing at 3 percent plus 3 percent inflation, the result would be estimated nominal import growth of 1.7 × 6% = 10.2%. The overstatement equals 10.2% − 8.1% = 2.1% = 3% × (1.7 − 1).

Figure 3.6 US current account under alternative elasticity, exchange rate, and rate of return assumptions, 2004–10 (percent of GDP)

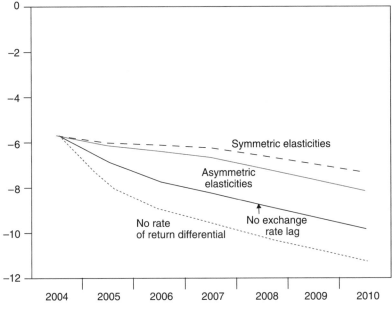

Source: Author's calculations.

Figure 3.6 uses the KGS and HMA models applying the successive changes just described to show the contribution of each of these differences to the overall difference between the Mann baseline and those projected here. The first (most moderate deficit) path has symmetric income elasticities and capacity elasticities, and is the KGS baseline. The second has asymmetric elasticities and is the HMA baseline. The third trajectory takes the HMA baseline and forces the lagged effects from depreciation after 2002 to zero. The fourth trajectory further removes the differential between the rate of return on foreign direct investment assets and liabilities.

As already discussed, the use of asymmetric elasticities boosts the 2010 current account deficit from 7.3 percent of GDP to 8.1 percent (KGS versus HMA). When in addition the influence of the depreciation after 2002 is suppressed, the resulting current account baseline is systematically about 1½ percent of GDP lower than in the main HMA baseline, and by 2010 the current account deficit stands at 9.8 percent of GDP instead of 8.1 percent. When in addition the differential rate of return on foreign direct investment is removed, the current account baseline falls further by about 1 percent of GDP as early as 2005, widening to 1.4 percent of GDP lower by 2010. This brings the 2010 deficit to 11.3 percent of GDP.

The upward bias from application of the import income elasticity to nominal rather than real GDP growth adds another 0.9 percent of GDP to the current account deficit by 2010.[20] Inclusion of this increment brings the projected deficit to 12.1 percent of GDP by 2010, close to Mann's estimate of 12.7 percent. The key economic differences lie in whether one expects lagged exchange rate effects to help arrest the speed of current account deterioration, and in whether one expects the large differential in direct investment returns to continue as it has persistently done in the past (see chapter 2).

The Roubini-Setser baseline projections assume nominal US import growth at 7.25 percent annually and nominal export growth at 5.5 percent annually. Roubini and Setser argue that this was the average over 1990–2003, and that the 2004 level of the dollar was the same as the average for that period (JP Morgan index) and hence trade growth should be about the same. Whatever the merits of this premise, it implicitly adopts asymmetric income elasticities, although not by as much as in the Mann (and HMA) specification. Thus, in the KGS baseline, by 2008 and after, when the pipeline effects of 2002–05 depreciation are complete, nominal imports grow at 8 percent and nominal exports at 7.4 percent, the difference arising solely from differences between US growth at 3.5 percent versus export-weighted foreign growth at 3.1 percent (table 3.1). Nominal import growth relative to export growth at 1.32 to 1 (the Roubini-Setser ratio) implies that the import elasticity is 1.17 times the export income elasticity, a mild asymmetry. On this basis alone, however, the Roubini-Setser baseline should be less favorable than KGS but not less favorable than HMA.

It is in the rate of return assumptions that Roubini and Setser differ more sharply from the projections here. They assume that the differential return will disappear by 2008, and that thereafter the return paid to foreign holders will exceed that earned by US holders of foreign assets. They work at the level of aggregate external assets and aggregate liabilities, rather than applying specific asset class returns as in the model here.[21] Their interpretation not only discards the persistent historical pattern of much higher return on US foreign direct investment abroad than on foreign direct investment in the United States. It also incorporates a major judgment that US creditworthiness will deteriorate and its risk premium escalate because of rising net external debt. This assumption might be valid for an emerging-market economy, but it seems unlikely to be war-

---

20. Applying the cumulative 7.8 percent overstatement to the 2004 import base.

21. Roubini and Setser judge that between 2004 and 2008, nominal return on external assets will rise from 3.7 to 4.7 percent. They project that over the same period, nominal return on external liabilities will rise from 2.4 to 4.8 percent, and that this return will then rise further to 5.1 percent in 2010 because "growing U.S. debt will lead the returns foreigners demand on U.S. [assets] to rise. . . ." (Roubini and Setser 2004, 28).

ranted for the United States under circumstances in which the "economic" net foreign liabilities position remains far more modest than that of emerging-market economies below investment grade.

The reversal from favorable to unfavorable return differential on foreign assets versus liabilities is the driving force in the more unfavorable Roubini-Setser current account baseline than that projected here. They project that (without exchange rate or other adjustment) the current account deficit will reach 10.2 percent of GDP in 2010, and that the capital services deficit will be 2.9 percent of GDP. In contrast, even in the asymmetric elasticity HMA model here, the current account deficit stands at only 8.1 percent of GDP in 2010, and the capital services deficit reaches only 1.3 percent of GDP. Their capital return assumptions thus generate three-fourths of the difference from the HMA baseline here. Their trade deficit by 2010 is 0.5 percent of GDP wider than in the HMA baseline, accounting for virtually all of the rest of the difference. This appears to reflect less allowance for the lagged effect of dollar depreciation in 2002 and 2003 on the trade baseline than in the HMA model here.

Overall, both the Roubini-Setser and the Mann baseline projections would appear to overstate the size of prospective current account deficits. However, the differences in the alternative baselines from the estimates here are ones of degree, not direction. Both the KGS and HMA models also indicate a deteriorating path for the already large US current account deficit, even though the deterioration is not as great as projected by the other two studies. A need for external adjustment is thus implied by all of the projections.

Adjustment Scenarios

This section examines the scope for external adjustment in alternative scenarios for the real exchange rate and foreign and domestic growth. These scenarios may be seen as essentially "policy reduced-form," in the sense that they do not spell out the specific fiscal and monetary policies that generate the postulated exchange rate and growth paths, but they do calculate the resulting current account trends given these paths. In broad terms, all of the adjustment paths implicitly involve tighter fiscal policy in the United States, which reduces domestic dissaving and tends to put downward pressure on the interest rate and hence the exchange rate. The paths also involve more stimulative fiscal policy combined with unchanged or tighter monetary policy abroad, which tends to maintain or boost growth while putting upward pressure on interest rates and hence foreign exchange rates. Structural policies that boost foreign growth on the one hand and increase US saving on the other would also ideally contribute.

Figure 3.7 Current account as a percent of GDP under alternative scenarios, 2004–10

percent of GDP

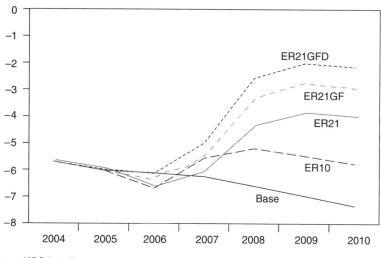

Base = KGS baseline
ER10 = 10 percent real trade-weighted foreign appreciation
ER21 = additional 10 percent real foreign appreciation in 2007 (cumulative foreign appreciation of 21 percent)
ER21GF = additional temporary rise in foreign growth above baseline
ER21GFD = additional temporary reduction in US domestic growth

Figure 3.7 shows the projected path of the current account deficit as a percent of GDP using the preferred KGS model under alternative scenarios. The "base" case is the same as that shown in table 3.2. Case ER10 assumes a 10 percent real trade-weighted appreciation of foreign currencies against the dollar (9.1 percent real depreciation of the dollar) in 2006. Case ER21 has a 10 percent real foreign appreciation against the dollar in 2006 and an additional 10 percent foreign appreciation in 2007, for a cumulative real foreign appreciation of 21 percent (or real depreciation of the dollar by 17.4 percent).[22] Case ER21GF also assumes 10 percent real foreign appreciation in both 2006 and 2007, and additionally assumes that foreign growth temporarily rises above the baseline. Case ER21GFD is the same as ER21GF, but in addition assumes a temporary reduction in US domestic growth.

The growth change scenarios are as follows. In ER21GF, export-weighted foreign growth increases by 0.75 percentage point above the base case assumption for three years (2006–07), reaching 3.85 percent. Allowance is made for some corresponding rise in import-weighted potential growth

---

22. That is, the real price of foreign exchange rises 21 percent, meaning that the real value of the dollar changes by the proportion: $[(1/1.21) - 1] = -0.174$.

capacity based on a 0.5 percentage point increase in foreign growth for the same three years when weighting by US imports, considering that economies with already high growth such as China bulk larger in US imports than exports. For the case with a change in US domestic growth (ER21GFD), it is additionally assumed that US growth is only 3 percent during 2005–07 before returning to the 3.5 percent base case rate. This ease in growth also reduces the 3-year average rate used in the capacity variable on the export side.

A 10 percent real foreign appreciation in 2006 (9 percent dollar depreciation) at first causes a J-curve worsening of the current account deficit from its baseline 6.1 percent of GDP in 2006 (table 3.2) to 6.7 percent in that year, but by 2008 the result is a lower current account deficit at 5.2 percent of GDP instead of the baseline 6.6 percent. The difference of 1.4 percent of GDP provides a useful summary relationship from the model: A 10 percent foreign real appreciation improves the current account balance by 1.4 percent of GDP after two years (as discussed further below). Nonetheless, the adverse baseline trend means that the adjustment is limited and, after narrowing to 5.2 percent of GDP by 2008, the deficit widens again to 5.8 percent of GDP by 2010.

Most analysts consider that an appropriate target for a sustainable current account deficit for the United States is in the range of 2 to 3 percent of GDP. Chapter 5 discusses the sustainable threshold and how it is affected by differential returns on equity. The analysis shows that there would be a cushion from differential returns that might justify a somewhat higher current account deficit, but nonetheless concludes that prudence, as well as uncertainty about the persistence of the differential return over much longer time spans than considered in the projections here, justify adhering to the more traditional target range of about 3 percent of GDP.

The scenario with 21 percent real foreign appreciation (ER21, with 10 percent in 2005 and another 10 percent in 2006) closes much, but not all, of the gap from such a target. In this scenario, the current account deficit narrows to about 4 percent of GDP by 2008, but remains at about that level thereafter. The 21 percent real foreign appreciation of this scenario would bring the dollar from its average level of 96.6 in the first five months of 2005 on the broad Federal Reserve real index to 79.8, which is 8.2 percent lower than its previous annual trough of 86.9 in 1995.

In contrast, if in addition to the 21 percent depreciation there is a temporary acceleration of foreign growth from the baseline, case ER21GF, the current account deficit does narrow to about 3 percent of GDP by 2008, and stays at about that level thereafter. If, in addition, US growth temporarily slows from the baseline, easing demand for imports, the current account would narrow to an estimated 2 percent of GDP by 2009–10. It would be difficult to argue, however, that this additional narrowing would provide welfare gains that would offset those from the lost growth.

Because of the special interest of the just-successful scenario involving 21 percent real foreign appreciation and temporary acceleration of foreign growth, it is useful to examine this case in more detail (table 3.4).

In this case of successful adjustment, the accounting NIIP erodes from −21.7 percent of GDP in 2004 to −29.8 percent in 2010, in comparison to −50.3 percent of GDP in the baseline (table 3.2). The rise in this net external debt is temporarily arrested in 2006 and 2007 by large exchange valuation effects, over $500 billion in each year, thereby trimming about $1 trillion off of the projected NIIP debtor position that would be projected if there were no attention to the exchange rate valuation effect. The erosion of the economic NIIP is sharply curbed from the baseline, as the CNCI reaches only −6.9 percent of GDP by 2010 instead of −21.7 percent.

As noted in chapter 2, Roubini and Setser (2004) argue that there is little future exchange rate valuation gain in the NIIP to be expected from dollar depreciation, because the countries that are home to US direct and portfolio investment have already done their appreciation (Europe), whereas the countries that will be doing the rest of the appreciation do not count for much in US foreign equity assets (e.g., East Asia). However, it is estimated in chapter 2 that only about 35 percent of US foreign non-dollar assets are in the euro or currencies of other countries that arguably have already appreciated as much as could be expected in an overall adjustment (Sweden, Australia, and New Zealand). About 34 percent is in currencies of three industrial countries that have not appreciated nearly as much (United Kingdom, Canada, and Japan). The rest is in currencies of Asian, Latin American, and other emerging-market economies that have appreciated very little or even depreciated against the dollar.

As discussed in chapter 2, if the incremental exchange rate changes beyond end-2004 calculated in the optimal realignment exercise of chapter 6 are weighted by US foreign (equity) asset shares, the weighted incremental foreign appreciation is about three-fourths as large as the trade-weighted incremental appreciation. Moreover, in practice, industrial countries may continue to participate relatively more in the exchange rate correction needed for US external adjustment, and the emerging-market economies relatively less, than recommended in the optimal realignment profile. If so, the gap between the trade- and equity-weighted exchange rate changes would be even smaller. Overall, there may be some upward bias in the size of the favorable exchange rate valuation effect on the NIIP in the adjustment scenarios of this chapter, but any such bias should be moderate.

It is important to note that the external adjustment scenario set forth in table 3.4 (case ER21GF in figure 3.7) is far more favorable than those projected in Mann (2004). She estimates that a decline of the dollar to a

Table 3.4 US external deficit and net foreign assets under exchange rate adjustment and acceleration of foreign growth, 2004–10 (in billions of dollars, in percent, and in ratios)

	2004	2005	2006	2007	2008	2009	2010
Exports, GS	1,151.5	1,296.9	1,501.2	1,792.1	2,132.4	2,348.6	2,522.3
Imports, GS	1,769.0	1,938.4	2,157.9	2,368.6	2,439.4	2,582.3	2,792.6
Trade balance	−617.6	−676.5	−691.7	−611.6	−341.9	−268.7	−305.3
Transfers	−80.9	−80.4	−84.7	−89.2	−94.0	−99.0	−104.4
Capital services	36.2	12.6	−53.8	−53.1	−42.8	−53.5	−60.6
Current account	−668.1	−739.7	−830.2	−753.9	−478.7	−421.2	−470.3
CA/Y	−5.7	−6.0	−6.4	−5.5	−3.3	−2.8	−2.9
Net foreign assets							
Accounting: NIIP	−2,542.3	−3,341.8	−3,543.1	−3,558.4	−3,990.4	−4,363.0	−4,782.8
NIIP/Y (percent)	−21.7	−27.0	−27.2	−25.9	−27.6	−28.6	−29.8
Economic: CNCI	848.6	286.1	−978.6	−965.7	−778.4	−972.0	−1,102.6
CNCI/Y (percent)	7.2	2.3	−7.5	−7.0	−5.4	−6.4	−6.9
ERvaladj	272.3	−81.3	608.0	705.8	0.0	0.0	0.0
Real dollars/FC	0.968	1.0	1.1	1.21	1.21	1.21	1.21
Real dollars/FC (-2)	0.869	0.925	0.968	1.0	1.1	1.21	1.21
Bond rate (ppa)	4.3	4.4	5.5	5.5	5.5	5.5	5.5
FDI return difference (ppa)	4.3	4.6	4.6	4.6	4.6	4.6	4.6

CA/Y = current account balance as percent of GDP
CNCI = capitalized net capital income
ERvaladj = exchange rate valuation change
FC = foreign currency
FDI = foreign direct investment
GS = goods and services
NIIP = net international investment position
ppa = percent per annum

Notes: Assumptions: 10 percent real foreign appreciation in 2006 and again in 2007; and foreign growth accelerates above baseline by 0.75 percent per year during 2006–08.

real index of 85 (Federal Reserve broad index), which would be between cases ER10 and ER21 examined here, would leave the current account deficit at 10 percent of GDP by 2010. Mann attributes this to the elasticity asymmetry and the large initial gap between imports and exports. A depreciation of the dollar to 85 on the Federal Reserve real broad index would correspond to two-thirds of the distance between the "base" and "ER21" scenarios of figure 3.7. This would place the current account deficit in 2010 at about 5 percent of GDP, using the KGS model developed here, likely too large for sustainability but by a much smaller margin than a deficit of 10 percent of GDP. Mann reaches the pessimistic conclusion that it would require not only a 15 percent depreciation of the real dollar but an ongoing 10 percent depreciation every year thereafter, bringing the real dollar index to only 35 by 2010, in order to do no more than compress the 2010 current account deficit to 6 percent of GDP. That outcome, however, would depart from historical experience internationally, in which "purchasing power parity" tends to be maintained for real exchange rates within relatively moderate ranges over time. Instead, Mann's path for the real dollar as just described would cause it to lose two-thirds of purchasing power parity in just six years.

In contrast, Roubini and Setser (2004) call for the achievement of a "strong, smooth, sustained adjustment" scenario in which the current account deficit falls to 4.5 percent of GDP by 2010. However, this scenario is premised on a particular trade outcome (nominal exports grow at 9 percent while import growth is only 5 percent) rather than developed through a projection model with the real exchange rate and domestic and foreign growth as the variables determining the trade outcome. They only state that in this scenario the real exchange rate "depreciates substantially over time" (and, in addition, that the fiscal deficit is cut to 2 percent of GDP by 2008 and zero by 2012).

The scenario exercises presented here would tend toward the conclusion that US external adjustment will be difficult but not impossible. The magnitudes of the implied real depreciation and relative growth rates are within reasonable levels. However, in the absence of any change in real exchange rates and baseline growth, the United States would remain on a dangerous path of escalating current account deficits and net international debt in both accounting and economic terms, even if the pace and extent of this deteriorating path may be less severe than suggested by some other estimates.

Impact Parameters

The various scenario results (and additional runs of the model) can be used to identify parameters for the impact of alternative macroeconomic events on the current account. These parameters are "partial equilibrium"

Table 3.5 Partial equilibrium macroeconomic impact parameters: Change in current account from baseline (percent of GDP)

Parameter for:	In year:		
	1	3	5
10 percent real foreign appreciation against the dollar (sustained)	−0.57	1.41	1.57
1 percent faster foreign growth for one year	0.39	0.39	0.44
1 percent faster US growth for one year	−0.42	−0.43	−0.48
1 percent higher interest rate (sustained)	−0.31	−0.43	−0.56

in that they assume no parallel macroeconomic phenomenon is induced by the "event" in question that has the effect of reducing or increasing the direct effect of the event itself. Four events are considered: a real depreciation of the dollar, a decrease in US domestic growth, an increase in foreign growth, and a rise in the US interest rate. The terminology "event" is used instead of "policy instrument" to recognize that, with the possible exception of the interest rate, these macroeconomic phenomena are endogenously determined and not direct policy instruments.

First, it is necessary to add one scenario not included above: a rise in the interest rate. When the projection model is shocked by applying a baseline for the 10-year Treasury bond rate that is 1 percentage point higher during 2006–10 than in tables 3.2 through 3.4, the result is to boost the KGS baseline current account deficit from 6.1 to 6.4 percent of GDP in 2006; from 6.2 to 6.6 percent in 2007; and from 7.3 to 7.9 percent by 2010.

Impact simulations of the KGS model can similarly be conducted for a 1 percent shock to US growth in 2006, and for a 1 percent shock to foreign growth in 2006. The resulting impact parameters can then be synthesized (table 3.5).[23]

Comparison of the ER10 scenario against the baseline (figure 3.7) yields the parameters for exchange rate change (foreign appreciation, or dollar depreciation) shown in table 3.5. The first-year effect is adverse because of the J-curve effect. By year 3, however, the 10 percent real foreign

23. Note that these parameters are broadly consistent with those in Cline (1989, 209) once changes in trade relative to GDP are taken into account (and after translating absolute impact estimates in that earlier study into percent of GDP; p. 187). In that study, a 1 percent real depreciation was estimated to produce a 0.15 percent of GDP current account improvement, versus 0.13 percent here. One percent of additional foreign growth was estimated to yield 0.17 percent of GDP improvement in the current account deficit, and 1 percent less domestic growth, a 0.22 percent of GDP improvement. The estimates here are higher because both exports and imports of goods and services have risen relative to GDP since the 1987 base in Cline (1989) (from 7.4 to 10 percent and from 10.6 to 15 percent, respectively). The current study's estimates also incorporate a strong cyclical elasticity for trade, which was absent in the earlier study.

appreciation carried out in year 1 (and with the real exchange rate held constant thereafter) induces a 1.41 percent of GDP rise in the current account balance from the baseline it would otherwise follow, and by year 5, this parameter rises to 1.57 percent of GDP. For the third year (mid-point), this parameter means that each percentage point of foreign appreciation translates into a reduction of about $16.5 billion in the current account deficit, gauged against 2004 GDP, or $20 billion when applied to GDP for the projection year in question (2008).

An increase in the export-weighted foreign growth rate by 1 percent for one year improves the current account balance by 0.39 percent of GDP by year 3.[24] Another run of the model finds that an increase in US growth by 1 percentage point from the baseline in 2006 increases the current account deficit by 0.43 percent of GDP by 2008. Finally, boosting the interest rate by 1 percentage point from the baseline during 2006–10 causes a rising increment in the deficit, reaching 0.43 percent of GDP by 2008 and 0.56 percent of GDP by 2010.

A useful rule of thumb from these results is that three effects have about the same impact on the current account by the third year. A 1 percent reduction in foreign growth for one year, a 1 percent increase in US growth for one year, and a 1 percentage point sustained increase in the interest rate would each cause the current account deficit to widen by about 0.4 percent of GDP by the third year. However, the influence of the higher interest rate grows over time.

---

24. Again it is assumed that the corresponding rise in US import-weighted foreign capacity growth is based on a smaller rise in growth, set here at 0.67 percent for one year, because of the greater prominence in US imports than in US exports of already high-growth economies such as China.

4

US Fiscal Imbalance
and the External Deficit

Understanding the Linkages

Correcting the large US external imbalance in a manner that avoids crisis will almost certainly require correcting the large US fiscal deficit. The reason is that the two deficits are closely linked. At the intuitive level, when a nation runs a current account deficit it is "living beyond its means." If the country is a developing one that is building up productive capacity financed by capital from abroad, such a deficit can be quite appropriate, as long as the size of the current account deficit is not so large as to trigger a collapse in confidence in the capital market. However, if the country is a wealthy one that is using the resources from abroad to finance consumption and government spending rather than capital investment, the current account deficit is a manifestation of distortions in an economic policy that is dubious at best and dangerous at worst. The presence of a fiscal deficit in this case indicates that the public sector is living beyond its means, and therefore reducing the public sector deficit is a prime vehicle for achieving external adjustment.

The central message of this chapter is that both further real depreciation of the dollar and fiscal adjustment will be required to substantially reduce the US current account deficit. This is a mainstream diagnosis. One alternative extreme position is that no change in exchange rates is necessary or desirable, and that only fiscal adjustment can bring about the external adjustment (McKinnon 2005). Another alternative extreme is the "Ricardian equivalence" proposition that fiscal adjustment has no effect on the domestic use of resources (and hence the current account balance) because any reduction (or increase) in the fiscal deficit is fully offset by a reduction (or increase) in private saving, on grounds that "rational expectations" lead households to expect future taxes to be lower (higher) as a consequence of the fiscal change (Barro 1974). The view that exchange rate change is not helpful contradicts past adjustment experience (Krugman 1991). The view that household saving changes to fully offset fiscal changes has always strained credulity, and has been flatly contradicted in recent years as private saving has continued to plunge even as government accounts have swung from surplus to large deficit.

This chapter develops a general equilibrium model to illustrate the importance of a combined contribution from both exchange rate change and fiscal adjustment in obtaining external adjustment. The discussion in chapter 5 returns to the question of the potential contribution of fiscal adjustment by assessing certain recent studies, especially Erceg, Guerrieri, and Gust (2005); Bernanke (2005); and Ferguson (2005).

Accounting Link

The national accounts provide a formal framework for thinking about how the excess claim on resources from abroad divides into excess use of resources by the respective public and private sectors. The national income accounts identity on the side of "product demand" is

$$Y = C + I + G + X - M \tag{4.1}$$

where Y is GDP, C is private consumption, I is private investment, G is government spending on consumption and investment (but not on interest payments or transfers), X is exports, and M is imports. Each of the elements on the right-hand side represents demand of a particular type. All of the demand components generate demand for domestic production except imports, which subtract from the amount that must be produced domestically to provide the product needed for the other components of demand.[1]

On the "factor supply" side of the national accounts, GDP is divided into the payments to the labor and capital that produce it. The household owners of labor and capital in turn use these payments for three possible purposes: consumption, saving, and tax payments. So on the factor payments side,

---

1. Government spending on interest and transfers, in contrast, does not generate a direct purchase of goods and services that enters into the national accounts estimates of production. The indirect effects of this spending, primarily induced consumption by recipients of transfers and interest, show up in the national accounts as consumption, not government activity.

$$Y = C + S_p + R \qquad (4.2)$$

where S_p is private saving and R is government tax revenue. We can subtract equation 4.2 from equation 4.1 and then rearrange the result to obtain

$$I + G + X - M - S_p - R = 0;$$
$$I - S_p - [R - G] = M - X; \qquad (4.3)$$
$$I - S_p - S_g = M - X;$$
$$I - S_p + D^F = M - X$$

The third line of equation 4.3 provides the fundamental link between the external and fiscal deficits. It states that *the excess of investment over domestic private and public sector saving equals the excess of imports over exports.* Investment must equal domestic saving plus "foreign saving," which is the excess of imports over exports. Domestic saving equals private saving (S_p) plus government saving (S_g, which is simply the excess of tax revenue over government spending, or $[R - G]$). The fourth line of equation 4.3 rewrites the same relationship using the definition of the fiscal deficit, D^F, which is the negative of government saving.

The excess of investment over saving amounts to a gap between the amount of resources used and the amount available domestically. This resource gap is made up by drawing on resources from abroad, in the form of imports in excess of exports. Because "government saving" is one source of domestic resources, a decline in government saving—i.e., a rise in the fiscal deficit—widens the resource gap and the external deficit. Thus, in the final line of equation 4.3, if the fiscal deficit rises and neither investment nor private saving changes, there must be an increase in the trade deficit.[2]

Because investment and private saving do not necessarily remain unchanged, however, what has sometimes been called the "twin deficits" relationship between the trade and fiscal deficits is by no means a lockstep (or Siamese-twin) relationship.[3] It is blindingly clear in figure 4.1 that, in fact, for the past quarter-century, the two deficits have moved in opposite

---

2. If the focus is on net foreign assets rather than the trade deficit, it is necessary to take net factor income on capital (NFI) into account as well as the above identities. Gross national income (GNI) equals GDP + NFI. The change in net foreign assets arises both from the trade balance and the balance on net factor income: $\Delta NFA = (X - M) + NFI$. At present, US NFI is still positive, although much smaller relative to GDP than in earlier decades. As the NFI turns negative and reaches large magnitudes, as in the baseline projections of net capital services income in chapter 3, the annual deterioration of net foreign assets will be considerably larger than just the trade deficit. Yet it will be only the trade deficit that provides real net resources to cover the gap between domestic investment and domestic saving.

3. For recent discussions of the twin deficits, see Gramlich (2004) and Truman (2004).

Figure 4.1 Fiscal balance and current account balance as a percent of GDP, 1978–2004

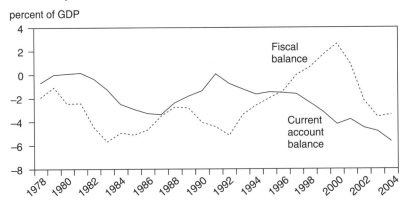

percent of GDP

Sources: IMF (2005a); BEA (2005c).

directions much more frequently than in the same direction.[4] For 1979 through 2004, the change in the fiscal and current account balances from the prior year had the same sign in only 10 of the 26 years, or 38 percent of the time. The relationship has been even less evident for the past 21 years; the two balances moved in the same direction during only six of 21 years, or only 29 percent of the time. The two deficits moved in the same direction in 2002–03, but diverged again in 2004.

The most sustained and dramatic divergence between the external and fiscal deficits was from 1992 to 2000, when the current account swung from near balance to large deficit even though the fiscal accounts swung from large deficit to sizable surplus. The source of this paradox was the upsurge in private investment combined with a collapse in the private saving rate. As shown in figure 4.2, from 1992 to 2000, net private investment (i.e., gross investment less depreciation) rose from 5.6 to 9.2 percent of GDP. From national accounts equation 4.3 above, this would have been expected to drive a downswing in the current account balance by the difference, or 3.6 percent of GDP. Adding to the widening resources gap, personal saving fell from 7.7 percent of disposable income to 2.3 percent.[5] Corporate saving (undistributed profits) fluctuated but was basically unchanged from 1992 to 2000, and thus did not finance rising investment, let alone make up for falling household saving.

Any "twin" relationship between the external deficit and fiscal deficits thus vanished in the 1990s. Fiscal restraint and the booming economy eliminated the fiscal deficit and turned it into surplus. But for two related

---

4. Figure 4.1 shows the current account and consolidated (federal, state, and local) fiscal balances.

5. Personal disposable income averaged 73.4 percent over 1992–2003, with little variation.

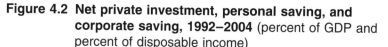

Figure 4.2 Net private investment, personal saving, and corporate saving, 1992–2004 (percent of GDP and percent of disposable income)

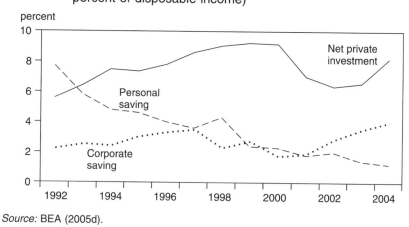

percent

- Net private investment
- Personal saving
- Corporate saving

1992 1994 1996 1998 2000 2002 2004

Source: BEA (2005d).

reasons, that did not head off a wider external deficit. First, there was a boom in investment, partly associated with lower interest rates aided by the fiscal correction, but also spurred by "the new economy" and the information technology sectors in particular. Second, there was also a sharp decline in household saving as measured for national accounts purposes, probably in considerable part because households perceived their wealth to be rising from increased asset prices for their holdings of equities in the stock market boom and from rising valuations of their homes (as discussed below).[6] The result was the opening up of a large gap between personal saving and private investment that more than offset the reduction in the fiscal deficit. In terms of the national accounts relationship, from 1992 to 2000, we can write the following trends: $\Delta I > 0$; $\Delta S_p < 0$; $\Delta S_g > 0$; $[\Delta I - \Delta S_p > \Delta S_g] \rightarrow \uparrow[M{-}X]$.

Table 4.1 summarizes the relationships between the swings in investment, saving, and the external balance from 1992 to 2000 and then to 2004. All of the data are gross, so neither investment nor saving figures deduct depreciation. The bottom line for the external accounts was a widening of the deficit on goods and services, from net exports of -0.5 percent of GDP in 1992 to -3.9 percent in 2000 and -5.2 percent by 2004, using the national income and product accounts (NIPA) concept. The balance of payments concept of the current account balance, which differs slightly by the amount of net capital services and transfers (as well as statistical differences from NIPA data), closely followed this path. A

---

6. It could also be argued that falling rates of saving reflected a rational response to the falling interest rate incentive.

Table 4.1 National accounts investment, saving, and external balance, 1992, 2000, and 2004
(in billions of dollars and in percent of GDP)

		1992		2000		2004	
		Billions of dollars	Percent of GDP	Billions of dollars	Percent of GDP	Billions of dollars	Percent of GDP
GDP	Y	6,337.7	100.0	9,817.0	100.0	11,735.0	100.0
Personal consumption	C	4,235.3	66.8	6,739.4	68.7	8,229.9	70.1
Gross private investment	Ip	864.8	13.6	1,735.5	17.7	1,927.3	16.4
Government consumption and investment	G	1,271.0	20.1	1,721.6	17.5	2,186.8	18.6
Exports, goods and services	X	635.3	10.0	1,096.3	11.2	1,175.5	10.0
Imports, goods and services	M	668.6	10.5	1,475.8	15.0	1,781.6	15.2
Net exports	X–M	−33.3	−0.5	−379.5	−3.9	−606.1	−5.2
Current account	CA	−48.0	−0.8	−411.5	−4.2	−665.9	−5.7
Government investment	Ig	223.1	3.5	304.5	3.1	379.7	3.2
Private saving	Sp	1,100.4	17.4	1,334.1	13.6	1,749.0	14.9
Government saving	Sg	−152.1	−2.4	436.4	4.4	−129.0	−1.1
Resource gap: Ip+Ig−Sp−Sg	—	139.6	2.2	269.5	2.7	687.0	5.9
Trade deficit	M–X	33.3	0.5	379.5	3.9	606.1	5.2
Statistical discrepancy	—	106.3	1.7	−110.0	−1.1	80.9	0.7

Source: BEA (2005c, d).

rise in private investment by 4.1 percent of GDP from 1992 to 2000, combined with a decline in private saving by 3.8 percent of GDP over the same period, widened the domestic resource gap by more than it was narrowed by the upswing in government saving (by 6.8 percent of GDP) and the slight moderation in government investment (-0.4 percent of GDP). Surprisingly, however, the measured rise in the resource gap was much smaller (from 2.2 to 2.7 percent of GDP) than the rise in the NIPA net deficit on goods and services (from 0.5 to 3.9 percent of GDP). The result was a large swing in the statistical discrepancy of the resource gap, from 1.7 percent of GDP in 1992 to -1.1 percent of GDP in 2000.

Table 4.1 also shows the further widening of the external deficit in association with the fiscal collapse over 2000–04. The downswing of government saving from 4.4 percent of GDP in 2000 to -1.1 percent of GDP in 2004 was only partially offset by a moderation in private investment by 1.3 percent of GDP (itself slightly offset by a rise in government investment by 0.1 percent of GDP) and by a modest recovery in private saving (from 13.6 to 14.9 percent of GDP). The result was a widening of the resource gap (investment minus saving) amounting to 3.2 percent of GDP, bringing the external deficit to about 6 percent of GDP.

It is fairly well known that the potential positive effect of fiscal adjustment in the 1990s on the external balance was more than offset by the even greater negative effect of rising investment and falling household saving. Perhaps less well known is that at least some part of the weak response of the external deficit to the fiscal adjustment was attributable to the difference between the budgetary fiscal deficit and the national accounts fiscal deficit. The traditional relationship of the fiscal deficit to the external balance weakens if the driving force in fiscal trends is changes in transfer and interest payments, which do not enter into the NIPA concept of government spending.

Consider a government that has been downsized to zero spending on defense, education, environment, and all other tangible goods and services demand. This government has only one function: to collect taxes and use them for transfers (e.g., Social Security and Medicare-Medicaid) and to pay interest on past debt. In the national accounts, this government's contribution to real product demand would be $G = 0$. Yet this government could be running a large fiscal deficit. For such a government, *reduction in the fiscal deficit would have no direct impact ex ante on the external balance*, because there would be no change in G in the national accounts relationships of equation 4.3. Reduction in the deficit would have to work strictly indirectly, by reducing the interest rate and thereby inducing downward pressure on the dollar (as discussed below); and by reducing disposable income to transfer-receiving households, thereby reducing their purchases of imports.

In the framework of traditional Keynesian income determination, the change in equilibrium income equals a "multiplier" times the initial

**Figure 4.3 Federal revenue, total spending, and NIPA
spending, 1992–2003** (percent of GDP)

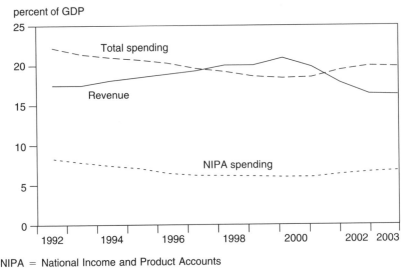

NIPA = National Income and Product Accounts
Sources: BEA (2005d); CBO (2005d).

change in government purchases of goods and services. The first two
rounds of the chain of spending in the multiplier are the change in government spending itself, ΔG, and the induced change in consumption by
households selling the goods and services to the government, which is
the marginal propensity to consume c times the amount purchased by
the government. Aggregate demand thus rises by $\Delta G(1 + c)$ just in the
first two rounds. In contrast, when the government increases transfer
payments rather than real purchases for its own use, by amount ΔGT,
there is no initial round of change in aggregate demand. The second,
induced, round is the same as before, and amounts to $c\Delta GT$. On just the
first two rounds in the spending chain, then, a change in government
transfers has less than half as much impact on aggregate demand (assuming $c < 1$) as a change in government purchases of goods and services.

Figure 4.3 indicates that so far the distinction between budgetary and
NIPA fiscal accounts has made only a modest difference in the extent
of changes in resource pressure exerted by the federal government on
aggregate demand. From 1992 to 2000, budgetary federal spending fell
from 22.2 to 18.4 percent of GDP, or by 3.8 percent. Federal government
purchases counted in the national accounts (NIPA in the figure) fell from
8.4 to 5.9 percent of GDP over the same period, or by 2.5 percent.[7] The

---

7. National accounts purchases by state and local governments hovered at a relatively
steady 11.5 percent of GDP, placing total G at 20 percent of GDP in 1992, and falling to an
average of about 17.5 percent in 1998–2000 before rebounding to 18.6 percent by 2004.

other 1.3 percent of GDP reduction in federal spending was mainly in lower interest payments (as discussed below). Even so, this divergence does suggest that *a modest part of the paradoxical divergence between falling fiscal deficits and rising external deficits from 1992 to 2000 was attributable to a smaller decline in real national accounts government purchases than in total government spending including interest and transfers.*

The difference between the NIPA and budgetary concepts of government spending could become much more important in the future. As discussed below, over a long-term horizon of several decades, transfer payments to recipients of Social Security and especially Medicare-Medicaid are projected to rise sharply. Fiscal adjustment programs involving cutbacks in these or other transfer payments would have no direct effect in reducing resource pressure from government spending. The ex ante effect of government spending cuts on the external balance would thus be absent in this area. The ex post effect would depend on induced exchange rate, investment demand, and consumer demand effects.

Induced Exchange Rate Effects

Whereas a focus on the national accounts identity tends to emphasize the role of government saving in aggregate demand for resources relative to supply as the transmission mechanism from fiscal to external deficits, the "trade elasticities" approach tends to emphasize the importance of the exchange rate in setting the relative price of tradables versus nontradables in the economy. There is a central linkage from fiscal balance to the exchange rate, which under normal times runs as follows. Fiscal adjustment to reduce the fiscal deficit takes pressure off of the domestic capital market, as there is less government "crowding out" of private borrowing. With a resulting fall in the interest rate, investment by foreigners in the US market is less attractive, so demand for the dollar will fall. As a consequence, fiscal adjustment prompts a decline in the value of the dollar. The resulting trade price "signal" working through trade response to price ("elasticities approach") then becomes the transmission mechanism through which fiscal adjustment leads to external sector adjustment.[8]

As discussed below, the national accounts identity and the trade price elasticities equations are merely parts of a set of simultaneous equations that must all hold in a general equilibrium for the economy. It is useful to recognize at the outset, however, that the sign of the fiscal adjustment's impact on the exchange rate is potentially ambiguous. Even in benign times, there is also a relationship of the exchange rate to expected growth rates, because higher domestic growth relative to foreign growth will

---

8. This has been called the "Massachusetts Avenue model" after the addresses of economic research centers in Cambridge and Washington (Krugman 1991).

tend to attract foreign investors who are searching for more investment opportunities than are available in their home countries. If the fiscal adjustment sends the signal of slower domestic growth, discouragement of foreign investment inflows will reinforce the influence of lower interest rates in pushing down the exchange rate and making exports more attractive and imports less attractive. But if fiscal adjustment sends the signal that future growth instead will be higher because of lower domestic interest rates (broadly the "Rubinomics" of the mid-1990s, named after President Bill Clinton's Secretary of the Treasury, Robert Rubin), then the boost in demand for dollars in response to the more favorable growth outlook may exceed the cut in demand for dollars by interest-sensitive foreign investors. This appears to have occurred in the late 1990s, when large inflows of foreign investment influenced by the sustained economic boom boosted the dollar even though interest rates had fallen.[9]

These alternative potential expectations effects on the exchange rate are both within broadly benign environments. However, there can also be "confidence shock" expectational effects. The dollar began to fall relatively rapidly following the reelection of President George W. Bush.[10] One plausible interpretation is that foreign investors judged that the new administration was less likely than an administration of candidate John Kerry to carry out fiscal adjustment, and that this contributed to at least a temporary loss in confidence in the dollar.

The possibility of a confidence break suggests a potentially highly non-linear relationship between the fiscal deficit and the exchange rate, such as that shown in figure 4.4. In a "normal" zone, such as a move in the fiscal balance from a moderate fiscal deficit at A to a modest fiscal surplus at B, the real exchange rate would depreciate from E_A to E_B in response to a moderation in the interest rate as the fiscal balances improve. If instead the fiscal deficit widens further, at some point there is a break in confidence and the exchange rate plunges to a level such as E_C at fiscal balance C. This occurs even though the interest rate is even higher at C than at A, because there is a sharply rising risk spread for exchange rate or (more typically for developing countries) debt default risk. Although the simple general equilibrium model developed later in this chapter assumes that, for any given growth rate, the exchange rate-fiscal balance relationship remains in the benign zone, the possibility of a confidence break must be kept in mind.

---

9. Thus, inflows of direct private investment into the United States soared from $58 billion in 1995 to $301 billion in 1999, even though the 10-year Treasury bond rate fell from 6.6 to 5.6 percent (IMF 2004b).

10. From November 2 to December 31, 2004, the dollar fell 6.2 percent against the euro and 3.4 percent against the yen.

Figure 4.4 Relationship of the exchange rate to the fiscal deficit

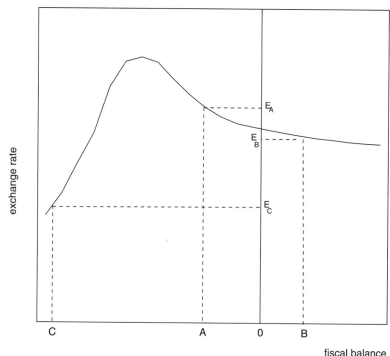

Note: Exchange rate = foreign currency/home currency.

Fiscal Adjustment and Consumption

Fiscal adjustment can influence the external balance working through induced reduction in consumption, as well as through the exchange rate mechanism. An increase in the tax rate will tend to reduce disposable income, which in turn will reduce consumption and imports of consumer goods. Similarly, a reduction in government spending (NIPA) will reduce payments to factors of production, hence income, hence consumption, and hence imports. In the case of transfer spending, a reduction will tend to reduce consumption in the same way as an increase in taxes, that is, by reducing disposable income.

From Fiscal Surplus to Deficit

The United States has experienced a stunning fiscal roller-coaster ride during the past decade. After a history of chronic fiscal deficits in the postwar period, and particularly large deficits in the 1980s, the federal fiscal accounts by the late 1990s moved into surplus with help from the stock market bubble and the sustained economic boom. The projected future surpluses were so large that serious economists began to think about the implications of the eventual elimination of federal debt (Truman 2001). Then, during 2001–04, with the bursting of the bubble, a brief recession, increased military spending, and the tax reductions enacted by the first administration of George W. Bush, large fiscal deficits returned. The federal fiscal balance fell from a surplus of 2.4 percent of GDP in 2000 to a deficit of 3.6 percent of GDP in 2004. The long-term outlook suddenly shifted from potential elimination of federal debt to protracted deficits and debt buildup over a decade or so, and even worse prospects later when the rising Social Security and Medicare costs of the retiring baby boom generation would begin to take effect.

In the 2004 presidential campaign, both President George W. Bush and Senator John Kerry pledged to cut the fiscal deficit in half over four years. The actual outcome for fiscal 2004 (ending September) was a deficit of $412 billion, which amounted to 3.6 percent of GDP for October 2003 to September 2004 (OMB 2005b, BEA 2005d). The second Bush administration seeks to cut the deficit to 3.5 percent in fiscal year 2005, 3 percent in 2006, 2.3 percent in 2007, 1.7 percent in 2008, 1.5 percent in 2009, and 1.3 percent in 2010 (OMB 2005a). As discussed below, however, it seems much more likely that in the absence of forceful and even radical action, the deficit will amount to about 3 to 3½ percent of GDP during the full period 2007–12. This section first diagnoses how the US fiscal accounts collapsed so swiftly. It then turns to baseline fiscal prospects.

The Congressional Budget Office (CBO) successively revised downward its fiscal projections for the period 2001–11, from a prospective 10-year cumulative surplus of $5.6 trillion in its January 2001 estimates to a cumulative deficit of $3 trillion. The downswing amounted to 6 percent of average projected GDP. Of the total change in the baseline, and summing over the 11-year period, 40 percent was attributable to "economic and technical changes," 33 percent to higher spending, and 27 percent to lower taxes. Much of the economic and technical change was for persistent rather than cyclical reasons. These include smaller than expected capital gains tax revenues, lower growth of incomes taxed at the highest marginal rates, and unexplained revenue weakness (OECD 2004b, 68–69, 94).

To provide historical perspective on the present imbalance, figure 4.5 shows the paths of the nominal and real federal fiscal deficits over the past 40 years. The real deficit is calculated as the nominal deficit less the inflationary erosion of outstanding federal debt in the hands of the public, estimated by applying the rise in the GDP deflator for the year in question to the debt at the end of the previous year.[11] It is the real deficit that

---

11. The series are from Council of Economic Advisers (2005). The federal fiscal deficits and federal debt held by the public are for fiscal years.

Figure 4.5 Nominal and real federal fiscal balances, 1963–2004 (percent of GDP)

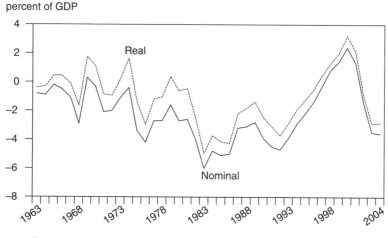

Sources: See text.

matters for the evolution of fiscal sustainability, because the inflationary component of rising debt will tend to be offset by corresponding inflation in the nominal GDP base. The nominal deficit was 3.5 percent of GDP in 2003 and 3.6 percent for 2004. These rates compare unfavorably with the average of 2.2 percent for the last four decades. The corresponding real deficits are 2.9 percent of GDP in 2003 and 2.8 percent in 2004. This outcome is even worse relative to experience over the past four decades: an average real deficit of only 1.1 percent of GDP. It is sometimes argued that today's deficits are not large by historical standards, but that impression is implicitly drawn against the period 1975–93, and in most of that period, the real deficit was considerably smaller than the nominal deficit because of relatively high inflation.

It is also natural to think that the recent deficits must be to a considerable extent transitory because they reflect in part the recession of 2001. Estimates by the Organization for Economic Cooperation and Development (OECD) of the cyclically-adjusted deficit suggest instead that the great bulk of the deterioration of the fiscal accounts has been for reasons other than the business cycle. Figure 4.6 reports OECD (2003) estimates of the US "general government" (federal, state, and local) fiscal balances for 1986–2003. The figure shows the actual deficit and the cyclically-adjusted deficit, for both the total and "primary" balances (the primary balance excludes net interest payments). The economic boom from 1999–2000 contributed a cyclical component of about +0.5 percent of GDP to the fiscal outcome for both the total and primary balances. Then by 2002–03, following the 2001 recession, the cyclical component had swung to about

Figure 4.6 General government fiscal balance and primary balance, actual and cyclically adjusted, 1986–2003
(percent of GDP)

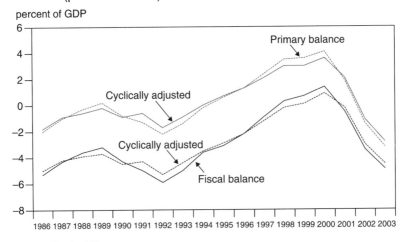

Source: OECD (2003).

−0.4 percent of GDP for both the total and primary balances. So the cyclical reversal contributed about 0.9 percent of GDP to the erosion of the fiscal balance between the two periods. Yet the total deterioration from the 1999–2000 average to the 2002–03 average amounted to about 5 percent of GDP for the actual deficit and 6 percent for the primary deficit. So the adverse cyclical effect can only account for about one-fifth to one-sixth of the erosion in fiscal performance.

Besides showing that the 2001 recession was not the main cause of fiscal deterioration, figure 4.6 illustrates another key development: The decline in interest rates has substantially shrunk the difference between the primary and total deficits. In part this reflects the decline in inflation, and hence the inflationary component of interest rates, since the late 1980s. In part, however, the unusually narrow gap by 2001–03 reflects unusually low real interest rates. This in turn suggests that the fiscal accounts are vulnerable to an increased interest burden as real rates return to more normal levels.

Figure 4.7 shows the evolution of actual federal revenue, expenditure, and fiscal balance as well as the CBO's baseline projections over the past 15 years and through 2012. It must be emphasized that the CBO is required by law to make projections based on current legislation, so its forecasts do not include the effect of the president's proposed extension of tax cuts and other changes that could make the outlook considerably worse. Focusing on the actual record to date, however, it is evident that the driving force in the fiscal collapse has been a decline in revenue. From

Figure 4.7 **Actual and Congressional Budget Office baseline projection of federal revenues and expenditures and fiscal balance, 1990–2012** (percent of GDP)

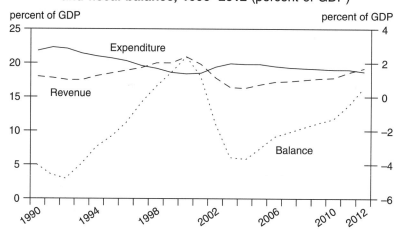

Note: Revenue and expenditure on left scale; fiscal balance on right scale.

Source: CBO (2005a, b).

2000 to 2004, federal revenue fell from 20.9 to 16.3 percent of GDP, or by 4.6 percent of GDP. Spending also rose, but only by 1.5 percent of GDP, from 18.4 to 19.8 percent (CBO 2005a, b).

Figure 4.8 decomposes federal revenue into taxes on incomes of individuals, incomes of corporations, social contributions (Social Security and Medicare-Medicaid), and all other taxes (excise, estate, customs, and other). The figure shows clearly that the driving force in the fiscal turnaround was a swing in personal income tax revenue, from a strongly rising trend in 1997–2000 to a sharply falling trend in 2001–04. Taxes on individuals rose from an average of 8.3 percent of GDP in 1995–96 to an average of 10 percent in 2000–01, but then plunged to 7 percent by 2004. In contrast, corporate income taxes were virtually unchanged from 1995–96 to 2000 (at 2.1 percent of GDP) but then fell to a low of 1.2 percent of GDP in 2003 before partially reviving to 1.6 percent in 2004. The rise and then fall of personal income taxes also suggests that a major part of the problem was an unsustainably high pace of personal income tax revenue by the latter part of the financial market and economic boom of the late 1990s.

Capital gains tax revenues in particular appear to have played a key role in the rise and fall in personal income taxes. As indicated in figure 4.9, the total of net capital gains reported on personal income tax returns surged from about 2 percent of GDP in 1990 and 1995 to about 6 percent of GDP in 1999 and 2000 before plunging again (with the stock market) to 2 percent of GDP in 2002 (Internal Revenue Service 2004). The corres-

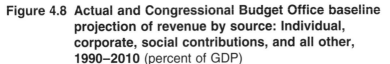

Figure 4.8 Actual and Congressional Budget Office baseline projection of revenue by source: Individual, corporate, social contributions, and all other, 1990–2010 (percent of GDP)

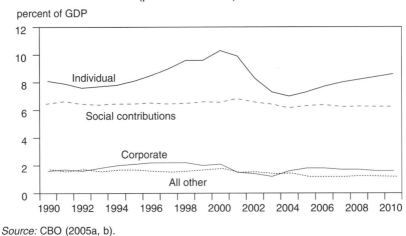

percent of GDP

Source: CBO (2005a, b).

ponding magnitudes of tax revenues on capital gains would probably have been about 25 percent of the amount of capital gains (considering the 20 percent rate on long-term gains plus the normal marginal rate for short-term gains), so an upswing of 4 percent of GDP in capital gains might have contributed an additional 1 percent of GDP to revenues during the stock market bubble culminating in 1999–2000. This would have been about half of the increase in personal income tax revenue (from 8.1 percent before and just after the bubble to about 10 percent in 1999–2001).

Tax cuts were also a key part of the decline in revenue, however, especially by 2003–04 as the recovery was well under way. The OECD (2004b, 69) estimates that tax cuts enacted in 2001 (the Economic Growth and Tax Relief Reconciliation Act—EGTRRA) and 2003 (the Jobs and Growth Tax Relief Reconciliation Act—JGTRRA) reduced revenue by 1.9 percent of GDP in 2003 and by 2.6 percent of GDP in 2004 from levels otherwise obtained.[12] The OECD estimate implies that in the absence of the tax cuts, the 2004 fiscal deficit might have been only 1 percent rather than 3.6 percent of GDP.

---

12. The two tax bills cut the top marginal tax rate from 39.6 to 35 percent and the minimum rate from 15 to 10 percent; increased the standard deduction for married couples; increased the child tax credit; temporarily increased the exemption from the alternative minimum tax; and, for 2003–08, cut the long-term capital gains tax rate from 20 to 15 percent and made dividends taxable at 15 percent instead of the earned-income rate.

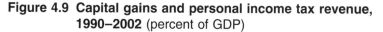

Figure 4.9 Capital gains and personal income tax revenue, 1990–2002 (percent of GDP)

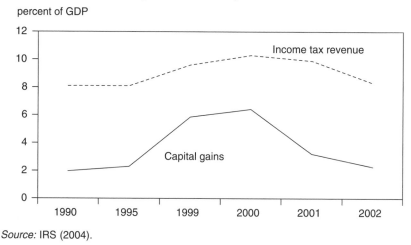

percent of GDP

Source: IRS (2004).

Whether the economy would have recovered from the 2001 recession as well as it did without the tax cuts is, of course, a central issue. Boskin (2004) argues that the tax cuts were ideal for reviving the economy. Krugman (2003) argues persuasively, however, that they were part of a longer-term agenda to reduce taxation of capital and higher-income households, and that cuts oriented toward lower-income households on a more temporary basis would have been much less dangerous for long-term fiscal equilibrium. The main point for the present analysis is that the much longer-term nature of the cuts than would usually be adopted for fighting a recession poses a major challenge to restoring fiscal balance, especially if the Bush administration achieves the objective of making the cuts permanent despite their initial phase-out dates.

Figure 4.10 shows past trends in the main components of federal spending along with the CBO baseline projections. The future projections again tend to understate the deficit by accepting the administration's projection that non-defense discretionary domestic spending will fall relative to GDP.

An important long-term trend evident in figure 4.10 is the sharp decline in defense spending in the 1990s, from an average of 5.3 percent of GDP in 1990–91 to 3.6 percent by 1995–96 and 3 percent by 2000–01. This "peace dividend" of 1.7 percent of GDP following the end of the Cold War played a major role in the early phase of the reduction in the fiscal deficit, contributing about half of the deficit reduction from 5 percent of GDP in 1990–92 to 1.8 percent in 1995–96. Conversely, the military buildup as a result of the Afghanistan and Iraq wars following the September 11, 2001 attacks brought defense spending back up to 3.9 percent of GDP by 2004. The lack of any real prospect for a sharp decline in defense spending

Figure 4.10 Federal spending: Defense, non-defense discretionary, mandatory, and net interest, 1990–2010 (percent of GDP)

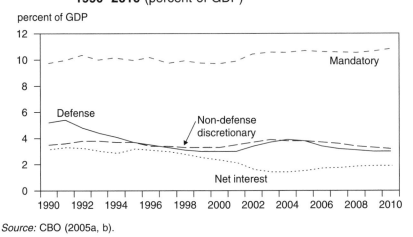

Source: CBO (2005a, b).

going forward is one of the main reasons that it is difficult to envision a repeat of the favorable swing into surplus in the 1990s.

Figure 4.10 also shows that the largest broad spending category has persistently been mandatory social spending, at about 10 percent of GDP, broken down as about 4.3 percent for Social Security, 2.3 percent for Medicare, 1.2 percent for Medicaid, 1.4 percent for income support, 1.2 percent for other retirement and disability programs, and 0.4 percent for other programs.[13] The mandatory category rose by about 1 percent of GDP from the 1997–2001 average to the 2002–04 average, mainly as a result of an increase in income support (reflecting in part unemployment after the 2001 recession) and higher Medicaid spending.

Once again, the spending relief from lower net interest is evident. Net interest fell from an average of about 3.2 percent of GDP in the early 1990s to only 1.4 percent of GDP in 2003–04. (The rebound to 1.9 percent of GDP by 2008 reflects not only accumulating debt but also the CBO assumption that 10-year Treasury bonds will be up to 5.4 percent by 2006 and 5.5 percent by 2007 and after, compared with 4.3 percent in 2004). Non-defense discretionary spending eased from an average of about 3.7 percent of GDP in the early 1990s to a low of 3.3 percent in 1999–2000, but jumped to an average of about 3.9 percent of GDP in 2003–04.

---

13. "Income support" includes unemployment compensation, supplemental security income, earned income tax credits, food stamps, family support, child nutrition, and foster care. Net total mandatory spending has typically been moderated by about 1 percent of GDP in "offsetting receipts."

De Rugy (2004) emphasizes that the first Bush administration sharply increased real discretionary spending. She estimates that the average annual real increase of 9.4 percent in the three fiscal years from 2002–04 was exceeded during the past 40 years only by the 13.6 percent average annual real increase in fiscal years 1967 and 1968. In contrast, the average annual increase for the past four decades was only 1.7 percent. She finds further that real non-defense spending will have risen almost as much as defense spending from fiscal year 2001 to fiscal year 2005, by 25 versus 36 percent respectively.

It is sometimes argued that non-defense spending on homeland security can explain the rise in discretionary non-defense spending. The budget for the Department of Homeland Security in fiscal year 2004 was $31 billion, or 0.26 percent of GDP, but much of this was supposed to replace spending in other agencies. In terms of budgetary impact, major increases in non-defense discretionary spending from fiscal year 2001 to fiscal year 2004 occurred in health, excluding Medicare (from 1.71 to 2.14 percent of GDP), education (0.57 to 0.77 percent), international affairs (0.16 to 0.3 percent), administration of justice (0.3 to 0.37 percent), transportation (0.54 to 0.6 percent), and regional development (0.12 to 0.16 percent) (OMB 2005b).[14]

To summarize, the collapse of the US fiscal accounts from surplus to deficit was driven at first by recession and an end to high capital gains tax revenues as the stock market bubble burst, and then increasingly by a large reduction in tax liabilities through new legislation. A rise in defense and non-defense discretionary spending as well as mandatory social spending also contributed to the large reversal in the fiscal accounts, from a surplus of 2.4 percent of GDP in 2000 to a deficit of 3.6 percent of GDP in 2004.

The Decline in Personal Saving

The swing from fiscal surplus to deficit in recent years has not been the only source of falling domestic saving that has prompted the need for more saving from abroad, and hence a widening current account deficit. Personal saving also has fallen sharply. The principal alternative measures of personal saving reported in figure 4.11 show a large decline over the past 15 years. The US Commerce Department's measure of personal saving relative to disposable income fell from an average of 7.3 percent in 1990–92 to an average of 1.6 percent in 2002–04. The less familiar corresponding

---

14. Farm spending actually fell thanks to stronger international agricultural prices, but could also have widened given the generous subsidy framework of the 2002 farm bill, a reversal of the 1996 farm bill that had attempted to "wean farmers from federal price supports and subsidies" (de Rugy 2004).

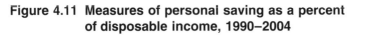

Figure 4.11 Measures of personal saving as a percent of disposable income, 1990–2004

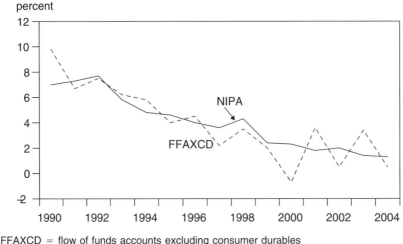

FFAXCD = flow of funds accounts excluding consumer durables
NIPA = National Income and Product Accounts

Sources: BEA (2005d); Federal Reserve Board (2005c).

estimate in the Federal Reserve's Flow of Funds Accounts (FFA) fell similarly from 8 to 1.5 percent over the same period (Federal Reserve Board 2005c).[15] Averaging the two series, the decline over this period has thus amounted to 6.1 percent of disposable income. Considering that disposable income has averaged 73.5 percent of GDP over this period, this means that the decline in personal saving has amounted to about 4.5 percent of GDP. In comparison, the current account balance, and hence the excess of domestic investment over saving, declined by 4.3 percent from 1990–92 to 2002–04.

The saving concept that is relevant for the external imbalance is current saving out of the stream of domestic production. The external imbalance is the excess of the annual flow of domestically used resources over domestically available resources. When personal saving out of current income declines, this excess rises, because the increase in consumption is not accompanied by a rise in the flow of domestic resources. This saving concept is quite different from the individual household concept of saving defined as the change in total stock of assets. That concept includes not only saving as a set-aside in a stream of current income, but also appreciation on previously held assets (capital gains). Some would argue that

---

15. The FFA also reports personal saving measured to include consumer durables. This series also fell sharply, from an average of 9.2 percent of disposable personal income in 1990–92 to 4.1 percent in 2002–04.

concern about personal saving in the United States has been misplaced, because households' saving defined to include asset appreciation has held up much better than saving out of current income. The problem with including asset appreciation from the standpoint of evaluating external resource use is that it is a zero-sum game across households. Unrealized capital gains are just that—unrealized. The attempt of all households to sell off and realize them at the same time would drive prices back down. While it may well be true that households' individual saving rates have not fallen much if their capital gains are included, it would be a fallacy of composition to argue that as a result the decline in personal saving out of current income has not contributed to the rising current account deficit.

Yet rising capital gains are probably the main factor in the decline in saving out of current income. The reason is precisely that households judge that they need to do less current saving if their assets have appreciated. For most of the past decade, there has been a large run-up in the prices of two categories of assets that matter most to US households: residential real estate and equities. As a result, as shown in table 4.2, US households enjoyed total increases in net worth that far surpassed their cumulative saving out of current income. From end-1990 to end-1999, net worth of households (and nonprofit institutions) rose by $22 trillion. During the same period, cumulative personal saving amounted to only $2.7 trillion, or only 12 percent of the total net worth increase.

The bursting of the stock market bubble cut equity assets from $17.3 trillion at the end of 1999 to $10 trillion at the end of 2002, although those assets partially recovered to $14.3 trillion by the end of 2004. An acceleration in housing price increases softened the overall decline in net worth during 2000–01 and contributed to the return to large net worth gains in 2003–04. Residential housing is much more widely owned across the spectrum of US families than are stocks, so the shift in asset appreciation (asset inflation?) from stocks to housing may have sustained rising consumption (and continued slim saving) despite the stock market's decline.[16] The impact of housing values on consumption is also bolstered by the use of home equity loans that increase the consumption potential of credit-constrained households.

One way to gauge the impact of asset appreciation on the personal saving rate is to apply the conventional range for the marginal propensity to consume out of wealth. Most of the literature places this marginal rate at about 3 percent.[17] As indicated in table 4.2, in the period of the stock

---

16. In 1998, the top 5 percent of households accounted for 57.4 percent of net worth. They owned 74.9 percent of stocks, but a much lower 35.3 percent of housing equity. See Poterba (2000).

17. See Poterba (2000). Note, however, that Juster et al. (2004) arrive at empirical estimates indicating a marginal propensity to consume out of wealth increases as high as 19 percent for capital gains in equities, despite finding the usual range of 3 percent for aggregate capital gains.

Table 4.2 US household wealth and saving, 1990–2004 (in billions of dollars and in percent)

	Assets				Net worth			Personal saving		
Year	Real estate	Equities	Other	Total	Liabilities	Level	Change	Rate (percent)	Amount	As a percent of change in net worth
1990	6,576	3,124	14,366	24,066	3,719	20,347		7.0	300	
1991	6,810	4,347	14,729	25,886	3,934	21,952	1,605	7.3	326	20.30
1992	7,122	4,887	15,042	27,051	4,139	22,912	960	7.7	366	38.11
1993	7,358	5,684	15,557	28,599	4,407	24,192	1,280	5.8	285	22.26
1994	7,523	5,680	16,386	29,589	4,734	24,855	663	4.8	247	37.30
1995	7,991	7,606	17,194	32,791	5,071	27,720	2,865	4.6	249	8.68
1996	8,320	9,194	18,206	35,720	5,428	30,292	2,572	4.0	228	8.85
1997	8,779	11,829	19,186	39,794	5,785	34,009	3,717	3.6	216	5.80
1998	9,545	13,736	20,423	43,704	6,242	37,462	3,453	4.3	275	7.96
1999	10,395	17,257	21,498	49,150	6,818	42,332	4,870	2.4	161	3.30
2000	11,401	15,333	22,624	49,358	7,399	41,959	−373	2.3	165	n.a.
2001	12,492	13,076	23,525	49,093	7,978	41,115	−844	1.8	135	n.a.
2002	13,683	10,028	24,379	48,090	8,673	39,417	−1,698	2.0	157	n.a.
2003	15,099	13,037	25,812	53,948	9,583	44,365	4,948	1.4	114	2.31
2004	17,242	14,347	27,597	59,186	10,719	48,467	4,102	1.3	112	2.74

n.a. = not applicable

Notes: Figures include nonprofit organizations. Equities include directly and indirectly held. "Other" includes deposits, credit market instruments, and other assets.

Sources: Federal Reserve Board (2005c); BEA (2005d).

market boom, total net worth rose by $4.9 trillion in 1999 alone. Applying the rate of 3 percent, this could have been expected to boost consumption by $146 billion. As it turns out, there was a drop of personal saving by $114 billion from 1998 to 1999, in the right order of magnitude for consistency with a special impact of rising wealth. Similarly, the rise of net worth by $4.9 trillion in 2003 (as the stock market improved and housing price increases accelerated) would once again have been expected to boost consumption by about $150 billion. If instead saving had been $150 billion higher, the personal saving rate in 2003 would have been 3.2 percent of disposable income rather than the actual 1.4 percent.

Whether the decline in personal saving fueled by asset appreciation has been a serious distortion that has unduly bloated US borrowing from abroad, or rather a socially efficient response to real economic changes, depends largely on whether the increase in asset prices has been mainly due to bubble dynamics or to a rise in the future stream of output expected from the assets because of higher productivity growth. In the first case, borrowing from abroad to finance extra consumption will have been shortsighted. In the second case, doing so will arguably have been optimal, because the increase in future productive capacity will easily repay the extra external debt.

There is no doubt that some of the stock market price increases in the 1990s could be warranted by rising productivity growth and the "new economy." By the late 1990s, however, the excesses of an equity bubble were the driving force, as most dramatically illustrated by the surge and then collapse of high-technology stocks.[18] As for real estate, there is no basis on which it can be argued that price increases reflect an increase in productivity and the future stream of output. Instead, rising housing prices seem likely to have been attributable mainly to historically low interest rates, and to the rotation of investor asset allocation from the stock market to housing once equities stumbled, especially as the specter of deflation was replaced by nascent signs of inflation and as real assets once again held attraction as a hedge against inflation.

The overall effect of the great asset appreciation of recent years, for the external accounts, seems likely to have been mainly that it contributed to a rise in current consumption beyond what was consistent with longer-term optimality for the economy as a whole. The implication is that, at some point, asset appreciation will slow down or reverse (as it did in 2001–02 for total net worth). As asset prices return to a path much closer to, and, possibly lower than, general inflation, households may increasingly return to saving out of current income, raising the personal saving rate

---

18. The NASDAQ index of high technology stocks rose from 752 in December 1994 to a monthly peak of 4,697 in February 2000 before falling to 1,321 in January 2003 (Bloomberg LP 2005).

back closer to its range of 7 percent of disposable income in the early 1990s from its recent level of about 1.5 percent. When and if that occurs, there will be much less pressure on the balance between domestic use and availability of the annual flow of goods and services, facilitating a correction in the external deficit.

Fiscal Outlook for 2005–10

The United States has two fiscal problems: a medium-term deficit similar to those of the past, and a long-term deficit involving more severe structural trends in Social Security and especially Medicare-Medicaid accounts. The medium-term problem is marked by the need to address the revenue already lost and the risk that it will not be regained if tax cuts initially enacted with expiration dates timed to the 10-year budget horizon are extended as the administration desires. The longer-term problem has so far been dominated by discussion of such measures as shifting part of Social Security rights to private accounts.

The baseline fiscal projections of the CBO (2005a) are shown in figures 4.7, 4.8, and 4.10. The baseline fiscal balance eases to 3 percent of GDP in 2005, then narrows by about 0.3 percent annually during 2006–08 and 0.2 percent annually in 2009–10, to reach a deficit of 1.2 percent of GDP in 2010. There is further improvement to a surplus of 0.4 percent of GDP by 2012, thanks mainly to expiration of the tax cuts of 2001 and 2003.

The CBO makes clear, however, that it is constrained by law about the assumptions it must make in the projections, and it illustrates what would happen to the projections if alternative assumptions were made. The projections must be made under the assumption that current tax law does not change. For discretionary spending, the projections must assume that the most recent year's spending holds constant in real terms, with no allowance for growth in real GDP.

For defense, moreover, the CBO states that its baseline projections omit supplemental appropriations for the wars in Iraq and Afghanistan, and for certain other expenses in the war against terrorism, amounting to about $30 billion in 2005 and rising to about $75 billion annually by 2006–08 (including extra interest costs) before easing. If allowance is made for these additional defense expenditures, the fiscal deficit reaches 3.3 percent of GDP in 2005 instead of the CBO baseline of 3 percent.

By July 2005, higher than expected revenues suggested instead that the fiscal year 2005 deficit could amount to about 2.7 to 2.9 percent of GDP ($325 billion to $350 billion; see CBO 2005c). The extra revenue was concentrated in corporate taxes, possibly reflecting expiration of 2002 corporate tax breaks, and income taxes not withheld, perhaps from capital gains in real estate. Reflecting the likely transitory nature of the higher revenue, the director of the CBO indicated that the medium-term fiscal outlook had not changed.[19]

Over the medium term, there are considerably more important additional unfavorable factors. The baseline projection of discretionary spending is likely understated. The Deficit Control Act requires the CBO to project discretionary spending at the level of the most recent appropriations with adjustment only for inflation (based on the GDP deflator and the employment cost index for wages and salaries). If instead discretionary spending is projected to grow at the same rate as nominal GDP, the result is to boost spending from the baseline by about $75 billion by 2008 and $220 billion by 2012.

Similarly, the baseline projection using current law provides for termination of the tax cuts (EGTRRA and JGTRRA, discussed above). If instead the Bush administration is successful in extending these cuts, there would be revenue loss (and associated increased interest on additional debt) amounting to about $30 billion annually in 2008 and $50 billion in 2010, rising sharply to $205 billion in 2011 and $325 billion in 2012.

Finally, there is widespread expectation that the alternative minimum tax (AMT) will have to be reformed to avoid its extension to large numbers of middle-class households not originally intended to be covered as inflation boosts nominal income levels. The CBO calculates that if the AMT is instead indexed for inflation after 2005, the revenue (and interest) loss would amount to about $40 billion annually by 2008 and $70 billion by 2010, easing to about $40 billion by 2012. The magnitude of the correction amounts to a peak of 0.43 percent of GDP in 2010, somewhat smaller than might have been expected given the salient political profile of this issue.

Figure 4.12 shows the field of alternative baseline projections that would result from the changes in key assumptions just discussed. The official baseline is the top line. The next (lower) path adjusts for the extra expenses for Iraq, Afghanistan, and other costs of the war on terrorism. The next alternative additionally allows for discretionary spending to rise at the same rate as nominal GDP. The next alternative assumes that the administration successfully extends the tax cuts otherwise scheduled to expire. The final alternative assumes additionally that the AMT is indexed for inflation after 2004.

All four of the adjustments to the CBO baseline are reasonable assumptions. Their combined effect would be to freeze the fiscal deficit at about 3.2 percent over the next eight years, a sharp contrast to the (required) official CBO baseline showing gradual elimination of the deficit and achievement of a small surplus by 2012. Similar calculations under alternative assumptions have been made by the OECD (2004b) and by Gale and Orszag (2004, 3). The latter conclude that under the most plausible

---

19. Paul Krugman, "Un-Spin the Budget," *New York Times*, July 11, 2005.

Figure 4.12 Congressional Budget Office baseline and alternative fiscal balance projections, 2004–12 (percent of GDP)

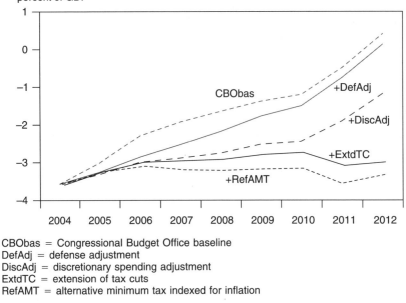

percent of GDP

CBObas = Congressional Budget Office baseline
DefAdj = defense adjustment
DiscAdj = discretionary spending adjustment
ExtdTC = extension of tax cuts
RefAMT = alternative minimum tax indexed for inflation

Source: CBO (2005a).

assumptions, the baseline fiscal deficit will hover around 3.5 percent of GDP each year from 2005 through 2014. On the basis of the CBO alternative paths shown in figure 4.12 as well as these other recent studies, it seems likely that *the United States is on a path of continued fiscal deficits of about 3 to 3.5 percent of GDP rather than a path of gradually eliminating the deficit, especially if the tax cuts are made permanent.*

Some would argue that these deficit projections are too pessimistic because they do not include the dynamic effects of the tax cuts. Indeed, there has been ongoing debate on whether budget "scoring" of fiscal proposals should include dynamic macroeconomic effects. The implicit assumption is usually that tax cuts will spur incentives, increase growth, and hence cause less revenue loss than expected based solely on applying the change in rates to an unchanged GDP or income baseline. This issue is essentially a current incarnation of the "supply side" debate and the "Laffer curve" argument dating from the 1980s—that tax revenue could actually be higher if tax rates were lower because of incentive effects.

The dynamic effects of tax cuts can be ambiguous, however. Consider the important EGTRRA tax revisions of 2001. Gale and Potter (2002) estimate that even after taking account of improved incentives for labor, private saving, and investment from the changes in this act, there would be a net loss in national saving and capital formation because of the dominant effect of lower fiscal revenue. They conclude that "EGTRAA will slightly reduce the size of the economy by 2011" (Gale and Potter 2002, 134). Orszag (2002, 1) argues more broadly that macroeconomic knowledge is insufficient to provide reliable estimates of dynamic macroeconomic effects of fiscal changes, and that to adopt dynamic scoring of fiscal proposals "would exacerbate ... the bias in the official baseline toward unrealistically favorable budget outcomes." In short, there would seem to be little firm basis for adopting more optimistic fiscal projections than those shown in figure 4.12 on grounds that dynamic macroeconomic effects of tax cuts should be added.

In the medium term, then, the challenge is to narrow the fiscal deficit sharply from a persistently high baseline. This will require some combination of spending cuts and tax increases. Many would argue that spending cuts are preferable on grounds, for example, that labor income taxes discourage effort and taxes on capital income discourage investment. However, the United States has already exhausted the easy defense spending cuts following the end of the Cold War, and parts of the social infrastructure (road systems, education) are arguably underfunded. Moreover, the tax cuts of recent years have reduced federal tax revenue to historically low levels gauged against the experience of the past half-century, suggesting at the least that some of the cuts should not be made permanent.

Long-Term Fiscal Problem

The longer-term problem is potentially much more severe. The CBO (2003) calculates that if spending growth is "intermediate" and if revenues recover by 2012 to their historical average of 18.4 percent of GDP (versus about 16.5 percent in 2004), then the fiscal deficit would be 6.1 percent of GDP in 2030 and 14.4 percent of GDP by 2050.[20] Federal debt in the hands of the public would rise from 37 percent of GDP in 2004 to 65 percent in 2030 and 185 percent by 2050.

The driving force behind this adverse long-term fiscal outlook is the prospective rise in Medicare-Medicaid spending, from 3.9 percent of GDP in 2004 to 8.4 percent in 2030 and 11.5 percent in 2050. Even this already high path assumes that the "excess cost" growth rate (excess of growth in Medicaid spending per enrollee above the annual GDP growth per capita) decelerates from 1.7 percent annually in 1990–2003 to only 1 percent annually in 2004–2050. In the high-spending scenario, this excess-

---

20. This scenario (intermediate spending, lower revenue) is one of six that the CBO calculates, comprising three spending cases (high, intermediate, low) combined with two revenue cases (higher, lower).

cost rate is 2.5 percent annually and Medicare-Medicaid spending would mushroom to 21.3 percent of GDP by 2050.[21]

Ironically, although most of the political discussion about radical fiscal reform has focused on Social Security (e.g., shifting from a public defined-benefit toward a private defined-contribution structure), spending on Social Security even without reform is only projected to rise from 4.2 percent of GDP today to 5.9 percent in 2030 and 6.2 percent in 2050. This increment of 2 percentage points of GDP not only pales in comparison to the 7.6 percent of GDP rise in Medicare-Medicaid spending (intermediate case), but is smaller than the 2.6 percent of GDP revenue lost by 2004 from the recent tax cuts. The 48 percent rise in projected Social Security spending as a share of GDP by 2050 is actually smaller than the 58 percent rise in the share of seniors in the total population.

Although the CBO (2003) projects that the ratio of workers to Social Security beneficiaries will fall from 3.3 today to 2.2 by 2030, various studies suggest that relatively modest changes in benefits and contributions could eliminate the prospective deficit in Social Security accounts. Remarkably, a single, arguably fair reform would seem capable of resolving the Social Security problem. At present, the initial benefit level of each cohort rises not only to offset inflation but also to accompany the growth of real average wages in the economy. Removing the increase for average real wages (projected by the CBO at 1.3 percent annually) but otherwise indexing for inflation would scale back Social Security spending from its projected 6.2 percent of GDP in 2050 to 4.1 percent, slightly below today's level (CBO 2003, 22).

It is a fair bet that a large majority of especially younger workers today do not expect the real level of their eventual Social Security benefits to be even as high as those paid to seniors today, let alone higher, and that most would favor stripping out the "real wage growth" component of current promised benefits if they could be assured in exchange that they

---

21. This much public spending on mandatory health programs would seem to border on the fanciful, however, because it implies (although the CBO does not state so explicitly) that more than half of GDP would be devoted to health care. Public and private health care together amount to 14.1 percent of GDP today. Medicare-Medicaid spending is thus about 28 percent of total health spending. The age group over 65 currently accounts for 12 percent of the population, and this will rise to 19 percent by 2030 and thereafter. The intensity of health spending is thus about 2.8 times as high for seniors as for the rest of the population (i.e., $[28\%/12\%]/[72\%/88\%] = 2.8$). If Medicare-Medicaid spending expands to 21.3 percent of GDP (high case) when seniors reach 19 percent of the population, then maintenance of comparable health care for the rest of the population would imply $[81/19] \times [21.3/2.8] = 32.4$ percent of GDP spent on nonsenior health. So 53.7 percent of GDP would be spent on health all together. This strains credulity. Even the "intermediate" Medicare-Medicaid excess cost growth rate of 1 percent per year, and Medicare-Medicaid spending at 11.5 percent of GDP in 2050, implies by the same calculus that total health spending would reach 29 percent of GDP, about double the share today.

would receive benefits no lower in real terms than those paid today.[22] Many might thus favor a reform that would assure maintenance of today's real benefits at the expense of delinking from further real wage growth. Nevertheless, removing the link between benefits and average real wages would make it much more explicit that Social Security is a "redistribution program" intended to assure a minimum income for the elderly, rather than a "savings program" in which workers get back at retirement what they themselves have saved and invested through the Social Security system. A true savings program instead would have a close link between the benefits and what the worker contributed (and thus, on average, a close link with average real wages). Of course, in reality the actual benefits received in the past have substantially exceeded the investment value of what the beneficiaries had contributed during their careers, a luxury made possible only by the pay-as-you-go structure of Social Security combined with the fact that in the first few decades, the ratio of active workers to retirees was very high.

In the CBO long-term scenarios, cutting the Medicare-Medicaid excess cost rate from 1 percent per annum to zero reduces that spending from 11.5 percent of GDP to 6.4 percent in 2050. Suppose instead that the excess cost growth rate were cut to 0.5 percent per annum. Call this "plausible health reform." By implication, Medicare-Medicaid spending would be curbed halfway, to 9 percent of GDP in 2050. If real wage growth (but not inflation adjustment) were stripped from the future escalation of Social Security benefits, Social Security spending would fall from 6.2 percent to 4.1 percent of GDP in 2050. Call this "real benefit maintenance Social Security reform." The CBO intermediate-spending scenario projects defense spending at 1.4 percent of GDP and all other primary (non-interest) spending at 4.2 percent of GDP in 2050. So if long-term fiscal adjustments included both "plausible health reform" and "real benefit maintenance Social Security reform," total primary spending in 2050 would be only 18.7 percent instead of 23.4 percent of GDP. Even with just the "lower" CBO revenue assumption of 18.4 percent of GDP, the primary balance would be close to zero. A modest increase of taxes by 1 percent of GDP—smaller than that in almost all International Monetary Fund (IMF) adjustment programs for developing countries—would yield a primary surplus of 0.7 percent of GDP.[23] Federal debt held by the public

---

22. A 1998 survey on Social Security by Paine Webber found that only 12 percent of respondents under the age of 30 expected to receive "all or most of the benefits to which they are entitled." The corresponding results for other age groups were 21 percent for those 31 to 49 years old and 57 percent for those near retirement (UBS 1998).

23. This could be accomplished through a "corporate activity tax," which would be a type of value-added tax that could be set at a rate sufficient to replace all present corporate income tax plus a modest additional amount. This approach has been recommended by Hufbauer and Grieco (2005), who moreover suggest that the corporate activity tax could be the primary mechanism for raising far larger incremental amounts if needed because of less success in scaling back the prospective growth of Medicare-Medicaid and Social Security expenses.

could be maintained at about 50 percent of GDP or less, implying interest payments of 2.8 percent of GDP or less under the CBO's baseline interest rate assumption (5.5 percent on 10-year Treasury bonds). The overall deficit of 2.5 percent would be small enough to stabilize the debt-to-GDP ratio at about 50 percent if nominal growth were 5 percent annually (e.g., 2.5 percent real growth plus 2.5 percent inflation) or higher. The long-term fiscal problem would thus appear surmountable. But the longer the political effort needed is delayed, the larger and more dangerous the problem will become. The single most important part of the solution will be identifying an equitable and efficient means of limiting the pace of rising health care expenses.

This excursion into the United States' long-term fiscal problem has been necessary because that issue is the elephant in the room that can only be ignored by the uninformed or the disingenuous. In terms of correction of the external sector deficit and the sustainability of external debt, however, the next few years are the ones that will be crucial in determining whether the United States can carry out a smooth adjustment or instead will face a financial crisis. In particular, if global investors—and US citizens—begin to see progress in reducing the large recent fiscal deficits, as well as signs that the longer-term problem is beginning to be addressed, then the risks of a dollar crisis and hard landing will be substantially reduced. The rest of this chapter thus returns to the central question of the extent of fiscal adjustment needed, in combination with exchange rate adjustment, to carry out sufficient external adjustment to attain sustainability of external economic debt (or capitalized net capital income, CNCI, as discussed in chapter 3).

General Equilibrium Framework

The purpose of this chapter is to clarify the complementary roles of exchange rate and fiscal adjustments in achieving external adjustment. For this purpose, appendix 4A develops a simple general equilibrium model relating the external and fiscal accounts. This model contains seven underlying economic equations.[24] The first economic equation (4A.1) is the set of national income accounts identities (equations 4.1-4.3). The second is an equation relating imports to the real exchange rate (price variable) and the level of GDP (income variable). The third equation relates exports to the real exchange rate (price) and the level of foreign GDP (income). Thus, the first three equations in the appendix enforce a general equilibrium solution in which the conditions of both the "absorption approach" to

---

24. There are also five definitional equations: for disposable income; for the fiscal deficit; and for specifying the exogenous initial levels of government spending, the tax rate, and foreign income.

external correction and the "elasticity approach" are simultaneously met. The "absorption approach" emphasizes that reducing a trade deficit requires reducing the fiscal deficit or reducing private investment relative to private saving (national accounts identity). The "elasticities approach" emphasizes that reducing the external deficit requires real depreciation of the exchange rate and/or a slowdown in domestic growth or acceleration in foreign growth (price and income determination of trade). These three joint equations overcome the frequent critiques of each of these two schools against calculations made by the other, by forcing the system to take account of both approaches simultaneously.[25]

The remaining economic equations of the model state that (i) consumption is a function of disposable income and the interest rate; (ii) investment is a negative function of the interest rate and a positive function of the level of GDP; (iii) the real exchange rate varies positively with the interest rate and the level of domestic relative to foreign GDP; (iv) the interest rate rises in response to a larger fiscal deficit ("crowding out"), as GDP rises toward or above its potential (full employment) level, and in response to a rise in the general price level; and (v) prices respond to the level of GDP and the level of the exchange rate. To make the system highly transparent and to facilitate calculation of the solution, all equations are specified in linear terms. Finally, although the model is in real terms, for interpretation of the results it is necessary to convert the import estimates into nominal values. When the real exchange rate depreciates, there is an adverse terms of trade effect that raises the price of imports.

The parameters used in the model are similar to those in chapter 3 for the trade equations. The price elasticity is unity for both exports and imports; the pass-through ratio is 0.5 for imports and 1.0 for exports; and the import income elasticity is 1.8 and that for exports is 1.2, providing some "Houthakker-Magee asymmetry" (chapter 3). The marginal propensity to consume is set at 0.9.

The parameters for investment, the real exchange rate, and interest rate equations are plausible but less based on "typical" or "stylized-fact" magnitudes. It is postulated that a 1 percentage point rise in interest rates depresses investment by 0.6 percent of GDP and also curbs automobile consumption, and that a 1 percent rise in GDP induces a 1.1 percent rise in investment (accelerator effect). It is similarly assumed that a 1 percent rise in the interest rate induces a 5 percent rise in the real exchange rate, and that a rise of 1 percent in US GDP relative to rest-of-world GDP causes a 1.67 percent rise in the real exchange rate. Estimates by Gale and Orszag (2004) form the basis for a parameter stating that a rise in the fiscal deficit by 1 percent of GDP causes a 0.3 percentage point rise in

---

25. For example, in the US external adjustment episode of the 1980s, it was often argued by supporters of a "strong dollar" that real depreciation of the dollar would accomplish nothing because the external deficit was determined solely by the fiscal deficit.

the interest rate. The "Taylor rule" is invoked to obtain the parameter of an increase of 0.5 percentage points in the interest rate for an increase in GDP by 1 percent of its potential level (Taylor 1993). The same rule leads to a 0.5 percent rise in the interest rate in response to a 1 percent rise in the price level. The price equation states that a 1 percent depreciation of the exchange rate raises prices by 0.1 percent, and that a 1 percent rise in GDP boosts the price level by one-fourth of 1 percent (based on the nonaccelerating inflation rate of unemployment [NAIRU] formulation of the Phillips curve and on Okun's law; see appendix 4A).

The main overall result of the various simulations is that fiscal adjustment will be crucial to achieving external adjustment. An experiment with an exogenous initial depreciation of the dollar without fiscal adjustment generates very little external adjustment. Thus, a 20 percent ex ante decline in the dollar (for example, from a sharp fall in confidence) reduces the trade deficit by only 0.5 percent of GDP (from 5.2 to 4.7 percent) if it is unaccompanied by fiscal adjustment. The reason is partly that the ex ante depreciation of 20 percent turns into an ex post depreciation of only about 9 percent, because the dollar is bid back up by the rise in interest rates induced by the tendency of output to rise above the capacity-based potential level (as exports begin to expand in the absence of fiscal adjustment).[26]

In experiments with only a fiscal correction, the size of the trade balance adjustment is only about 40 percent as large as the fiscal adjustment.[27] In contrast, the most favorable external adjustment is achieved when there is a combination of ex ante exchange rate adjustment, fiscal adjustment, and some acceleration in foreign growth. In the most forceful and favorable example modeled, with an ex ante 25 percent real depreciation of the dollar, 2 percent of GDP reduction in government spending, 2 percent of GDP increase in taxes, and 1.5 percent rise in foreign GDP, the trade deficit is cut from 5.2 to 3.1 percent of GDP.

These relationships may be on the pessimistic side for judging the scope for external adjustment through fiscal and exchange rate adjustment. For example, as will be discussed in chapter 5, when there is a perceived need to accomplish a correction of fiscal and external deficits, monetary

---

26. Note, however, that a special run of the Federal Reserve Board's Global Model (FRB/Global) shows that a considerably larger portion of the initial exchange rate shock persists after taking account of induced macroeconomic effects, including an increase in interest rates. An initial 10 percent decline in the dollar (modeled by a change in the risk premium required by foreign investors) results in a dollar that is 7 percent below the baseline by year 3. This simulation also shows a trade balance improvement from the baseline by 0.5 percent of GDP by year 3. (Christopher Erceg, personal communication, May 17, 2005.)

27. A much-cited recent study by Federal Reserve Board economists (Erceg, Guerrieri, and Gust 2005) places the ratio of the change in the current account to fiscal change at an even lower 20 percent. However, as argued in chapter 5, that model estimate and others like it may understate the potential for fiscal adjustment to contribute to external adjustment.

authorities could be much less likely to adhere to usual rules relating interest rates to output and inflation. Specifically, in the face of a reduction in the fiscal deficit, they might reduce the interest rate by less than a standard Taylor rule would suggest. If so, there would be less induced increase in investment and consumption to offset the reduction in government spending, leaving a larger rise in the domestic resource balance available to reduce the external deficit.[28] The relationship of the induced change in the trade balance to the change in the fiscal balance might thus be higher than 40 percent. If, in addition, there is an exogenous decline in the exchange rate, the overall external adjustment would be still larger.

Moreover, it should be kept in mind that the current account adjustment should be larger than the trade balance adjustment. Revaluation of foreign assets from exchange rate depreciation improves the base for capital service earnings, and an ease in interest rates associated with fiscal adjustment reduces interest payments on external debt.

The general equilibrium structure serves to underscore the importance of feedback effects. For exchange rate adjustment, these feedback effects tend to be negative (self-defeating) for external adjustment, whereas for fiscal adjustment, they tend to be positive (reinforcing). Exchange rate depreciation by itself causes an incipient rise in exports and a decline in real imports that boosts GDP by the national accounts equation. This raises disposable income and hence consumption, narrowing the potential reduction in the resource gap. The incipient rise in real GDP also boosts the interest rate (Taylor rule), which in turn curbs the extent of the exchange rate depreciation from its otherwise (ex ante) magnitude. In contrast, when a cut in government spending is the only ex ante change, the resulting incipient decline in GDP tends to reduce consumption and import demand, and reduces the exchange rate through the effect of domestic relative to foreign GDP level. The fiscal correction also tends to reduce the interest rate, both through the direct fiscal variable and the indirect effect of incipient decline in GDP relative to the full employment level, and the lower interest rate exerts further downward (and hence corrective) pressure on the exchange rate.

The simple model is designed to be illustrative rather than a definitive quantification of results from alternative policies. Nonetheless, it serves broadly as a caveat that suggests that the direct exchange rate impact estimates of chapter 3 may tend to overstate rather than understate external adjustment effects. Most importantly, the general equilibrium model serves as a sharp reminder that fiscal adjustment will need to be a central part of the external adjustment process.

---

28. Truman (2005) has argued implicitly that the Federal Reserve should be tightening monetary policy to curb demand and pave the way for external adjustment.

Toward Fiscal and External Adjustment

The partial equilibrium trade and factor services model developed in chapter 3 found that the US external accounts remain on a baseline path of widening external deficits, rising from 5.7 percent of GDP in 2004 to 7.3 percent of GDP by 2010 (preferred model). The simulations found that a further 21 percent real foreign appreciation against the dollar beyond the January–May 2005 level could trim the baseline path to about 4 percent of GDP by 2010, and the additional effect of plausible foreign growth acceleration might reduce it further to about 3 percent.

The principal purpose of the simulations in appendix table 4A.3 is to show that the exchange rate adjustment will likely need to be accomplished by sizable fiscal adjustment. The specific calibration of the parameters may overstate the amount of fiscal adjustment required. In chapter 3, the ratio of the current account adjustment to the trade balance adjustment is about 1.22 to 1 in the favorable scenario shown in table 3.4.[29] This scenario involves a 21 percent real foreign appreciation against the dollar and a cumulative 2.25 percentage-point-years in additional foreign growth (0.75 percent annually over three years). In comparison, in the most favorable scenario conducted in appendix 4A, the general equilibrium model shows a 2.1 percent of GDP reduction in the trade deficit for a 33 percent foreign real exchange rate appreciation (25 percent dollar depreciation), 1.5 percent cumulative increase in foreign GDP, and 4 percent of GDP fiscal adjustment. By implication, the current account adjustment would be $1.22 \times 2.1 = 2.6$ percent of GDP, reducing a 7.3 percent of GDP baseline deficit to 4.6 percent. The implied impact parameter would be only 0.79 percent of GDP for each 10 percent foreign appreciation, much lower than the impact estimate of chapter 3 of 1.4 percent by year 3 and 1.6 percent by year 5. One reason for a smaller impact is that the general equilibrium model does not capture exchange rate valuation effects on foreign assets, and with a larger dollar depreciation in the general equilibrium scenario (case G), the amount of current account adjustment for a given trade balance adjustment would be somewhat larger than in table 3.4.

After taking into account a possible bias toward understating the current account adjustment, the broad implication is that it will probably require *complete elimination* of the prospective fiscal deficit of about 3¼ percent of GDP as the necessary fiscal adjustment to accompany further real foreign appreciation of 20 percent or so to reduce the current account deficit in 2010 from its baseline value of about 7½ percent to the range of 3½ percent of GDP.

---

29. Against the baseline, in the favorable scenario, the 2010 trade balance improves by 3.6, percent of GDP and the current account by 4.4 percent of GDP.

Neither the simulations of chapter 3 nor those here envision contraction-ary external adjustment premised on a serious slowdown in US invest-ment and growth. However, if serious fiscal correction is not pursued, a loss in growth could well turn out to be the way in which external adjustment occurs. The present commitment of the administration to reduce the fiscal deficit from 3.6 percent of GDP in 2004 to 1.7 percent by 2008 does not seem sufficient to carry out the fiscal role needed to complement exchange rate adjustment and cut the external deficit to the range of 3 to 4 percent of GDP from a baseline level of 7½ percent of GDP in 2010. Moreover, at present, the most realistic fiscal outlook is for a deficit still at about 3¼ percent of GDP by 2008–10, rather than 1.7 percent, given the Bush administration's commitment to making the recent tax cuts permanent and in view of more plausible trends for discretion-ary spending.

If even the promised fiscal adjustment does not take place, the chances of a currency crisis would increase, as could the chances of a hard landing for the economy (recession). The calculations of the general equilibrium model suggest that exchange rate adjustment alone will accomplish only limited external adjustment. If one combines this judgment with the judg-ment that financial markets will become increasingly convinced that a baseline path of ever-widening current account deficits cannot be sus-tained, then the implication would seem to be ample potential for a large decline in the value of the dollar in the absence of perceived firm progress on reducing the fiscal deficit. Whether a hard landing for the dollar would translate into a hard landing for the economy would depend primarily on whether interest rates rose sharply. Although the Federal Reserve would likely be reluctant to significantly raise the policy interest rate (federal funds rate) solely to "defend the dollar," it might raise the rate if higher import prices posed an increased risk of inflation; and the long-term interest rate determined in the private capital markets might surge because of reduced capital inflows. The next chapter considers the various sides in the debate about the risk of a hard landing and the sustainability of the external deficit.

The analysis of this chapter also suggests another important nuance about fiscal adjustment. Important as curbing transfer payments will be for addressing the long-term fiscal problem, limiting fiscal adjustment solely to reductions in transfer payments would tend to be less effective in curbing the external deficit than would cuts in direct government purchases of goods and services and increases in taxes. A dollar cut in trans-fer payments may have significantly less impact in reducing the external deficit than a dollar cut in government purchases or a dollar raised in additional taxes, as set forth above.

Correspondingly, if the baseline for the fiscal deficit by 2050 really is 14.4 percent of GDP, the only silver lining might be that the resulting external deficit would be somewhat less than would be expected if the bulk of the projected spending were on goods and services rather than transfers (Social Security and Medicare-Medicaid) and interest. An analysis of the external sector implications of such large deficits would also have to take account of the fact that other industrial countries under similar baselines would show large fiscal deficits driven by transfers to the elderly population, with the implication that those countries at least would not be likely candidates for providing the external sector surpluses to match US external sector deficits.

Appendix 4A
A Simple General Equilibrium Model Relating the Trade and Fiscal Balances

To examine the relationship between the fiscal and trade deficits, it is necessary to consider multiple general equilibrium feedback effects. Depending on the principal causal force operating at any given time, these feedback effects will sometimes mean that the two deficits move closely together (the "twin deficits") and sometimes that they will not do so and may even move in opposite directions. This appendix constructs a simple general equilibrium model to analyze the relationship and consider the interaction between alternative adjustment policy instruments.

The Model

The national accounts identity is the first equation that must be met in general equilibrium determination of the external and fiscal balances. This identity leads to the familiar relationship that the trade deficit must equal the excess of investment over saving.[30] Thus:

$$Y = C + I + G + X - M \qquad (4A.1)$$

where Y is GDP, C is consumption, I is investment, X is exports, and M is imports. This is the "product demand" side of the economy. On the factor payments side, output must equal income paid to workers and owners of capital, and this income must be used for consumption, saving, or tax payments. Thus, the basic national accounts identities also require that

$$Y = C + S_p + R \qquad (4A.1a)$$

where S_p is private saving and R is government tax revenue. Subtracting equation 4A.1a from equation 4A.1 and rearranging yields the key external sector relationship in the national accounts identities:

$$I - S_p + G - R = M - X;$$
$$I - S_p - S_G = M - X \qquad (4A.1b)$$

where S_G is "government saving" or R–G. Equation 4A.1b confirms that the trade deficit (right-hand side) equals the excess of investment over saving, defined to include private saving (S_P) and government saving (S_G).

---

30. For the purposes of this appendix, "trade" refers to both goods and services.

The second building block of a general equilibrium framework is the partial equilibrium relationship between trade and the exchange rate and levels of activity. Abstracting from time lags, these traditional relationships show imports as a function of the real exchange rate and domestic GDP, and exports as a function of the real exchange rate and foreign GDP. In order to construct a simple model that can be solved by standard matrix methods, the relationships are specified here as being linear. Thus:

$$M = \alpha_M + \beta E + \mu Y \qquad (4A.2)$$

$$X = \alpha_X - \gamma E + \varepsilon Y_F \qquad (4A.3)$$

where E is the real exchange rate, defined as the amount of foreign currency per US dollar after deflating both sides by domestic prices (so that a rise in E means a stronger dollar), and Y_F is foreign GDP.

The addition of equations 4A.2 and 4A.3 already establishes a system in which the two traditional approaches to external balance must be met simultaneously: the "absorption approach," concentrating on aggregate resource use compared to resource availability (the $I-S_p-S_g = M-X$ identity); and the "elasticities approach," which determines changes in exports and imports by consideration of changes in the price and income variables as applied to the respective price and income elasticities.[31]

Simple specifications of the other components of a general equilibrium system relating the trade accounts to the fiscal accounts include the following. Consumption depends on disposable income, which in turn depends on the level of taxes. Consumption is also responsive to the interest rate, not so much because of the traditional theoretical effect of interest rates on the trade-off between consumption now and consumption in the future (and hence saving), but because of the influence of consumer finance on such durables as automobiles in particular (as discussed below). Thus:

$$C = \alpha_C + \delta Y^D - \eta r; \qquad (4A.4)$$

$$Y^D \equiv Y - R = Y(1 - \tau) \qquad (4A.5)$$

where r is the interest rate, Y^D is disposable income, and τ is the tax rate (assumed for simplicity to be both the average and marginal tax rate).[32]

For its part, investment may be specified as a negative function of the interest rate, which determines the cost of capital. An important part of this relationship is the influence of the interest rate on residential investment.

---

31. The classic statement of the absorption approach is by Alexander (1952). The elasticities approach dates back much further, notably to 19th-century economist Alfred Marshall and 20th-century economist Abba Lerner.

32. That is: $R = \tau Y$.

Investment is also a positive function of the level of GDP, considering that rising GDP generates demand for increased productive capacity. Thus:

$$I = \alpha_I - \theta r + \psi Y \qquad (4A.6)$$

The real exchange rate is also a function of the interest rate, and in addition, is influenced by the rate of domestic growth relative to foreign growth in response to greater capital inflows when relative growth appears likely to be stronger. In a simple linear formulation, the exchange rate is determined as

$$E = \alpha_E + \rho r + \Omega(Y - Y_F) \qquad (4A.7)$$

The interest rate is influenced by the size of the fiscal deficit, as government "crowding out" exerts pressure on the capital market. Monetary authorities influence the interest rate, seeking to increase it when inflation increases. Monetary authorities are also likely to vary interest rates in response to the level of output relative to potential output. This means that the interest rate is likely to rise with GDP.[33] Thus:

$$r = \alpha_r + \phi D^F + \pi P + \lambda Y \qquad (4A.8)$$

where P is the level of the domestic price index.

The level of prices depends on whether the economy is overheated or below potential output. It also depends on the exchange rate, because of the influence of the exchange rate on the price of tradables, especially imports. Thus:

$$P = \alpha_P + \omega Y + \Gamma E \qquad (4A.9)$$

For its part, the fiscal deficit is the excess of total government spending over revenue. Total spending includes spending on real activity, G, which enters into the national accounts, as well as the interest paid on public debt, which is a transfer rather than a production concept and is thus not included in the national accounts activity concept of G. Because the model is "comparative static" in that it describes a single solution at a point in time once all of the variables settle to their equilibrium levels, rather than "dynamic" in the sense of tracing out a path over time, the level of public debt is a given constant, which may be designated Δ. Interest payments on the debt will then be $r\Delta$. There is another discrepancy between the national accounts concept of G and federal budgetary spending. The national accounts concept excludes other transfers as well, but it includes

33. A specification using $(Y-Y^*)$ where Y^* is potential GDP, rather than just Y, would simply shift the constant term downward by λY^*.

government activity at the state and local levels. These two differences largely offset each other, but there is a remaining difference between them, designated here as α_{DF}. The fiscal deficit is then

$$D^F = G + (0.01)r\Delta + \alpha_{DF} - R = G + (0.01)r\Delta + \alpha_{DF} - \tau Y \quad (4A.10)$$

Equations 4A.1 through 4A.10 constitute a system of 10 simultaneous equations for 10 endogenous variables ($Y, C, I, X, M, E, Y^D, r, P, D^F$) and three exogenous variables ($G, \tau,$ and Y_F). Fiscal policy is thus explicitly exogenous. In addition, monetary policy can be made exogenous by imposing a shift in the constant term α_r in equation 4A.8. Similarly, if it is believed that policymakers can affect the exchange rate by jawboning, coordinated intervention, special foreign withholding taxes, capital controls, or other direct measures (beyond monetary and fiscal policy), then there can also be an exogenous "exchange rate policy," expressed through a shift in the constant term α_E.

The system in equations 4A.1 through 4A.10 can be expressed in matrix form, as follows:

$$\underset{10x10}{A}\ \underset{10x1}{Z} = \underset{10x1}{K} \quad (4A.11)$$

where A is a matrix of coefficients, Z is a vector of the ten endogenous variables, and K is a vector of constants. Table 4A.1 presents this matrix equation in the form of a table.

The set of equations can then be solved for the values of the variables in vector Z by applying Cramer's rule to each successive variable.[34]

Calibration

The base year for the macroeconomic aggregates in the general equilibrium model is 2004.[35] The calculation of parameters in the various equations applies the following approach. In each linear equation, there is a constant term and a series of coefficients applied to explanatory variables. For each of these relationships, there will typically be a "stylized" (or

---

34. Cramer's rule states that the solution to the vector of unknowns Z in a matrix equation $AZ = K$ can be obtained as a ratio of two determinants: $z_i = |B_i|/|A|$, where z_i is the equilibrium value of unknown variable i, and B_i is a matrix constructed by replacing column i in matrix A with vector K.

35. Note that because the model was estimated before final data for 2004 were available, the values applied compared with final official data in parentheses were as follows: GDP, $11,715 billion ($11,735 billion); exports of goods and services, $1,152 billion ($1,151 billion); imports of goods and nonfactor services, $1,760 billion ($1,769 billion); consumption, $8,221 billion ($8,230 billion); gross private investment, $1,915 billion ($1,927 billion); and government consumption and investment, $2,187 billion ($2,184 billion).

Table 4A.1 General equilibrium matrix equation

Equation:	Y	C	I	X	M	E	Y^D	r	D^F	G	τ	Y^F	P		K:
A:															
1	1	−1	−1	−1	1					−1				=	0
2	−μ				1	−β								=	α_M
3				1		γ						−ε		=	α_X
4		1					−δ	−η						=	α_C
5	τ−1						1							=	0
6	−Ψ		1					θ						=	α_I
7	−Ω					1		−ρ				Ω		=	α_E
8	−λ							1	−φ				−π	=	α_r
9	−ω					−Γ							1	=	α_P
10	τ							−.01Δ	1	−1				=	α_{DF}
11										1				=	G_0
12											1			=	τ_0
13												1		=	Y^F_0

139

"Bayesian") value for the "elasticity," which indicates the percentage change in the dependent variable for a 1 percent change in the independent variable. The equations seek instead the "marginal" relationship. There is a fundamental identity whereby for any relationship between a dependent variable y and an independent variable x, the elasticity = [marginal]/ [average]. That is: $e = [\partial y/\partial x]/[y/x]$. Given a stylized estimate of e, it is possible to estimate the marginal coefficient $\partial y/\partial x$ as $e[y/x]$. The base values of x and y are known, so the equation parameter in question can be estimated. Then, when each of the estimated marginal coefficients is applied to each of the independent variables, and the sum is subtracted from the base level of the dependent variable, the residual is the constant for the equation in question.

For the import and export equations, the simplest formulation is to adopt the traditional Houthakker-Magee asymmetry structure. As it is found in chapter 3 that this structure can understate export growth relative to import growth, a relatively mild degree of asymmetry is adopted here, with the income elasticity set at 1.8 on the import side and 1.2 on the export side. The parameter $\mu = \partial M/\partial Y$ can then be estimated as follows: $\mu/[M/Y] = 1.8$. Applying base values of $M = 1760$ and $Y = 11{,}715$ the result is $\mu = 0.27$.

For the import coefficient on the exchange rate, we have $\beta = \partial M/\partial E$. Following chapter 3, the underlying price elasticity is set at unity. However, the formulation here treats the import price pass-through and elasticity jointly. With pass-through at 0.5 and the underlying elasticity at 1, the effective elasticity is 0.5. So we have: $\beta/[M/E] = 0.5$. The base value of E is index level 100. So $\beta = 0.5 [1760/100] = \$8.8$ billion change in import volume per percentage point change in the real exchange rate. As the national accounts are in real terms, change in volume equals change in value. However, a subsequent adjustment must be made in price to examine the corresponding change in import value. In effect, with an underlying import price elasticity of unity, there is no change in the nominal value of imports from an exchange rate change, because the reduction in volume from a 1 percent price increase (or 0.5 percent price increase after pass-through dampening) is just offset by the 1 percent (or 0.5 percent) increase in terms of dollar prices. For the constant term, given the estimates of μ and β, from equation 4A.2 we have: $\alpha_M = 1760 - (0.27 \times 11715) - 8.8 \times 100 = -\$2{,}283$.

For exports, the price elasticity is also set at unity. For simplicity, full pass-through is assumed (close to the 0.8 pass-through suggested in chapter 3). The exchange rate coefficient is thus: $\gamma = 1 \times [X/E] = [1152/100] = \$11.52$ billion per percentage point change in the real exchange rate index. Foreign GDP is estimated as follows. In 2002, global output at market exchange rates was \$32.3 trillion, of which the United States accounted for \$10.38 trillion (World Bank 2004a, 188). Applying the same relationship for 2004, rest-of-world output is set at a base of $24,740 billion. With an export income elasticity of 1.2, we have for the export income coefficient: $\varepsilon = 1.2 \times [1152/24740] = 0.0559$. Applying the price and income coefficients and subtracting from the base export level, we obtain the constant term as: $\alpha_X = 1152 + 11.52 \times 100 - 0.0559 \times 24740 = \$921$ billion.

For consumption, national accounts data for 1982–2003 show that, as a simple average of the change in consumption from the prior year relative to change in GDP, the marginal propensity to consume is: $\delta = 0.90$ (BEA 2004e). As indicated in the main text, tax revenue in 2004 is set at 16 percent of GDP ($\tau = 0.16$), so disposable income is $0.84 \times \$11,715$ billon.

In recent years it has also become evident that consumption responds to the interest rate. The classical argument for such a response is that the interest rate is the relative price between current and future consumption, and households will consume less and save more if the reward for delaying consumption increases. Against this price effect, however, there is an income effect working in the opposite direction, because higher interest rates raise the income of households owning interest-bearing assets.

In contrast to the ambiguous classical relationship resulting from opposing price and income effects, the influence working through the availability of consumer finance, and in particular financing "incentives" from producers, appears to have been clear and significant at least in the case of automobiles. In the 2001 recession especially, real consumption of automobiles rose by a surprising 5 percent, up from 3.8 percent in 2000 (BEA 2004e). Over 1991–2004, the income elasticity for real automobile consumption was approximately unity.[36] In 2001, real GDP growth dropped to 0.8 percent from 3.7 percent the year before. Based on the income elasticity, auto consumption growth should have fallen commensurately. However, the prime interest rate eased as well, from 9.23 percent in 2000 to 6.92 percent in 2001 (IMF 2004b). If all of the unexplained strength of auto consumption growth in 2001 is attributed to the decline in the interest rate, the parameter obtained is that a 1 percentage point decline in the interest rate boosts auto consumption by 1.8 percent.[37] Automobile consumption stood at 4 percent of GDP in 2003 (BEA 2004e). So we can estimate that a 1 percentage point decline in interest rates boosts automobile consumption by an amount equivalent to 1.8 percent of 4 percent of GDP, or by $8.4 billion. This amount is used as the coefficient of consumption on the interest rate (η) in equation 4A.4.

---

36. Based on a simple regression of percent changes with statistics too non-robust to bother reporting.

37. That is, instead of falling to 0.8 percent growth in 2001, auto consumption rose to 5 percent growth. The 4.2 percent unexplained growth divided by the 2.31 percentage point drop in the prime rate yields a coefficient of a 1.8 percentage point change in auto consumption for a 1 percentage point decline in the interest rate.

Consumption in 2004 was $8,221 billion. The constant term in the consumption equation is thus: $\alpha_C = 8221 - 0.90 \times 0.84 \times 11715 + 8.4 \times 4.1 = -\$601.1$ billion.

The coefficient relating investment to the interest rate is perhaps one of the weakest areas for identifying a "stylized-fact" value. However, suppose the real interest rate were to rise by 10 percentage points, and suppose that the consequence would be to suppress real gross investment down to a level where it would just cover depreciation (leaving zero net investment). Real investment for 2004 is estimated at 16.3 percent of GDP. On the basis of national accounts for 2002–03 (BEA 2004e), private capital consumption (depreciation) amounted to 10.3 percent of GDP. So if a rise in the real interest rate by 10 percent cut net private investment to zero, this would amount to a reduction in gross investment by 6 percent of GDP. A rise in the interest rate by 1 percentage point would then reduce investment by 0.6 percent of GDP, so in equation 4A.6 the coefficient $\theta = 0.006 \times 11715 = \$70.3$ billion.

Once again a closer look at financing helps firm up this estimate. Falling mortgage rates in recent years, as interest rates generally have fallen, have contributed to a boom in residential construction. (The bursting of the stock market bubble may also have spurred portfolio shifts toward housing and hence construction.) Residential investment amounts to about one-third of total gross fixed investment (BEA 2004e). Real residential investment growth averaged only 0.6 percent in 2000–01, but surged to an average of 8.25 percent in 2003–04 (BEA 2004e). Allowing a one-year lag, the corresponding change in the 10-year bond rate (which influences mortgage rates) was from 5.84 percent (1999–2000) to 4.32 percent (2002–03). So a decline in the interest rate by 1.52 percentage points was associated with a rise in residential investment by 7.65 percentage points, giving a relationship of about 5 to 1 between the change in residential investment growth and the change in the interest rate. Residential investment in 2003 was 5.2 percent of GDP. This implies that a decline in the interest rate by 1 percentage point induces a rise in residential investment equivalent to about $30 billion.[38] This amount is in the correct order of magnitude to be consistent with an overall decline in investment by $70 billion for a 1 percent rise in the interest rate, considering that residential investment is about one-third of the total.

The relationship of investment to GDP is also set to incorporate some "accelerator" influence, with an elasticity of 1.1 (i.e., a 1 percent rise in GDP induces a 1.1 percent rise in investment). On this basis, the coefficient ψ in equation 4A.6 is: $\psi = 1.1 \times [1915/11715] = 0.180$. The base year value for the interest rate is estimated at 4.1 percent (10-year bond). Applying the interest rate and GDP coefficients to equation 4A.6, the

---

38. That is, $0.052 \times \$11,715$ billion $\times 5 \times .01 \cong \$30$ billion.

constant term then becomes: $\alpha_I = 1915 + 70.3 \times 4.1 - 0.18 \times 11715 =$ $94.5 billion.

The base year value of 100 for the real exchange rate index (E) conveniently is approximately the actual level of the Federal Reserve's broad real index for 2004 (see chapter 3). How much should we expect the real exchange rate to rise in response to a rise in US interest rates? All else being equal, it is assumed here that a 3 percentage point rise in the interest rate will induce sufficient additional capital inflow to cause the real exchange rate to rise by 15 percent. This implicitly assumes that interest rates remain unchanged abroad. In equation 4A.7, the coefficient ρ is thus set at 5 percentage points on index E for each percentage point rise in interest rate r. For the response of the exchange rate to differential growth, the calculations assume that a 3 percent rise in the level of US GDP relative to rest-of-world GDP induces a 5 percent rise in the real exchange rate. On this basis, an increase in US GDP by $351 billion induces a 5 percent rise in the real exchange rate, or coefficient $\Omega = 5/351 = 0.0142$. The constant term for the exchange rate equation is then estimated as: $\alpha_E = 100 - 5 \times 4.1 - 0.0142(11715-24740) = 264.5$.

For the relationship of the real interest rate to the fiscal deficit, Gale and Orszag (2004) estimate that an additional 1 percent of GDP in the fiscal deficit increases the long-term interest rate by 25 to 35 basis points. On this basis, an additional deficit of $117.15 billion translates into a 0.3 percentage point increase in the interest rate, so in equation 4A.8 the corresponding coefficient is $\varphi = 0.3/117.15 = 0.00256$ percentage point per billion dollars of additional fiscal deficit.

It is important to note that the experience of the 1990s tended to support a strong influence of fiscal deficit reduction on the interest rate and, in turn, on investment and consumption. This virtuous circle of fiscal adjustment rewarded by expansion of the economy became known as "Rubinomics," after US Treasury Secretary Robert Rubin (see Krugman 2003, xxi). At the extreme, this influence implies that an increase in the fiscal deficit (usually called "fiscal expansion") is contractionary for the economy, and a reduction in the deficit (usually called "fiscal contraction") is expansionary. That is, in an extreme formulation, the indirect effects on investment and consumption demand, working through the interest rate effect, would swamp the direct effects of changes in government spending (or taxes). The parameters used in the model of this chapter are not this extreme, however, and fiscal expansion (contraction) remains expansionary (contractionary) for the economy.

With respect to the impact of GDP expansion on the interest rate, the "Taylor rule" describing monetary policy provides a basis for determining the needed parameter (Taylor 1993). This rule states that the change in the real policy interest rate (federal funds rate) is determined half on the basis of the deviation of inflation from the target inflation rate and half on the basis of the deviation of actual from potential output.[39] Backcasts applying this rule for 1987–2003 and using a target inflation rate of 2 percent obtain a very close fit with actual federal funds interest rates (Carlstrom and Fuerst 2003).

The CBO (2004b) has estimated that the "output gap," or shortfall of actual from potential GDP, stood at 3.1 percent at the beginning of 2003 and 1.3 percent at the beginning of 2004. If we use a 1 percent output gap for base year 2004, then potential output will have been $11,832 billion for this year. Each increment of 1 percent of this base, or $118.32 billion, generates a Taylor-rule tightening of monetary policy by 0.5 percentage points. So in equation 4A.8, the corresponding coefficient $\lambda = 0.5/118.3 = 0.00423$ percentage point change in the interest rate for each additional $1 billion in GDP.

The other half of the Taylor rule concerns inflation. For this component the coefficient is simply 0.5. That is, if inflation rises by 1 percent, the Federal Reserve raises interest rates by 0.5 percent. As discussed below, the model applies the change in the price *level* as this change in the inflation rate. Given the parameters φ, λ, and π, and using 4.1 percent as the base level of the nominal interest rate and $422 billion as the base fiscal deficit (CBO 2004b), the constant in the interest rate equation can be estimated as: $\alpha_r = 4.1 - .00256 \times 422 - .00423 \times 11715 - 0.5 \times 100 = -96.53$ percent.

For prices (equation 4A.9), the specification requires translation of annual rates of inflation into a price level. As a model of comparative static equilibrium, the model is best suited to identifying an equilibrium *level* of prices (price index level), not an equilibrium rate of change for prices (rate of inflation). In equation 4A.9, use of the price level fits naturally with inclusion of the level of the exchange rate as an explanatory variable (E). The coefficient on the exchange rate, Γ, is obtained as follows. The import pass-through ratio is 0.5, so a 1 percent rise in the real exchange rate E reduces the price of imports by 0.5 percent. (Export pass-through is complete, so dollar export prices do not change when the exchange rate changes.) Imports of goods and services amount to 15 percent of GDP. Allowing for spillover into tradables more generally, we can place "importables" at, say, 20 percent of GDP. So if a 1 percent decline in the exchange rate boosts import prices by 0.5 percent, then applying a weight of one-fifth for importables in the overall price index will result in an increase of one-tenth of 1 percent for prices overall. With the price index at 100, this means that a 1 percent depreciation in the real exchange rate

---

39. Taylor assumed target inflation of 2 percent and a long-term average real federal funds rate of 2 percent, giving a nominal interest rate of 4 percent under target conditions warranting "neutral" monetary policy. For other conditions, the rule implies: $r^* \equiv r - \pi = 2 + 0.5(\pi - 2) + 0.5\,(100 \times [Y/Y_p - 1])$ where r^* is the real interest rate, π is the inflation rate, and Y_p is potential output.

causes a 0.1 percent rise in the price index, giving a parameter value of: $\Gamma = -0.1$.

The parameter relating prices to GDP is more difficult to assess. The approach here is to use the modern formulation of the Phillips curve to arrive at this parameter. Gordon (1996) judges that a decline of the unemployment rate by 1 percentage point below the nonaccelerating inflation rate of unemployment (NAIRU) will generate a 0.5 percent increase in the rate of inflation, if sustained for one year. He also indicates that, from Okun's law, a 1 percentage point change in unemployment is associated with a 2 percent change in GDP.[40] This means that a 4 percent rise in GDP will be associated with a 1 percent rise in prices (i.e., [2%∂Q/ ∂u] / [0.5%∂P/∂u] = 4%∂Q/1%∂P). Four percent of GDP for 2004 amounts to $469 billion. If an increase in the price level by 1 percent is associated with this amount of additional GDP, then the coefficient ω in equation 4A.9 is: $\omega = 1/469 = 0.00213$ percentage point increase in the price index for a $1 billion increment in GDP. The constant term is then: $\alpha_P = 100 + 0.1 \times 100 - 0.00213 \times 11715 = 85$.

Deriving this coefficient further requires mapping the percent price change (inflation rate) to price levels. The Phillips curve and Okun's law are stated as annual percentage rates. The treatment here assumes that the impacts in question are sustained only one year, so changes in the inflation rate also equal the change in the price level. It could alternately be assumed, for example, that the cumulative comparative static impact should be based on, say, three years or more of annual inflation. However, the central role of the price variable in the model is as an influence on the interest rate, and the specification in the interest rate equation applies the change in the price level for one year only. For consistency, the price equation cumulates inflation for only one year as well.

Finally, in the fiscal deficit (equation 4A.10), the contribution of interest on the debt is simply the interest rate as applied to debt at the end of the previous year. The CBO estimate of net interest for 2004 is $159 billion, and end-2003 federal debt in the hands of the public was $3.9 trillion. This is consistent with the 4.1 percent interest rate used here as the base year rate.[41] The term α_{DF} is set at $-\$50$ billion to adjust for the difference between the national accounts concept of government activity (federal,

---

40. The idea is that firms tend to hold on to workers during recessions but are slow to hire additional workers during expansion, so that employment varies less than proportionately with swings in output over the business cycle.

41. Note that this is the 10-year rate. Although the Taylor rule cited above applies to the short-term federal funds rate, the incremental coefficient λ discussed above will apply to both the 10-year rate and the short-term policy rate if the yield curve remains unchanged. In practice, the yield curve is likely to flatten as the economy strengthens.

Table 4A.2 Parameter values

Parameter	Concept	Value	Units
α_M	Import (M) equation constant	−2,283.0	Billions of dollars
μ	Marginal impact of GDP on imports	0.27	Pure number
β	Marginal impact of exchange rate on M	8.8	Billions of dollars/index
α_X	Export (X) equation constant	921.0	Billions of dollars
γ	Marginal impact of exchange rate on X	11.52	Billions of dollars/index
ε	Marginal impact of foreign income on X	0.0559	Pure number
α_C	Consumption equation constant	−636.0	Billion of dollars
δ	Marginal propensity to consume	0.90	Pure number
η	Marginal impact of interest rate on consumption	−8.4	Billions of dollars
α_I	Investment (I) equation constant	94.5	Billions of dollars
θ	Marginal impact of interest rate on I	70.3	Billions of dollars/percent
Ψ	Marginal impact of GDP on investment	0.180	Pure number
α_E	Exchange rate (E) equation constant	264.5	Index
ρ	Marginal impact of interest rate on E	5.0	Index/percent
Ω	Marginal impact of $Y-Y^F$ on E	0.0142	Index/billions of dollars
α_r	Interest rate (r) equation constant	−96.53	Percentage points
φ	Marginal impact of fiscal deficit on r	0.00256	Percent/billions of dollars
λ	Marginal impact of GDP on r	0.00423	Percent/billions of dollars
π	Marginal impact of price level on r	0.5	Pure number
α_P	Price level constant	85.0	Index
ω	Marginal impact of GDP on price level	0.00213	Index/billions of dollars
Γ	Marginal impact of exchange rate on prices	−0.1	Pure number
α_{DF}	Budget vs. national accounts adjustment	−50.0	Billions of dollars
Δ	Government debt held by public	3,914.0	Billions of dollars
G_0	Base case government spending	2,187.0	Billions of dollars
τ_0	Base case tax rate	0.16	Pure number
Y^F_0	Foreign GDP	24,740.0	Billions of dollars

state, and local spending excluding transfers) and the corresponding budgetary concept for the federal deficit, as discussed above.[42]

The full set of parameter estimates is reported in table 4A.2.

Because the model so far is stated solely in real terms, and because the dollar price of imports changes with the exchange rate, it is necessary to consider further the translation of the equilibrium outcome into consequences for the nominal trade balance. When the real exchange rate depreciates (e.g., from $E_0 = 100$ to $E_1 = 90$), and if the pass-through ratio is σ, then the dollar price of imports rises from $PM_0 = 1$ to PM_1, and the nominal value of imports becomes M^{nom}, where:

---

42. Thus, the federal fiscal deficit is estimated at $422 billion (CBO 2004b). With $G = \$2,187$ billion, interest at $160 billion, and revenue at $0.16 \times$ GDP or $1,874 billion, the adjustment constant is $\alpha_{DF} = 422 - 2187 - 159 + 1{,}874 = -\$50$ billion.

$$P_1^M = 1 + \sigma\left(\frac{E_0}{E_1} - 1\right); \quad M^{nom} = MP_1^M \qquad (4A.12)$$

This relationship of the nominal to the real equilibrium import level is needed to evaluate the equilibrium trade balance, but it does not constitute a direct part of the general equilibrium system of equations 4A.1 through 4A.11 and table 4A.2.

Simulation Results

Table 4A.3 reports the results of alternative simulations of the model. The first column of the table reports estimated "actual" values for 2004, the base year. The second column reports the corresponding estimates of the model applying Cramer's rule to the matrix shown in table 4A.1 with the parameter values indicated in table 4A.2. The only divergences of the model's base values from "actual" values are small rounding errors. The base value of the trade deficit (goods and nonfactor services) is 5.2 percent of GDP; the base fiscal deficit is 3.6 percent of GDP.

The first policy simulation, case A, applies a fiscal adjustment reducing government spending (NIPA concept) by 3 percent of GDP. The fiscal deficit falls to 0.4 percent of GDP. It is worth noting that the reduction in the fiscal deficit outcome by 3.2 percent of GDP exceeds the initial cut in government spending, because of favorable induced effects from lower interest payments on government debt. The easing of pressure on the domestic capital market allows the interest rate to fall from 4.1 to 2.7 percent. A lower interest rate exerts downward pressure on the real exchange rate, which falls by about 9 percent. The lower interest rate also boosts investment by about 3.5 percent. GDP falls by 1.4 percent, however, because the rise in investment is not enough to offset the reduction in government demand and induced reduction in consumption as disposable income falls. The more competitive exchange rate boosts exports by about 9 percent and, together with weaker domestic output, curbs imports by about 7 percent in real terms (but only about 2 percent in nominal terms). The trade deficit falls from 5.2 to 4 percent of GDP.

The second simulation, case B, also imposes a 3 percent of GDP ex ante fiscal adjustment by raising the tax rate from 16 to 19 percent. The results for GDP and for the trade balance are similar but slightly weaker than those from the cut in government spending. The principal difference is that personal consumption is lower and government spending remains higher than in the first case, where the adjustment is through lower government spending. Once again the interest rate falls and so does the real exchange rate. The fiscal adjustment is the same as in the first case— a cut in the deficit by 3.2 percent of GDP. The external adjustment is slightly smaller—a reduction in the trade deficit by 1.1 percent of GDP. On the basis of simulations A and B, it would appear that *a reasonable*

Table 4A.3 General equilibrium model simulations (in billions of dollars, in ratios, and in percent)

Variable	Base		Simulation						
	Actual	Model	A	B	C	D	E	F	G
GDP	11,715	11,714	11,549	11,578	11,909	12,129	11,758	11,825	11,823
Consumption	8,221	8,220	8,107	7,815	8,354	8,506	8,093	8,139	8,085
Investment	1,915	1,915	1,982	1,979	1,839	1,754	1,905	1,884	1,888
Exports	1,152	1,152	1,258	1,247	1,259	1,380	1,361	1,404	1,465
Imports, real	1,760	1,760	1,634	1,651	1,731	1,698	1,613	1,614	1,567
Real exchange rate	100.00	100.02	90.78	91.77	90.69	80.20	81.88	79.92	74.65
Disposable income	9,841	9,839	9,701	9,378	10,003	10,188	9,700	9,756	9,695
Interest rate percent	4.1	4.1	2.7	2.8	5.7	7.5	4.3	4.8	4.8
Price level	100.0	100.0	100.6	100.5	101.3	102.9	101.9	102.2	102.8
Fiscal deficit	422	423	44	48	454	488	74	80	−39
Government spending (NIPA)	2,187.0	2,187.0	1,835.6	2,187.0	2,187.0	2,187.0	2,011.3	2,011.3	1,952.7
Tax rate	0.16	0.16	0.16	0.19	0.16	0.16	0.175	0.175	0.18
Foreign GDP	24,740	24,740	24,740	24,740	24,740	24,740	24,740	25,111	25,111
Import price	100.0	100.0	105.1	104.5	105.1	112.4	111.1	112.6	117.0
Imports, nominal	1,760	1,760	1,718	1,725	1,820	1,908	1,791	1,816	1,833
Trade balance percent of GDP	−5.2	−5.2	−4.0	−4.1	−4.7	−4.4	−3.7	−3.5	−3.1
Fiscal balance percent of GDP	−3.6	−3.6	−0.4	−0.4	−3.8	−4.0	−0.6	−0.7	0.3
GDP percent change from base	0	0	−1.4	−1.2	1.7	3.5	0.4	0.9	0.9

A. 3 percent of GDP cut in government spending.
B. 3 percent of GDP increase in taxes.
C. 20 percent ex ante fall in dollar.
D. 20 percent ex post fall in dollar.
E. 1.5 percent of GDP cut in government spending, 1.5 percent of GDP rise in taxes, 20 percent ex ante decline in dollar.
F. E plus 1.5 percent rise in foreign GDP.
G. 2 percent of GDP for both lower spending and higher taxes, 25 percent ex ante decline in dollar, 1.5 percent rise in foreign GDP.

NIPA = National Income and Product Account

expectation for the external adjustment solely from fiscal correction is only about 40 percent as large as the initial fiscal adjustment.[43]

In simulation C, in contrast, it is assumed that by some means there is an ex ante exogenous reduction in the real exchange rate by 20 percent.[44] This is implemented in the model by reducing the constant in the exchange rate (from α_E = 264.5 to 244.5, or by 20 index points against an index base of 100). The results of this case show that there are strong general equilibrium influences tending to offset the ex ante weakening of the exchange rate. Most importantly, because of the incipient upward pressure on GDP as exports expand and imports contract, the interest rate rises briskly (driven by the Taylor rule response). The rise in the interest rate substantially diminishes the size of the exchange rate reduction as foreign capital responds to higher interest rates, leaving the net exchange rate decrease at only about half of the ex ante potential reduction. The rise in GDP also boosts demand for imports by enough to leave the real import volume approximately unchanged from the base case, and the nominal import bill increases as a result, considering that the dollar price of imports is now higher. The overall extent of adjustment is surprisingly modest given the depth of the ex ante exchange rate reduction; the trade deficit eases by only 0.5 percent of GDP (from 5.2 to 4.7 percent).

A more extreme case of "exchange rate only" adjustment is shown in simulation D. In this case, the constant term in the exchange rate equation is successively reduced until the general equilibrium solution shows approximately a 20 percent reduction in the ex post exchange rate.[45] This time the upward pressure on interest rates is even more severe, as GDP rises by an outsized 3.5 percent (to well above potential). Once again the external adjustment in nominal terms is modest (from 5.2 to 4.4 percent of the GDP nominal trade deficit) in view of the major reduction in the real exchange rate. Interestingly, the sharp depreciation scenario also boosts the federal deficit. The reason is that the large rise in the interest rate increases the interest burden in fiscal accounts.

Simulation E, in contrast, assumes a more balanced set of adjustment influences. Government spending is cut by 1.5 percent of GDP; taxes are raised by 1.5 percent of GDP; and the ex ante real exchange rate is cut by 20 percent (α_E falls from 264.5 to 244.5). This case achieves a somewhat greater external correction than under the "fiscal only" scenarios (A and

---

43. That is, in scenario A, the trade deficit falls from 5.2 to 4 percent of GDP or by 1.2 percent of GDP, which is 40 percent of the initial 3 percent of GDP reduction in government spending. Note, however, the discussion of possible downward bias in the relationship of the current account adjustment to fiscal adjustment in the main text of this chapter and also in chapter 5 and appendix 5A.

44. From 100 to 80. This represents a 25 percent rise in the dollar price of foreign currencies.

45. This requires cutting the ex ante real exchange rate by 29 percent, as the constant α_E is cut from 664.5 to 635.5, or by 29 index points.

B), as the trade deficit is cut from 5.2 to 3.7 percent of GDP. Moreover, this adjustment occurs with a GDP increase of 0.4 percent rather than a GDP decline of about 1.3 percent in the fiscal-only cases. Considering that US GDP in 2004 was about 1 percent below potential, this "balanced" case of fiscal and exchange rate adjustment with some expansionary effect is relatively favorable.

Simulation F adds foreign GDP expansion to the "balanced" package of simulation E. Foreign GDP is assumed to rise exogenously by 1.5 percent. This scenario gives the largest increase in real exports (by 21.9 percent from the base level). It also gives the largest reduction in the real exchange rate, considering the additional downward pressure from a larger foreign GDP relative to US GDP (the "relative growth" influence in the exchange market). Under the more favorable conditions of simulation F, the trade deficit eases to 3.5 percent of GDP. One reason the external adjustment is not larger is that, with a 20 percent decline in the ex post real exchange rate, the dollar price of imports rises by 12.6 percent, and after taking account of the increase in GDP on import demand, the nominal value of imports is 3 percent higher than in the base case, even though the import volume is 8.3 percent lower.

Simulation G applies a more forceful package of adjustment, involving a 2 percent of GDP cut in government spending, a 2 percent of GDP rise in taxes, an ex ante 25 percent reduction in the real exchange rate, and once again the favorable assumption of a 1.5 percent rise in foreign income. This time the fiscal adjustment is strong enough to swing the fiscal balance to a surplus of 0.3 percent of GDP. The nominal trade deficit falls to 3.1 percent of GDP.

Implications

The principal implication of the general equilibrium experiments is that fiscal adjustment will be an indispensable part of external adjustment. Without substantial fiscal adjustment, much of the potential trade correction from even a large decline in the dollar will tend to be thwarted by a partial dollar rebound in response to rising interest rates and offsetting increases in import volume in response to the rise in aggregate demand. The particular quantitative estimates obtained here should be interpreted as primarily illustrative rather than definitive. They probably err on the side of pessimism in finding that, under plausible scenarios, the size of the nominal external adjustment is considerably smaller than the size of the fiscal adjustment, even when there is help from an exogenously falling dollar. At the same time, as discussed in the main text of this chapter, it should not come as a surprise that fiscal adjustment by a given percent of GDP will not necessarily be accompanied by an "identical twin" reduction in the trade deficit by the same percent of GDP.

In chapter 3, it was estimated that, using an elasticities model approach, a 10 percent real depreciation of the dollar can be expected to reduce the current account deficit by 1.4 percent of GDP after two years (although in the first year there is a perverse J-curve effect). In contrast, in the general equilibrium model presented in this appendix, even in the most favorable and strongest adjustment package considered (simulation G), a 25 percent real depreciation, accompanied by a fiscal adjustment of about 4 percent of GDP, only reduces the trade deficit by 2.1 percent of GDP (from 5.2 to 3.1 percent). The adjustment impact of 0.084 percent of GDP for each percentage point of real depreciation is considerably smaller than in the partial equilibrium estimate of 0.14 percent of GDP per percentage point depreciation. Moreover, if the exchange rate moves alone with no help from fiscal adjustment (simulation D), the impact shrinks to an even smaller 0.067 percent of GDP for 1 percentage point depreciation.

It is important to recognize, however, that the size of the real external adjustment is larger than the size of the nominal adjustment, because of the adverse terms of trade effect from the rise in the price of imports. Thus, in the most favorable case (G), whereas the nominal trade deficit falls by 2.1 percent of GDP, the real trade deficit at base period import prices falls from $608 billion to $102 billion, or by 4.3 percent of GDP. The fiscal adjustment is 3.9 percent of GDP, so the size of the two deficit corrections is approximately the same in real terms. The underlying economics is that enough room must be made in aggregate demand for the shift of real resources away from domestic use to foreign use as the real trade deficit declines. A key implication, however, is that whereas the required fiscal adjustment will be approximately the same size as the real trade balance adjustment obtained, the observed reduction in the dollar value of the trade deficit will be considerably smaller than both of the real adjustments because of the rising unit price of imports. More generally, the various simulations involving at least some fiscal adjustment find that the size of the adjustment in the real trade deficit is approximately 60 percent as large as the fiscal adjustment (in cases A-B of fiscal-only adjustment) to 100 to 115 percent (in the fiscal *cum* ex ante exchange rate adjustment cases E-G) as large as the fiscal adjustment, but that the corresponding nominal external adjustment in these cases tends to be in the range of one-third to one-half the size of the fiscal adjustment respectively.[46]

The difference between the real and nominal adjustment also means that the larger nominal external adjustment impact parameters estimated

46. In contrast, when there is no ex ante fiscal adjustment but only ex ante exchange rate reduction, the real external adjustment is far larger than the ex post fiscal adjustment. However, in these cases (C and D), the magnitude of the external adjustment is very limited, and even so there is strong upward pressure on GDP and hence potential inflationary pressure.

in chapter 3 than in this appendix also imply larger real adjustment impacts. Thus, in the model of chapter 3, given the pass-through parameters and trade elasticities, the ratio of the real to nominal external adjustment is approximately 1.5 to 1 (Cline 1989, 360). On this basis, the results in chapter 3 imply that a 10 percent real decline of the dollar generates a real external adjustment of about 2 percent of GDP after two years.

It is normal for general equilibrium estimates to damp down the size of policy impact parameters. General equilibrium systems tend to generate negative (damping) rather than positive (amplifying) feedback. The large difference between the estimated partial and general equilibrium impacts of a decline in the dollar on the trade balance suggests relatively strong negative feedback in this system. One of these is the induced increase in GDP when exports begin to rise, which in turn induces increased imports through the income demand effect. Another is the induced rise in the interest rate as GDP rises relative to potential output, which in turn tends to arrest the decline in the dollar. At the same time, however, the results here suggest that when fiscal adjustment is the initial policy measure, the feedback effects tend to be positive (reinforcing) for external adjustment. As one example, the smaller fiscal deficit exerts downward pressure on the interest rate, which induces a real depreciation of the exchange rate, which in turn contributes to external adjustment through the price effect.

Overall, the simulations here suggest that it will be essential for sizable fiscal adjustment to accompany dollar adjustment if US external adjustment is to make much progress. Moreover, although primarily illustrative, the estimates tend to suggest that the size of the external adjustment, in terms of the change in the ratio of the nominal deficit to GDP, will tend to be moderate, even for what can only be regarded as large changes in the value of the dollar and the size of the fiscal deficit.

5

Sustainability of the US Current Account Deficit and the Risk of Crisis

The large and growing US external deficit and the associated shift into net external debt pose potential problems for the US and world economies. The United States runs the risk that the external imbalance will eventually trigger a "hard landing." For the rest of the world economy, a large ongoing US external deficit has mixed effects because although it provides a source of demand for exports, it also absorbs the lion's share of global capital flows (as will be examined in chapter 6). If there is a recessionary hard landing for the US economy, moreover, it is highly likely that the adverse effects will spill over to the rest of the world economy. Even if the United States were to escape any serious short-term disruption from an ever-widening external deficit, the long-term consequences would be to support additional consumption in the current decade at the expense of consumption in future decades, when the external debt would eventually have to be repaid, posing the same questions of intergenerational equity raised by the long-term fiscal problem.

This chapter examines the risks and sustainability of the US current account deficit and emerging net external debt from various vantage points. It first considers whether the US deficit has grown so large that the necessary foreign financing is likely to be difficult to mobilize because of constraints on the amount of US assets foreigners are prepared to hold relative to their overall portfolios. Trends in dollar reserve holdings by foreign central banks are an important part of this question. The discussion then turns to traditional benchmarks in terms of safe levels of external debt, and considers whether these thresholds—largely based on developing country experience—are of relevance to the United States. The chapter concludes with a review of the evolving policy debate among economists on whether the external imbalance poses a potentially serious risk.

US Share in Global Portfolios

Potential risk to debtor countries can be viewed from both a stock and a flow perspective. Traditional rules of thumb tend to identify a range of about 40 percent of GDP as a zone in which the stock of external debt may begin to cause problems. As discussed in chapter 1, however, several industrial countries have exceeded this threshold without experiencing debt crises. More broadly, industrial countries have not defaulted on debt since the 1930s, and the safety thresholds have been based on the experiences of developing countries. For decades, Canada had net external debt in the range of 30 to 40 percent before its recent relative debt reduction; Australia and New Zealand have reached external debt ratios of 55 to 80 percent, respectively, over the past decade. More dramatically, Finland's net debt surged from 30 percent of GDP in 1988–93 to 70 percent in 1994–99 without causing capital markets to bat an eye (see figure 1.3 in chapter 1).[1] One likely reason is that capital markets have not viewed external net liabilities in equities as comparable to liabilities in pure debt (and surging prices of Finnish corporate stocks held by foreigners were the driving force in the sharp increase in net external liabilities).

US net external liabilities, at 22 percent of GDP at the end of 2004, are not yet at even the developing-country threshold of 40 percent, where debt stock might arguably pose a risk. As argued in chapter 2, moreover, in economic terms based on the burden of capital services payments, the United States has remained a small net creditor. In 2004, its "economic" net foreign asset position as measured by capitalized net capital income (CNCI) was still positive at 7.2 percent of GDP (chapters 2 and 3).

These considerations suggest that the United States remains well below levels of external indebtedness at which the stock of debt might begin to pose a serious risk to the economy. It seems considerably more likely, however, that the size of the annual current account deficit is so large that the United States could encounter external debt difficulties because of flow problems. The possibility of a flow crisis despite a comfortable stock situation is familiar among some developing countries with relatively low debt stocks that nonetheless experienced acute liquidity problems (a notable example being Korea at end-1997). The United States itself has experienced episodes of balance of payments flow crises when its net external asset position was considerably more favorable. The sharp decline

---

1. On the contrary, Finland's sovereign rating by Moody's rose from Aa2 in 1992 to the agency's highest level, Aaa, by 1998, and has stayed there since (Moody's Investors Service 2003, 16).

of the dollar in 1977–79 played at least a modest role in the severe tightening of US monetary policy in 1979–80, even though high inflation was the more prominent factor; and disagreement between US and German officials in mid-1987 about dollar policy at the height of the US current account imbalance likely contributed to the stock market crash of October 1987.

For the United States, the potential flow problem is not excessive short-term debt in the face of a fixed exchange rate, as was the case in Korea. Instead, the risk is that a change in expectations will make foreigners much less willing to finance the large current account deficit, placing pressure on the dollar and potentially forcing the Federal Reserve to boost interest rates to keep the currency from falling too rapidly, with recessionary consequences.[2] As examined below, already by 2002–03, there were signs of growing potential for such an event, as the composition of financing of the US current account deficit shifted substantially from private to official purchases of US assets. The largest official purchasers were China and, at least until March 2003, Japan, both intent on preventing appreciation of their currencies against the dollar.

Flow thresholds for external crises are not as familiar as debt stock thresholds. However, some recent studies have suggested that industrial countries have tended to enter into external difficulties and faced adjustment typically involving a slowdown in growth once their current account deficits reached 4 to 5 percent of GDP (Freund 2000, Mann 1999). The United States is already well beyond the 5 percent mark, and the baseline in chapter 3 shows the current account deficit rising to about 7½ percent of GDP by 2010.

The constraint usually invoked in considering why the US current account deficit cannot keep widening indefinitely is the limit that foreign investors are likely to place on the share of US assets in their portfolios. It is in the portfolio share that the flow perspective intersects with the stock perspective. If there is a ceiling portfolio share, then the question is whether the existing stock places the present portfolio share close enough to that ceiling to pose a meaningful obstacle to continuation of the present pace of deficit flows.

Recent Trends

One gauge of the US portfolio share is simply the share of the US current account deficit in the global sum of current account surpluses for countries in surplus in the year in question. This current account share is essentially

---

2. It is unclear whether the Federal Reserve would have tightened just as much in 1979 because of inflation even if the dollar had not fallen. The dollar's fall presumably had some role in aggravating inflationary expectations. The reaction of the Federal Reserve to a dollar decline is discussed further below.

Figure 5.1 US current account deficit (left) **and share in world
current account surpluses** (right), **1992–2002**

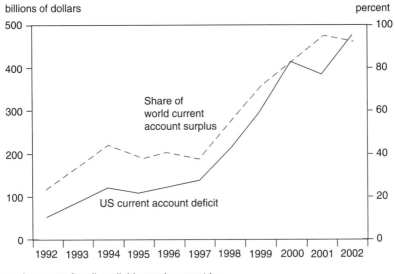

billions of dollars

percent

Note: Aggregate for all available surplus countries.
Source: IMF (2005b).

a "marginal portfolio share," because the current account is the annual
increment to the stock of the net international investment position (NIIP).
Figure 5.1 shows the path of the US current account deficit (absolute
value) in billions of dollars, on the left scale, and the US deficit as a
percent of the total current account surpluses for surplus countries for
each year in question (right scale) using data from the International Monetary Fund (IMF 2005b). As the figure shows, the US deficit rose from
about 25 percent of the global surplus total in 1992 to a plateau of about
40 percent in the mid-1990s, before surging to an average of about 90
percent in 2000–02. The inordinate US share in global current account
surpluses in recent years is a vivid illustration of the point that, because
the US economy is so large relative to the economy of the rest of the
world, there may be additional "portfolio constraints" limiting how long
other countries are prepared to finance the ongoing US external deficits.

From the standpoint of shares in asset stocks as opposed to current
account flows, the data compiled in chapter 1 provide a basis for examining the share of US assets in foreign portfolios. There are two alternative
ways to gauge this share using these data. The first is to think of each
country as a net debtor or net creditor, and to make the judgment that
net debtor countries are competing for shares in an aggregate portfolio
of net asset positions of the net creditor countries. If this "net" formulation

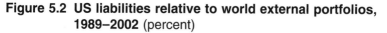

Figure 5.2 US liabilities relative to world external portfolios, 1989–2002 (percent)

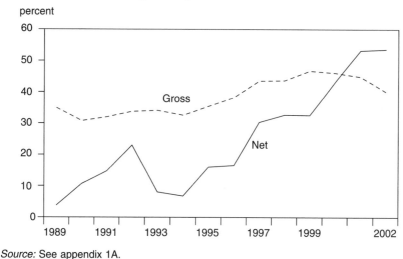

percent

Source: See appendix 1A.

is used, then the trend in the US external liability position would seem to give cause for concern about a rapid advance toward some plausible limit on the US share in foreign portfolios. Figure 1.9 in chapter 1 showed the time path of global net assets of net creditors and global net liabilities of net debtors. To address the global balance sheet discrepancy discussed in chapter 1, the more meaningful aggregate is that for global net liabilities of countries in net liability positions. This aggregate rose from $1.2 trillion in 1989 to $4.9 trillion in 2002. The stock of net US liabilities as a share of the global total rose sharply, from 4 percent in 1989 to 54 percent in 2002 (figure 5.2). (Note that the surprising fall in the portfolio share in 1993 reflected the large reduction in US net external liabilities that year as a consequence of enormous price valuation effects; see table 2.1 in chapter 2).

An alternative way to think about the US share in foreign external portfolios is in terms of gross external assets. In this framework, all foreign countries, not just net creditors, would be seen as potential holders of US external liabilities, and foreign holders would assess the US share against their gross holdings of foreign assets, not their net holdings. In this "gross" portfolio approach, also shown in figure 5.2, there is a far milder rise in the US share, and even some decline since 1999. By this measure, the US share rose from a low of 31 percent in 1990 to a peak of 47 percent in 1999 before easing to 40 percent in 2002. The gentler trend for gross external liabilities than for net liabilities simply reflects the much greater proportionate rise for the net figure, which, as emphasized in chapter 1, is a residual between two large gross measures (assets and liabilities).[3]

Still another way to consider the US share in global portfolios is against total portfolios including domestic assets within foreign countries.[4] Data from the Organization for Economic Cooperation and Development (OECD) place gross household financial assets for the seven large industrial countries at $74 trillion at end-2001, or 3.6 times their combined GDP of $20.3 trillion (at market exchange rates).[5] At end-2002, gross financial assets of households stood at $35.7 trillion for the United States and an estimated $34.4 trillion for the other six major industrial nations that make up the Group of Seven (G-7): Japan, Germany, France, Italy, the United Kingdom, and Canada.

Considering total financial assets immediately helps place the external assets and liabilities into perspective. Gross US external assets and liabilities at end-2002 were 19.1 and 25.9 percent, respectively, of gross household financial assets, somewhat higher than the stylized fact of "home bias" in portfolios might suggest.[6] The main perspective provided by the total financial asset estimate is that net US foreign liabilities are small relative to total portfolios of US households. Thus, the end-2002 net external liabilities of $2.5 trillion amounted to only 7 percent of gross financial assets. Although they were relatively larger compared with net financial assets (about 11 percent), they were smaller relative to the net wealth of households, including housing and other nonfinancial assets (about 5 percent). Americans' net debt abroad is dwarfed by their net wealth at home.

Returning to the question of shares in foreign portfolios, figure 5.3 shows the path of gross household financial assets for the United States and for the other G-7 countries over the past decade, along with the trend in US gross external liabilities. It is evident that US gross external liabilities remain modest compared with the gross household financial assets of both the United States and the other G-7 countries. It is also evident,

---

3. Note further that the seeming tension between the exceptionally high US share in resources provided by global current account surpluses in 2000–02, on the one hand, and the easing of the US gross liability share in the non-US global stock of gross external assets in those years, on the other, reflects the sizable contribution of exchange rate valuation changes in boosting the dollar value of the latter by 2002.

4. This section partly follows the data approach suggested in Mann (2003).

5. Calculated from OECD (2004a) for assets relative to disposable income and (2004d) for disposable income. End-2002 assets for Italy are based on end-2001 data and the percent change from 2001 to 2002 for Germany and France.

6. The ratio is not significantly biased upward by excluding the government, as US external reserves are small. Although the corporate sector is excluded, in principle, the value of corporate assets is already captured in the financial assets of households, because all corporate shares are owned ultimately by households.

Figure 5.3 Household gross financial assets and gross US external liabilities, 1992–2002 (trillions of dollars)

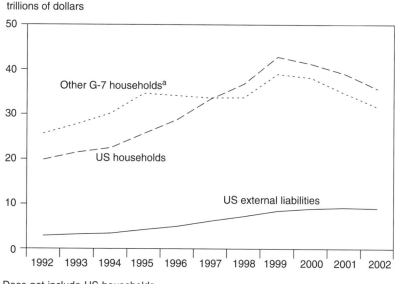

trillions of dollars

Other G-7 households[a]

US households

US external liabilities

a. Does not include US households.
Sources: OECD (2004a, b); IMF (2004a, b).

however, that US gross external liabilities have risen substantially relative to both US and other G-7 nations' gross financial assets.

Another trend evident in figure 5.3 is the decline in household financial assets following their peak in 1999–2000. The decline was driven by a plunge in equity assets as a percent of disposable income from end-1999 to end-2002 (from 182 to 91 percent in the United States, 120 to 57 percent in the United Kingdom, 178 to 101 percent in France, and 153 to 102 percent in Italy).[7]

Still another important trend is the rise in US financial assets relative to those of the other main industrial countries. In 1992, gross household financial assets of the United States were only 77 percent as large as those of the other G-7 nations; by 2002, this ratio had reached 104 percent. Over the period, US gross financial assets rose 80 percent, whereas those of the other main industrial countries rose only 34 percent.[8] This means that the ratio of US financial assets to those in the other G-7 countries rose by

---

7. The latter figure for Italy is for end-2001. The bursting of the global equity bubble had much less impact in Japan (48 to 42 percent), Germany (75 to 54 percent), and Canada (an increase from 92 to 95 percent).

8. The slowest growth, but not by much, was in Japan (31 percent expansion versus 36 percent for the other G-7 countries, excluding the United States).

Figure 5.4 Share of US gross external liabilities in rest-of-world gross financial assets, 1992–2002 (percent)

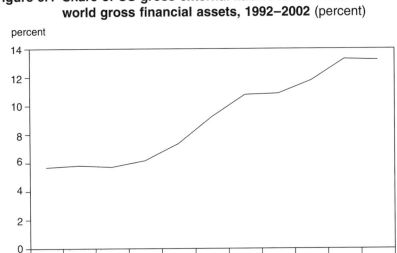

percent

Sources: See figure 5.3.

about 35 percent over the decade. It is perhaps less surprising than otherwise might be thought, then, that many US financial aggregates (including gross liabilities abroad) would have risen over the period relative to those of other industrial countries.

The more proper comparison for gauging the share of US assets in the portfolios of foreigners is against global rather than other G-7 nation assets. In the absence of data for other countries, such an estimate requires extrapolating from the other G-7 industrial-country aggregates to world portfolios. One basis for this expansion is GDP. In 2002, the other G-7 countries accounted for 51 percent of non-US global GDP at market prices (World Bank 2004a). An alternative benchmark is the global stock of capital. Cline (1997, 183) uses World Bank capital stock estimates to calculate that in 1993, the United States accounted for 20.8 percent of global capital stock, the European Union, 20.7 percent, Japan, 10.5 percent, and Canada, 2 percent. On this basis (and overstating the other G-7 nations a bit by treating the European Union as just the four largest European economies), the other G-7 nations accounted for 42 percent of non-US world capital stock. Considering that financial intermediation in the industrial countries is higher than in developing countries, this is also consistent with the other G-7 nations representing about half of non-US global financial assets. On this basis, a reasonable approximation of non-US global financial assets is simply twice the amount held by households in the other G-7 nations.

Figure 5.4 shows the results of comparing gross US external liabilities against the estimated total of financial assets for the rest of the world, calculated simply as twice the amount for the other G-7 nations. This exercise shows the US share in foreign portfolios rising from 5.7 percent in 1992 to 13.2 percent in 2002. This rapid increase in share, coupled with continued (if lessening) home bias in portfolios, is suggestive of eventual limits in the pace of the US buildup of external liabilities, and perhaps sooner rather than later.

Baseline Projections

The baseline projections in chapter 3 for US external accounts provided corresponding projections of gross and net US external liabilities. For the average of the two models developed in chapter 3, with the dollar unchanged from its average real level in the first five months of 2005, and with baseline US and foreign growth, the US current account deficit would reach 7.7 percent of GDP in 2010. Gross US external liabilities would rise from $12.5 trillion at the end of 2004, or 107 percent of GDP, to $20.6 trillion at the end of 2010, or 128 percent of GDP. Net liabilities would rise correspondingly from 22 to 52 percent of GDP. This is on an accounting rather than an "economic" basis. It is the accounting gauge of financial liabilities that is more relevant for concerns about shares in foreign portfolios, whereas the economic concept of external liability burden (based on capital services rather than accounting net liabilities) is more relevant for diagnosing the underlying debt burden.

The size of foreign financial assets over the same horizon depends on the pace of foreign growth, the ratio of disposable income to GDP, and the trend in the ratio of financial assets to disposable income. Figure 5.5 shows that for the G-7 countries, there was a trend toward rising financial assets relative to disposable income during the past decade. For the G-7 excluding the United States, a simple linear regression (including country dummy variables) finds a highly significant annual increase in the assets/income ratio by about 8 percentage points per year over this period.[9]

As shown in figure 5.3, gross financial assets of households in G-7 nations excluding the United States reached an estimated average of $34.6 trillion in 2001–02. This represented a weighted average of 410 percent of household disposable income. A trend rise of 8 percentage points per year thus amounts to a 2 percent annual increase in the ratio of financial assets to disposable income for those G-7 nations. The projections of chapter 3 assume foreign real GDP growth of 3.5 percent per year and US inflation at 1.8 percent annually (GDP deflator). If the same inflation

---

9. The regression is: $z = 286.1 \ (29) + 7.93 \ T \ (8.1) + 109 \ J \ (10) - 82.6 \ G \ (-7.6) - 27.8 \ F \ (-2.6) - 51.6 \ I \ (-4.6) + 79.5 \ U \ (7.5)$; adj. $R^2 = 0.90$, where z is gross financial assets as a percentage of disposable income, T is time (1992 = 1 to 2003 = 12), with t-statistics in parentheses. Dummy variables (1 if applicable, 0 otherwise) J, G, F, I, and U are for Japan, Germany, France, Italy, and United Kingdom.

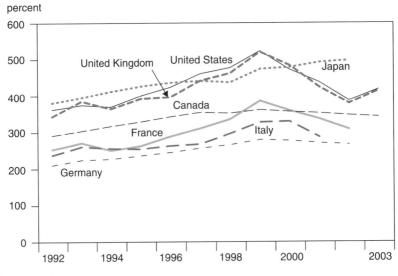

Source: OECD (2004a).

rate is applied to foreign economies, their nominal growth rate is 5.4 percent.

As a first approximation, then, the global non-US stock of gross financial assets begins from a 2001–02 base of about $70 trillion (twice the aggregate of the other G-7 countries) and grows at a nominal rate of 5.4 percent to accompany nominal GDP, plus 2 percent to capture financial deepening. A further adjustment of the base is needed to take account of the change in exchange rates from 2001–02 to 2004. From the end of 2002 to November 2004, the other G-7 currencies rose against the dollar by 18.8 percent, weighting by shares in gross household financial assets. This would have boosted the other G-7 nations' aggregate financial assets from $34.4 trillion to $41 trillion for exchange valuation. Adding 4 percent for two years' financial deepening and 9 percent for nominal GDP growth, the other G-7 nations' gross household financial assets in late 2004 stood at an estimated $46 trillion. Gross financial assets in the rest of the world will not have risen as fast in dollar terms because of much lesser appreciation of currencies against the dollar in this period. Omitting exchange rate movements for the non-G-7 nations, but incorporating annual financial deepening by 2 percent and GDP growth in dollar terms at 6.4 percent annually (4.5 percent real and 1.8 percent inflation), gross financial assets for this group would have risen from about $35 trillion to about $40 trillion from end-2002 to end-2004. So the end-2004 base for non-US global financial assets is an estimated $84 trillion. This aggregate can then be

**Figure 5.6 Baseline projected share of US gross external
liabilities in rest-of-world gross financial assets,
2004–10** (percent)

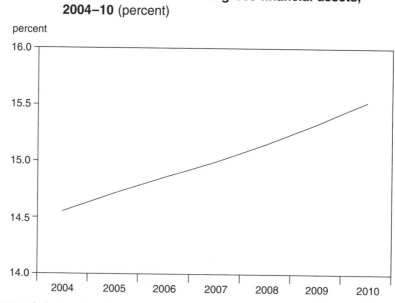

Source: Author's calculations.

projected to grow at 7.5 percent annually in the future, reflecting 2 percent
annual financial deepening, 3.5 percent real GDP growth, and 1.8 percent inflation.

Figure 5.6 shows the resulting baseline projection for US gross external
liabilities as a percentage of non-US global financial assets. This share in
global portfolios is estimated at 14.6 percent for end-2004, about one-
tenth higher than the 13.2 percent at end-2002. The rise in the dollar value
of rest-of-world portfolios from depreciation of the dollar against the
other G-7 currencies, combined with nominal GDP growth and some
financial deepening, has substantially offset the brisk rise in gross external
liabilities (from $9.3 trillion at end-2002 to $12.5 trillion at end-2004, a
rise of 35 percent).

The baseline rise of US gross external liabilities, from 14.6 percent of
rest-of-world gross financial assets to 15.5 percent over six years, is not
dramatic, but it does pose the question of compatibility with the traditional
"home bias" in financial portfolios. Feldstein and Horioka (1980) first
identified this bias in statistical tests showing an extremely high correlation between national saving rates and investment rates; major divergences from investing in the home market would instead have generated
lower correlation. Greenspan (2004a) has argued that the home bias has
declined thanks to the growing integration of world capital markets. He
notes that whereas the correlation between national saving and investment

was persistently about 0.95 for the postwar period up through the mid-1990s, by 2002, it had fallen to only 0.8. The share of foreign assets in the portfolios of US residents (including equity and debt securities as well as direct investment) rose from less than 9 percent in the 1970s to 15 percent in the mid-1990s.

Mann (2003) cites the estimate by Lewis (1999) that home bias preempts 70 percent of non-US world financial assets, making only 30 percent available for investment in the United States or other non-home countries. Mann (2003, 68) calculates that in 1998–2000, net foreign purchases of US assets represented 79 percent in the change in this "available" portion of foreign portfolios, climbing to 98 percent in 2001.[10] That pace would seem to indicate that the United States has already been testing the upper bounds of foreign portfolio availability to finance its external deficits. Nonetheless, if the 30 percent availability benchmark is used, then the baseline projections here placing gross US external liabilities by 2010 at about 16 percent of non-US gross financial assets (figure 5.6) would seem to leave significant room for increased foreign holdings of US assets.

It is important, however, to keep in mind that for virtually all other countries in the world, the question of a global portfolio constraint would simply not arise. Other countries' external liabilities are simply too small to even raise the question of absorbing more than a ceiling amount that other countries in the aggregate are prepared to hold for the foreign portion of their portfolios. Yet there obviously have been ceilings on foreign willingness to hold more liabilities of individual countries in the past, not because of overall foreign portfolio limits, but because of expected return. In particular, when foreign creditors become concerned about solvency or even liquidity of the debt obligations, they will begin to run down their holdings or avoid accumulating more. So even if the United States could continue to find enough room in aggregate foreign portfolios to keep running large external deficits, it could find it infeasible to do so once foreign creditors become convinced that the rate of return on claims on the United States would be unattractive and quite possibly (or probably) negative in view of likely depreciation of the dollar.

Trends in Central Bank Portfolios

Even if foreign private holdings of US assets are not bumping up against ceilings of portfolio shares set by the home bias, foreign private investors

---

10. The corresponding absolute amounts averaged approximately $750 billion annually over 1999–2001. The higher percentage for 2001 reflects the economic slowdown and lesser expansion of non-US wealth.

Figure 5.7 US current account deficit and capital flows, 1995–2004 (billions of dollars)

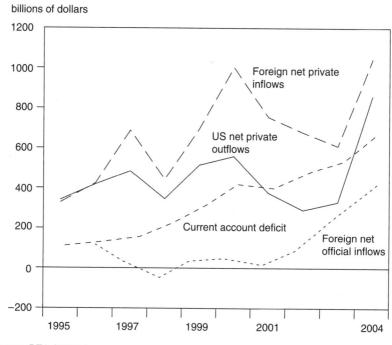

Source: BEA (2005c).

will be unlikely to continue financing the US external deficit if they find prospective returns insufficient relative to risk and opportunities at home. As the US current account deficit has widened and the new-economy boom and stock market bubble have given way to recession and recovery, private foreign capital inflows have moderated and foreign government intervention has increasingly made up for the resulting potential gap in financing of the current account deficit. But this in turn has raised the question of whether foreign central banks have begun to reach limits in their exposure to the dollar.

Figure 5.7 shows annual capital flows and the US current account deficit for recent years, with 2000 marking the most extreme phase of large net private inflows. Private inflows that year reached about $1 trillion, exceeding private outflows by about $450 billion, or more than enough to cover the current account deficit of about $415 billion. Official capital inflows, which means foreign official buildup of their reserve holdings, were only about $40 billion. There then began a scissors movement that involved falling private inflows, somewhat offset by falling private outflows, in the face of a rising current account deficit. Although private inflows rebounded to the $1 trillion range in 2004, private outflows also soared to some $860 billion, leaving a private capital surplus of only about $185 billion or only 28 percent of the current account deficit of $668 billion.

The growing gap between the current account deficit and net private capital flows during 2001–04 could have led to an even sharper decline in the dollar than occurred. Instead, such central banks as those of Japan, China, India, Korea, and many others intervened in increasing magnitudes.[11] Foreign official capital inflows ballooned to $114 billion in 2002, $278 billion in 2003, and $395 billion in 2004 (BEA 2005c). Financing by foreign central banks thus shifted from a cumulative average of 10.6 percent of the current account deficit during 1997–2001 to 24 percent in 2002, 54 percent in 2003, and 59 percent in 2004. If the central bank share is calculated against total gross capital inflows rather than the current account deficit, the corresponding shares reached 15 percent in 2002, 31 percent in 2003, and 27 percent in 2004.

The stock of foreign official holdings of US liabilities correspondingly rose rapidly, from $1.11 trillion at the end of 2001 to $1.98 trillion at the end of 2004 (BEA 2005e). The bulk of these holdings were in US government securities ($1.5 trillion at the end of 2004). By September 2004, foreign official and private holdings of US Treasury securities amounted to $1.85 trillion (US Treasury 2004a). This amounted to 43 percent of total US public debt held by the public (US Treasury 2004b).

The dollar experienced a phase of relatively rapid decline in the fourth quarter of 2004. From end-September to end-December 2004, against the dollar the euro rose 11 percent, the yen 6.6 percent, and the Canadian dollar 5 percent (IMF 2005a). In the face of prospective losses on reserve holdings in dollars, a number of central banks reportedly considered not only desisting from accumulating dollars but also shifting some of their dollar holdings to euros. Some authorities in Russia and China seemed to indicate that they were considering shifting reserves out of dollars, although subsequent denials typically followed.[12] The head of the European Central Bank (ECB) called the rise of the euro against the dollar "brutal."[13]

In contrast, in the first half of 2005, the dollar rebounded, especially against the euro in the face of French and Dutch referendums rejecting

---

11. The Bank of Japan intervened massively from March 2002 to March 2004, boosting reserves from $394 billion to $816 billion, but largely desisted thereafter, placing reserves at $833 billion by May 2005 (IMF 2005a).

12. *Financial Times*, November 23, 2004; *New York Times*, December 4, 2004. Members of the Organization of Petroleum Exporting Countries (OPEC) reportedly had already cut back the share of their reserves in dollars from 75 percent in September 2001 to 62 percent by late 2004 to limit loss of reserve value as the dollar declined, and also in view of a shift away from pricing oil solely in dollars (*Financial Times*, ibid.). There were also signs of a shift out of US Treasury bonds into claims on the private sector (still in dollars), such as US mortgage-backed bonds held as part of China's reserves (*New York Times*, ibid.).

13. *The Economist*, November 16, 2004.

the new EU constitution. From end-December to June 30, the dollar rose 12.7 percent against the euro, 6.4 percent against the yen, and 2.1 percent against the Canadian dollar (Federal Reserve Board 2005d). Although the pressure was temporarily off the dollar, any major sell-off of dollar reserve holdings by central banks abroad in exchange for purchases of euros or other currencies would still contribute substantially to a renewed decline in the dollar. However, diversification out of the dollar would probably be mainly by central banks other than the ECB and the Bank of Japan. The ECB would have no practical alternative currency to diversify into, and by selling dollars, Japan's central bank would only risk driving the dollar down further, thereby increasing its accounting losses on reserves. Indeed, in late 2004, Japanese authorities were suggesting instead joint intervention with the ECB to purchase dollars (although the ECB showed no intention of doing so, at least in the absence of any approval by the United States of such joint intervention).

Roubini and Setser (2005) have argued that if foreign central banks were to quit accumulating more dollar reserves, there would be a major shock to US interest rates. Their ballpark estimate is a rise of 200 basis points. They emphasize that the entire new net supply of US Treasury obligations since 2000 has been purchased by nonresidents, with foreign central banks accounting for 80 to 90 percent of those purchases. They also stress that if foreign central banks stopped accumulating additional dollar reserves, the effect would be magnified by a cutback in foreign private capital inflows because private investors would begin to perceive more foreign exchange risk in purchasing US assets.

Truman (2005) has suggested that the interest rate impact of external financing is analogous to that of a fiscal deficit. Using this approach, and applying the Gale-Orszag (2004) rule of thumb that each 1 percent of GDP increase in the fiscal deficit boosts the long-term interest rate by about 30 basis points, if foreign central banks had not provided the $395 billion in net capital inflows (3.4 percent of GDP) to the United States that they did in 2004, then interest rates might have been about 100 basis points higher. It can also be argued, however, that there is a high degree of substitutability between private and official financing, and that a cutback of official financing would be offset by a rise in private financing in response to just a modest rise in the interest rate. Overall, it would seem likely that the impact of a cessation in foreign central bank financing of the US external deficit would boost long-term interest rates in the range of 50 to 100 basis points, rather than the 200 basis points suggested by Roubini and Setser.

Debt Ratios and Critical Thresholds

As there is an extensive literature on indicators of creditworthiness for developing countries, it is worth considering whether the benchmarks from that literature might apply to the United States as a basis for identifying a possible future crisis, and if so, whether the United States is headed toward what have traditionally been regarded as danger zones for creditworthiness.

Crisis Indicators for Developing Countries

The traditional literature on developing country debt crises has focused on debt rescheduling or "default" events and examined the economic indicators associated with their occurrence (see Frank and Cline 1971; Cline 1984; Goldstein, Reinhart, and Kaminsky 2000; and Peter 2002). The formal econometric estimates typically apply binary-outcome techniques, such as logit analysis, and incorporate multiple variables (e.g., debt/export ratio, debt service ratio, reserves/imports, amortization rate, and in more recent studies, indicators of banking sector stability), rather than identifying single-variable thresholds. Nonetheless, various stylized-fact thresholds have emerged.

In the early 1970s, a popular benchmark was that debt service (interest on all debt plus amortization on long-term debt) should not exceed 25 percent of exports of goods and services. By the late 1970s, considerably higher debt service ratios were being maintained, largely thanks to an outward shift in the global supply of capital to developing countries associated with the recycling of petrodollars after the OPEC oil price increase of 1973–74. The debt crisis of the 1980s underscored the need for fiscal solvency (the internal transfer problem) as well as external solvency (availability of foreign exchange to service external debt), which increased attention to the debt burden relative to GDP. Stylized-fact critical thresholds for middle-income countries tended to be in the range of 40 percent for the external debt-to-GDP ratio and 300 percent for the debt–to-exports ratio.[14]

Cline (1995b, 50) emphasized that the debt burden depended crucially on the interest rate (which had soared in the early 1980s with the Volcker interest rate shock, discussed below), and suggested that the best measure was the ratio of net interest payments to exports of goods and services.[15] This ratio for 17 major countries involved in the 1980s debt crisis reached

---

14. Cline (1995b, 45) estimated that the GNP-weighted average ratio of net external debt (gross debt minus reserves) to exports of goods and services for the 17 countries included in the "Baker Plan" of concerted debt rollover rose from 290 percent in 1982 to 384 percent at its peak in 1986, and then declined to 225 percent by 1993, when most of these countries had regained access to capital markets. Cohen (1997) reported the average debt-export ratio for African and Latin American countries that experienced debt crises in the 1980s to be 270 percent.

15. That analysis omitted amortization on the grounds that in the 1980s debt reschedulings, principal on long-term debt was typically rolled over.

a GNP-weighted 30 percent in 1982, eased to 25 percent by 1984–88, and was down to only 11 percent by 1992–93, suggesting a critical threshold of perhaps 20 percent on this measure.

For the ratio of external debt to GDP, a 40 percent benchmark threshold has received recent statistical support from Reinhart, Rogoff, and Savastano (2003). They find that the median ratio of external debt to GNP for emerging-market economies that did not experience external default any time during 1970–2000 was 33 percent, whereas the median for countries that did experience default was 41 percent.[16]

The international effort in the late 1990s to reduce the debt of countries that qualified for relief under the Heavily Indebted Poor Countries (HIPC) initiative provided the occasion for policy reviews of debt thresholds considered sustainable. It was recognized that the debt of these countries had to be calculated in net present value terms to take account of "illusory" concessional debt at near-zero interest rates. The first incarnation of the HIPC initiative in 1996 set the range of 200 to 250 percent as the critical threshold for net present value of debt relative to exports of goods and services, and 280 percent as the critical threshold for the ratio of net present value of debt to fiscal revenue (van Trotsenberg and MacArthur 1999, 2). The second version of the initiative, the "enhanced" HIPC in 1999, lowered the debt-to-exports threshold to 150 percent "to allow some leeway for debt burdens to increase in the future without pushing countries straight back into unsustainability" (Birdsall and Williamson 2002, 32). The threshold for net present value of debt to fiscal revenue was similarly lowered to 250 percent. These thresholds, of course, were for poor countries, and thus presumably well below levels that could be considered sustainable for middle-income countries with greater access to capital markets.

The other experience of the late 1990s that generated new metrics for risk was the East Asian currency crisis. In particular, the crisis in Korea in late 1997 underscored the fact that even strong economies can get into an external sector crisis if they encounter a liquidity squeeze. The dominant indicator that came out of this experience was the ratio of short-term debt to reserves. Although there is no stylized-fact threshold for this measure, somewhere in the vicinity of 200 to 250 percent would seem consistent with the experience of the late 1990s. Thus, this ratio rose from 159 percent in 1991 to 955 percent in 1994 in Mexico's crisis; from 129 percent in 1994 to 177 percent in 1997 in Indonesia; from 206 percent to 315 percent over the same period in Korea; and from 80 percent in 1995 to 444 percent in 1998 in Russia (IIF 1999, 25).

---

16. The authors also conclude, however, that the safe level is far lower, perhaps as low as 15 percent of GDP, for those countries that have shown themselves to be "debt intolerant" by a record of serial defaults.

The prominence of banking sector problems in the East Asian crises also focused attention on financial indicators such as the ratio of M2 to base money and the real interest rate on deposits.[17] The shift of the nature of the crises from debt to currency collapse underscored the importance of such measures as the extent of mismatch in currency denomination of assets and liabilities (Goldstein and Turner 2004).

Are the Thresholds Relevant for the United States?

Those who are prepared to apply the traditional crisis threshold metrics for developing countries to the United States can find grounds for concern.[18] The accounting NIIP shows net liabilities at 221 percent of exports of goods and services for 2004 (see table 3.2 in chapter 3), three-fourths of the way toward a 300 percent critical ratio, and the NIIP stands at 22 percent of GDP, about halfway toward the 40 percent threshold. Nevertheless, there are several reasons why the conventional benchmarks for developing countries are unlikely to apply to the United States.

The first reason is that the debt ratios do not take account of the fact that the United States does not yet have a real debt burden, as it has still been earning more on its external assets than on its external liabilities. Thus, the economic net foreign asset measure (capitalized net capital income, or CNCI) suggested in chapter 2, which equals the net capital services flow discounted by the 10-year bond rate, was still modestly positive in 2004 (+7.2 percent of GDP). The United States does not yet have a debt problem if it does not yet have economically meaningful net debt.

My preferred indicator of the debt burden—the ratio of net interest to exports of goods and services—is highly relevant for the United States, because (when the concept includes equity earnings as well as interest) it accurately captures the fact that net US capital services are still slightly positive, indicating no debt burden at present. That does not mean, however, that the United States is not on its way to developing a sizable debt burden and eventually even a debt problem.

The central point about the debt-to-GDP ratio is not so much that it does not apply to the United States in principle, but that the debt must be carefully defined in economic terms to be meaningful. If a concept such as the CNCI suggested in this study is used as the debt measure,

---

17. See Goldstein, Reinhart, and Kaminsky (2000). Note, however, that these authors gauged each country's vulnerability against its own past averages rather than seeking to establish internationally applicable threshold levels.

18. Roubini and Setser (2004, 3) state, "at an estimated 280 percent of exports at the end of 2004, [the] US debt to export ratio is in shooting range of troubled Latin economies like Brazil and Argentina."

then the traditional benchmark of 40 percent of GDP would seem to be a reasonable criterion for defining a threshold where growing concern is warranted.

In contrast, the traditional debt ratios relative to the export base may not be relevant for the United States even when the economic as opposed to accounting net debt is used. The reason, as set forth more fully below, is that the United States is atypical in having its external debt largely denominated in its own currency, so the usual concern about the adequacy of foreign exchange availability from the export base is inapplicable.

The second reason that developing-country debt thresholds do not apply is that there is ample evidence that industrial countries such as the United States have less debt vulnerability. A central reason is that in the past, developing-country debt crises often arose because the government defaulted on its debt, whether owed to its domestic public or to foreign creditors. Yet industrial countries simply have not defaulted on public debt in the postwar era. Formal statistical tests by Reinhart, Rogoff, and Savastano (2003) find, in fact, that for advanced economies, the ratio of external debt to GNP is positively rather than negatively related to credit ratings by Institutional Investor over 1979–2000. In contrast, for developing countries, there is a strong negative relationship of these ratings to the debt-to-GNP ratio.

The third reason why many of the standard indicators are not applicable is that the United States borrows in its own currency rather than foreign currency. This means that the classic trigger for debt crises in developing countries—lack of foreign exchange to pay debt service coming due—is not relevant. The United States enjoys a status superior even to that of most other advanced economies in this regard. Indeed, the US situation is just the opposite of that of a developing country forced into devaluation. Typically, the developing country has a mismatch between external debt in foreign currency and domestic government receipts as well as private firm earnings in local currency. When there is a large depreciation of the currency, there is a severe balance sheet loss for both the government and the private sector. (Argentina is perhaps the most recent and most extreme example.) The local currency burden of the foreign-currency denominated debt soars with little rise in the local currency income base for servicing the debt (except for export-oriented firms, and for a moderate offset from induced domestic inflation).[19] In contrast, the balance sheets of US firms actually *improve* when the dollar declines, because foreign equity assets are denominated in foreign currency so their dollar value balloons, whereas liabilities to foreigners are in dollars and stay unchanged.

---

19. Note that the inflationary relief appears to have fallen as well. In the 1980s, there was a high feedback from depreciation to domestic inflation, but in the past decade emerging-market economies have experienced remarkably low induced inflation in the face of sudden and large depreciations.

(The US government also experiences a windfall gain on the small amount of foreign exchange it holds in reserves.)

The irrelevance of some of the standard debt indicators when considering the United States with its own-currency debt denomination is most evident in the popular reserves/imports (or short-term debt/reserves) ratios. The United States has a reserve currency itself, and with no need for reserves, has a minimal amount of them. Gold and non-gold reserves stood at $85 billion at the end of 2003. This amounts to only about three weeks' worth of imports, which by international standards would be considered disastrously low. In contrast, in 2002, for other countries the median ratio of reserves to imports was 35 percent (about four months' imports), and the average was 54 percent (six months) (World Bank 2004a).

Sustainability Benchmarks for the United States

Analyses of sustainability of the US external imbalance usually focus on the size of the current account deficit relative to GDP. The framework for identifying the sustainable current account deficit, however, usually reflects an underlying judgment about the amount of net external liabilities the United States should prudently accumulate relative to GDP. With the target net liabilities relative to GDP in mind, the sustainable current account deficit is derived working backwards. The current account deficit is the change in the net liabilities position (aside from the equity price and exchange rate valuation influences examined in chapter 2).

Suppose that what is desired is to stabilize the ratio of net external liabilities to GDP at a target ratio "λ". If the nominal growth rate of GDP is g percent, it turns out that the sustainable current account deficit z, as a percent of GDP, consistent with this target is $z = \lambda g$.[20] This result excludes any valuation changes. The exchange rate valuation effects should be set to zero, because a sustainable current account deficit target should presumably be premised on a constant real exchange rate rather than requiring secular real depreciation. Although there are also price change valuation effects, these should be relatively small when the equity base is approximately the same size on the asset and liability sides.[21]

---

20. Define D as "net foreign debt," broadly interpreted to include both credit instruments and equity liabilities. Let z be the ratio of the current account deficit to GDP. The condition for stability of a ratio is that at the margin this ratio equals the previous average of the ratio. So it is desired that $\Delta D / \Delta Y = D/Y = \lambda$, where Y is GDP and Δ indicates change. The change in nominal GDP is the nominal growth rate times the base level of GDP, or: $\Delta Y = gY$. The increase in net external debt is the current account deficit, or: $\Delta D = zY$. So we have: $\Delta D / \Delta Y = [zY]/[gY] = D/Y = \lambda$; $z = \lambda g$.

21. See the discussion in chapter 2 of the possible annual favorable valuation drift from equity price effects. Note that at the end of 2004, US direct and portfolio equity assets abroad were $5.8 trillion, while equity liabilities were $4.6 trillion, so each percentage point increase in equity prices adds about $8 billion to the US NIIP.

Williamson (2004, 30) and Mussa (2005, 189) arrive at a range of 2 to 2.5 percent of GDP as target current account deficits on this basis. Williamson suggests this would allow the NIIP to stabilize at "a reasonable value"; Mussa explicitly arrives at the target based on a prudential limit of 50 percent of GDP for net liabilities relative to GDP, combined with an expectation of 5 percent nominal growth for US GDP (3 percent real plus 2 percent for inflation).[22]

The present study has emphasized the point that because of asymmetric returns on equity investment, the NIIP tends to overstate the net liability position of the United States in terms of economic burden. A reasonable modification of the sustainability criterion is thus to consider a target for the alternative concept of CNCI relative to GDP. At the same time, however, it would seem appropriate to set the ceiling for economic net foreign liabilities (CNCI) at perhaps 40 percent of GDP rather than 50 percent. The unique role of the US economy in the world economy, as well as the questionable if not perverse nature of sustained capital flows from developing countries to the United States instead of the reverse, is cause for prudence in setting an acceptable level of net US liabilities, even expressed as CNCI.

The preferred baseline projections of chapter 3 show the current account deficit at 7.3 percent of GDP by 2010, the accounting NIIP at -50 percent of GDP, and the CNCI at -22 percent. The favorable adjustment simulation in that chapter for a 21 percent real foreign appreciation against the dollar and a modest acceleration in foreign growth leaves the current account at a plateau of about -3 percent of GDP in 2008–10, the NIIP at about -30 percent (but still deteriorating slowly), and the CNCI net liability at only 7 percent (but still rising slowly). However, in that simulation much of the rise in both the NIIP and CNCI relative to the baseline stems from the exchange rate valuation gains from a large depreciation. In setting a sustainable current account, the expected real exchange rate should presumably be constant, and such gains would not be present.

The baseline nominal growth rate of the economy assumed in chapter 3 is 5.3 percent (3.5 percent real, 1.8 percent inflation). By the relationship $z = \lambda g$, if it is desired to limit the NIIP net liabilities to 50 percent of GDP, in the long term, the current account deficit would need to be limited to 2.65 percent of GDP. The paradox of a lower than 50 percent of GDP level of net NIIP liabilities by 2010 in the adjustment scenario (30 percent as just described), despite a higher current account deficit than 2.65 percent of GDP, stems from the fact that it takes a long time for a higher marginal ratio to bring up the average ratio to a 50 percent ceiling from a starting point about half that large in 2004.

---

22. Mussa (2005, 187) judges that "a net liability ratio of 50 percent of GDP is still not a critical problem [for the United States]; but I would worry a great deal about ratios rising toward 100 percent of GDP."

Overall, a reasonable long-term target for the US current account deficit would seem to be in the range of 3 percent of GDP. This is modestly higher than the 2.65 percent rate based on the expected nominal growth rate of 5.3 percent times a notional ceiling of 50 percent for the ratio of NIIP net liabilities to GDP. It is lower, however, than might be justified by judging sustainability by the alternative concept of economic burden of net liabilities as measured by CNCI/GDP. One reason to aim for a lower deficit is uncertainty that the size of the asymmetry between return on foreign equity assets and liabilities will remain as large as in the past. In particular, the substantially higher return on equity might not continue over a span of decades as opposed to a few years.[23]

The more fundamental reasons for a cautious current account target are that the United States should err on the side of prudence, both for its domestic economic welfare objectives and because of its central role in the global economy. Market behavior might not give full weight to persistent differential returns, leading to a confidence crisis despite continued long-term "solvency" as measured by either the NIIP or CNCI. In addition, the United States should at some point return to providing net capital to the rest of the world rather than borrowing on a net basis from it, especially from developing countries.

Hard Landing, Long-Term Burden, and Protectionist Pressures

International experience with the debt of middle-income countries has tended to identify crisis with disruption in payments, involving either temporary default or eventual forgiveness of a portion of the debt. For the various reasons just outlined, and especially on the basis of the still-valid assumption that the US government will not default on its public debt owed at home and abroad, many of the standard gauges of the severity of external debt would not seem to apply to the United States. However, this does not mean that the external sector is incapable of provoking a serious disruption in the US economy. In the short to medium term, the rising trade deficit and net foreign liabilities pose the risk of a "hard landing" for the dollar and the US economy (as well as the world economy). In the longer term, there are serious questions about the desirability of placing a large foreign debt burden on households in the next generation in return for increased consumption today. The outbreak of protection, moreover, has in the past been a forcing mechanism that has

---

23. As noted in chapter 2, if the difference in rates of return between assets and liabilities disappears, and if all rates of return equal the long-term bond rate, the CNCI becomes the same value as the NIIP.

mobilized corrective measures even when the financial markets might have allowed external deficits more latitude to continue growing.

Parsing the Hard-Landing Scenario

The principal means by which US external deficits and debt might pose an economic burden on the United States in the short to medium term is through a sharp reduction in foreign capital inflows in the face of a confidence shock. This could precipitate a severe, disorderly decline of the dollar and sharply higher interest rates. The interest rate shock, in turn, could provoke a decline in the equity and housing markets, curb investment and consumption, and precipitate a recession. This is the classic "hard-landing scenario" outlined by Marris (1985) in the previous round of severe dollar overvaluation in the mid-1980s. As noted below, Obstfeld and Rogoff (2004) have added an important nuance that is more modern. The extensive presence of derivatives in today's global economy suggests that an extremely large and sudden decline in the dollar could cause financial crises.

The simplest way to think about how a sharp decline in the dollar (hard landing for the dollar) might trigger a recession (hard landing for the economy) is probably the least relevant: a framework in which monetary authorities cared acutely about the value of the dollar and were prepared to defend it at all costs. In such a world, a plunge in the dollar would lead directly to a sharp hike in the policy interest rate (federal funds rate), and the higher interest rate would curb investment and consumption, provoking recession. Although there was some relevance of this framework under the Bretton Woods system of fixed exchange rates, it is much less germane today under flexible rates.[24] Today, central banks remain committed in principle to intervention to counter "disorderly" currency movements, implicitly defined as large movements in a short period of time. However, at no time was the recent decline of the dollar against the euro by 37 percent over 34 months (end-February 2002 to end-December 2004) considered sufficiently precipitous to trigger joint intervention.

A look back at Marris's hard-landing scenario in the mid-1980s indicates that even then the simple "dollar defense" dynamic was not the main concern. Instead, concern focused on supply and demand in the private capital markets. The fear was that if the dollar were to fall sharply, foreign suppliers of capital would seek to protect themselves from further exchange losses by cutting off new lending to the United States, creating a vicious downward spiral in the exchange rate and squeezing the supply of private capital, thereby boosting market interest rates.[25]

---

24. Something very much like this happened, however, in the case of Argentina's crisis in 1999–2001, under its fixed peg of the peso to the dollar.

25. In Marris's words, "The hard-landing scenario assumes that a 'crunch' in the financial and exchange markets is inevitable as people try to avoid the exchange rate losses involved

It is useful to consider the implications of a "market interest rate shock" unaccompanied by a change in the Federal Reserve's policy interest rate, which is the federal funds rate for interbank lending. The result would be a rise in the spread between the long-term interest rate, which the Federal Reserve does not control, and the short-term federal funds rate, which it does (and which moves virtually in lock-step with the short-term Treasury bill rate and the commercial paper rate).[26] But this would then involve a steepening of the "yield curve," which is usually associated with a subsequent economic expansion rather than a recession.

Despite an unusual combination of steep yield curve with incipient recession, a surge in long-term market rates without a rise in the federal funds rate could occur. Indeed, as recently as the second quarter of 2004 the 10-year Treasury bond rate stood 360 basis points (3.6 percent) above the federal funds rate (IMF 2005a). If a yield curve this steep were imposed on a federal funds rate in the range of 4 to 5 percent (instead of 1 percent as in early 2004), the long-term market rate would be high enough to do considerable damage to the economy.

The interest rate shock would be greater and more certain, of course, if an initial rise in the long-bond rate were followed by a substantial increase in the federal funds policy rate. However, to prompt the Federal Reserve to boost the federal funds rate, a falling dollar would probably have to be seen by the Fed as heightening the risk of inflation by raising exports, curbing imports, and thereby pushing up output demand uncomfortably high relative to capacity. A second, more direct inflationary threat would also be perceived if monetary authorities expected dollar depreciation to translate directly into higher import prices. However, as discussed below, the emerging view that the import price pass-through has fallen would likely moderate this second potential channel of response by the Federal Reserve. Even if the Federal Reserve did increase policy interest rates due to such inflationary concerns, in the first instance, the impact would be to dampen overheating of the economy from excess demand. To get a hard landing, there would somehow have to be an overshooting in the extent of the interest rate increase and the size of the economy's reaction beyond the monetary authorities' expectations. Otherwise, the Federal Reserve's tightening would moderate excessive expansion rather than push the economy into recession.

Another way of looking at the hard landing is to ask whether currency depreciation in the face of the need to curb an external deficit is expansionary or contractionary for the domestic economy. In the classic literature on internal and external equilibrium (Meade 1951), a currency depreciation is

---

in so sharp a decline of the dollar. . . . With inflation accelerating and the dollar falling sharply there would be little scope to ease monetary policy" (Marris 1985, 138, 141).

26. Simple regressions on the federal funds rate (r_{ff}), expressed as percent rates, show the following results for quarterly data from 1982 to 2004 (from IMF 2005a). Treasury bill: $r_T = 0.244$ (4.6) $+ 0.961\ r_{ff}$ (119.7); adj. $R^2 = 0.994$. Commercial paper: $r_c = 0.239$ (4.0) $+ 0.880\ r_{ff}$ (97.6); adj. $R^2 = 0.991$. T-statistics are in parentheses.

expansionary because it stimulates a rise in exports, reduces supply from imports, and hence raises demand for domestic output. In some contexts, such as conditions that may be found in developing countries, depreciation on balance may be contractionary because of a delay in domestic output response (or inelastic demand for exports) in the face of a contractionary demand effect from the reduction in real incomes from higher import prices (Krugman and Taylor 1978). Recession could be aggravated where domestic firms suffer windfall losses because of large debt denominated in foreign currency, as happened in the East Asian financial crisis of 1997–98.

Under US conditions, in the first instance, the dominant influence of a dollar depreciation would likely be the classical expansionary effect, operating through the trade expansion channel. The principal question, then, is whether the contraction in total capital supply from a reduction in external financing would sufficiently raise long-term interest rates to curb investment and consumption by more than enough to offset the expansionary influence on net exports. A key related question would be whether the timing would be unfavorable, with immediate contractionary effects from higher interest rates but a longer lag for the boost in output in exports and import substitutes.

If the market impact were in the range of the increase of 50 to 100 basis points discussed above for a cessation of foreign central bank accumulation of dollar reserves, then in the absence of a conscious tightening by the Federal Reserve solely to "defend the dollar," a contractionary effect for the economy would be unlikely.[27] However, a considerably larger increase in interest rates could occur if private inflows declined substantially as well. The overall effect could be substantial relative to the scale of the credit market. Total net borrowing in the US economy in early 2005 was running at an annual pace of about $3 trillion (Federal Reserve Board 2005c). Suppose that, including private lending, net lending from abroad fell by two-thirds of the amount of the current account deficit, or by $400 billion. This would amount to an ex ante cutback of 13 percent in total net financing in the US economy. This would seem large enough to require a substantial increase in interest rates to curb credit demand and call forth more credit supply.

The hard-landing scenario has probably been rendered at least temporarily less likely, moreover, by the partial reversal of the dollar's 2002–04 decline during the first half of 2005. This development has reminded markets that even with an outsized US current account deficit, the dollar's path is not a one-way bet. This in turn reduces the likelihood of "extrapolative" or "bandwagon" expectations in the currency market and increases

---

27. This would especially be the case if the Federal Reserve continued its recent view that the narrowing of the yield curve spread, offsetting tightening in the federal funds rate, was an unwelcome "conundrum," and was thus content to see some widening in the spread as a consequence of the shrinkage in foreign capital supply.

the likelihood of "stabilizing expectations," thereby reducing the chances that the dollar will sharply overshoot downward in its path toward an equilibrium level. Of course, if the resurgent dollar were to persist too long, the effect would be to aggravate the medium-term path of the current account deficit, setting the stage for a potentially more severe adjustment (harder rather than softer landing) in the future.

Overall, nonetheless, prudence suggests that policymakers should attach some significant probability to a hard-landing scenario in which a severe decline in the dollar triggers a recession. One reason is the potential for adverse effects in the stock market and the derivatives market. Another reason is the much larger external disequilibrium today than in previous historical experiences.

Even so, the appropriate policy framework would probably only place the probability of a hard landing for the economy from external imbalance in the range of 30 percent or so, albeit rising along with the current account deficit. This means that in the principal outlook, policy concern about the external deficit may not be dominated by the hard-landing risk. Instead, two other concerns may appropriately be more prominent. First, the external gap can impose a long-term burden on the economy and the next generation; and second, more immediately, the external deficit may provoke a political response of increased protection against imports. These risks are discussed in the next two sections.

First, however, it is useful to complete this consideration of the hard landing by recognizing that the United States has come close to such an outcome at least once and arguably twice in the past three decades. On the first episode, Marris (1985, 148–49) has summarized the events as follows.

> . . . [I]n 1978–79 . . . [there was] an initially expansionary fiscal policy, a deteriorating current account, and an inflation performance deteriorating relative to other countries. The first [anti-inflation program] . . . came in May 1978, including smaller pay increases for federal workers and . . . [a] reduction in planned tax cuts. Another package in October 1978 included a pledge to reduce the share of federal spending in GNP from 23 percent to 21 percent. . . . On November 1, 1978, a $30 billion line of foreign credits was mobilized to help support the dollar.[28] . . . On October 5, 1979, the discount rate was raised—for the tenth time since January 1978—to 12 percent, and the Federal Reserve Board announced a major change in the conduct of monetary policy. . . . [N]one of this did much to stem the loss of confidence in the dollar, which fell by 35 percent against the DM [deutsche mark] in the four years to December 1979. . . . The shift to fiscal restraint, and more particularly the change in monetary policies, did, however, pave the way for the 1980–82 recession. . . .

It can be reasonably argued, however, that even this closest case for the hard landing was not really driven by the external imbalance and the falling dollar, but by the determination of the Federal Reserve Board

---

28. This would translate to $150 billion at today's size of the economy.

under then-chairman Paul Volcker to finally put a halt to the high inflation of the 1970s. Consumer prices had risen by an average of 12.5 percent annually in 1974–75 and 8.7 percent in 1976–79 before peaking at 12.3 percent in 1980 (IMF 2005a). The minutes of the Federal Open Market Committee for the crucial meeting of October 6, 1979, when the Federal Reserve shifted to targeting money supply rather than the interest rate, suggest that inflation was the primary concern and the dollar only a secondary concern.[29]

A second close flirtation with the hard landing arguably occurred in 1987. From end-October 1986 to end-January 1987, the dollar fell 10 percent against the deutsche mark (DM) and 6 percent against the yen, despite a hike in the federal funds rate by 60 basis points (IMF 2005a). US Treasury Secretary James Baker organized the Louvre Agreement of February, 1987, in which the United States and other G-7 members sought to assure that the corrective decline of the dollar previously agreed to in the Plaza Agreement of 1985 did not turn into an overshooting rout of the US currency. The Louvre Agreement sought to keep the dollar within certain ranges against the DM and the yen. Arguably, for some months the agreement successfully calmed the currency markets, as the dollar rose by about 2 percent against the DM from end-January to end-September. However, implementing the agreement meant either that the United States had to raise interest rates, or Germany and Japan needed to lower rates to support the dollar, posing problems of consistency of monetary policy with domestic goals. When German authorities instead raised interest rates following a US interest rate increase, the agreement broke down in an atmosphere of heated disagreement between US and German officials. The ensuing financial market uncertainty was a pivotal force contributing to the US stock market crash, which saw the Dow Jones Industrial Average fall by 23 percent in a single day (October 19, 1987) and about one-third from August to December (albeit from "bubble" heights following a run-up earlier in the year). US interest rates rose relatively sharply—from 7.25

---

29. In the opening briefing, the Federal Reserve staff expert did not even mention the status of the dollar. Chairman Volcker stated at one point, "I don't think we are talking about a program here just to support the dollar. . . . The psychology in the foreign markets is the same as the psychology at home . . . it is the inflationary psychology. . . . So I don't think of this as a program specifically directed to the foreign side. If anything, it is specifically directed to the domestic side, but it will have foreign repercussions" (Federal Reserve Board 2005e, 15). Henry Wallich, perhaps the most internationally oriented member of the Board of Governors at that time, stated, "I think the main argument of the reserve strategy [the new policy of targeting money supply] is that it allows us to take stronger action than we probably could by the other technique. We are much more constrained in the other technique by the appearance of very high interest rates. . . . I think we need stronger action because of the resurgence in inflation and the behavior of the aggregates and the dollar" (ibid, 19). He thus cited the dollar but only after enumerating inflation and money supply growth as grounds for action.

percent in February to 8.4 percent in June and 9.5 percent in October for 10-year Treasury bonds (IMF 2004b)—although the shock was not enough to precipitate a recession.

Long-Term Debt Burden Versus Short-Term Crisis Risk

In evaluating the potential risks of a large external deficit, it is important to recognize that even under favorable assumptions about the willingness of foreigners to finance an ever-widening deficit, there is the problem of what in the context of the domestic fiscal deficit used to be called the "termites in the woodwork." The problem is not so much that there will be a sudden financial crisis as much as that, over a long period of time, the cumulative deficits will weaken the economy and, in particular, pose a large repayment burden for the next generation.

In the fiscal context, the problem of burdening the next generation is well understood (see Peterson 2004). In the external sector context, this potential problem is less widely recognized. It is often argued that it makes no difference to a typical future American household whether debt is owed to foreigners or to other (e.g., richer) Americans. But easy access to foreign financing and running a large current account deficit tend to facilitate consumption today at the expense of the future, when the external debt must be repaid. Moreover, there will be an adverse terms of trade effect of carrying out the external transfer to pay back the external debt in the future, as well as a reduction in future consumption needed to cut the external deficit.

It is possible to extrapolate the current account model of chapter 3 over a 20-year period to illustrate the issues involved in judging the long-term burden of delaying external adjustment. Figure 5.8 shows three alternative long-term paths for the US current account (panel A) and NIIP (panel B). The path with no adjustment shows the current account deficit reaching about 14 percent of GDP by 2024, and the NIIP reaching −135 percent of GDP. Neither level is credible, and some form of crisis would occur long before the end of the two decades. The path with early adjustment applies a foreign appreciation of 10 percent in 2006, another 10 percent in 2007, and a further 8.5 percent appreciation in 2008, for a cumulative foreign appreciation of 31 percent. This cuts the current account to a range of about 3 percent of GDP over 2009–15, although the deficit widens again to an average of about 4.5 percent of GDP by 2024. In early adjustment, the NIIP net liabilities are held to about 30 percent of GDP through 2015, but then gradually rise to 50 percent of GDP by 2024. In the path with late adjustment, in contrast, there is no real exchange rate adjustment until 2015, but then there is a sharp real foreign appreciation of 53 percent over three years. The late adjustment scenario follows the path of no adjustment until 2015, so the current account deficit reaches 11 percent of GDP and the NIIP reaches about −70 percent of GDP. Thereafter, the large foreign

Figure 5.8 Long-term current account and NIIP, 2005–24

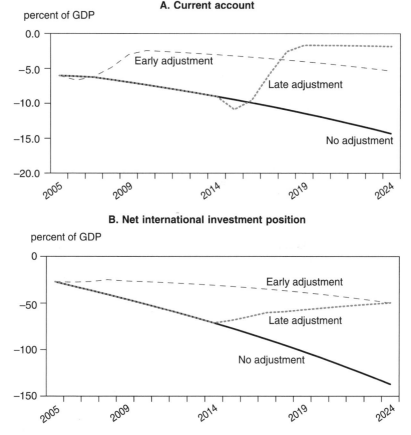

A. Current account

percent of GDP

Early adjustment

Late adjustment

No adjustment

B. Net international investment position

percent of GDP

Early adjustment

Late adjustment

No adjustment

Source: Author's calculations.

appreciation cuts the current account deficit sharply to about 1.7 percent of GDP by 2019–24. Nonetheless, the larger deficits in the first decade mean that the NIIP position by 2024 is the same as that under the early adjustment scenario, at −50 percent of GDP.

The larger required depreciation of the dollar in the late adjustment scenario means a greater terms of trade loss. With 50 percent import price pass-through, real import prices are about 10 percent higher in the second decade under late adjustment than under early adjustment. The cost of adjustment under the two alternative scenarios can be measured by the reduction in cumulative consumption associated with the cutback in the real trade deficit. It turns out that the cumulative adjustment cost is almost the same under the two scenarios.[30] The extra loss in terms of trade under

---

30. At 2005 prices, cumulative GDP during 2005–24 is $350 trillion. The sum of (unsustainable) baseline trade deficits (goods and nonfactor services) is $27.8 trillion. The corresponding

late adjustment is offset by earlier (but smaller) terms of trade loss in early adjustment, combined with the fact that there is a greater contribution of exchange valuation gains under late adjustment because of the greater depreciation and its application to a larger (because it is later) foreign equity stock.[31]

If some recessionary cost of adjustment is imposed on the late adjustment scenario, then the comparison could reverse to show early adjustment more favorable than late adjustment. The chances of a hard landing are much greater under late adjustment, considering that, whereas the current account narrows by 3.6 percent of GDP over five years under early adjustment, it must narrow by 7.3 percent of GDP over five years in late adjustment. This sharper reduction would be more likely to require recession to depress import demand. If it is assumed that a hard landing under late adjustment costs 4 percentage points of GDP (e.g., 2 percent in each of two years), then the cost of adjustment is greater under late than early adjustment, but the two scenarios still have nearly the same adjustment cost.[32]

The true cost of late adjustment, then, is not that it sharply increases total adjustment costs above early adjustment (although the specific assumptions for the comparison may understate the extra adjustment costs). Instead, the true cost of delayed adjustment is its inequitable distributional impact on the future versus the present. Under early adjustment, households cut consumption (reduce the real trade deficit) from the baseline by a cumulative $7.5 trillion (at 2005 prices), or 4.6 percent of GDP, in the first decade; and by a cumulative $16.4 trillion, or 8.8 percent of GDP, in the second decade. Under late adjustment, households do not cut consumption from the baseline at all in the first decade, but must cut consumption by a cumulative $23.4 trillion, or 12.5 percent of GDP, in the second decade. The cutback necessary in the second decade thus rises by 43 percent under late as compared with early adjustment. So the essence of the cost of delay is a distributional cost: the inequity of postponing the burden of external adjustment and placing it entirely on the "next generation" in the second decade.[33]

---

sum of trade deficits with adjustment is $3.95 trillion under early adjustment and $4.38 trillion under late adjustment. The difference of $430 billion amounts to 0.12 percent of total period GDP.

31. Both scenarios cut the NIIP net liabilities from $45.8 trillion to $16.6 trillion in 2024. Exchange rate valuation effects directly contribute $2.1 trillion to this reduction in the early adjustment scenario, compared with $5.7 trillion in the late adjustment scenario.

32. Adding 4 percent of 2016 real GDP to the consumption loss under late adjustment boosts its total costs by $722 billion, causing the comparison between early and late adjustment to swing from −$430 billion to +$292 billion in favor of the early adjustment scenario. The latter amount would be only 0.08 percent of full-period GDP, however.

33. This analysis applies a zero discount rate, the framework usually applied in US policy discussions on long-term fiscal choices. Discounting at plausible rates would somewhat increase the marginal advantage of late over early adjustment but leave the unequal distribu-

Finally, it should be emphasized that the cost of delay in adjustment assumes all current account deficit resources are used for consumption. If somehow they could all be channeled to increase investment above levels otherwise attained, the calculus would shift more toward delaying adjustment because of additional future output from additional investment. However, the persistent decline in personal saving analyzed above suggests that, in contrast to the late 1990s, the United States has recently been in a persistent phase of using the resources from the external deficit to finance private consumption and government dissaving, rather than investment. No allowance for extra future output from persistent current account deficits thus seems the more prudent assumption.

The Risk of Protection

In past episodes of dollar overvaluation and US external imbalances, rising pressures have sometimes reached action-forcing levels first in the realm of trade protectionism rather than in the financial arena. Overvaluation and large trade deficits in the late 1960s and early 1970s "coincided with the deepest protectionist pressures of the postwar period . . . despite modest levels of aggregate unemployment" (Bergsten and Williamson 1983, 111). These pressures led to long-lasting protectionist measures, including the extension of textile and apparel quotas to synthetic fibers and import restraints in steel.

Similarly, in the mid-1980s, an overvalued dollar and large trade deficits spurred proposals for sweeping trade legislation to impose import surcharges on countries with large bilateral surpluses against the United States, quotas on footwear, "reciprocity" clauses mandating retaliation against countries whose markets were closed to US exports, and pervasive changes in trade law to facilitate petitions by US firms for relief from import competition (Destler 2005, 88–95). The threat of protection was a key factor prompting the second Reagan administration to switch from being unconcerned about the strong dollar and large deficit to making a conscious effort at dollar adjustment, led by Treasury Secretary James Baker and coordinated with other major economies through the Plaza Agreement in late 1985 on joint currency intervention to achieve appreciation of other principal currencies against the dollar.

Partly because of correction of the dollar and subsequent signs of trade adjustment, and partly because of chastening by the stock market crash of October 1987, negotiations between the administration and Congress on the omnibus trade bill began to take a more positive direction. The

---

tion of adjustment costs between the two decades essentially unchanged. Thus, if there is no recessionary disruption from the sharper, later adjustment in 2015 and beyond, discounting at 1 percent per annum boosts the advantage of late over early adjustment from 0.12 percent of full-period GDP to 0.7 percent.

eventual Omnibus Trade and Competitiveness Act of 1988 was far less protectionist than earlier drafts, and included the "fast-track" presidential negotiating authority needed for bilateral agreements as well as the Uruguay Round of multilateral trade negotiations. Nonetheless, the new law kept its Section 301 "reciprocity" directive to the US Trade Representative to seek retaliation against "unjustifiable and unreasonable" trade protection in other countries.

Today, there are signs that a large US trade deficit is once again exerting protectionist pressures. The principal target has been China, with the main issue proposed being retaliation for an undervalued Chinese currency, but there also have been calls for restrictions in textiles and apparel, furniture, and color television sets (Hufbauer and Wong 2004). Similarly, ratification of the Central American Free Trade Agreement (CAFTA), the Bush administration's top priority in trade legislation for 2005, faced serious difficulties in Congress, in part because of an overall environment of unprecedented trade deficits.[34] Even if the overall trade deficit is invoked as political cover for interest group politics (such as opposition to CAFTA from sugar growers), the consequence is to strengthen protectionist forces.

As discussed in chapter 6, the threat to impose trade penalties against China if it does not substantially revalue the renminbi may be salutary rather than pernicious, in view of the importance of this policy adjustment not only for the Chinese exchange rate but also for several other key Asian currencies. However, the risk of a stalling out of new free trade agreements, and more importantly, the Doha round of the World Trade Organization (WTO) negotiations, is a potentially high-cost ramification of the US trade imbalance. A key question is whether, as in the past, such protectionist risks will help focus the minds of top policymakers on the importance of taking corrective measures, ideally on macroeconomic policy and in the area of fiscal policy in particular.

The Evolving Crisis Debate

As the US current account deficit has continued to widen, and especially as the decline of the dollar after its peak in early 2002 gathered momentum in early 2004 and again in the fourth quarter of 2004, the debate has sharpened on whether the external imbalance poses a serious problem. In broad terms, from the late 1990s to late 2004, there was an increasing

---

34. As Senate Minority Leader Harry Reid (D-NV) put it: "I don't like CAFTA; I am not going to vote for it, and I will do whatever I can to kill it. . . . We are approaching a trillion-dollar trade deficit. We can't survive as a viable, strong country doing that" ("Free Trade Pact in Americas Faces Trouble," *New York Times*, May 10, 2005, C1). In late July 2005, CAFTA did finally pass the US House of Representatives, but only by a margin of two votes.

evolution away from the view that the strong dollar and external deficit were benign to the view that they pose a problem, despite some prominent contrary diagnoses by early 2005 (see the discussion of recent Federal Reserve studies and the global saving glut argument later in this chapter). The earlier benign diagnosis was premised mainly on the fact that the strong dollar was being driven by large private capital inflows and was going to finance a sharp increase in investment in the United States. US authorities typically averred that a "strong dollar" was good for the United States. As the sourcing of the inflows shifted from the private to the official sector, and the external resources shifted from financing high levels of US investment to high fiscal deficits and high personal consumption, the center of gravity in the debate shifted toward the diagnosis that the external imbalance posed a significant risk. This section reviews some of the principal arguments in this evolving debate.

Bellwether Policymakers

The evolution of the debate is perhaps best illustrated by the positions of two leading economic officials: Alan Greenspan and Lawrence Summers. In October 1999, Federal Reserve Chairman Greenspan (1999) stated that "imports presumably can continue to expand for awhile, since the rising rate of return on U.S. assets has attracted private capital inflows, particularly a major acceleration of direct foreign investment. . . . But a continued widening of that deficit could eventually raise financing difficulties, ultimately limiting import growth." The current account deficit was 3.1 percent of GDP in 1999.

In 2002, the current account deficit reached 4.6 percent of GDP, and by March of that year Greenspan showed somewhat more concern:

> During the past six years, about 40 percent of the total increase in our capital stock in effect has been financed, on net, by saving from abroad. This situation is reflected in our ongoing current account deficit. . . . But this deficit is also a measure of the increase in the level of net claims, primarily debt claims, that foreigners have on our assets. As the stock of such claims grows, an ever-larger flow of interest payments must be provided to the foreign suppliers of this capital. Countries that have gone down this path invariably have run into trouble, and so would we. Eventually, the current account deficit will have to be restrained. (Greenspan 2002, 4)

After the current account deficit had reached 4.9 percent of GDP in 2003, Greenspan seemed to suggest in March 2004 that the imbalance could continue for a long time, because a declining "home bias" in international capital markets "has enabled the United States to incur and finance a much larger current account deficit than would have been feasible in earlier decades" (Greenspan 2004a, 5). He cited a Federal Reserve staff study indicating that in developed countries since 1980, current account deficits had "risen as high as double-digit percentages of GDP before markets enforced a reversal." He judged that "the odds are favorable that current imbalances will be defused with little disruption to the economy or financial markets" but acknowledged that "there are other outcomes that are less benign" and urged that "one avenue by which to lessen the risk of a more difficult adjustment is for us to restore fiscal discipline."

The current account deficit for 2004 reached 5.7 percent of GDP, and in November of that year, Greenspan signaled still greater concern:

> ... [N]et claims against residents of the United States cannot continue to increase forever in international portfolios at their recent pace. Net debt service cost, though currently still modest, would eventually become burdensome. At some point, diversification considerations will slow and possibly limit the desire of investors to add dollar claims to their portfolios. Resistance to financing, however, is likely to emerge well before debt servicing becomes an issue . . . [as] a continued buildup of dollar assets increases concentration risk. This situation suggests that international investors will eventually adjust their accumulation of dollar assets or, alternatively, seek higher dollar returns to offset concentration risk, elevating the cost of financing of the U.S. current account deficit and rendering it increasingly less tenable. If a net importing country finds financing for its net deficit too expensive, that country will, of necessity, import less. (Greenspan 2004b, 2–3)

The evolution in the views of former US Treasury Secretary Lawrence Summers arguably has been even more pronounced. Summers was closely identified with a "strong dollar policy." In January 2000, he stated:

> Any current account deficit is a reflection of. . .the amount invested domestically relative to the amount that is saved. When, as it does now in the US, the imbalance reflects a period of strong growth relative to the rest of the world, accelerating productivity gains and relatively high investment in our productive potential, and takes place in a context of rising public sector savings, it is unlikely to pose an immediate risk to the well being of the economy. Indeed, quite the reverse. (Summers 2000a, 1)

Summers (2000b, 1) also stated that ". . . our policy with respect to the dollar remains unchanged: a strong dollar is in the interest of the United States."

In contrast, by October 2004, the former secretary worried that "the U.S. current account deficit . . . is perhaps receiving less attention than it should" (Summers 2004). After noting that the size of the US current account deficit was "without precedent" and on track to rise even further, he asked: "Is this current account deficit a sign of economic vitality or an incipient problem?" His implied answer was that it was a problem because it reflected a decline in saving to "the lowest net national savings rate in American history." He noted that "net investment has declined over the last four or five years . . . suggesting that all of the deterioration of the current account deficit can be attributed to reduced savings and increased consumption rather than to increased investment." He added that the investment that was taking place was not being channeled into tradable goods for future "export capacity that can ultimately service debt" but into nontraded goods as manifested by the "dramatic increases in the price of residential real estate. . . ." He indicated that the solution required both "an increase in U.S. national savings" as well as an appropriate adjustment in the "relative price" of US goods, including a "coordinated adjustment of exchange rates that are quasi-fixed to the dollar" (Summers 2004, 1, 3, and 7).

It should be stressed that the evolution in thinking about the current account deficit by both Chairman Greenspan and Secretary Summers reflects not only the widening of the deficit over time but perhaps more fundamentally, the transition of the US fiscal position from surplus to large deficit. So there are two basic reasons for their growing concerns. The first is normative: Policymakers can hardly be sanguine about a large current account deficit when the fiscal accounts show a large deficit, because the foreign resources are going to finance public overspending rather than private investment. The second is operational. In 1999–2000, those US policymakers who were concerned about the external deficit would have faced a quandary about what to do about it. The budget was already in sizable surplus. The most natural policy measure to curb the external deficit is to reduce the fiscal deficit or raise the fiscal surplus. Doing so not only cuts the investment-saving gap but also tends to reduce interest rates, in turn reducing the attractiveness of the home capital market to capital inflows, and thereby contributing to a decline in the exchange rate and an increase in the competitiveness of exports. But with the fiscal accounts already in sizable surplus, it would have strained policy credulity to call for an even larger fiscal surplus because of the potential future risks of the external deficit.

A New Bretton Woods "System"?

In the emerging debate about the sustainability of large and growing US current account deficits, an intriguing argument has been advanced by Dooley, Folkerts-Landau, and Garber (2004). They maintain that today's international monetary system has in effect reestablished a sort of Bretton Woods system of fixed exchange rates for "periphery" countries' currencies against the dollar, and that this system coexists alongside a flexible exchange rate regime for the "center" industrial countries. The periphery includes most notably China and the rest of emerging Asia, but also Japan. The authorities in the periphery have struck an implicit bargain with the United States: They will intervene in the foreign exchange market to accumulate dollar reserves and keep their currencies at low valuations. In exchange, the United States will purchase their manufactured exports, which will enable the periphery countries to continue to absorb their unlimited supplies of unskilled labor. Whereas the dollar may fall further against the euro and other flexible exchange rates at the center, the Bretton Woods-like fixity of the periphery exchange rate will guarantee that the US current account deficit will persist for years to come. Part of the motivation of the implicit bargain is that the monetary authorities of the periphery understand that they will eventually take large capital losses on their dollar reserves, but they are more concerned about assuring continuation of rapid export-oriented growth in the present than about future reserve value losses.

There are several serious problems with the revised Bretton Woods hypothesis (BW2 for short). First, Japan does not fit in the periphery. It has, if anything, a labor shortage (aging population) rather than an unlimited labor supply. Although Japanese authorities aggressively intervened to keep the yen from appreciating from April 2002 (right after the dollar's peak) to March 2004, they intervened very little in the year ending March 2005.[35]

Second, the numbers do not add up. The plausible periphery candidates do not have a large enough current account surplus to assure financing for the US current account deficit. The combined 2004 current account balances of China, Hong Kong, India, Indonesia, Korea, Malaysia, the Philippines, Singapore, Taiwan, and Thailand amounted to only $196 billion (IMF 2005b), or 29 percent of the US current account deficit for 2004. The BW2 periphery is simply too small by itself to finance the large US current account deficits. Even if Japan is added (with a current account surplus of $171 billion in 2004; ibid.), the total amounts to only about half of the US deficit.

Third, the BW2 hypothesis envisions a robust continuation of large US deficits and periphery surpluses over a decade or more, but there are already signs that protectionist pressures would cause a collapse in the arrangement much sooner. Legislation has already been proposed and widely supported in the US Senate to impose a 27 percent penalty tariff on China for manipulating its exchange rate to maintain undervaluation, given its continued exchange rate peg against the dollar despite a large current account surplus (4.2 percent of GDP in 2004; IMF 2005b). The BW2 authors count on the vested interests of US multinational firms as direct investors in China to assure lobbying pressure against any protectionist response by the United States, but this insurance looks increasingly unreliable. Moreover, although economists rightly argue that a country's exchange rate policies should be considered in light of its overall current account balance, not the bilateral trade balance, the large US bilateral deficit with China—$162 billion in 2004, or 70 percent of bilateral exports

---

35. Japan's foreign exchange reserves soared from $394 billion in March 2002 to $816 billion in March 2004, but changed little thereafter and stood at $827 billion in March 2005 (IMF 2005a).

plus imports (US International Trade Commission 2005)—exerts an inevitable political pressure towards a protectionist response.

In short, BW2 cannot be counted on to ensure comfortable financing of ever-larger US external deficits over a time span of a decade or more. The key kernel of truth in the hypothesis is its insight that many developing countries (and, on occasion, Japan) do pursue formal or informal exchange rate pegs against the dollar, and that this pattern amounts to returning a significant portion of the world economy to the Bretton Woods monetary regime with its associated problems. That regime of pegged exchange rates against the dollar imposed a straitjacket that kept the US currency from readily depreciating to contribute to external adjustment. Whereas other countries could devalue their currencies against the dollar, the United States could not achieve a generalized devaluation of the dollar against all other currencies by itself. Instead, it required a multicountry agreement reached at the Smithsonian Institution in December 1971 to revalue most currencies against the dollar. The implication is that if periphery countries de facto peg to the dollar today, some coordinated agreement for generalized realignments against the dollar may once again be needed.

Global Portfolio Optimists

Other international economists have argued more generally that there is ample room in foreign portfolios for further accumulation of claims against the United States and hence, continuation of a large and growing current account deficit. Mann (2004, 25) argues that there is a systematic "co-dependency" in which "[t]o an inordinate degree, all countries and regions in the rest of the world have depended on net exports to the United States—both directly and indirectly—for economic growth." This imbalance, Mann maintains, is particularly apparent for Asia's net exports to the United States. On the US side, she judges that "the U.S. structural tendency toward consumption and a savings-investment imbalance is reflected in a trending downward in household savings and a structural predilection toward imported consumer goods and autos" (Mann 2004, 24). The resulting co-dependency of foreign countries on US demand and of US consumers on foreign saving has underpinned the persistent and growing US external deficit, but Mann judges that the path of the external deficit is unsustainable, and that correction is unlikely to be achieved by exchange rate adjustment alone. As a result, "[t]here is a real possibility that the entanglements created by this co-dependency cannot be undone by anything short of a global economic crisis." So although for the relatively near term, Mann is by implication optimistic about further scope in foreign portfolios for financing US deficits, and even sees the system as structurally biased in this direction, her longer-term diagnosis is highly cautionary.

Cooper (2001; "Two Views on the US Deficit," *Financial Times*, October 31, 2004) has been more squarely in the portfolio optimist camp. He emphasizes that rates of return on capital have been higher in the United States than in Europe and Japan, and more "reliable" (i.e., less risky) than in many developing countries. He also stresses the advantages of the US capital market for stocks and bonds in being larger, more liquid, and providing better protection to creditors and minority shareholders than most foreign countries. The United States also tends to be more attractive because its growth is typically higher than that in Europe and Japan and less volatile than that in emerging markets. When Cooper wrote in 2001, he added that investment had been strong and that unlike in the 1980s, foreign capital had been financing investment rather than budget deficits (although by now the 1980s pattern has returned).

Cooper argues, moreover, that the potential attraction of the US capital market for foreign investors will not be thwarted soon by problems of portfolio satiation. He uses back-of-the-envelope calculations to make the point. He illustrates the case of a $500 billion current account deficit continuing indefinitely. With nominal GDP growing at 5 percent (3 percent real plus 2 percent inflation), this constant deficit would cause the net international liabilities to rise from 25 percent of GDP in 2002 to a peak of 46 percent after 15 years, but thereafter, this liability ratio would persistently decline. The current account deficit would correspondingly fall to 2.2 percent of GDP by 2018, despite remaining constant in nominal dollar terms. Turning to the capital supply side, Cooper estimates that global saving outside the United States amounts to $6 trillion annually, so by comparison, his postulated $500 billion capital inflow into the United States, plus an allowance for financing needed to cover US capital outflows, amounts to only about 10 percent of global saving. With the US economy representing one-fourth of the world economy and one-half of world marketable financial assets, and given the favorable return-risk features of the US capital market, he finds it likely that foreigners will be comfortable placing 10 to 15 percent of their savings in the United States, especially as this share would decrease over time. He also emphasizes that any attempt to reduce the US current account deficit abruptly "would undoubtedly produce a world recession" ("Two Views on the US Deficit," *Financial Times*, October 31, 2004).

The real problem with Cooper's portfolio optimism is that it is not optimistic enough to cover the much wider US external deficits projected in the baseline of chapter 3, or the even wider future deficits predicted in such estimates as Roubini and Setser (2004) and Mann (2004). It is difficult to take strong exception to Cooper's view that the rest of the world could easily continue to finance a US current account path trending downward from 5 percent of GDP at the start to 2.2 percent 15 years from now. The problem is that the baseline is now starting at 5.7 percent of

GDP and is headed for about 7½ percent of GDP in just five years and 12 percent in 15 years (see figure 5.8). Cooper does not clarify what forces or policy changes will turn around the baseline from an ever-widening gap relative to GDP to a gradually falling share of GDP.

Substitutability Pessimists

Obstfeld and Rogoff (2004) have provided one of the more influential and rigorous recent studies on the pessimistic side of the debate over whether the United States faces a potential external sector crisis. Their approach is in the Chicago tradition that emphasizes the relative price of tradables versus nontradables. This approach differs from both the workhorse "elasticities" model and the national accounts-oriented "absorption" approach (see chapter 4), although its results are influenced by price elasticities and by the extent of the reduction in domestic absorption of tradables needed for adjustment.

The central conclusion of Obstfeld and Rogoff is that any event or process that forces the elimination of the US current account deficit will as a consequence significantly reduce the real exchange rate of the dollar. They cite a range of 20 percent if the adjustment is gradual and 40 percent if it is abrupt and involves overshooting. The essence of their model is that the trade deficit is large relative to the tradable goods sector, and that the substitutability in demand between tradables and nontradables is limited, so that it will take a large rise in the relative price of tradables to curb demand enough to close the external gap. By symmetry, the rest of the world needs to have a decline in the price of tradables relative to nontradables. The increase in the real price of foreign exchange can thus be even greater than the increase in the relative price of tradables to nontradables domestically. The exchange rate adjusts as a consequence of the trade adjustment, not as a cause. The cause is some demand shock that reduces the relative price of nontradables, such as a collapse in the housing market.

Obstfeld and Rogoff do not see forced external adjustment as injurious to real activity in a direct sense, and they see the extent of US net international liabilities as easily manageable rather than a severe debt burden. Instead, their principal concern is that, in view of the integration of global financial markets, and the extensive presence of derivatives in particular, a sharp decline in the dollar might precipitate international financial crises in a manner similar to the threat posed by the collapse of the Long Term Capital Management hedge fund in 1998. This concern is different from the traditional hard-landing concern about an abrupt rise in the US interest rate in the face of a collapsing dollar and a cutoff in capital inflows, with domestic recession in response to the higher interest rate.

Appendix 5A describes the Obstfeld-Rogoff model in greater detail. Although the authors' analysis is typically considered to be at the pessimistic end of the spectrum of US external adjustment difficulty, it would appear to be no more so (and perhaps less) than the calculations of chapters 3 and 4 of the present study. Indeed, chapter 3 suggests that an additional 21 percent real foreign appreciation against the dollar beyond the January–May 2005 average level would be required just to reduce the US external deficit down to 3½ to 4 percent of GDP (versus complete elimination in Obstfeld-Rogoff), rather than growing to its 2010 baseline of about 7½ percent of GDP. The analysis of chapter 4 indicates that even this real depreciation could be insufficient for this task in the absence of large fiscal adjustment. The Obstfeld-Rogoff results are more consistent with the exchange rate estimates of the present study if their 5 percent of GDP correction is taken against the future baseline deficit of 7½ percent of GDP, however.

Whether the Obstfeld-Rogoff model is pessimistic also depends on whether their assumed parameter values are appropriate. They set the tradable sector of the economy at only 25 percent, yet in an earlier paper they cite a 50 percent share of GDP as nontradable as a "popular rule of thumb" based on the share of services, construction, and transport (Obstfeld and Rogoff 2000, 22). If the tradable share is boosted to 50 percent, then in their first case, with $\theta = 1$ and $\eta = 2$ (see appendix 5A), the required real exchange rate depreciation to eliminate the 5 percent of GDP external deficit (now only one-tenth rather than one-fifth of tradables) amounts to only 21 percent rather than 31 percent.

Long-Term Equilibrium Analyses

Blanchard, Giavazzi, and Sa (2005) also conclude that potentially large real depreciation is in store for the dollar, but that it can be stretched over time. They revive Kouri's (1983) portfolio preference approach to exchange rate determination, and augment it with special attention to exchange rate effects on the valuation of foreign assets and differential returns at home and abroad. The core idea in the portfolio approach is that when the United States runs a current account deficit, home bias causes the net demand for US assets to fall as wealth shifts from US to foreign citizens. The resulting excess supply of US assets will only disappear when there is enough dollar depreciation to reduce the foreign currency valuation of foreign holdings of US assets (original plus the new increment from the current account imbalance) to the desired foreign portfolio share for US assets.

The central result is that a country persistently running external deficits will face a secular depreciation of its currency. The pace of the depreciation can be slowed or even temporarily halted by shifts in foreign preferences (for example, reduction in home bias globally), but the depreciation will eventually occur. As discussed in appendix 5A, with the parameters used by Blanchard, Giavazzi, and Sa, the current level of the US current account deficit of about $750 billion annually would imply an induced dollar depreciation of about 3.4 percent annually to meet the portfolio preference requirements, prior to taking into account exchange rate valuation and differential return effects. After taking account of valuation and differential return effects, the authors note that if the baseline for the NIIP is a steady decline of 5 percent of GDP annually, the upper bound for the anticipated rate of dollar depreciation would be 2.7 percent annually (Blanchard, Giavazzi, and Sa 2005, 47). However, they acknowledge that an adverse shift in portfolio preferences (such as diversification by foreign central banks away from dollars) could lead to a considerably larger short-term depreciation.

Blanchard, Giavazzi, and Sa examine the size of dollar depreciation that would be needed to stabilize the NIIP at -25 percent of GDP, an ambitious target. They set the trade balance as a function of the exchange rate, calibrated at a 1 percent of US GDP adjustment from a 15 percent depreciation. They take account of valuation effects assuming all US assets abroad are denominated in foreign currency and all US liabilities abroad are denominated in dollars. However, because about 42 percent of gross US foreign assets are in bonds and loans rather than equity (see table 2A.1), and these credits are typically denominated in dollars, their calibration would appear to overstate the valuation effect.[36] After also taking account of differential return on assets, and setting a target of 0.75 percent of GDP for the US current account deficit (rather than zero, based on 3 percent growth and maintenance of 25 percent of GDP in net external liabilities), they estimate that a depreciation of the dollar by 56 percent would be required to adjust the US deficit from its rate of about 6 percent of GDP.[37] This estimate is broadly consistent with the analyses of chapters 3 and 6 of the present study, if the less ambitious current account target here (a deficit of about 3 percent of GDP) is taken into account and the decline of the dollar that has already taken place from 2002 to the present is included in the total (as the Blanchard-Giavazzi-Sa analysis abstracts from lagged effects).[38]

---

36. Thus, their estimate for the NIIP valuation effect from a 15 percent depreciation of the dollar is 10 percent of GDP (Blanchard, Giavazzi, and Sa 2005, 22), considerably larger than the 5 to 6 percent of GDP impact implied by the analyses in chapters 2 and 3 of the present study.

37. The authors abstract from inflation, however, which would raise the permissible deficit given the target NIIP/GDP ratio. In a private communication (May 17, 2005), Blanchard indicated that inflation should be added. However, he also noted that adjustment for inflation would approximately offset adjustment for a higher actual current account deficit—about 6.5 percent of GDP rather than 6 percent. That is, if inflation is 2 percent, then the adjusted current account target would be 2% $\times$ 0.25 = 0.5 percent of GDP higher; but the actual deficit base is also about 0.5 percent of GDP higher than in the exercise in the paper.

38. Note further that the 56 percent "depreciation" indicated by the authors is the rise in the real value of the foreign currency, as in chapter 3 here, not the proportional loss in value of the dollar (which would correspond to a decline of about 36 percent).

Blanchard, Giavazzi, and Sa (2005, 23) also note, however, that the US adjustment to a sustainable current account deficit does not have to occur immediately, because the rest of the world continues to be willing to lend to the United States, even "if perhaps not at the current rate." Their central analysis thus implies a slow but steady dollar depreciation for a long time to come.

Gourinchas and Rey (2005) have developed a model of US external adjustment that emphasizes exchange rate and asset price effects, adding asset valuation changes to trade balance change as the means of external adjustment. Their two key conclusions are that (1) "stabilizing valuation effects contribute as much as 31 percent of the external adjustment" (2005, i), and that (2) "the 2001–04 imbalance is less pronounced than that of the second half of the 1980s . . . due to the positive impact of the depreciation of the dollar in 2002–04 on US gross foreign assets and increased cross border holdings" (2005, 26). As noted in chapter 2, their finding on the importance of exchange rate valuation effects is similar to that identified in the present study.

As set forth in appendix 5A, Gourinchas and Rey develop a variable *nxa* that is a weighted sum of the logarithm of exports minus the logarithm of imports and the logarithm of foreign assets minus the logarithm of foreign liabilities. The weights applied to each of these variables are determined in statistical regressions of *nxa* on the discounted sum of expected future net asset returns and increases in net exports.

The authors' underlying framework seems to be that the United States is pursuing a long-term downward path of net foreign assets relative to GDP, reaching ever-larger net external debt while running trade deficits. It is unclear in the model at what level the net US external debt stabilizes relative to GDP, if ever. What the model emphasizes is that whenever the net asset earnings and net export receipts are high enough to deflect the United States upward from this secular path, investors will push the dollar up, and conversely.

They thus argue that current imbalances as gauged by their summary measure *nxa* must predict either future export growth, or future movements in the net foreign asset portfolio, or both. Statistically, they find that "deviations from trend of the ratio of net exports to net foreign assets predict net foreign asset portfolio returns one quarter to two years ahead and net exports at longer horizons."[39] The main driver in the change in returns is the exchange rate. The exchange rate also drives the trade balance. Correspondingly, the authors find that their *nxa* variable successfully explains future exchange rate changes. They conclude that "the curse

39. Their terminology is heuristic, because "net exports to net foreign assets" taken literally would explode as net assets transit through zero (from positive to negative), as has been the US experience.

of the random walk seems therefore to be broken. . . ."[40] Indeed, they can explain 60 percent of the variation in the exchange rate over a 3-year horizon, which would seem to be the econometric equivalent of capturing a unicorn if not finding the holy grail.

Gourinchas and Rey find that the US external imbalance as measured by their *nxa* was smaller in the first quarter of 2004 (at only −7 percent of exports) than in 1985 (−27 percent). This conclusion at first seems to be a major paradox, considering that the current account deficit in 2004 was nearly twice as large relative to GDP as the previous peak deficit in 1987 (at 5.7 versus 3.4 percent). The resolution of this paradox is partly that gross US foreign assets are also proportionately much larger today (7.7 times exports in 2004 compared with 4.5 times exports in 1985), providing a more robust base upon which the leveraged effect of depreciation can act.

The more important part of the paradox of "lesser imbalance," however, seems to be the authors' implicit assumption that the trend line for US net foreign liabilities can continue to plumb depths that are beyond the ranges considered prudent for the United States by most analysts. The authors most decidedly do not mean that a reduction in the current account deficit by only 7 percent of exports, or about $80 billion, would be sufficient to hold the eventual ratio of net liabilities to GDP to anything like −25 percent or even −50 percent of GDP. Instead, the authors are focusing on what magnitude of imbalance it takes to generate market pressure on the exchange rate, in view of historical dynamics and after taking account of both valuation and trade effects. They predict that these pressures will cause the dollar to decline by 12 percent from the first quarter of 2004 to the first quarter of 2007. Considering that the actual change from the first quarter of 2004 to the first quarter of 2005 was a decline of 2.8 percent (Federal Reserve broad real index), it could be said that so far, their prediction is almost on track.

The paradox may also reflect the fact that by examining the intertemporal current account balance over an infinite horizon, Gourinchas and Rey may implicitly be allowing very large current account deficits at present because at some distant future date, the power of compound interest favoring asset returns will overwhelm the cumulated deficits. However, market participants may not have as much patience as the infinite horizon model requires, and instead may apply a risk discount factor that from their perspective turns the present value of future external balances negative. Indeed, the authors themselves do not specifically rule out a market panic that involves a departure from past behavior.

The main point is that their method focuses on current market pressures, not on eventual sustainability of the current account and net external

---

40. Meese and Rogoff (1983) first showed the long-standing proposition that economic models do no better than a "random walk" in predicting exchange rates.

debt. It would have been highly informative if the authors had included the long-term path of the current account and net external liabilities implied by their analysis (e.g., over the next 20 years), as it seems likely that this path would involve much larger deficits and net debt than most analysts would consider sustainable. In a sense, their finding is discouraging, because it suggests that the market left to its own devices will allow the United States to accumulate far more external debt than might be consistent with long-term equity or optimality, along the lines analyzed above in the discussion of early versus delayed adjustment. At the least, it is important that readers of their provocative analysis recognize that they are not claiming that the United States is close to external equilibrium when judged against the more conventional benchmarks for longer-term sustainability. In this regard, the quantitative results of Gourinchas and Rey may be much closer to the diagnoses of major long-term depreciation prospects identified by Obstfeld and Rogoff and by Blanchard, Giavazzi, and Sa than might appear to be the case at first reading.

Recent Federal Reserve Analyses

In early 2005, certain Federal Reserve staff studies and governors' speeches seemed to challenge the growing concern that the US external deficit was a serious problem, and especially that it had been caused by US policy mistakes.[41]

The first study, by Croke, Kamin, and Leduc (2005, ii), explicitly addressed growing concerns in the press about a "disorderly correction" involving "a sharp fall in the exchange rate that boosts interest rates, depresses stock prices, and weakens economic activity." They found "little evidence" in past adjustment episodes for the disorderly correction hypothesis, maintaining instead that "it was among the episodes where GDP growth picked up during adjustment that the most substantial depreciations of real exchange rates occurred."

The methodology of the study is highly transparent. The authors identify 23 current account adjustment episodes in industrial countries over the past several decades.[42] They compare the seven most expansionary

---

41. Edwin C. Truman, a former senior official of the Fed, has written that ". . . too many Federal Reserve officials are interpreted as being cheerleaders for the view that the adjustment process when it comes will be smooth, rather than warning that the process might well be disruptive and unpleasant" (Truman 2005). He notes, however, that two prominent Federal Reserve representatives—Geithner (2005) and Gramlich (2004)—have been more cautious.

42. Following Freund (2000), Croke, Kamin, and Leduc defined an adjustment episode as one in which the current account deficit exceeded 2 percent of GDP before being reversed, and fell by at least 2 percent of GDP, and at least one-third, over three years; and one in which the maximum deficit in the five years following adjustment did not exceed the maximum in the three years before adjustment.

episodes (largest increase in growth rate from before the onset of adjustment to after) against the seven most contractionary episodes (largest declines in growth rate). The US adjustment episode beginning in 1987 is in the expansionary group.

The differences they identify include the following. First, the size of the current account imbalance was larger for the contractionary episodes (designated here as C) than in expansionary cases (E). Whereas both groups had current account deficits averaging 2 percent of GDP two years prior to the adjustment, for the C group, the deficit had widened to an average of 6 percent by year zero, whereas for the E group it had reached only 3 percent of GDP. Curiously, the authors do not note that by this metric, the United States would presently qualify as a good candidate for a contractionary episode in its near future, as the US current account deficit has reached 6 percent of GDP. In any event, this difference would seem to confirm the intuition: that the potential for an unfavorable growth experience with external adjustment is greater if the current account deficit to be corrected is larger.

Second, growth starts out above the OECD average before adjustment in the C group and then falls well below it, whereas growth in E episodes starts out well below the OECD average and then moves toward that average in adjustment. For the E group, growth averaged only 1 percent annually prior to adjustment, but climbed to an average of about 2½ percent in the two years after the onset of adjustment. In contrast, for the C group, growth averaged about 4 percent prior to adjustment, but fell to an average of about zero in years 1 and 2 after the onset of adjustment. The authors infer that the C episodes involve overheating of the economy before the adjustment. Again, although the authors do not so state, the recent pace of US growth relative to OECD growth would seem at present to make the United States more a candidate for future C rather than E adjustment. Even though US growth may not involve overheating of the economy as in some of the C cases, for external accounts the foreign-domestic growth differential may matter more than whether overheating has occurred. As for inflation, there is little difference between the two groups.

Third, the real exchange rate behaves differently between the groups. For the E group, the real exchange rate depreciates through most of the period, consistent with lagged current account adjustment in response to the real exchange rate. For the C group, however, the real exchange rate remains essentially unchanged, suggesting that the burden of adjustment fell to demand contraction through slow growth or recession. It is this result—the real exchange rate story—that the authors emphasize in dispelling the "disorderly adjustment" hypothesis (also known as the "hard landing," although the authors do not use that term), which typically depicts problems as stemming from a plunge in the exchange rate. The implication is that the significant downward movement in the real value of the dollar already, and likely substantial further real depreciation, would be more likely to prompt US expansion (à la group E) than precipitate a hard landing.

Fourth, real stock market prices decline for both C and E groups from two years before the adjustment to year 0. In contrast, once adjustment begins, real stock market prices rise for the E group but fall sharply in the C group before rebounding.

Fifth, neither real long-term interest rates nor real policy rates differ much between the C and E groups. This too undermines the disorderly adjustment hypothesis, which turns importantly on a surge in interest rates.

Sixth, there is a sharp contrast between the two groups in the behavior of saving and investment. In the C group, the external imbalance is associated with a large rise in investment that outstrips saving, and the adjustment involves a sharp decline in investment. In the E group, the preadjustment gap is narrower, and the correction involves a more even allocation of adjustment between moderately higher saving and moderately lower investment. This pattern also sets the E group apart from the sample as a whole, for which reduction in investment is the dominant adjustment mechanism.

Seventh, whereas real export growth is steady and about the same for the two groups, in the C group, imports decline during the adjustment, but in the E group they continue to grow. The authors find, however, that ". . . the ratio of imports to exports is much lower among the expansion episodes than the contraction episodes. For a given growth rate of exports and imports, the smaller the ratio of imports to exports, the larger the reduction in the trade deficit. Thus, the expansion episodes are able to achieve the same degree of current account adjustment as the contraction episodes, but with less import compression" (Croke, Kamin, and Leduc 2005). Here again is a smoking gun for the United States, although the authors do not draw the inference. The ratio of exports to imports is extremely low for the United States, so past episodes would seem once again to suggest that the United States is more a candidate for contractionary future adjustment than for expansionary adjustment.

Finally, the authors do not find significant differences between the two groups for movements in cyclically adjusted fiscal balances or for changes in NIIPs.

Overall, the findings of Croke, Kamin, and Leduc (2005) would seem to bolster their critique of the usual formulation of the hard-landing scenario—that a sharp real depreciation is the trigger for a surge in interest rates and a recession. Instead, they emphasize that a sharp real depreciation has been a feature of expansionary adjustments. However, reading between the lines, their findings also paint a darker picture for the United States, which currently seems consistently to have features associated with past contractionary adjustments: a high ratio of imports to exports, an imbalance on the order of 6 percent of GDP rather than 3 percent, and recent growth well above the OECD average rather than below it. By focusing on the "disorderly" hypothesis, the authors (and those who cite their study) may have called insufficient attention to the prospect that the adjustment could nonetheless be painful (i.e., contractionary). Indeed, if the United States comes to resemble a contractionary episode adjustment, the expected path of growth would be a decline from about 4 percent to a couple of years of zero growth. Such a path might be orderly but it would be unpleasant.

In early 2005, several Federal Reserve officials cited an important recent staff study by Erceg, Guerrieri, and Gust (2005) to the effect that $1 in fiscal adjustment would only bring about 20 cents in adjustment of the current account deficit. Bernanke (2005) and Ferguson (2005), in particular, invoke this estimate to downplay the role of the widening US fiscal deficit in explaining the rise in the current account deficit. A closer look at the new macroeconomic model developed in that study, called SIGMA, suggests instead that this type of interpretation may be misleading and that a more appropriate interpretation is that fiscal deterioration probably did play an important role and fiscal correction will be central to US external adjustment.

The SIGMA model is in the "new" school of central bank models that are dynamic general equilibrium models of intermediate size, heavily based on consistency with microeconomic theory and dependent on "calibration" (as distinct from econometric estimation) of numerous parameters. Several key features of the model suggest that it is inappropriate to use it in the summary fashion that, for example, Bernanke (2005) does to downplay the scope for external adjustment through fiscal adjustment.

First, the model applies "Ricardian equivalence" to half of consumers. This principle means that when households see the government's deficit rising, they reduce their consumption and increase their saving against the day when they will have to pay higher taxes once the government finally comes to its senses. Placing the Ricardian offset to fiscal policy at something like 50 percent is increasingly common in macroeconomic modeling (see Campbell and Mankiw 1989). This means that any fiscal expansion (contraction) of $1 only reduces (increases) national saving by 50 cents, all else being equal, because of induced changes in private saving in the opposite direction. SIGMA incorporates this effect by treating half of all households as Ricardian and the rest as having "rule of thumb" behavior (spending whatever is their disposable income).

The Ricardian assumption should be increasingly suspect, however. In recent years, the private saving rate has not shown a strong rebound to offset the sharp swing of the fiscal balance from surplus to deficit. Personal saving fell from 3.4 percent of GDP in 1995 to 1.7 percent in 2000 and only 0.87 percent in 2004 (BEA 2005d). If instead Ricardian equivalence applied to even half of households, personal saving should have risen from 1.7 percent of GDP in 2000 to 4.5 percent in 2004 in response to the collapse of total government saving from 4.4 percent of GDP to −1.2 percent (see table 4.1 in chapter 4). It is highly implausible to argue that if the government now improved its fiscal balance (and hence government saving) by, say, 3 percent of GDP, households would offset this by plunging into negative saving at about −2 percent of GDP (or, if the Ricardian offset is only one half, to −0.63 percent of GDP (= 0.87 − 0.5 × 3). But without the Ricardian assumption, the model would show much more effective change in national saving from each dollar of change in fiscal saving. As a result, there would be a stronger current account adjustment resulting from fiscal adjustment.

Second, SIGMA and other models like it implicitly begin from a state of long-term equilibrium. Any shock is treated as a disturbance. There are fiscal and monetary "reaction functions" that are premised on returning the economy back toward equilibrium. It is not appropriate, however, to apply this setup when the underlying path of the economy is toward disequilibrium, as is currently the case with both the US fiscal and external deficits. In particular, the model assumes that when there is a $1 shock of increased government spending, there is a "fiscal reaction function" that subsequently raises taxes in order to reduce the deficit back toward a level consistent with the long-term target ratio of debt to GDP. But surely the whole point, in the present context, is that $1 in reduction of the fiscal deficit (whether by higher taxes or reduced spending) would not induce an eroding "fiscal reaction" because it would move the economy closer to rather than away from long-term fiscal equilibrium. In short, it is inappropriate to leave the fiscal reaction function unchanged when the underlying baseline of the economy is not in long-term equilibrium.

The consequence of the fiscal reaction function in SIGMA is that the "fiscal shock" of $1 is itself shrunk relatively to a much smaller amount: only 45 cents by the fifth year (Erceg, Guerrieri, and Gust 2005, 36). The trade balance impact of 15 cents by this time is thus a higher fraction of the actual fiscal change, or one-third, than the 0.2 fraction emphasized in recent statements by Federal Reserve officials. Moreover, the trade balance effect does not include the interest earnings effects or changes in equity capital earnings from currency valuation effects on the stock of foreign equity assets. In the principal macro model used by the Federal Reserve Board for international analysis (FRB/Global), the total current account impact of a fiscal shock is about three-fourths larger than the trade balance impact.[43] So the overall ratio of the current account adjustment to the de facto fiscal adjustment is even higher, and likely in the same vicinity as

---

43. A sustained government spending reduction of 1 percent of GDP generated a three-year average increase of 0.18 percent of GDP in the trade balance and a 0.3 percent of GDP increase in the current account balance in the 1997 version of FRB/Global. See Levin, Rogers, and Tryon (1997, 18).

the 40 percent ratio identified just for the trade balance in the simple general equilibrium model set forth in chapter 4. (For further discussion of the issues involved in interpreting the SIGMA model, see the discussion of interpreting macroeconomic model simulations in appendix 5A.)

Federal Reserve Vice Chairman Ferguson (2005) provides an important statement and analysis by a leading Federal Reserve official. His diagnosis assigns an even smaller role to fiscal deterioration in explaining the widening US current account deficit. On the basis of special runs of the FRB/Global model, he estimates that a 3 percent of GDP structural erosion in the US fiscal position from the beginning of 2002 to the end of 2004 (comprised of 1 percent from higher spending and 2 percent from tax cuts) contributed only 0.15 percent of GDP to the total 4 percent of GDP decline in the trade balance of goods and services (from −1.3 to −5.3 percent of GDP) from 1997 to 2004.[44] On the face of it, this estimate is extraordinarily small and seemingly inconsistent with other Federal Reserve model estimates, which typically show an impact of about 0.2 percent of GDP for each 1 percent fiscal shock (Erceg, Guerrieri, and Gust 2005; Levin, Rogers, and Tryon 1997). In contrast, the corresponding implied parameter in the Ferguson runs is only a 0.05 percent of GDP trade balance change for each 1 percent of GDP fiscal shock (i.e., 0.15/3).

Ferguson instead emphasizes the increase in productivity growth as another directly measured impact, as well as three effects treated residually: reduction in investment in the G-7 (excluding the United States) and in East Asia (excluding China); autonomous reduction in US private saving; and increased global financial integration (reduction in home bias, treated as a reduction in the US "risk premium" levied by foreign investors). However, the residual treatment of the latter three influences means their measurement is at best speculative and dependent on proper measurement of the other two influences. The method allocates one-third of the residual to each of the three. They wind up each accounting for a 0.5 percent of GDP reduction in the US trade balance.[45] There is perhaps important information on the ambiguity of these measurements in the finding that whereas Bernanke (2005) attributes the lion's share of US external balance erosion from 1997 to the global saving glut (also known as the global investment collapse), Ferguson at best attributes a lamb's share (one-eighth).

The direct measurement in Ferguson for the productivity acceleration impact is based on the model's corresponding calculation of an induced increase in investment by 1 percent of GDP, and a reduction in private saving by 1 percent of GDP in response to households' expectations of

---

44. The fiscal impact of only 0.15 percent is inferred by measurement from figure 2 of the appendix to Ferguson (2005).

45. Again inferred by physical measurement of the graphs provided in the study.

higher future incomes. An offsetting influence is a depreciation of the real exchange rate, caused by the model treatment of domestic versus foreign inflation. The productivity shock curbs US inflation, whereas foreign inflation continues apace, contributing a real depreciation of the dollar. This is just the opposite of what many argue was the main influence of the productivity growth shock: an appreciation of the dollar spurred by an inflow of capital in response to improved investment opportunities.

As for the autonomous saving effect, foreign investment collapse effect, and dollar risk premium effect, their calibration as the residual necessary to fill the gap would seem to make them of limited use other than as reminders that these influences may have been present. Overall, while the Ferguson study usefully reminds us of major possible explanations of the US current account erosion, its seeming precision based on its use of the FRB/Global model would appear basically misleading. On the most important policy issue—the role of fiscal policy—the study gives a de minimus impact that is inconsistent with larger effects implied by other model estimates at the Federal Reserve and elsewhere.

Global Saving Glut?

The "global saving glut" argument of Ben S. Bernanke (2005), formerly a Federal Reserve Board governor and now chairman of the Council of Economic Advisers, is a particularly trenchant version of the approach downplaying both the severity of the problem of external imbalance and the role of fiscal policy in either causing or resolving it. Bernanke rejects the idea that the growing US external deficit "*primarily* represents economic policies" (2005, 1). Instead, he argues that the decline in US saving is largely an endogenous reaction to the "emergence of a global saving glut in the past eight to ten years" associated with rising saving in wealthy countries with aging populations and, more importantly, the "metamorphosis of the developing world from a net user to a net supplier of funds to international capital markets" (2005, 4). He notes that the counterpart of the increase of the US current account deficit by $546 billion from 1996 to 2004 was primarily in developing countries, whose aggregate current account shifted by $416 billion (from a deficit of $90 billion to a surplus of $326 billion). He points to the financial crises in East Asia and Russia in 1997–98, Brazil in 1999, and Argentina in 2002 as motivating forces that started many developing countries on a path of building up reserves as a "war chest" and promoting export-led growth by preventing exchange rate appreciation. East Asian countries maintained their high saving rates even as their domestic investment fell.

Bernanke argues that the global saving glut contributed to low interest rates in the United States, and that this in turn spurred a housing boom that increased home values. This, together with a recovery in the stock market, boosted the ratio of household wealth to income back to 5.4, well above its 1960–2003 average of 4.8 (albeit below the peak of 6.2 in 1999). With rising wealth, households felt less need to save. As for the fiscal deficit, Bernanke cites the Erceg, Guerrieri, and Gust (2005) model result that each dollar of fiscal correction leads to only 20 cents of current account adjustment as a basis for downplaying the importance of fiscal erosion (and the efficacy of fiscal adjustment for external adjustment). Although he laments that "for the developing world to be lending large sums on net to the mature industrial economies is quite undesirable," he sees little reason why the adjustment process should not be smooth. He expects that "the various factors underlying the U.S. current account deficit— both domestic and international—are likely to unwind only gradually. . ." and that "we probably have little choice except to be patient as we work to create the conditions in which a greater share of global saving can be redirected away from the United States and toward the rest of the world— particularly the developing nations" (2005, 14).

This view undoubtedly contains a kernel of truth. For example, the decline in East Asian investment rates no doubt contributed to weaker exchange rates and a shift of demand from investment to exports. However, there is no reason that the entirety of the external impact should have shown up in the US external deficit rather than being much more widely dispersed, in the absence of strong domestic US influences and especially fiscal erosion to shape this outcome. Ultimately, the argument, which amounts to saying that the US current account deficit is mainly attributable to causes from abroad rather than policies and behavior at home, is unconvincing. Worse, it is counterproductive in terms of keeping attention focused on the need to implement forceful US fiscal adjustment.

At one level, the statement that the US current account deficit represents a global saving glut is a tautology. By definition, the current account equals the excess of investment over domestic saving. Also by definition, if the United States has a current account deficit, the rest of the world in the aggregate has a corresponding current account surplus (aside from statistical discrepancies). If "glut" is defined as "excess," then it follows that the rest of the world has a saving glut and the United States has a saving "dearth" or shortfall.

The economic content of the argument turns on understanding the sources of swings in the saving-investment imbalances. Table 5.1 shows the change in saving and investment rates by major countries and regions from 1997 to 2004. Aggregate saving and investment rates are obtained weighting by GDP. The differences between the saving and investment rates in principle equal the current account balance as a percent of GDP, although there are relatively small statistical discrepancies. These data confirm that there was a decline in the investment rate in East Asia excluding China—from 32 to 25 percent of GDP in the newly industrial-

Table 5.1 Global saving, investment, current accounts, and GDP, 1997 and 2004 (in percentage of GDP and in billions of dollars)

	1997					2004				
	s	i	s–i	ca	GDP (billions of dollars)	s	i	s–i	ca	GDP (billions of dollars)
United States	17.6	19.8	−2.2	−1.6	8,304	13.6	19.6	−6.0	−5.7	11,734
Euro area	21.7	20.3	1.4	1.5	6,534	20.9	20.2	0.7	0.4	9,397
Japan	30.9	28.7	2.2	2.2	4,313	27.6	23.9	3.7	3.7	4,668
United Kingdom	17.0	17.1	−0.1	−0.1	1,327	14.8	17.0	−2.2	−2.2	2,295
NIEs	32.8	32.4	0.4	0.5	1,087	31.3	24.9	6.4	7.1	1,258
China	41.8	38.0	3.8	3.8	898	51.2	47.0	4.2	4.2	1,649
ASEAN-4	28.0	38.0	−10.0	−3.0	570	26.5	22.0	4.5	5.5	624
Latin America	19.2	22.6	−3.4	−3.3	2,003	21.0	19.8	1.2	0.8	1,998
Middle East	26.1	24.6	1.5	1.7	545	32.0	25.4	6.6	17.3	822
Africa	17.6	19.8	−2.2	−1.4	444	20.6	21.0	−0.4	0.2	680
Subtotal	22.8	23.1	−0.3	0.1	26,025	21.1	21.9	−0.7	−0.4	35,125
o/w non-US	25.2	24.7	0.5	0.9	17,721	24.9	23.0	1.9	2.2	23,391
o/w NAL	24.6	27.9	−3.3	−2.1	3,660	24.9	21.7	3.3	3.6	3,880
Rest of world	n.a.	n.a.	n.a.	n.a.	3,742	n.a.	n.a.	n.a.	n.a.	5,546
World	n.a.	n.a.	n.a.	n.a.	29,768	n.a.	n.a.	n.a.	n.a.	40,671

s = saving
i = investment
ca = current account
NIEs = newly industrialized economies (Korea, Hong Kong, Singapore, and Taiwan)
ASEAN-4 = Association of Southeast Asian Nations (Indonesia, Malaysia, Philippines, and Thailand)
NAL = includes the NIEs, the ASEAN-4, and Latin America
n.a. = not applicable

Sources: IMF (2005b) and Rajan (2005).

ized economies (NIEs) and from 38 to 22 percent of GDP in the Association of Southeast Asian Nations (ASEAN-4)—and, to a lesser extent, in Latin America (from about 23 to 20 percent). In China, in contrast, investment rose sharply, but so did the rate of saving. The table also shows the sharp drop in the saving rate in the United States, by 4 percentage points of GDP, and the corresponding rise in the US current account deficit by the same amount.

One test of the Bernanke hypothesis would be to see whether the size of the investment decline in the developing countries facing financial difficulties in this period can explain the drop in US saving, based on the argument that these countries' excess saving induced saving reductions in the rest of the world including the United States. If the NIEs, ASEAN-4, and Latin America are aggregated to a grouping labeled NAL, their average investment rate fell from about 28 to 22 percent of GDP, while the saving rate remained unchanged at about 25 percent. So it can be postulated that the financial crises and the resulting drop in investment (as well as aggressive export responses to the crises) caused these countries to generate a swing of 6.6 percent of their GDP into excess saving imposed on the rest of the world. Applied to 2004 GDP, that amounted to $256 billion.

Global GDP outside the affected NAL countries stood at $36.8 trillion in 2004. So the upswing in excess saving from the NAL countries amounted to 0.7 percent of non-NAL GDP. By this test, the Bernanke thesis is rejected. The new saving glut should only have induced excess saving for the United States equal to 0.7 percent of GDP. Instead, US saving fell by 4 percent of GDP. Bernanke (2005, 9) addresses this discrepancy by arguing that the United States disproportionately absorbed the upswing in net foreign saving because of the attractiveness of investment there during the technology boom of the 1990s and because of the sophistication of the country's financial markets. Suppose these advantages made it twice as likely that the excess saving would flow to the United States as to other countries. Then the discrepancy would still remain and still be large—a 4 percent of GDP US saving decline versus a 1.4 percent of US GDP infusion of excess saving from the NAL group.

The "Occam's razor" principle applied by economists—the simplest explanation for a phenomenon—would surely suggest instead that the driving force in the drop in US saving was the conscious adoption of fiscal policy changes that reduced the contribution of the fiscal accounts to US saving. As noted in chapter 4, the OECD has estimated that after taking out cyclical influences, the US tax cuts of the past four years have eroded the fiscal balance by 2.6 percent of GDP. On the basis of the comparisons just discussed, *US fiscal policy is responsible for two to four times as much reduction in US saving as can plausibly be attributed to developing country financial crises.* (The lower figure assumes US attractiveness doubles its global share; the higher figure assumes the share is only proportional to US GDP.)

A crucial policy judgment in Bernanke's analysis is that fiscal deterioration was not much to blame for the widening US external deficit. In support, he cites the Erceg, Guerrieri, and Gust (2005) simulations indicating only 20 cents of trade adjustment for each dollar of fiscal adjustment. However, as discussed here, this parameter is likely to understate both the role of recent fiscal erosion in driving the rising external deficit as well as the potential for fiscal correction to narrow the current account deficit. Instead, it is more reasonable to stick to the "smoking gun" of 2.6 percent of US GDP saving erosion from fiscal policy change and the decline in the personal saving rate as the driving forces in the widening US external imbalance than it is to blame an inflow of excess global saving. After all, foreigners did not force the United States to cut taxes, nor did they force US households rather than European ones to cut back their saving.

Another of Bernanke's arguments, however, is that the global saving glut is the source of low US interest rates, which in turn spurred the housing boom and curbed household saving as higher home prices provided wealth accumulation without saving. But how strong is the evidence that external saving was the source of lower interest rates? There is a problem for this argument with respect to the timing. The height of the East Asian, Russian, and Brazilian crises was 1998–99. Allowing for some lag, a major saving glut, supply-side push on capital markets should have depressed the interest rate in 1999–2000. Instead, the 10-year bond rate rose from 5.3 percent in 1998 to an average of 5.8 percent in 1999–2000.

The most dramatic subsequent influence on US interest rates was the reduction in the Federal Reserve's policy rate in an effort to counter the 2001 recession. The federal funds rate fell from 6.0 percent in 2000 to 1.7 percent in 2002 and 1.1 percent in 2003 (IMF 2005b). But the test of external interest rate influences would have to show up in the rate not controlled by the Federal Reserve—the long-term bond rate. Unfortunately for the Bernanke hypothesis, the gap between this rate and the federal funds rate—the "yield curve spread"—widened rather than narrowing. By 2003, the spread between the 10-year bond rate and the federal funds rate stood at 294 basis points, up from virtually zero in 1998 and −20 basis points in 2000. To be sure, the main cause of the shift from an inverted to a steeply positive yield curve was the swing from over full employment in 2000 to recession in 2001 and low-employment recovery thereafter, as the Federal Reserve kept the policy rate at historically low levels in light of low inflation and unused capacity. Nonetheless, if by 2003, there had been enormous downward pressure on US interest rates from an external saving glut, surely the yield curve spread between the long-bond rate and the federal funds rate would have been relatively low. Instead, the nearly 300 basis point spread in 2003 and again in 2004 was among the highest on record. In comparison, the simple average spread between the federal funds and 10-year bond rates for 1960–2004 was only 89 basis points (IMF 2005b). Low US interest rates after 2001 were thus made in America, not in East Asia and Latin America.

Finally, another weak link in the saving glut argument is its premise that private saving abroad has come in large volume to the United States in the absence of sufficient investment opportunities abroad, whereas increasingly it has been foreign buildup of official reserves that has financed the increase in the US current account deficit. In gauging private versus official flows for purposes of examining the saving glut argument, it is appropriate to consider the net private inflows after deducting US private outflows. After all, if the argument is that there are few investment opportunities abroad compared with saving abroad, then we would not expect that phenomenon to be siphoning private capital out of the United States; American investors would also find the pickings slim abroad. When US private outflows are deducted, net private capital inflows to the United States averaged $276 billion annually in 2003–04, compared with official capital inflows averaging $302 billion.[46] With more than half of net capital inflows coming from the foreign public sector rather than the private sector, the argument that the US current account deficit is caused primarily by private savers abroad seeking investment opportunities rings hollow. On the contrary, the major role of foreign central banks means that the large US current account deficit is being sustained despite the lack of adequate financing for it from the private sector alone. In contrast, foreign official capital inflows during 1998–2001 averaged a meager $24 billion annually (BEA 2005c).

Macro Model Biases?

There may be a danger of downward bias in judging the potential impact of fiscal adjustment in correcting the external deficit in the class of models represented by FRB/Global and the "new" generation of smaller but more theoretically elegant models now being tested in many central banks (Faust 2005), as exemplified by Erceg, Guerrieri, and Gust (2005). In short, the problem is that this type of model may exaggerate the extent to which a fiscal shock induces output change in the short run (Keynesian structure), while exaggerating changes in domestic consumption and investment rather than changes in the trade balance in the long run. Both effects will downplay the trade balance change.

Consider the fiscal experiment in Ferguson (2005). In this experiment, the private saving rate rises by 2 percent of GDP when there is fiscal expansion of 3 percent of GDP (appendix figure 2 in the paper). But this

---

46. The corresponding gross private averages were $554 billion annually in outflows versus $829 billion annually in inflows.

change is not the consequence of a Ricardian offset (absent in the FRB/ Global model); nor is it the consequence of lower absolute consumption from a higher interest rate. Instead, it reflects approximately unchanged consumption in the face of higher output.[47] That then turns our attention to what is happening to output, and how this influences the impact of fiscal expansion on the external balance.

As shown in appendix 5A, the macroeconomic models will tend to understate any impact of fiscal adjustment on the current account in the short run because of their Keynesian feature, whereby output changes by almost exactly the same amount as the change in government spending, leaving no room in the national accounts identity for a change in the trade balance. Yet in the medium or longer run, when output is constrained to potential capacity, the same class of models may also tend to understate the external adjustment because of parameter calibration of effects from induced monetary policy change, induced fiscal policy change, and Ricardian-equivalence household saving changes. So the models may show little impact of fiscal adjustment on the external accounts in either the short run or the medium to longer run.

Allowing output to revert toward capacity through trade balance change rather than these sorts of offsets can, however, imply a much larger space for the trade balance to improve in response to fiscal tightening. The fiscal adjustment curbs income and hence the demand for imports ("expenditure reduction"). It also reduces interest rates—the lower interest rate induces a depreciation, and the more attractive exchange rate stimulates exports and curbs imports ("expenditure switching"; see Meade 1951). If the overall trade response is strong enough, then the maintenance of output at capacity level may occur considerably more through external adjustment, and considerably less through domestic demand revival by induced monetary loosening, induced fiscal (reaction-function) loosening, or a Ricardian household consumption increase than the models permit.

The FRB/Global and SIGMA models may indeed understate the scope for exchange rate change in response to the interest rate in particular, and as a consequence, understate the scope for change in the trade balance to contribute to equilibration of total demand back toward domestic output supply in response to an expansionary fiscal shock. The simulations in Ferguson (2005) certainly seem to imply an understatement of the impact on exchange rates. The shock is 3 percent of GDP fiscal expansion, but the real exchange rate rises only 1 percent. The small trade balance change (0.15 percent of GDP) approximately reflects applying an export price elasticity of 1.5 to the export base of nearly 10 percent of GDP combined with a 1 percent real exchange rate appreciation (and with

---

47. Christopher Erceg, personal communication, May 13, 2005.

minimal adjustment of the nominal import bill because the price effect is working against the volume effect).

With a short-term multiplier of about unity, a 3 percent of GDP fiscal expansion would boost output 3 percent above capacity, and by the Taylor rule, cause the Federal Reserve to boost interest rates by 150 basis points. By the Gale-Orzag parameter for crowding out effects, moreover, the 3 percent of GDP deficit would add another 0.9 percentage point to the interest rate. Overall, the interest rate increase would be on the order of 2.5 percent. The calibration of the simple model in chapter 4 assumes that a 1 percentage point rise in the interest rate boosts the exchange rate by 5 percent, implying a rise by about 12 percent in the real exchange rate— an order of magnitude larger than the 1 percent rise in the Ferguson fiscal simulation. On this basis, there are grounds for suspecting that the responsiveness of the exchange rate to the interest rate is understated in the FRB/Global and SIGMA models, and that this in turn leads to an understatement in the adjustment of the trade balance even if the trade price elasticities are appropriate.

Pass-through and Adjustment Prospects

Finally, recent statistical work has tended to show a decline of the import price pass-through ratio over time. Marazzi, Sheets, and Vigfusson (2005) estimate that the pass-through ratio has fallen from about 0.6 in the early 1990s to about 0.4 during 1998–2004.[48] As possible causes of the decline, they cite the falling share of industrial supplies (excluding oil) in imports, considering that industrial supplies have typically had higher import pass-through ratios than other goods; the rising share of China in imports, considering that China has maintained a fixed exchange rate against the dollar; and a seeming shift of East Asian economies toward more fully pricing to the US market in the aftermath of the 1997–98 financial crisis than before. They find a statistically significant relationship between the size of the decline in the pass-through ratio by sector and the size of the increase in China's market share by sector.

Some observers appear to be concerned that a decline in the import price pass-through would be adverse to US external adjustment. However, as Marazzi, Sheets, and Vigfusson (2005) explicitly recognize, if the price elasticity of demand for imports is unity rather than greater than unity, the size of the pass-through does not affect adjustment of the nominal

---

48. This is their result for the model excluding commodity prices as a separate explanatory variable. There is no clear reason why commodity prices should be included, because to the extent that they affect foreign production costs, their impact should already show up in foreign prices as translated through the exchange rate. The authors emphasize instead their results with commodity prices directly included in the regression equation; in this case the decline is from about 0.5 in the 1980s to about 0.2 during the past decade.

import bill. That is, with a price elasticity of -1, the decline in the quantity imported just offsets the rise in the import price to leave the dollar value of imports unchanged when the dollar declines, so it does not matter whether the import price change "passed through" from the exchange rate is high or low. The import price elasticity is usually estimated at about unity, so the pass-through issue should not cause much if any difficulty for US adjustment in nominal terms.

Moreover, in terms of the real welfare loss to be expected from eventual US correction of the external imbalance, it is actually more favorable for the United States to have a low than a high import price pass-through. The reason is that the United States will not need to give up as much in real import volume to accomplish the same external adjustment. Another way of looking at the same point is to recognize that if foreign suppliers adjust to a decline in the dollar by reducing their profit margins and holding their dollar price in the US market almost unchanged, there will be much less terms of trade loss for the United States than if foreign suppliers keep profit margins unchanged and boost dollar prices to make up for the lesser value of the dollars earned. With unitary import price elasticity, the nominal adjustment must occur on the export side in any event. Similarly, monetary policy faces a less difficult task in the external adjustment process if import pass-through is lower, because there will be less upward pressure on the US price level from a given depreciation of the dollar. In broad terms, then, if import price pass-through has indeed declined, it should be a cause for comfort rather than concern regarding the scope for US external adjustment.

Appendix 5A
Key Features of Leading Recent Analyses

Obstfeld and Rogoff (2004)

The Obstfeld-Rogoff model summarized in the main text is as follows. There are two countries: the home country and the foreign country (indicated by an asterisk). Each country has a tradable sector (T) and a nontradable sector (N). Capital and labor in each sector are assumed to be fixed, which is an important source of potential rigidity and hence difficulty of adjustment in the model. The home country is forced to eliminate a deficit of 5 percent of its GDP (i.e., approximately the size of the US current account deficit), and can only do so by cutting back consumption of tradables. The authors place T at 25 percent of GDP and N at 75 percent, so the cutback amounts to 5/25 = 20 percent of tradable goods production. This is their first point: The US external adjustment is much larger relative to tradables than it is relative to GDP.

Figure 5A.1 shows how adjustment occurs in this type of model. The supply-demand graph applies to each country. It shows the quantity of tradables relative to the quantity of nontradables on the horizontal axis, and the price of tradables relative to the price of nontradables on the vertical axis. The home country is at a point such as a, where the relative quantity of tradables sought by consumers along the demand curve exceeds the relative quantity produced domestically. The foreign country is at a point such as b, where the opposite is true. When the home country is forced to adjust, it must reduce its ratio of tradables consumed relative to nontradables to point c, because eliminating the trade deficit means consumption matches domestic production. With fixed output in each sector, the only way to do this is to suppress consumer demand for tradables by raising their price, thereby reducing the quantity of tradables demanded by enough to eliminate the trade deficit.

Obstfeld-Rogoff define the real exchange rate as the ratio of the average price in the foreign country to that in the home country: $q = E(P^*/P)$, essentially the ratio of the two GDP deflators. This is the Latin American definition rather than the US definition, because a higher real exchange rate means the home country is more competitive. The economy-wide price level is the weighted average of the sectoral price levels, using a constant-elasticity of substitution demand structure: $P = [\gamma P_T^{1-\theta} + (1 - \gamma)P_N^{1-\theta}]^{1/(1-\theta)}$, where γ is the share of tradables in GDP (set at 0.25) and θ is the elasticity of substitution in demand between the two sectors (defined as $\theta > 0$).

If the elasticity of substitution between tradables and nontradables in demand is unity, and the demand for tradables in the home country needs to decline by 20 percent, the price of tradables relative to nontradables

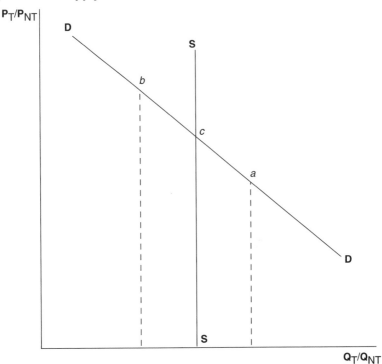

Figure 5A.1 Supply and demand for tradables and nontradables

must increase 20 percent. The mirror image occurs in the foreign country, but is dampened because the foreign country is the rest of the world and is larger than the home economy. The authors put the foreign country at about three times the size of the US (home) economy.

The key equation in the model shows the real exchange rate as a function of the nominal exchange rate and, ultimately, the ratio of nontradable to tradable goods prices in the foreign country relative to the same ratio in the home country. Thus:

$$q = \frac{EP^*}{P} = E\frac{P_T^*}{P_T} \times \frac{[\gamma + (1 - \gamma)(P_N^*/P_T^*)^{(1-\theta)}]^{1/(1-\theta)}}{[\gamma + (1 - \gamma)(P_N / P_T)^{(1-\theta)}]^{1/(1-\theta)}} \qquad (5A.1)$$

where E is the nominal exchange rate, P is price (the asterisk is for the foreign country and the absence of an asterisk refers to the home country), subscript T is the tradable sector, subscript N is the nontradable sector, θ is the elasticity of substitution, and γ is the share of tradables in consumption.[49] The term P_T^*/P_T reflects the terms of trade for traded goods.

---

49. The final ratio on the right hand side derives from the ratio of the two countries' consumer price indexes. For the home country, this index is:
$$P = [\gamma P_T^{(1-\theta)} + (1-\gamma)P_N^{(1-\theta)}]^{[1/(1-\theta)]}.$$

Now consider the impact of a demand shift sufficient to curb home demand for tradables by 20 percent. With $\theta = 1$, P_T/P_N must rise by 20 percent. In the foreign country, $P_N{}^*/P_T{}^*$ rises by a smaller amount because of the larger size.[50] For its part, the term $P_T{}^*/P_T$ will rise by an amount corresponding to a terms of trade loss of about 7 percent, when the elasticity of substitution between the foreign good and the home tradable (η) is 2. This turns out to mean that $EP_T{}^*/P_T$ rises by 2.7 percent, using $\alpha = 0.7$ for the share of the home good in tradables.[51] So the real exchange rate rises (depreciates) from $q = 1$ to:[52] $q = 1.027 \times [(1.105)^{0.75} / [(0.802)^{0.75}]$ $= 1.306$.[53] This real depreciation by about 31 percent (real loss of value by about 23 percent) can be carried out by a rise in the foreign price level, with a fixed exchange rate E; or by a rise in the nominal exchange rate E that is proportionate to the rise in the real exchange rate q with no rise in the foreign price level on average (and/or no decline in the average home price). The authors imply that with today's flexible exchange rates and the tendency of central banks to implement inflation targeting, the latter mode of adjustment would dominate.

Even when the authors apply optimistic substitution elasticities ($\theta = 2$, $\eta = 3$), the real exchange rate depreciates 15 percent, with alternative combinations yielding depreciations of 20 to 25 percent. Hence their central conclusion: the real depreciation of the dollar would need to be 20 percent to close the trade gap. They also cite an alternative figure of 40 percent, however, as "a large potential overshoot in the event of a rapid reversal" rather than gradual adjustment (Obstfeld and Rogoff 2004, 19).

Dividing the first and second terms of the bracketed expression by $P_T{}^{(1-\theta)}$ yields the form in equation 5A.1. Note further that when the elasticity of substitution is unity ($\theta = 1$), the constant elasticity of substitution (CES) form used by Obstfeld and Rogoff transforms into a Cobb-Douglas form (Henderson and Quandt 1971, 88). In this case, the final right-hand-side ratio in equation 5A.1 becomes: $[(P_N{}^*/P_T{}^*)^{1-\gamma}/(P_N/P_T)^{1-\gamma}]$.

50. Taking account of the various parameters, the mirror-image rise in the relative price of nontradables abroad works out to 10 percent.

51. Specifically: $E(P_T{}^*/P_T) = [\alpha \tau^{1-\eta} + (1-\alpha)]^{[1/(1-\eta)]} / [\alpha + (1-\alpha)\tau^{1-\eta}]^{[1/(1-\eta)]}$, where α is the weight of the home-produced tradable and $(1-\alpha)$ is the weight of the foreign tradable in tradable goods consumption, τ is the terms-of-trade ratio (price of foreign-produced tradable relative to home-produced tradable), and η is the elasticity of substitution between the home- and foreign-produced tradable goods.

52. The actual Obstfeld-Rogoff figure is 1.336, reflecting small differences in the approximation here. They call this a depreciation of 33.6 percent, which using their definition amounts to a loss of real value of 25.1 percent.

53. The implementation here of the Obstfeld-Rogoff model, using the "goal-seek" spreadsheet function to solve for τ, gives a slightly different estimate from the Obstfeld-Rogoff implementation. With $\theta = 1$ and $\eta = 2$, the estimate here is 30.6 percent depreciation, versus 33.6 percent in the Obstfeld-Rogoff results. With $\theta = 1$ and $\eta = 3$, the corresponding estimates are almost identical (25.3 and 25.4 percent, respectively).

Blanchard, Giavazzi, and Sa (2005)

A simplified version of the key exchange rate equation in Blanchard, Giavazzi, and Sa (2005) is

$$\partial E / \partial F = -\frac{\alpha + \alpha^* - 1}{(1 - \alpha^*)X^*} \tag{5A.2}$$

where E is the exchange rate (foreign currency units per dollar, normalized here to unity), F is net US external debt, α is the share of home assets in wealth, the asterisk denotes the foreign country, and X is the total stock of assets.[54] If there is no home bias, then $\alpha = \alpha^* = 0.5$ and the numerator on the right-hand side turns to zero. In a world with no home bias, a shift of wealth from the United States abroad has no consequences for the dollar because foreigners are just as happy to hold US assets as their home assets.

The authors instead place α at 77 percent portfolio share for home assets in the United States, and at $\alpha^* = 70$ percent abroad. This gives a value of 0.47 for the numerator of the right-hand side of equation 5A.2. They place X^* at about \$35 trillion. The impact of a \$1 trillion US current account deficit on the exchange rate will then be: $-0.47 \times \$1$ trillion/ $[0.3 \times \$35$ trillion$] = -0.045$. That is, a \$1 trillion increase in net US external debt would induce a 4.5 percent depreciation of the dollar because of home bias. On this basis, the present pace of US current account deficits at about \$750 billion annually would be expected to cause a 3.4 percent depreciation of the dollar (i.e., $= 0.75 \times 4.5\%$) annually, before taking account of foreign asset valuation and differential return considerations.

The dynamics of the system are driven by the fact that (i) a rise in F (net external debt) boosts interest payments, raising the current account deficit, and (ii) a rise in net external debt also induces a decline in the dollar, which improves the trade balance and reduces the current account deficit.[55] At the steady state equilibrium, demand and supply for US assets must be equal, and (in the no-growth version) the current account deficit

---

54. In the full formulation, the portfolio shares α and α^* depend on the rates of return at home and abroad and on expected depreciation. In simplified form, the authors arrive at the equation for change in the exchange rate as follows. US net foreign debt equals US assets minus US wealth, and conversely, so:
  1) $F = X - W = W^*/E - X^*/E$, where W is wealth. Demand for US assets is:
  2) $X = \alpha W + (1-\alpha^*)W^*/E = \alpha(X-F) + (1-\alpha^*)(X^*/E + F)$.
  Holding US and foreign assets constant so that $\partial X = \partial X^* = 0$, it can be shown that:
  3) $\partial E/\partial F = -[\alpha + \alpha^* - 1]/[(1-\alpha^*)X^*/E^2]$, which, for $E = 1$, becomes the text equation.

55. The stability condition, whereby an increase in net debt reduces the current account deficit, is that: $r/D_E < (\alpha + \alpha^* - 1)/[(1-\alpha^*)X^*/E^2]$, where D_E is derivative of the trade deficit with respect to the exchange rate and r is the return on assets (with $r = r^*$ for convenience in the dynamic analysis).

must be zero.[56] The authors consider two effects they believe characterize the US external accounts over the past decade: (1) an unexpected increase in the trade deficit from levels otherwise associated with activity levels and (2) an unexpected increase in foreign demand for US assets. The first leads to initial depreciation, followed by further anticipated depreciation; the second leads to initial appreciation, followed by anticipated depreciation.

Gourinchas and Rey (2005)

Gourinchas and Rey invoke the intertemporal budget constraint on the external deficit to arrive at the following key equation, estimated statistically:[57]

$$nxa = (x - \bar{x}) - 0.91(m - \bar{m}) + 0.79(a - \bar{a}) - .47(l - \bar{l}) \qquad (5A.3)$$

$$= - \sum_{j=1}^{\infty} \rho^j [r_{t+j} + \Delta nx_{t+j}]$$

where lower case refers to natural logarithm, X and M are quarterly exports and imports of goods and services, A is gross foreign assets, L is gross foreign liabilities, and the overbar represents the 1952–2004 mean. The term ρ is the ratio $(1 + r^*)/(1 + r)$ where r^* is the steady-state rate of return (equal for both assets and liabilities) and $r = w_a r^a + w_L r^L$, a weighted average of the return on assets and liabilities respectively. The term nx is the logarithm of exports minus the logarithm of imports. All underlying variables are in real per capita terms, deflating by producer prices for finished consumer goods and services (2000 = 100).

This measure is meant to capture the composite effect of the trade balance and portfolio earnings in meeting the intertemporal external balance constraint. The higher coefficient on assets than on liabilities reflects higher return on US foreign assets than liabilities. At the stationary ratios of exports, imports, assets, and liabilities to wealth, nxa should be zero. If $nxa > 0$, the exchange rate will appreciate and the trade balance decline, or the return on the net foreign asset position will decrease, or both; if $nxa < 0$, the currency will depreciate and the trade balance increase, or the return on the net foreign asset position will increase, or both.

Interpreting the Gourinchas-Rey analysis poses several difficulties. First, the analysis is relatively opaque. For example, as noted in the main

---

56. This requires, respectively, that: $X = \alpha(X - F) + (1 - \alpha^*)[(X^*/E) + F]$; and $0 = rF + D(E)$.

57. With lower case italics representing logarithms, the authors regress x on m and leads and lags of Δm; a on l and Δl; and x on a and leads and lags of Δa (dynamic ordinary least squares). They combine the estimated coefficients with theoretically required weights for stationary ratios of exports, imports, assets, and liabilities to wealth to obtain equation 5A.3.

text, it is never clarified what the eventual level of net foreign liabilities is at the steady state.

Second, some of the underlying assumptions seem potentially contradictory. In particular, the framework requires that a steady-state net creditor run a trade deficit and a steady-state net debtor run a trade surplus. But the United States is a net debtor running a trade deficit, and it is unclear whether it is to transit somehow to net creditor status while continuing a trade deficit or to transit to net debtor running a trade surplus—in which case it should be made clear when and how the trade balance might be expected to swing into surplus (certainly the small depreciation mentioned in association with the imbalance would be insufficient to achieve this result).

Third, a glance at the "estimating" equation 5A.3 immediately shows that somehow the authors must regress their key variable on a set of data that does not exist: the entire future history of trade and asset earnings. They must use "expected" values as a proxy for this unknown future, but again, their method in identifying the right-hand-side measures for the statistical tests is complicated at best and arguably opaque.

Fourth, although the analysis is postulated in a framework of a "stationary" pattern for the ratios of assets, liabilities, exports, and imports to total household wealth, implicitly, the future paths are anything but stationary in the usual sense. They involve a secular deterioration in the US net foreign asset position. Although the resulting downward path may be stationary in the sense that observed fluctuations are stationary around it, it is unclear that this first-derivative stationarity is consistent with the underlying framework.

Understanding the Macro Model Simulations

In the basic fiscal impact analysis using the national income accounting identity (as set forth in chapter 4), the implicit assumption is that output is constant and a reduction in government spending reduces resource use and hence induces a reduction in the trade deficit. But macroeconomic models such as the FRB/Global (and even the simple general equilibrium model developed in appendix 4A of this study) instead allow response of output to the fiscal shock. Consider the implications for the trade balance. In difference form, the trade balance change from the national accounts identity becomes:

$$\Delta TB = \Delta X - \Delta M = \Delta Y - \Delta G - \Delta C - \Delta I \qquad (5A.4)$$

In the short term, and with a (neo-) Keynesian multiplier of close to unity,[58] a fiscal stimulus of dG will prompt a rise in output by $dY = dG$.

---

58. See, in particular, Blanchard and Perotti (2002).

If the model treats consumption and investment responses as sluggish, then in the short run, all that happens is that there is a boost in output that is identical to the increase in government spending, and nothing else changes.[59] There is no impact on the trade balance whatsoever.

Now consider the long run, which may be anywhere from three to five years and beyond. No reasonable macro model will allow long-run output to exceed capacity, so a fiscal stimulus will eventually have to be offset by reduced demand elsewhere in the system if the economy starts at full capacity. The Erceg, Guerrieri, and Gust (2005) model, as described in the main text of this chapter, suppresses demand back to capacity levels by strong negative feedback working through higher interest rates and a strong impact of the interest rate on investment and consumption. The model also suppresses consumption through Ricardian equivalence that directly offsets half of the fiscal shock as well as a fiscal reaction function, which means that the fiscal shock itself is eventually reversed. But the central question for the trade balance is whether this specification of the system's adjustment overstates adjustment of the domestic demand variables rather than the change in exports minus imports.

The long-run adjustment can be represented as follows:

$$\Delta(X - M) = \Delta Y - \Delta G - \Delta I - \Delta C \qquad (5A.5)$$
$$= 0 - \Delta G - (\partial I/\partial i)(\partial i/\partial Y)d\hat{Y} - (\partial C/\partial i)(\partial i/\partial Y)d\hat{Y} - (\partial C/\partial G)\Delta G$$

Here the interim increase in output above full capacity is represented as $d\hat{Y}$. This excess output induces the monetary authorities to raise interest rates (i) by the amount $(\partial i/\partial Y)d\hat{Y}$. This increase in interest rates then induces a decline in investment by the amount: $(\partial I/\partial i)(\partial i/\partial Y)d\hat{Y}$. Similarly, the rise in the interest rate induces a corresponding decline in consumption (fourth right-hand side term). Consumption also falls because of Ricardian equivalence (fifth right-hand side term). If the partial derivatives of investment and consumption with respect to the interest rate are large enough, and if the Ricardian reduction in consumption is large enough, then the entire right-hand side can go to zero and leave no room for change in the trade balance on the left-hand side. This same result can obtain with even smaller responsiveness to the interest rate and smaller Ricardian offset if there is a fiscal reaction function that squeezes down ΔG to well below its initial level.

Now suppose instead that the coefficients of investment and consumption on the interest rate, and the degree of Ricardian offset and fiscal reaction, are smaller. Consider furthermore the effect of the exchange rate (e) on exports and imports. Then we can write:

---

59. That is, if $\Delta G = dG$ and $\Delta Y = \Delta G$ while $\Delta C = \Delta I = 0$, then equation 5A.4 becomes: $\Delta X - \Delta M = dG - dG = 0$.

$$\Delta X - \Delta M = (\partial X/\partial e)(\partial e/\partial i)(\partial i/\partial Y)(d\hat{Y}) \qquad \text{(5A.6)}$$
$$- (\partial M/\partial e)(\partial e/\partial i)(\partial i/\partial Y)(d\hat{Y}) = RHS$$

where RHS is the right-hand side of equation 5A.5. This time we specifically consider the impact of the exchange rate on exports and imports.[60] If the parameters for the partial derivatives of exports and imports with respect to the exchange rate are large enough, and if the derivative of the exchange rate with respect to the interest rate is large enough, the allocation of the adjustment back to capacity output will be distributed much more toward a decline in the trade balance rather than solely a decline in domestic demand. Neither the left-hand side (trade balance change) nor the right-hand side (domestic demand change) will be zero; instead, there will be a decline in the trade balance in addition to the decline in domestic demand for consumption and investment.

---

60. No income effect on imports is included because in the long-run version income must return to the original level.

6

Impact of the US External Imbalance on the Rest of the World

From the mid-1990s through 2004, the US economy served as the main source of demand growth among industrial countries, and hence as the locomotive for the global economy. This would have been true even if the United States had not experienced a rising trade deficit. The widening trade deficit has, however, amplified the role of the United States in leading world demand growth. At the same time, the rising US call on global capital flows to finance its external deficit means that there were potentially adverse effects on the rest of the world through higher interest rates. On balance, however, it would appear that the favorable output demand effects have greatly exceeded any adverse interest rate effects.

Impact on Global Demand

Figure 6.1 shows the share of the US economy in world GDP, which rose from 26.5 percent in 1992 to a peak of 32.5 percent in 2001 before easing to 28.9 percent in 2004.[1] The rise through 2002 reflected not only more rapid real growth in the US economy than in the rest of the world, particularly Europe and Japan, but also the valuation effect of a strengthening dollar and hence larger value of US GDP when compared with foreign currency GDPs translated into dollars. The downturn of the dollar in 2003 and 2004 was the main reason for the partial reversal of the rising share in world nominal GDP.

---

1. World dollar GDP data are from the International Monetary Fund (IMF 2005b). The US current account deficit is from the Bureau of Economic Analysis (BEA 2005c).

Figure 6.1 US share in world GDP (left) **and US current account deficit relative to rest-of-world GDP** (right), **1992–2004** (percent)

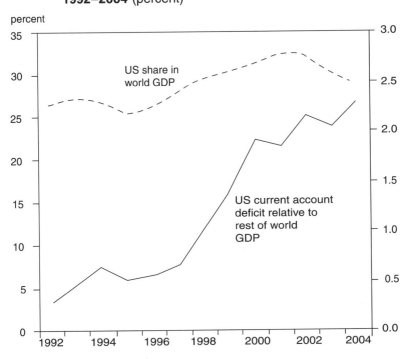

percent

Sources: IMF (2005b); BEA (2005c).

The figure also shows (on the right-hand scale) the US current account deficit expressed as a percentage of the dollar-equivalent GDP of the rest of the world. This rose from 0.28 percent in 1992 to 1.92 percent in 2000 and 2.31 percent in 2004. On this basis, it can be said that *the widening of the US current account deficit after 1992 contributed to an increase in demand for the rest of the world that reached the equivalent of about 2 percent of rest-of-world GDP annually by 2004.*

This positive demand shock for the rest of the world turns out to have been much more powerful for developing countries than for developed countries (figure 6.2). Based on merchandise trade data (IMF 2004d), the trade surplus of the industrial countries with the United States rose from about 0.3 percent of their aggregate GDP in 1992 to about 0.8 percent in 2002. The corresponding trade surplus of developing countries with the United States rose much more, relatively, from 1 percent of their GDP in 1992 to 4.7 percent in 2002.[2]

---

2. The dollar GDP magnitudes are from the World Bank (2004a). For compatibility with the World Bank GDP data, the IMF country categories for trade data are adjusted by shifting

Figure 6.2 Developed and developing countries' aggregate trade balances with the United States, 1992 and 2002 (percent of their aggregate GDP)

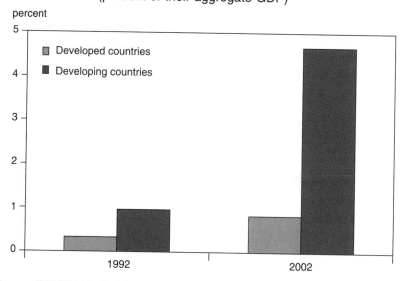

Sources: IMF (2004d); World Bank (2004a).

For some key US trading partners, the increase in demand from a rising trade balance with the United States was especially large. As shown in figure 6.3, Canada's trade surplus with the United States rose from about 1.5 percent of Canadian GDP in 1992 to about 6.5 percent in 2003.[3] For Mexico, the increase was even larger, from −1.5 percent of GDP in 1992 to +6.5 percent in 2003, with most of the increase occurring in a surge in 1995 following the Mexican peso crisis. China's trade surplus with the United States reached the highest share of GDP among the top five trading partners of the United States, at 8.8 percent of China's GDP in 2003 (up from 3.9 percent in 1992).

In contrast, the size of the trade surplus with the United States relative to partner GDP remained much more modest for the European Union, rising from near zero in 1992 to 0.9 percent in 2003; and in Japan, where the level was somewhat higher but the increase was smaller (from 1.3 percent of GDP in 1992 to a peak of 1.7 percent in 2000 before easing to 1.5 percent in 2003).

Figure 6.4 shows further detail within the broad pattern of more dramatic increases in the bilateral trade balance with the United States for

Hong Kong, Singapore, and Israel from developing (IMF) to developed (the World Bank's "high-income" countries).

3. For figures 6.3 and 6.4, bilateral trade balances are from US International Trade Commission (2005), and dollar GDP data are calculated from the IMF (2004b).

Figure 6.3 Trade balances with the United States relative to partner-country GDP: Five largest US trading partners, 1992–2003 (percent)

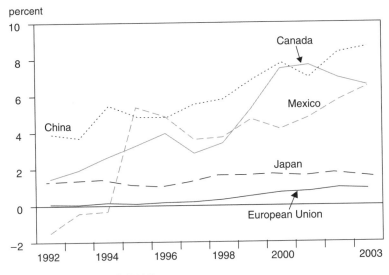

Sources: IMF (2004b); USITC (2005).

developing than for developed countries. The figure also shows a pattern of larger increases for Asian than for Latin American economies.[4] The timing of the Asian increases, moreover, shows the strong influence of external adjustment following the 1997–98 East Asian currency crises.

An obvious question raised by the pattern of large increases in trade balances with the United States is whether the adjustment of the US external imbalance will not only halt but at least partially reverse a strong source of demand contributing to growth in many trading partner countries over the past 12 years. In some cases, the magnitudes of the increases may be misleading for purposes of assessing total demand impact, because the countries in question may have experienced falling trade balances with other countries such that their overall trade balances did not rise by as much as their balances with the United States. Nonetheless, for the developing countries as a whole, the balance on goods and services swung from −1.8 percent of GDP in 1992 to +1.3 percent in 2002 (IMF 2000, 2002). This increase by 3.1 percentage points of GDP is broadly consistent with the 3.7 percentage point increase in their aggregate bilateral trade balances with the United States (figure 6.2).

---

4. With the remarkable exception of Venezuela, where the bilateral surplus with the United States reached 16 percent of GDP in 2003 and the overall trade surplus reached 20 percent of GDP.

Figure 6.4 Trade balances with the United States relative to partner-country GDP: Selected emerging-market economies, 1992–2003 (percent)

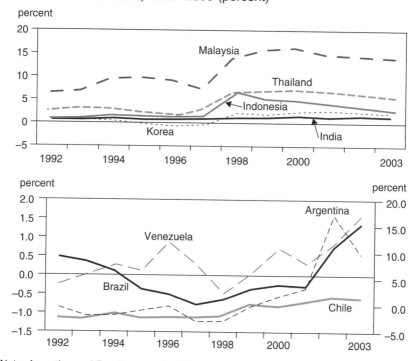

Note: Argentina and Brazil are on the left axis; Chile and Venezuela are on the right axis.
Sources: IMF (2004b); USITC (2005b).

The contribution of the rising US current account deficit to demand in other countries is of course related to the phenomenon of a decline in domestic investment demand in East Asia (excluding China) and Latin America examined in the previous chapter in connection with the "global saving glut" hypothesis. Even though the analysis there concluded that the widening of the US current account deficit was mainly the consequence of domestic US economic and policy developments (in particular, falling private saving and the swing from fiscal surplus to large deficit), it is nonetheless true that East Asia and Latin America in particular obtained an important source of demand stimulus from the rising US external deficit at a time when their domestic investment was weakening.

Impact on Interest Rates

Although the widening US current account deficit played an important role in the past decade in stimulating demand for net exports from the

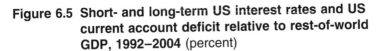

Figure 6.5 Short- and long-term US interest rates and US current account deficit relative to rest-of-world GDP, 1992–2004 (percent)

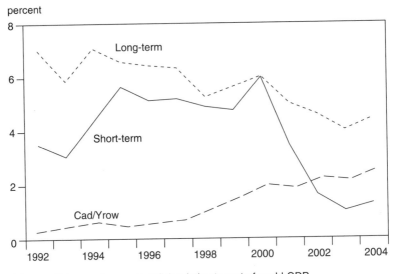

Cad/Yrow = US current account deficit relative to rest-of-world GDP

Sources: International Monetary Fund (2004b); see figure 6.1.

rest of the world, especially from developing countries, it is conceivable that this effect was offset by a contractionary influence of induced higher world interest rates. In the world capital markets, the rising US demand for financing its external deficit must have exercised some upward pressure on interest rates.

As it turned out, although rising interest rates might have been anticipated if all else had remained equal, all else did *not* remain equal, and instead this period was marked by falling rates. As shown in figure 6.5, the only subperiod when the US current account deficit (relative to rest-of-world GDP) and US interest rates moved notably in the same direction was 1998–2000.[5] This was the height of the domestic US economic boom and stock market bubble, and the modest uptick in interest rates (from about 5 to 6 percent for both short- and long-term rates) reflected more the response of US monetary authorities to domestic economic conditions than any tightening in world capital markets forcing the US government and firms to pay higher rates on borrowing abroad. The plunge in interest rates through 2003, in turn, reflected aggressive monetary and fiscal policy designed to ensure what the International Monetary Fund (IMF) Chief

---

5. Long-term rates are for the 10-year bond; short-term rates are for three-month treasury bills (IMF 2004b).

Economist Kenneth Rogoff called "the best recovery that money can buy" (IMF 2003b).

In short, it would be difficult to make the case that, in the past decade, the call of the United States upon the world capital markets to finance its external deficits has exerted a major contractionary influence abroad, operating through the induced effect on world interest rates. The net effect of the widening US external deficit on foreign demand and growth has thus almost certainly been positive.

This evaluation does not mean, however, that the net effect would necessarily continue to be benign into the indefinite future if the United States were to not adjust its external deficit. On the contrary, failure of the United States to adjust its external imbalance would progressively raise the probability of a financial crisis involving a sharp rise in the interest rate and a US recession, and hence reduction in demand for imports. The chances of a net adverse effect of continuation of the large US current account deficit on the rest-of-world economy would thus seem much higher in the future than revealed by the favorable (from this standpoint) experience of the past decade.

Emerging-Market Capital Supply and Current Account Performance

The US current account deficit remained in the vicinity of about 1.5 percent of GDP from 1993–97. It was only at the start of 1998 that the period of explosive widening of the deficit arrived, with the deficit rising to about 2½ percent of GDP in 1998 and 4½ percent by 2000 (see figure 3.2 in chapter 3). Undoubtedly, the driving force in the period of rapid increase in the deficit was the strong entry of foreign private capital in response to the economic and stock market boom. However, a contributing factor was the large swing in the external accounts of a number of emerging-market economies adopting sharp external adjustment following crises. These included the East Asian economies after their crises in 1997–98, and Russia, Brazil, and eventually, Argentina. Figures 6.3 and 6.4 above showed in particular the large rise in East Asian trade surpluses with the United States, a reflection of these external adjustments.

Two questions arise about these trends. First, did the surge in the US current account deficit in some way deprive emerging-market economies of capital that otherwise would have flowed to them instead of to the United States? Second, did the enormous increase in reserves of developing countries in this period constitute a heavy economic burden for these countries, somehow imposed on them by an unstable international financial system? The answer here to the first question is no, and to the second, largely no.

Figure 6.6 Net capital flows to the United States and emerging-market economies (total and private foreign), 1992–2004

billions of dollars

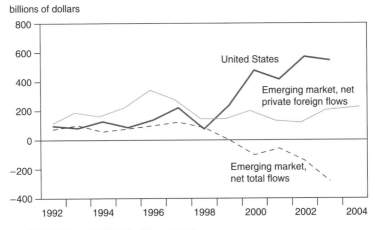

Sources: IMF (2004e); IIF (2004); Cline (2001).

As for the first question, it is certainly true that there was a sharp increase in capital flows to the United States that coincided with a period of weak capital flows to developing countries. As shown in figure 6.6, net capital inflows to the United States were in the range of $100 billion to $200 billion annually over 1994–99, but surged to the range of $400 billion to $600 billion annually over 2000–03 (IMF 2004e, 184–85). In contrast, total net capital inflows to emerging-market countries (defined broadly to include Hong Kong, Israel, Korea, Singapore, and Taiwan) fell from an earlier plateau of about $100 billion annually to about −$300 billion by 2003. If instead the focus is on net private *foreign* capital flows to major emerging-market economies, the bulk of the decline had already occurred by 1998, and flows were relatively flat, in a range of $150 billion to $200 billion during 1999–2004 (Institute of International Finance 2004, Cline 2001). The concept of foreign capital flows excludes capital flows of residents of these countries, and hence does not deduct resident outflows, which in some circumstances (as in the case of Russia) amounted to large capital flight.[6]

Whichever definition of capital flows to developing countries is used, it is evident that there was a substantial scaling back after their peak in 1996–97, just as the phase of much higher capital inflows to the United States began. Yet it would be incorrect to attribute the cutback in flows to emerging markets to a diversion into the United States. The principal cause of the cutback for emerging markets was the reaction to the series

---

6. Note also that the Institute of International Finance data on flows to major emerging-market economies exclude Hong Kong, Israel, Singapore, and Taiwan.

Figure 6.7 Current account balance, United States and developing countries, 1992–2004 (billions of dollars)

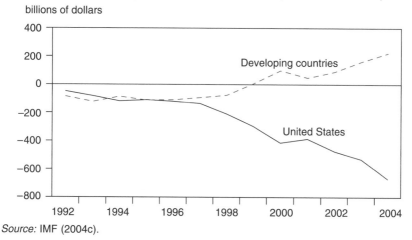

billions of dollars

Source: IMF (2004c).

of financial crises beginning with that of East Asia. This reaction included an initial phase of capital market confidence shock and rising risk premiums, followed by a phase of cutbacks in country demand for capital as trade balances surged in response to a sharp depreciation of exchange rates. The true test of whether a siphoning off of global capital by the United States was also a cause of shrinking flows to emerging markets is whether the period was characterized by rising or falling world interest rates. That is, the interest rate is the price of capital. If the dominant influence had been a surge in demand on global capital markets from the rising US trade deficits, the price of capital—the interest rate—would have risen. But as just seen (figure 6.5), at least after 2000, interest rates fell sharply rather than rising. As noted above, if the US deficits were to continue to worsen in the future, the claim on global capital markets could begin to push up interest rates and become a source of displacement of capital flows to developing countries. So far, however, that has not happened.

The counterpart of the trend toward higher net capital inflows into the United States and lower net inflows to developing countries has been a widening US current account deficit accompanied by a shift from deficit into surplus for developing country current account balances in the aggregate. From 1992 through 1997, both the US deficit and the developing country deficit amounted to about $100 billion annually (figure 6.7). But beginning in 1998, the two paths diverged sharply, as the US deficit rose to about $670 billion by 2004 and the developing countries continued a new pattern of a rising current account surplus (which reached about $200 billion).[7]

---

7. This time, the developing-country aggregate used is from the IMF's (2004c) *World Economic Outlook* grouping, except that Korea has been added back into the developing-country total.

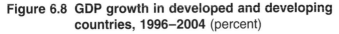

Figure 6.8 GDP growth in developed and developing countries, 1996–2004 (percent)

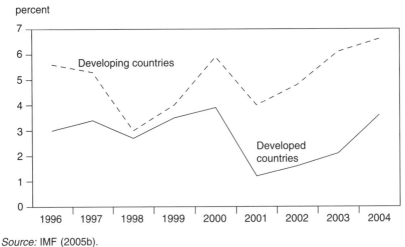

percent

Source: IMF (2005b).

In principle, the swing of developing countries into current account surplus could be a cause for concern. The current account deficit represents a net inflow of real resources that can contribute to development. A current account surplus indicates instead that the country is transferring real resources abroad. The result could be less availability of imported inputs for production and imported capital equipment for investment. But it turns out that far from undermining growth in developing countries, the shift into current account surplus in recent years has instead been associated with a return to rapid economic growth. As indicated in figure 6.8, after a severe drop with the East Asian crisis in 1998 (which was before the rising current account balance really began), growth in developing countries returned to high levels in 2000–04 (despite a moderate drop in the global recession year of 2001).[8]

The explanation of what otherwise might be a paradox is that, to a major extent, developing-country growth in recent years has been led by exports. Rising exports buoyant enough to bring a swing from current account deficit to surplus have been a leading force in overall GDP growth. So once again, although it might have been possible that a widening US trade deficit would curb developing-country growth by siphoning off global capital, increasing interest rates, and thereby pushing these countries into recession, which would have been a story consistent with rising

The *World Economic Outlook* excludes Hong Kong, Korea, Singapore, and Taiwan from developing countries and places them in the developed country category.

8. Once again, the growth figures are from the IMF's *World Economic Outlook* and hence place Hong Kong, Korea, Singapore, and Taiwan in the developed country category.

current account surpluses because of falling developing-country imports, the outcome was much more favorable. Not only did the larger US claims on global capital not impose high global interest rates, but in addition, the widening US trade deficit became a major source of stimulus for higher growth in developing countries through an export boom, so that the rising current account balances of these countries were a sign of economic strength rather than weakness. Indeed, the principal question has become whether this "co-dependency" (as so termed by Mann 2004), in which developing countries (and Japan and Europe) depend heavily on US demand for growth, can continue in light of the need for the United States to adjust its external imbalance.

Developing-Country Reserves: Burden or Bonanza?

The pattern of global growth associated with rising trade deficits in the United States and rising trade surpluses (or falling deficits) in emerging-market economies has resulted in a rapid run-up in the reserves of East Asian economies in recent years. As shown in figure 6.9, the reserves of the four newly industrialized economies (NIEs) of Hong Kong, Taiwan, Korea, and Singapore more than doubled from about $270 billion in 1997 to $580 billion in 2003. China's reserves nearly tripled to more than $400 billion during the same period. For all other developing countries as a group, reserves nearly doubled, from about $500 billion to about $1 trillion. Moreover, these increases sharply outpaced the corresponding increases in imports, boosting the ratio of reserves to imports to about 100 percent or more in the four NIEs and China by 2003, and from 41 percent in 1997 to 54 percent by 2003 for all other developing countries.

Stiglitz (2003) has argued that the rise in developing-country reserves is a serious burden for these countries that is imposed by flaws in the international financial system. Focusing on the aftermath of the East Asian financial crisis in 1997–98, he emphasizes that when a developing country adds another $100 million to reserves, and receives perhaps 1.5 percent interest on US treasury bills but must pay perhaps 8 percent in issuing domestic bonds to purchase the dollars, the country experiences a loss ($6.5 million annually, in this example) that could be avoided if the international system had some form of readily available special drawing rights or other financing to provide liquidity in a squeeze.[9] The Stiglitz critique raises the possibility that part of the overall pattern of global development in recent years associated with the widening US trade deficit has been a

9. His examples are more extreme—such as domestic interest rates at 16 percent—but also less representative.

Figure 6.9 Developing-country reserves: Total and relative to imports, 1992–2003

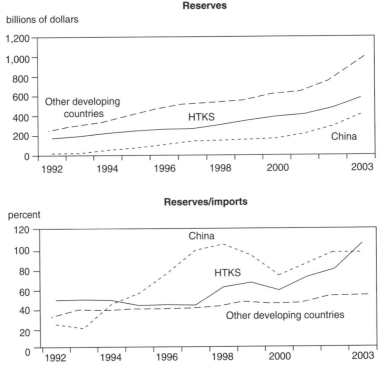

Reserves

billions of dollars

Other developing countries

HTKS

China

Reserves/imports

percent

China

HTKS

Other developing countries

HTKS = Hong Kong, Taiwan, Korea, and Singapore
Source: IMF (2004b).

burden placed on developing countries as a consequence of their associated rise in reserves.

The notion of involuntary recourse to building costly reserves may have been of some relevance at the peak of the East Asian financial crisis. However, by now, the buildup of reserves has far surpassed any magnitude that might be attributed to such externally imposed shocks, and is instead almost certainly a manifestation of a preferred policy of export-led growth. Certainly for East Asia, the ballooning of reserves by now has all of the characteristics of a bonanza rather than a burden.

Perhaps the simplest test of this proposition is whether the rise in reserves is well beyond what might be needed for security against a crisis. As noted, the ratio of reserves to imports has surged. Indeed, for the four NIEs, the nominal dollar value of imports was actually modestly lower by 2003 (at $540 billion) than in 1997 ($600 billion) (IMF 2004b). Surely by now, if the holding of reserves were such a burden, these countries would have begun to spend some of their reserve cache on more imports.

Nor is prudence against the risk of short-term debt runoff the explanation, at least not any more. For example, Korea's short-term external debt in 1997 reached a precariously high level of 315 percent of reserves (Institute of International Finance 1999, 25). But by 2003, much of Korea's short-term debt had been run down, and with higher reserves, the ratio of short-term debt to reserves was only 29.9 percent. Indeed, with rapid repayment of short-term debt after the end-1997 crisis, the ratio had already fallen sharply to 57 percent by end-1999 (Deutsche Bank 2004). So the continued buildup in reserves has reflected an export-led growth strategy and the desire to keep the currency from appreciating too rapidly, not an outwardly imposed need to hold costly reserves.

East Asian Exchange Rate Rigidity

Indeed, by now, far from being the victims of international financial imbalances, the East Asian economies are arguably an important part of the cause of these imbalances. The reason is that their exchange rates have remained relatively rigidly fixed against the US dollar at a time when major currencies of industrial countries have appreciated against the dollar in the beginning of a much-needed process of adjustment in the US external imbalance. China, Hong Kong, and Malaysia have all maintained unchanged fixed exchange rates against the dollar for the past several years. Figure 6.10 shows the paths of East Asian currencies against the dollar, along with those of the yen and the euro, against the base period of March 31, 2002 (essentially at the dollar's peak). Whereas the euro rose 55 percent and the yen 30 percent against the dollar (through end-2004), there was no rise for China, Hong Kong, and Malaysia ("ChHKM" in the figure), and the rise was only about 10 percent for Singapore, Thailand, and Taiwan. Although the Korean won finally rose to close to the yen's total appreciation by end-2004, its rise was substantially delayed.

Kamin (2005) convincingly argues that East Asian governments (excluding China) intervened to keep their exchange rates attractive for export expansion in the years after the 1997–98 East Asian financial crisis in order to maintain demand in the face of a collapse in domestic investment. Investment fell because it had been excessive and misallocated before the crisis, firms sought to correct excessive precrisis debt levels, and domestic banking systems nearly collapsed. Kamin draws the corresponding inference that once domestic investment demand returns to more normal levels, the monetary authorities will desist from intervention to keep exchange rates highly competitive, and indeed will need to do so in order to prevent the development of inflationary pressures.

On July 21, 2005, China announced that it was shifting to a managed floating exchange rate regime, and Malaysia also announced it had ended

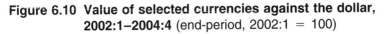

Figure 6.10 Value of selected currencies against the dollar, 2002:1–2004:4 (end-period, 2002:1 = 100)

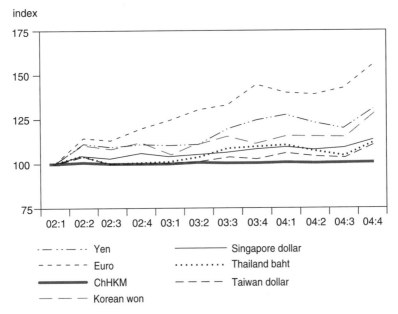

index

ChHKM = Chinese yuan, Hong Kong dollar, and Malaysian ringgit

Source: IMF (2005a).

its fixed rate against the dollar (although Hong Kong maintained its fixed peg to the dollar). China revalued the yuan 2.1 percent against the dollar and stated that it would henceforth manage the currency against a basket of other currencies, with weights not announced. It also indicated the maximum fluctuation against the dollar would be limited to $+/-0.3$ percent daily. Although the end of the long-standing fixed rate regime for the Chinese currency was potentially extremely important, most observers doubted that the float would be managed in a manner that would permit the yuan to rise by more than a few percentage points against the dollar within the next several months.[10]

Despite the new shift to a managed float, China's exchange rate policy may continue to be a serious obstacle to a return to less intervention (and hence currency appreciation) in the rest of East Asia. Goldstein (2004) had called for an appreciation of the Chinese currency against the dollar by 15 to 25 percent (far above the revaluation adopted), and a new peg set not just against the dollar but against a basket of currencies (as China decided to do). It is highly likely that without a much larger appreciation

---

10. "China Revalues the Renminbi," *Financial Times*, July 21, 2005, 1.

of the Chinese renminbi, the other main fixed or quasi-fixed exchange rates in the region (the Hong Kong dollar, Taiwan dollar, and possibly still the Malaysian ringgit) will remain essentially unchanged against the dollar, and that even the somewhat more flexible exchange rates of several other countries in the region (such as the Thai baht and Singapore dollar) will change little against the dollar because of concerns over loss of competitiveness against China. More exchange rate flexibility and significant appreciation of the East Asian currencies against the dollar will almost certainly have to be part of the solution to the problem of achieving a smooth US adjustment of its external imbalance.

It is a fair question to ask, however, whether an abrupt end to Chinese and East Asian currency intervention might not be a cure that at least temporarily aggravates rather than heals the disease. The vulnerability of US interest rates to a sudden cessation of foreign official purchases of US Treasury obligations is discussed in chapter 5. The basic answer to this question is that the size of any such shock would likely be limited. The appropriate adjustment would involve a parallel shift toward fiscal adjustment in the United States, which would tend to reduce interest rates and ameliorate or more than offset any upward pressure from an end to foreign official purchases of US government bonds. In any event, it would seem misguided to seek to perpetuate undervalued East Asian currencies, and hence prolong US external imbalances, for fear of interest rate pressures resulting from the correction of those currencies.

Achieving Global Adjustment

Lessons from the 1980s

The analysis above suggests that the widening of the US current account deficit over the past dozen years has provided an ongoing stimulus to demand for the rest of the world. Looking forward, a central question is whether and how the United States can achieve external adjustment without causing contractionary pressure on the world economy by shifting from creating to reducing demand for goods and services from the rest of the world. A useful place to start is to review what happened to the world economy the last time the United States went through a major balance of payments adjustment cycle, in the late 1980s.[11]

The United States swung into large current account deficit in the mid-1980s as a consequence of a strong dollar, high domestic growth, and a move into large fiscal deficits. The Reagan tax cuts stimulated the economy but left fiscal accounts much eroded. The federal budget deficit widened

---

11. For an analysis of that episode, see Cline (1994, chapter 2).

from 2.6 percent of GDP in 1981 to 5.1 percent in 1985 (Council of Economic Advisers 2004). The Treasury bill rate had peaked at 14.4 percent in 1981 as the Federal Reserve Board under Paul Volcker applied tight monetary policy to combat the inflation rate that reached nearly 14 percent in 1980. Monetary policy eased in response to the deep recession of 1982, but after falling to 8.6 percent by 1983, the interest rate rose to 9.4 percent in 1984 (when inflation edged up to 4.3 percent from its 3.2 percent pace in 1983) (IMF 2004b). The high US interest rate attracted capital from abroad, boosting demand for the dollar and raising the real exchange rate by 41 percent from its 1978 annual average to its 1985 average.[12] Real growth surged to 7 percent in 1984. With a strong income effect on imports, a strong price effect from the exchange rate, and a wide underlying fiscal gap, the external current account deficit widened rapidly. The deficit reached a peak of 3.4 percent of GDP in 1987, up from nearly zero in 1981–82.

The adjustment process in the 1980s episode included a coordinated effort by the Group of Seven (G-7) governments to correct the overvaluation of the dollar, notably through the September 1985 Plaza Agreement of G-7 finance ministers. Joint intervention in the exchange market helped ensure continuation of the nascent reduction in the value of the dollar begun earlier that year. The dollar fell in real terms by about 13 percent in 1986, another 8 percent in 1987, and another 7 percent in 1988. Concern that the dollar was overshooting downward led to the G-7 Louvre Accord in February 1987 calling for intervention to support the dollar, but the dollar continued to decline (for example, by 36 percent against the deutsche mark from end-1985 to end-1987).

The major reversal of the dollar was not accompanied by forceful US fiscal adjustment, as the 1986 fiscal reform was broadly revenue-neutral. Nonetheless, the US fiscal deficit narrowed to 3.2 percent of GDP by 1987 and 2.8 percent by 1989 (Council of Economic Advisers 2004). After the usual two-year lag from exchange rate signal to trade performance, the US current account deficit peaked in 1987 and then significantly narrowed by 1989, reflecting a response to the correction in the dollar and the improving fiscal accounts. Even so, it was not until the US economy slowed in 1990 and went into recession in 1991 that the current account deficit largely disappeared, suggesting that although the external adjustment process "worked" for the United States in the 1980s episode, it was less than fully satisfactory.

Figure 6.11 shows the course of the US current account deficit during this episode.[13] The cycle lasted a decade, with the initial period of wider

---

12. Or from 86.7 to 122.4 on the Federal Reserve's broad real exchange rate index (March 1973 = 100). See Federal Reserve (2005b).

13. The data for 1991 have been adjusted to place the current account at a deficit of $48 billion instead of the recorded surplus of $3.7 billion, to remove the aberrational influence of the large payments received from the Gulf states in support of the 1990 Gulf War. (US

Figure 6.11 US current account (percent of GDP) **and growth in the United States, other G-7 nations, and the rest of the world** (percent), **1981–94**

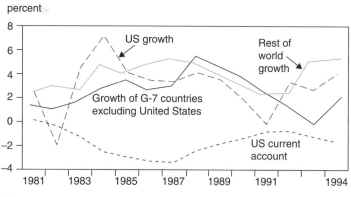

Source: See text.

deficits spread over six years and the reversal accomplished during the subsequent four years. The initial sharp decline in the current account coincided with extraordinary domestic growth (1984) and the endpoint of return to near balance coincided with recession (1991).

Figure 6.11 also reports growth in the major industrial countries (excluding the United States) as well as the rest of the world.[14] Although one should be extremely cautious in applying "ocular econometrics," there is an uncanny mirror image between the growth rate for the rest-of-world category and the size of the US current account deficit in this period. As the US current account deficit narrowed from 3.4 percent of GDP in 1987 to 0.8 percent in 1991–92, rest-of-world growth (excluding the G-7) eased from 5.2 to 2.5 percent. Average growth in the G-7 nations excluding the United States fell from 5.3 percent in 1988 to 2.2 percent in 1991. As reunification in Germany spurred higher interest rates and spillover recession in Europe, and as Japan entered the postbubble period of the early 1990s, growth in those six other G-7 nations fell to zero by 1993 before recovering moderately.

At the most aggregate level, then, the 1980s episode of US external adjustment showed successful correction of the dollar and external deficit, and this process avoided the severe "hard landing" feared by some at the time (Marris 1985). Even so, the extent of the correction was "helped" by a mild US recession, and the evidence at best shows a mixed perfor-

government grants reported in the balance of payments swung from net outflows of $10.4 billion in 1990 to net inflows of $29 billion in 1991 before returning to −$16.3 billion in 1992; BEA 2004c.)

14. G-7 growth (excluding the United States) and rest-of-world growth rates are calculated from the IMF (2004f).

mance in terms of the impact of the US adjustment on the rest of the world. Of course, many other influences played a role. These notably included an increase in average oil prices by about 30 percent in 1990 when Iraq invaded Kuwait, German reunification, the European exchange rate mechanism crisis that saw forced devaluations by Italy and the United Kingdom, and the collapse of the bubble economy in Japan.[15] Nonetheless, the growth record abroad during the correction of the US external imbalance in the late 1980s suggests, at the least, that policymakers will need to be alert to adverse growth effects internationally in the next few years as the United States experiences the corrective phase of the present balance of payments cycle.

A Blueprint for International Adjustment

Chapter 3 suggests that it would require a real appreciation of trade-weighted foreign currencies against the dollar by 21 percent from the January–May 2005 level, combined with an acceleration of foreign growth by 0.75 of a percentage point annually for three years, to reduce the baseline current account deficit from about 7½ percent of GDP by 2010 to about 3 percent.[16] Each 10 percent in real foreign appreciation cuts about 1.6 percent of GDP off the external deficit by the fifth year (see table 3.5 in chapter 3). Because the rest of the world will have to sustain growth in the face of lower US demand, it is probably unrealistic to count on much help for US adjustment from greater growth abroad than in the baseline. At the same time, it may prove unrealistic to assume that the United States can fully maintain potential growth (set at 3.5 percent in chapter 3) and at the same time achieve the desired external adjustment. The 21 percent real foreign appreciation against the dollar from the recent level thus remains a useful benchmark for examining the extent of further currency realignments required for US external adjustment.

The Federal Reserve's broad real exchange rate index for the dollar stood at an average of 96.6 for January through May 15, 2005.[17] Table 6.1 shows the weight of key individual currencies in the index (Federal Reserve Board 2005a), along with the real appreciation of each country in the index against the dollar from the year-average for 2002 to the average for March 2005, the midpoint of the base period for the projections

---

15. There are grounds for arguing that Japan's experience was in part attributable to the US adjustment process, as the large monetary expansion in Japan that contributed to the asset price bubble reflected the effort to prop up the dollar against the yen by 1987 and after.

16. The foreign appreciation in the adjustment scenario is from two annual tranches of 10 percent, for a total of 21 percent.

17. The base used in chapter 3. For the full first five months of 2005, the average was 96.88. See Federal Reserve Board (2005b).

Table 6.1 Real appreciation from 2002 average to March 2005
(percent)

Country	Weight for United States		Real appreciation against	
	Fed	SSB	Dollar	All countries
Argentina	0.44	0.35	23.1	3.2
Australia	1.25	1.17	44.6	25.5
Brazil	1.79	1.69	29.3	11.2
Canada	16.43	18.54	27.5	21.8
Chile	0.49	0.38	15.3	−1.0
China	11.35	11.09	0.7	−10.4
Colombia	0.41	0.56	16.8	5.3
Czech Republic	—	0.14	41.4	6.0
Denmark	—	0.34	37.3	6.2
Egypt	—	0.20	−12.2	−27.9
Euro area	18.80	17.57	37.5	15.4
Hong Kong	2.33	1.04	−8.8	−16.4
Hungary	—	0.22	49.2	14.3
India	1.14	1.01	15.6	−1.6
Indonesia	0.95	0.75	10.7	−2.6
Israel	1.00	1.00	2.7	−12.9
Japan	10.58	9.80	10.7	−1.0
Korea	3.86	3.46	27.3	15.4
Malaysia	2.24	1.87	−2.3	−12.0
Mexico	10.04	12.13	−8.3	−13.0
New Zealand	—	0.27	56.1	29.9
Norway	—	0.44	24.9	−3.6
Philippines	1.06	0.82	2.3	−6.8
Poland	—	0.18	33.0	−0.3
Russia	0.74	0.71	46.1	15.7
Saudi Arabia	0.61	1.20	−5.1	−18.9
Singapore	2.12	1.45	4.9	−5.2
South Africa	—	0.46	82.0	50.4
Sweden	1.16	0.85	35.4	5.8
Switzerland	1.44	0.98	27.4	−0.3
Taiwan	2.87	2.15	7.3	−2.3
Thailand	1.43	1.21	10.8	−0.9
Turkey	—	0.43	40.4	9.5
United Kingdom	5.17	4.26	28.5	2.0
Venezuela	0.30	1.31	−0.6	−7.3
Total	100.00	100.00		
Fed			16.3	
SSB			16.4	

— = not included

Sources: Federal Reserve Board (Fed) (2005a); Salomon Smith Barney (SSB) and Citigroup (2001); IMF (2005a).

in chapter 3. The (geometrically) weighted sum indicates a real appreciation of foreign currencies against the dollar by 16.3 percent over this period.[18] The table also shows US weights for a larger set of countries, based on estimates by Salomon Smith Barney (2001) and Citigroup. The two weighting schemes show virtually the same weighted foreign appreciation against the dollar.

Table 6.1 also reports the overall trade-weighted real effective appreciation of each of the currencies in question, based on the Salomon Smith Barney weights for the 36 countries listed in the table. These weights are based on both bilateral trade and multilateral trade, with the latter incorporated to capture the influence of competition in third-country markets.[19]

An important pattern evident in the table is that for most countries, the extent of overall real appreciation was far smaller than that of real appreciation against the dollar. For example, Sweden appreciated in real terms by 35.4 percent against the dollar, but because of its high proportion of trade with European countries that also appreciated sharply against the dollar, its currency rose only 5.8 percent on an overall real trade-weighted basis. Even so, for the euro area, the overall real appreciation was sizable, at 15.4 percent. This indicates that the real appreciation of the euro to date cannot be dismissed lightly on grounds that the euro area's trade with the United States alone is relatively small. Indeed, it turns out that in the Salomon Smith Barney weights, the US weight for the euro area is almost identical to the euro area weight for the United States.[20] On this basis, it can be said that changes in the dollar-euro rate are just as important for the United States as for the euro area, and represent about one-sixth of total exchange rate influences for both sides.

A key pattern is that most of the East Asian countries actually experienced real depreciations of their currencies on a trade-weighted basis, as they "rode the dollar downward" because of their pegs to it. China depreciated by 10.4 percent in real effective terms and Hong Kong by

---

18. The corresponding foreign appreciation in the Federal Reserve's broad index itself is 15.6 percent. The difference likely reflects different procedures for projecting consumer price index inflation for recent months with official data not yet available, as well as the fact that the estimates of table 6.1 apply the 2005 weights (essentially a Paasche index with end-period weights), whereas the Federal Reserve uses different weights for each year.

19. The underlying Salomon Smith Barney weights are for 49 countries. The analysis here normalizes by expanding proportionately the weights of each of the 36 countries considered so that they add up to 100 percent. The 36 countries constitute a median of 98 percent of the total trade weights for the 49 countries, and the coverage is 96 percent at the lowest quartile, so normalization to a 36-country set should be relatively reliable.

20. All trade shares for the euro area exclude intratrade among euro-area countries. The weight of the United States in euro-area trade, according to the normalized Salomon Smith Barney data, is 17.2 percent. The weight of the euro area in the trade weights for the United States is 17.57 percent (table 6.1).

16.4 percent. Malaysia and the Philippines depreciated in real effective terms by about 12 and 7 percent respectively. For its part, Japan experienced a slight overall real depreciation (-1 percent change), and even its appreciation against the dollar was modest (10.7 percent). Korea is a somewhat surprising exception to the East Asian pattern, as its real effective exchange rate appreciated by about 15 percent. Greater real appreciation of Korea's currency than that of Japan, despite a comparable nominal appreciation against the dollar, reflects the lower rate of inflation in Japan than in Korea.

Appendix 6A develops a method for identifying a set of "optimal" exchange rate realignments for the purposes of bringing the US current account deficit into a range about 3 percent of GDP by 2010. As set forth in chapter 5, this range would seem to be a reasonable benchmark for a sustainable current account deficit for the United States. In the analysis in the appendix, the idea is to specify the target overall trade-weighted rise in foreign currencies against the dollar needed for this purpose, and then to calculate the composition of currency changes on the basis of economically sensible criteria. The first criterion is that the resulting set of changes in individual-country current account balances should conform as closely as possible to a specified pattern. For purposes of the estimation here, this pattern is determined as a uniform proportionate reduction in the current account surpluses of countries with current account surpluses of 1 percent of GDP or larger. Modest reductions in current account balances are also specified for countries with smaller surpluses or with deficits.[21] It turns out that the proportion required for this approach to generate foreign reductions in current account balances compatible with the target rise in the US balance is a 40 percent cut in the surpluses of countries with current account surpluses of 1 percent of GDP or more.

There are two exceptions. First, the target for Australia is set at zero change, because its current account is already in large deficit. Second, following Williamson (2004), the target for the euro area is also set differently. Williamson called for cutting the euro-area current account surplus to zero, representing a reduction of about $70 billion against the 2004 outcome predicted by the IMF at the time. The actual outcome for 2004 was a surplus only about half as large (table 6A.1). Because of the large economic size of the euro area, its substantial participation in the foreign counterpart of US external adjustment will be especially important. The analysis here maintains the same absolute adjustment as suggested by Williamson, and hence sets the target change in the euro-area current account at -0.7 percent of GDP, or from $+0.4$ percent to -0.3 percent.

---

21. A fixed 0.35 percent of GDP reduction in the current account balance is specified for these countries.

Appendix 6A sets forth a simple method relating expected change in current account balance for each country to the overall (trade-weighted) real appreciation of the country's currency.

As discussed in appendix 6B, Williamson suggests current account adjustment targets of -1.5 percent of GDP for several key countries and regions (China, Japan, the four NIEs, other Asian developing countries, and the Middle East). The approach used here yields about the same adjustments as a percent of GDP for China (-1.7 percent), Japan (-1.5 percent), Korea (-1.6 percent), and the Philippines (-1.8 percent). However, the target adjustments of this study are considerably larger for Singapore (about -10 percent of GDP), Malaysia (-5 percent), and Hong Kong (-4 percent), and for the oil economies (-8 percent of GDP for Saudi Arabia, -5 percent for Venezuela, and -4 percent for Russia). The issue is whether countries with extraordinarily high current account surpluses (such as Singapore's 26 percent of GDP) should be expected to pursue larger adjustments; the judgment here is that they should.[22]

Except for the super-surplus countries, the current account adjustments assumed here are broadly comparable to those assumed by Williamson. Correspondingly, they should also generally conform to his diagnosis that the resulting magnitudes of demand change should be manageable. Even so, as discussed in appendix 6B, if the terms-of-trade effect is taken into account, the real demand changes could be about 1.5 times as high as the nominal changes. At the upper end of Williamson's range of adjustments (1.5 percent of GDP nominal), real demand contraction would be about 2.25 percent of GDP. If spread over three years, this implies that the adjustment process could trim real demand growth by approximately 0.7 percent of GDP per year from rates otherwise attained by Japan, the NIEs, China, and other Asian nations. The impact would be much larger for some of the super-surplus countries if instead their nominal adjustments were on the scale suggested in this study (e.g., a range of 4 to 5 percent of GDP).

The second criterion for the optimal realignment exercise is that although the final set of exchange rate changes can deviate from the amounts that would generate the target set of current account changes, a weighted function of the deviations should be minimized subject to achieving the target real depreciation of the dollar.[23]

---

22. This is also the judgment for oil economies if one expects the price of a barrel of oil to remain in the vicinity of $50, as assumed in chapter 3, so that the high recent surpluses are seen as persistent rather than transitory in the absence of special adjustment measures.

23. Specifically, the sum of GDP-weighted squared deviations of change in the current account as a percent of GDP from the target list of changes as a percent of GDP is chosen as the "objective function" to be minimized. Note further that the real exchange rate for Hong Kong against the US dollar is constrained to rise by no more than 10 percentage points above the increase for China, given the integration of the two economies. As a result,

Table 6.2 reports the results of this optimization exercise. The target overall real appreciation against the dollar on a trade-weighted basis is set at 39 percent from the 2002 average real level. This total appreciation is based on the amount that actually occurred from the 2002 annual average to the January–May 15, 2005 base used in chapter 3, plus another 21 percent for the effect of the favorable adjustment scenario in table 3.4 in chapter 3 (i.e., 1.151 × 1.21 = 1.39).

The table also reports the change in the trade-weighted real exchange rate of each country in the optimal solution. Once again it is evident that these appreciations are far smaller than the bilateral appreciations against the dollar. For the euro area, the optimal real appreciation against the dollar is 44.4 percent from the 2002 level, but the optimal trade-weighted real appreciation is only 7.3 percent.[24] For Japan, the bilateral real appreciation is about 53 percent and the trade-weighted appreciation is about 17 percent. The relatively high overall real appreciation found optimal for Japan reflects the relatively high ratio of its current account surplus to GDP (3.7 percent of GDP surplus in 2004) combined with its relatively low parameter relating change in the current account as a percent of GDP to change in the real exchange rate. As discussed in appendix 6A, this parameter is smaller for more closed economies.

Table 6.2 also shows the extent of real appreciation of each currency against the dollar that occurred from the average for 2002 to the average for March 2005, the midpoint of the base used for the adjustment scenarios of chapter 3. Correspondingly, the table also indicates the additional amount of real appreciation still to be completed to reach the optimal amount. The result is particularly informative for the euro. The euro is found to need an additional real appreciation of only 5 percent against the dollar from the March 2005 level to reach the level indicated in the optimal realignment calculation.[25] Moreover, with general realignment of other currencies, there would be a 7 percent trade-weighted real depreciation rather than appreciation of the euro from the March 2005 level, as the currency once again would become more competitive against those that have lagged behind in the correction against the dollar. The findings

---

Hong Kong is omitted from the objective function. The minimization problem is resolved using the SOLVER function in an Excel spreadsheet.

24. Note, moreover, that the optimal realignment exercise probably overstates somewhat the real effective appreciation for the euro area, because the analysis is implemented using the 26 countries in the Federal Reserve broad index plus the United States, rather than the 36 countries in the Salomon Smith Barney weights of table 6.1. Several omitted Eastern European countries are likely to keep their exchange rates moving closely with the euro, suggesting a somewhat smaller real effective appreciation for the euro area if those partners were included.

25. Note, however, that the March exchange rate of 1.315 $/€ was considerably stronger than the level of 1.206 on July 15, 2005 as this study went to press. Against the latter level, the optimal rise of the euro would be 14.5 percent.

Table 6.2 Optimal exchange rate realignments for US external adjustment^a (percent)

| Country | Real appreciation from 2002 average | | | | Remaining real appreciation to reach optimal amount | |
| | Optimal | | Actual to March 2005 | | | |
	Versus dollar	Overall^b	Versus dollar	Overall^b	Versus dollar	Overall^b
Argentina	40.7	5.2	23.1	3.2	14.3	1.9
Australia	44.2	2.6	44.6	25.5	-0.3	-18.3
Brazil	39.0	7.2	29.3	11.2	7.5	-3.7
Canada	16.9	4.6	27.5	21.8	-8.4	-14.1
Chile	38.3	3.4	15.3	-1.0	19.9	4.5
China	45.9	8.1	0.7	-10.4	44.8	20.6
Colombia	25.7	3.4	16.8	5.3	7.6	-1.8
Euro area	44.4	7.3	37.5	15.4	5.0	-7.0
Hong Kong	55.9	11.1	-8.8	-16.4	70.9	33.0
India	44.5	4.9	15.6	-1.6	24.9	6.6
Indonesia	49.8	5.8	10.7	-2.6	35.4	8.6
Israel	32.9	2.5	2.7	-12.9	29.5	17.7
Japan	53.3	16.7	10.7	-1.0	38.5	17.9
Korea	45.6	6.4	27.3	15.4	14.4	-7.8
Malaysia	55.7	13.3	-2.3	-12.0	59.4	28.8
Mexico	13.6	2.1	-8.3	-13.0	23.9	17.3
Philippines	47.3	6.3	2.3	-6.8	44.0	14.1
Russia	55.6	14.5	46.1	15.7	6.5	-1.0
Saudi Arabia	60.7	22.2	-5.1	-18.9	69.4	50.6
Singapore	87.5	46.2	4.9	-5.2	78.7	54.2
Sweden	49.9	10.2	35.4	5.8	10.7	4.1
Switzerland	55.7	14.9	27.4	-0.3	22.2	15.2
Taiwan	47.7	7.1	7.3	-2.3	37.7	9.6
Thailand	47.2	5.2	10.8	-0.9	32.8	6.2
United Kingdom	42.2	3.1	28.5	2.0	10.7	1.1
Venezuela	31.0	17.7	-0.6	-7.3	31.7	27.0

a. For weighted average real appreciation against dollar by 39 percent.
b. Trade weighted.

are qualitatively quite different for Japan, where real bilateral appreciation against the dollar amounted to only about 11 percent from 2002 to March 2005. This leaves a large additional 38 percent real appreciation of the yen to be completed to reach the optimal realignment. This would mean a further 18 percent real appreciation of the yen on a trade-weighted basis.

The broad pattern in table 6.2 is that the East Asian economies in particular have a long way to go in real appreciation of their currencies against the dollar to reach optimal realignment, but that once again the extent of their corresponding trade-weighted appreciations would be much smaller. For China, the optimal realignment calls for a 46 percent real appreciation against the dollar from the 2002 base, and almost none has occurred so far. Even so, after optimal realignment, the Chinese currency would rise by less than half as much (21 percent) from its March 2005 level on a trade-weighted basis. Korea, in contrast, has gone much further, and with the same target real appreciation against the 2002 base (46 percent) had already carried out well more than half by March 2005. This would leave an additional 14 percent real appreciation against the dollar to be completed, but there would actually be a real depreciation of the Korean won on a trade-weighted basis (by 8 percent) because the size of the remaining correction to be made is much larger for China and most of the other currencies in the region.

The results indicate a sizable real appreciation of the Mexican peso against the dollar, because even though its target total from 2002 is moderate (at 13.6 percent), the currency has depreciated significantly in the interim, meaning that the rise would be a substantial 24 percent against the March 2005 level against the dollar and 17 percent on a trade-weighted basis.[26]

The results for Canada also warrant special mention. The optimal realignment exercise finds that the Canadian currency has already moved by more than enough to contribute the target change in Canada's current account. The Canadian dollar appreciated in real terms by about 28 percent from 2002 to March 2005, which meant a real effective (trade-weighted) appreciation of about 22 percent. If the parameter relating current account change to real exchange rate change is correct, however, the size of the exchange rate change needed to reduce the current account from the 2.6 percent of GDP surplus in 2004 to 1.6 percent (40 percent cut) would be

---

26. Although this diagnosis contradicts the Bénassy-Quéré et al. (2004) result discussed in appendix 6B, it simply involves compatibility with an overall optimization that widens the current account deficit by a modest 0.35 percent of GDP. Even so, this result for Mexico does warrant caution. Note further that for the special case of Mexico, the outcome is constrained to limit the ratio of the calculated change in the current account to the target change to no more than 1.5. In the optimal solution, this constraint is binding, and Mexico's current account deficit rises from 1.3 percent of GDP to 1.82 percent rather than to just 1.65 percent.

smaller (about 17 percent bilateral, 5 percent trade-weighted), allowing some reversal of the Canadian appreciation (by about 8 percent bilateral, 14 percent trade-weighted) rather than requiring further appreciation.

As discussed in appendix 6B, Bénassy-Quéré et al. (2004) find a surprisingly similar profile of desired currency realignments against the dollar for many of the main economies, even though they use an extremely different methodology. Thus, when updated to end-2004, their results indicate needed realignments that are especially close to the estimates reported in table 6.2 for China (46 percent currency rise against the dollar versus 45 percent), Korea (19 versus 14 percent), the euro (-1 versus $+5$ percent), Brazil (5 versus 7 percent), and India (24 versus 25 percent). Their estimates are also broadly similar to those here for Australia (-9 versus -0.3 percent) and Canada (0.5 versus -8.4 percent). Their results are in the same direction but considerably more moderate in magnitude for Japan (22 versus 38 percent) and Indonesia (21 versus 35 percent).[27]

The optimization exercise sets as an absolute constraint that the various currency realignments must add up to a 39 percent real foreign *appreciation* against the dollar on a US trade-weighted basis (28 percent *depreciation* of the dollar) from the annual 2002 level. The resulting deviation of changes in current account balances for other countries from the set of targets is then minimized, but these deviations nonetheless remain significant. The median ratio of the optimal change of the current account balance (as a percent of GDP) to the target change is 1.3. This means that the optimization exercise generates larger reductions in foreign current account positions in the aggregate than would be required to offset the target increase in the US current account balance. This divergence implies either that the parameters chosen to state the responsiveness of the current account to the real exchange rate are too high for the 26 countries in the exercise excluding the United States, or that the responsiveness of the US current account to real depreciation of the dollar should be greater than estimated in the model of chapter 3. The likelihood is that the foreign response parameters tend to be overstated. However, for purposes of obtaining the optimal pattern of currency realignments, all that is needed is for this overstatement to be approximately the same for all of the countries in question. Even so, the optimal realignment results found here should be interpreted as being more robust in terms of overall patterns than for individual countries.

The Stakes for Developing Countries

Achieving a smooth external adjustment instead of a hard landing for the US economy is of great importance for developing countries. Their

---

27. The divergence between their estimates and those here is considerably larger for the United Kingdom (-7 versus $+11$ percent) and especially Mexico (-12 versus $+24$ percent) and Argentina (80 versus 14 percent).

export growth will of course tend to be curbed by deceleration in the growth of US imports and acceleration in growth of US exports. But their cumulative export growth over the medium term would likely be even lower if an additional few years of unsustainably high growth of exports to the US market were to be followed by a sharp fall in these exports because of a plunge in the dollar and recession in the US economy.

US external adjustment does imply some shift in developing-country demand from exports toward domestic investment and consumption. Such a shift would be desirable in terms of global development patterns. As shown in table 6A.1, at present, there is a distorted pattern of global trade and payments in which many developing countries are running current account surpluses rather than deficits. These include the oil-exporting developing countries, the East Asian developing countries, India, and the major Latin American countries (excluding Colombia and Mexico). This is a pattern of perverse resource flows from developing countries to the largest rich country in the world.

The developing countries will also stand to gain from a smooth US external adjustment because it is more likely to keep global interest rates moderate than would be the case with a hard landing. A severe break in confidence in the dollar, after additional years of ever-widening external deficits, would exert upward pressure on US interest rates as foreign capital inflows began to decline, and interest rates could also rise from a decision by the Federal Reserve that tighter monetary policy was required to weigh against the inflationary impact of a sharp decline in the dollar. Inflationary pressure would arise from the pass-through of the exchange rate change to imports, which account for 15 percent of GDP (goods and services), even with incomplete pass-through. Thus, suppose that as a consequence of delay in adjustment, the eventual exchange rate correction required a 60 percent rise in the price of foreign exchange (37.5 percent depreciation of the dollar). Such an exchange rate change, combined with a pass-through ratio of 0.5, would raise import prices by 30 percent, contributing a 4.5 percentage point (30×0.15) increase to the consumer price index. This would be a substantial inflationary shock if concentrated within a year or two. Inflationary pressure would be further aggravated as US supply began to be channeled toward exports and as the supply of foreign goods began to decline in response to the exchange rate change.

Delayed adjustment and an eventual hard landing would mean that a US recession would be part of the adjustment process. A recession would cause an even more severe reduction in developing-country exports to the United States than would a smoother, earlier US adjustment. As for interest rate effects, many developing countries have large outstanding debt that is sensitive to dollar interest rates. A scenario in which interest rates were to soar would increase the cash-flow burden of their external debt and make it more costly for them to issue new debt.

Whereas a hard landing for the US economy would thus tend to cause spillover damage for developing countries, a smooth landing involving some upward exchange rate realignment for these economies against the dollar would provide some benefit to them in the form of a reduction in the real burden of their existing dollar-denominated debt. Ratios of external debt to GDP for countries such as Brazil would ease substantially as the Brazilian currency appreciated relative to the dollar—but very little on a trade-weighted basis—as part of an overall adjustment process.

Policy Coordination Versus Laissez-Faire

For all of these reasons, it is in the broad interests of developing countries for the United States to achieve a smooth external adjustment, even taking into account that such an adjustment will almost certainly require substantial real appreciation of the currencies of many developing countries against the dollar. There is a major question about the feasibility of a general exchange realignment, however, and it turns on the phenomenon called the "new Bretton Woods" payments system by Dooley, Folkerts-Landau, and Garber (2004) (see chapter 5). Despite the doubtful policy conclusion these authors infer about the indefinite sustainability of large US deficits because of this system, they are right in diagnosing the similarity of the current arrangements to the regime of fixed exchange rates against the dollar that existed under Bretton Woods for a wide range of developing countries. The reason is that most of these countries tend to manage their exchange rates rather than allowing a free float—the "fear of floating" phenomenon emphasized by Calvo and Reinhart (2000). For the important cases of China, Hong Kong, and Malaysia, moreover, the fixed rate has been even more rigid, and there is no guarantee that the recent end to the fixed rates in China and Malaysia will mean major appreciations against the dollar.

In the final stages of the Bretton Woods exchange rate regime, it was recognized that achieving a general realignment of fixed exchange rates required coordination. The Smithsonian Agreement in December 1971 involved a devaluation of the dollar against gold, continuation of existing parities against gold for the French franc and British pound sterling, and appreciation against gold for the deutsche mark, yen, and Swiss franc (Cline 1976, 3). Something very much like the Smithsonian Agreement (without the gold) could well be necessary if the large number of countries otherwise essentially pegging to the dollar are to carry out a broad real appreciation against the dollar.

Game theory helps explain why some form of coordination is needed. The classic game of "prisoners' dilemma" shows that an inferior outcome for all parties can arise when they fail to coordinate. In this game, two thieves are arrested and questioned separately. Each is told he will receive a moderate sentence if he confesses but a harsh sentence if he does not confess and the other thief does. Because the thieves cannot communicate to arrive at a joint statement of innocence, there is an incentive for both thieves separately to confess, so that both wind up with a moderate sentence rather than going free.

In the same way, any individual developing country considering whether to allow its exchange rate to rise against the dollar is likely to be concerned about its general loss of competitiveness, and the risk that its currency will be appreciating not only against the dollar but also against all other currencies. In isolation, the country faces a strong incentive to keep its rate against the dollar unchanged. But if a large number of countries enter into a coordination process in which they all agree to appreciate against the dollar, then they can carry out their end of the action needed for US external adjustment while not facing the penalty of making their exports uncompetitive against those of other developing countries. This dynamic is the reason that most analysts consider substantial appreciation of the Chinese renminbi against the dollar to be the key to unlocking a broader set of currency appreciations by most of the East Asian economies against the dollar.

So far, neither the United States nor the other nations of the G-7 have formally called for a Smithsonian-type of general agreement on coordinated appreciation of exchange rates against the dollar. On the contrary, the US position appears to be to "let the market do it." For its part, the IMF has called for US external adjustment, including dollar adjustment, but it has not broached the possibility of a coordinated international initiative for exchange rate realignments. It is time for the United States, the other nations of the G-7, and the IMF to press for such a coordinated international effort. This effort would at the least set ground rules prohibiting further intervention in exchange markets to keep currencies from rising against the dollar for a set of countries diagnosed to be undervalued against the dollar in terms of the need for an overall adjustment of the US external accounts. A more aggressive agreement could call for intervention in the opposite direction (i.e., the selling off of reserves by such countries as China and Korea), as occurred in the Plaza Agreement among major industrial economies in 1987.

Appendix 6A
Optimal Exchange Rate Realignment

Given a target real effective exchange rate appreciation of all currencies against the dollar, what is the optimal country composition of exchange rate changes? Let i refer to countries other than the United States, and let z_i be the proportionate appreciation of country i's currency against the dollar. Let c_i be the desired change of country i's current account balance as a fraction of GDP, determined by some approach that arrives at consistency with the US current account adjustment and some allocational principle for counterpart adjustments by other countries. Let v_i be the actual (as opposed to desired) predicted change in the country's current account as a fraction of GDP; let y_i be the real effective overall appreciation of country i's currency; let γ_i be a parameter stating the change in country i's current account balance as a percent of GDP to be expected from a 1 percent appreciation in the country's real effective exchange rate; let φ_{ij} be the weight of partner j in the trade of country i; and let subscript u refer to the United States.

The objective is to obtain an optimal set of exchange rate appreciations against the dollar, z_i, such that the resulting set of current account changes is as close as possible to the desired set while meeting the condition that for the United States, the real effective appreciation of other currencies against the dollar equals the target amount Z^*. The real effective appreciation of country i will be

$$y_i = \varphi_{iu} z_{iu} + \sum_{j \neq u} \varphi_{ij} z_{ij} \tag{6A.1}$$

where z_{ij} is the real appreciation of the country's currency against the currency of trading partner j. However, whereas the country appreciates against the United States by $z_{iu} \equiv z_i$, it appreciates against another trading partner j by only $z_{ij} = z_{iu} - z_{ju} \equiv z_i - z_j$. So the equation for the effective real appreciation of country i's currency can be rewritten as

$$y_i = \varphi_{iu} z_{iu} + \sum_{j \neq u} \varphi_{ij} (z_i - z_j) = z_i - \sum_{j \neq u} \varphi_{ij} z_j \tag{6A.2}$$

(The final right-hand side follows from the fact that the sum of the US trade weight and all other trade weights must equal unity.) Overall, the country's effective real exchange rate change will depend on the share of the United States and each of the other countries in its trade, in combination with the respective real appreciation rates against the dollar.[28]

---

28. The actual implementation of the analysis uses geometric rather than arithmetic weights. If we redefine y and z as index levels rather than percent changes, it can be shown that the

The expected change in the country's current account as a fraction of GDP will be

$$v_i = y_i \gamma_i \qquad (6A.3)$$

The deviation of the predicted change in the current account from the desired change (both as a fraction of GDP) will then be

$$d_i = v_i - c_i = \gamma_i [z_i - \sum_{j \neq u} \varphi_{ij} z_j] - c_i \qquad (6A.4)$$

We then choose some form of a penalty function for deviation from the desired current account changes. A reasonable penalty function is the square of the deviation, but it is also reasonable to weight by country economic size (GDP). The optimization problem is then to select the set of currency appreciations so as to minimize the penalty function subject to the constraint that the resulting overall real appreciation of US trading partners against the dollar (using US trade weights) equals the target amount. The problem is thus

$$MIN\ W = \sum_i \theta_i d_i^2 \qquad (6A.5)$$

where θ_i is the share of country i in aggregate GDP of US trading partners, subject to

$$Z = \sum_i \alpha_i z_i = Z^* \qquad (6A.6)$$

where α_i is the weight of country i in the broad real exchange rate index of the Federal Reserve Board.

Table 6A.1 reports IMF (2005b) estimates of the 2004 current account balances and GDP values in dollar terms for the 26 trading partners included in the Federal Reserve's broad real exchange rate index for the dollar. A striking feature of this compilation is that several economies, including some oil exporters and also some of the East Asian economies, had exceptionally high current account surpluses of 10 percent of GDP or higher. These and several other countries with surpluses of, say, 3 percent of GDP and more would seem to be excellent candidates for surplus reduction as the counterpart of reduction in the US current account deficit.

More specifically, the table also indicates suggested values for the "desired" reduction in current account positions. The magnitudes indi-

---

geometric analogue to equation 6A.1 is: $y_i = z_i / (\Pi\ z_j\ \varphi_{ij})$, where Π is the product operator and j refers to $j \neq u$.

Table 6A.1 Current account balances, target changes, export ratios, and response parameters for major US trading partners (in billions of dollars, in percent, and in ratios)

Country	Current account[e]	GDP[a]	Current account as percent of GDP	Target change Percent of GDP	Target change Amount	Exports/ GDP[b, c]	Gamma[e]
Argentina	3.1	151.9	2.0	−0.8	−1.2	0.250	−0.23
Australia	−39.4	617.6	−6.4	0.0	0.0	0.181	−0.17
Brazil	11.7	599.7	1.9	−0.8	−4.7	0.169	−0.16
Canada	26.0	995.8	2.6	−1.0	−10.4	0.378	−0.32
Chile	1.4	93.7	1.5	−0.6	−0.6	0.364	−0.31
China	70.0	1,649.4	4.2	−1.7	−28.0	0.344	−0.30
Colombia	−1.0	95.2	−1.1	−0.4	−0.3	0.214	−0.20
Euro area	35.6	9,397.7	0.4	−0.7	−63.8	0.147	−0.14
Hong Kong	15.9	164.6	9.6	−3.9	−6.3	1.722	−0.16
India	2.1	661.0	0.3	−0.4	−2.3	0.146	−0.14
Indonesia	7.3	257.9	2.8	−1.1	−2.9	0.312	−0.27
Israel	0.1	116.3	0.1	−0.4	−0.4	0.384	−0.32
Japan	171.8	4,668.4	3.7	−1.5	−68.7	0.118	−0.12
Korea	26.8	681.5	3.9	−1.6	−10.7	0.382	−0.32
Malaysia	15.7	117.8	13.3	−5.3	−6.3	1.149	−0.47
Mexico	−8.7	676.5	−1.3	−0.4	−2.4	0.284	−0.25
Philippines	3.9	85.1	4.6	−1.8	−1.6	0.491	−0.38
Russia	59.6	582.7	10.2	−4.1	−23.8	0.350	−0.30
Saudi Arabia	49.3	248.8	19.8	−7.9	−19.7	0.470	−0.37
Singapore	27.9	106.8	26.1	−10.4	−11.2	1.580[d]	−0.27
Sweden	28.0	346.5	8.1	−3.2	−11.2	0.439	−0.36
Switzerland	42.9	358.0	12.0	−4.8	−17.1	0.437	−0.35
Taiwan	19.0	305.2	6.2	−2.5	−7.6	0.584	−0.43
Thailand	7.3	163.5	4.5	−1.8	−2.9	0.656	−0.45
United Kingdom	−47.0	2,125.5	−2.2	−0.4	−7.4	0.251	−0.23
United States	−668.1	11,735.0	−5.7	2.7	313.9	0.095	−0.10
Venezuela	14.5	107.5	13.5	−5.4	−5.8	0.370[d]	−0.31
Total	−124.5	37,109.7			−3.5		

a. 2004; b. 2003; c. Goods and services; d. Goods only; e. Change in current account as percent of GDP for 1 percent rise in real exchange rate.

Sources: IMF (2005b); author's calculations.

cated are simply set at a uniform 40 percent reduction in the current account surplus for all countries with surpluses of 1 percent of GDP or more. For other countries (including those in deficit), the adjustment is set at a fixed -0.35 percent of GDP. For Australia, which is already in large deficit, the target is no change in the current account. For euro-area countries, the target change in the current account surplus is set to shift the current account from a surplus of 0.4 percent of GDP to a deficit of 0.3 percent, as discussed in the main text. These targets are set such that the overall reduction in the surplus of these countries is approximately equal to the size of a targeted reduction in the US deficit. The US current account adjustment is set here at a target of $314 billion, which amounts to 2.7 percent of GDP and would cut the deficit to 3 percent of GDP (against the 2004 outcome). As indicated in table 6A.1, the sum of reductions in current account balances for the other countries falls only slightly short of the targeted reduction in the US deficit, which is easily compatible with global consistency when some allowance is made for countries not specifically covered as well as the likely shrinkage of the global current account discrepancy if the large US deficit declines.

The table also reports the ratio of exports of goods and services to GDP. This ratio can serve as the basis for estimating the parameter relating the change in the current account to the change in the real exchange rate. The approach here assumes that trade price elasticities of demand are unity for both exports and imports. This means that the entire adjustment takes place on the export side, because on the import side, the change in the price of foreign exchange offsets the change in the volume of imports, if the pass-through ratio is unity (and lesser pass-through means lesser change in volume).

When the export price elasticity is unity and the export pass-through is complete, then the percent change in exports will equal the negative of the percent real appreciation of the country's exchange rate. This change in exports, expressed as a fraction of GDP, will simply be the percent change in exports multiplied by the ratio of exports (goods and services) to GDP. For countries with relatively low ratios of trade to GDP, this approach should broadly hold. However, for countries with high ratios of trade to GDP, it is increasingly necessary to take into account the responsiveness of supply, as the change in exports can become large enough relative to GDP to invalidate the assumption that export supply elasticities are infinite. In the absence of specific econometric estimates by country, it is assumed here that the effective elasticity of export volume with respect to price facing the foreign market, which is meant to incorporate both supply and demand effects, is unity for a country with an export/GDP ratio of 10 percent (the case of the United States), and that this elasticity steadily falls to 0.5 for a country with exports as high as 100 percent of GDP (such as Malaysia). This set of assumptions yields the following simple linear equation for the effective elasticity of exports with respect to the real exchange rate: $e = -1.056 + 0.56x$, where x is the ratio of exports of goods and services to GDP. (The elasticity is negative and so falls in absolute value as the share of exports in GDP rises.)

With an estimate of the effective export elasticity in hand, the estimate for the change in the current account as a percent of GDP becomes this elasticity multiplied by the ratio of exports of goods and services to GDP. Thus, in equations 6A.3 and 6A.4, the parameter γ is: $\gamma = ex = -1.056x + 0.56x^2$. The term γ is reported in the final column of table 6A.1. For example, this term is -0.32 for Korea. With a target current account change equal to -1.56 percent of GDP for Korea, the implied appreciation of the real exchange rate is 4.88 percent ($= [-1.56]/[-0.32]$). (The actual optimal appreciation can differ because the deviation from the optimal target is being minimized but not eliminated.) Of course, the bilateral real appreciation against the dollar would be much larger.

Appendix 6B
Recent Alternative Profiles Proposed for Global Adjustment

Williamson (2004) set forth a proposed set of target current account adjustments by major country or region as the counterpart of a targeted correction in the US external deficit. He placed the goal for the US current account deficit at $250 billion, which amounted to 2.1 percent of 2004 GDP. This is a level he considers compatible with avoiding a further increase in the ratio of net international liabilities to GDP. Table 6B.1 shows the 2004 current account outcomes predicted in April 2004 by the IMF and used by Williamson, along with his proposed targets, and also reports the change from the predicted level to the target as a percent of each region's GDP.

Williamson's central point was that the reductions in demand coming from the counterpart of US external adjustment did not need to be punitively large for the rest of the world. For the euro area, for which he saw a near-zero balance as a reasonable target, the demand shift would amount to only 0.7 percent of GDP. For Japan, Williamson judged that a reduction of the current account surplus to 1.5 percent of GDP would be manageable. Given the expected surplus at the time of his study, this involved a reduction of demand amounting to 1.5 percent of GDP. For other industrial countries (including Canada), cutting the surplus to close to zero would have involved a reduction in demand somewhat smaller than that for the euro area, relative to GDP. For the NIEs (Hong Kong, Taiwan, Korea, and Singapore) he suggested a cut in the surplus of 1.5 percent of GDP, which would still leave their surplus at 4.7 percent of GDP. For China and other developing Asian countries, the cut would also have amounted to 1.5 percent of GDP. Williamson suggested current account reductions of 0.3 percent of GDP for transition economies, and set targeted adjustment at zero for both Africa and Latin America.

With even the maximum reductions in current account balances at only 1.5 percent of GDP, and with adjustment spread over three years or more, Williamson concluded that the foreign counterpart of US external correction would amount to only a mild impact on demand.

Williamson's estimates do not specifically address the translation of nominal changes to real changes for the current account relative to GDP. Because the rest of the world would be appreciating against the dollar, there would be a favorable terms of trade change from lower import prices expressed in domestic currencies. This means, however, that real imports would have to rise even more (and real exports fall more) in order to accomplish the same nominal change in the trade balances. Assuming pass-through ratios of 50 percent from exchange rate change to price change (see chapter 3), the ratio of the real trade balance change

Table 6B.1 Current account balances: 2004 expected and Williamson target (in billions of dollars and in percent of GDP)

	Expected[a]	Target[b]	Change	Change as percent of GDP
Advanced countries				
United States	−496	−250	246	2.1
Euro area	68	0	−68	−0.7
Japan	144	71	−73	−1.5
NIEs	77	58	−19	−1.5
Other	23	0	−23	−0.4
Subtotal	−184	−121	63	
Developing countries				
Africa	−8	−8	0	0.0
China	25	1	−24	−1.5
Other Asia	26	4	−22	−1.5
Middle East	44	33	−11	−1.5
Western Hemisphere	−7	−7	0	0.0
Subtotal	80	23	−57	
Economies in transition	6	0	−6	−0.3
Discrepancy	−98	−98	0	

NIEs = newly industrialized economies (Korea, Hong Kong, Singapore, and Taiwan)

a. In early 2004. IMF, *World Economic Outlook* (April 2004).
b. Williamson (2004).

to the nominal change would be about 1.25 (Cline 1989, 360).[29] If pass-through ratios were as high as 80 percent, this ratio would be about 1.9. Using a ratio of 1.5 for the real relative to nominal adjustment, Williamson's 1.5 percent of GDP ceiling for nominal adjustment would imply 2.25 percent of GDP in real terms, or 0.75 percent of GDP annually—not extremely severe but not trivial either.

At the same Institute for International Economics conference at which Williamson presented his estimates, Bénassy-Quéré et al. (2004) presented a paper calculating the extent of undervaluation of individual major currencies against the dollar, and by implication, indicating which currencies should bear the bulk of the appreciation against the dollar required for international adjustment. Their approach was rather different from the traditional fundamental equilibrium exchange rate (FEER) method of Williamson (1983), which identifies the exchange rate at which internal equilibrium (unemployment at the non–inflation accelerating level) and external equilibrium (some target appropriate or sustainable current account balance) are achieved. In essentially a more positive rather than normative approach, they estimate empirically the relationship of the real exchange rate to two explanatory variables: the ratio of net foreign assets to GDP

---

29. Assuming the underlying price elasticities are unity.

and the ratio of domestic consumer prices to producer prices. The idea is that a country with high levels of foreign assets will tend to enjoy a higher (stronger) real exchange rate (if only because it can pay for some of its imports with earnings on capital assets rather than exports). As for the internal price ratio, the approach invokes the Balassa-Samuelson effect, in which a secular rise in productivity of export goods at a pace faster than in domestic nontradables will yield a secular rise in the real exchange rate (as observed historically, most notably in the case of Japan). The consumer/producer price ratio is a gauge of the price of nontradables relative to tradables (as the consumer price index includes nontraded services) and is hence interpreted as a measure of relative productivity in tradables. The higher the internal price ratio, the higher the expected real exchange rate.

The merit of the Bénassy-Quéré et al. approach is unclear. It would seem highly subject to unstable multiple equilibria for the estimated equilibrium real exchange rate (ERE). The reason is that both variables in the equation for the ERE are highly likely to respond positively to a depreciation of the actual exchange rate, making the equilibrium rate endogenous rather than exogenous. That is, the ratio of external debt, which is typically in dollars, to GDP will balloon when the dollar equivalent of local currency GDP shrinks because of a depreciation of the currency. Similarly, the ratio of the consumer price index to the producer price index is likely to fall sharply when the exchange rate depreciates sharply, because the weight of traded goods is much higher in the denominator (producer price index) than in the numerator (consumer price index). Suppose that there is a collapse in the exchange rate because of a transitory loss of confidence. The measure of the ERE will also show a large drop, because the debt-to-GDP ratio will have risen and the ratio of the consumer price to the producer price index will have fallen.

The Bénassy-Quéré et al. estimates are for 15 countries during 1980–2001. They generate time paths of "equilibrium" real exchange rates predicted from the model as applied to the net foreign asset and consumer/producer price ratios. These are compared with actual real exchange rates to determine whether each country is overvalued or undervalued. These comparisons are then translated into overvaluation or undervaluation against the dollar. The method generates large gyrations in the predicted real exchange rate, in contrast to what might be expected for more meaningful equilibrium rates.[30] (The essence of a fundamental

---

30. For example, Brazil's estimated equilibrium real exchange rate over 1983–88 is about 30 percent higher than the 22-year average, about 20 percent below the average in 1996, and about 25 percent above the average in 2001. Australia's ERE rises (depreciates, as the definition is real home currency per foreign currency) steadily from 15 percent below the actual 1990 level in 1980 to 27 percent above the 1990 actual level in 2001. Note that the close adherence of the equilibrium rate index to the actual index for Brazil, and the wide fluctuation of both, is highly suggestive of the problem of positive feedback from the actual to the supposed equilibrium rate as discussed in the text.

equilibrium exchange rate is that it tends toward a central value that changes only slowly, and the whole objective is to compare the actual exchange rate—which can move much more rapidly—against the fundamental equilibrium level to judge exchange rate overvaluation or undervaluation.) This outcome is consistent with the diagnosis here that the method likely is subject to positive feedback from the actual rate to the supposed equilibrium rate, generating unstable multiple equilibria in the ERE.

The seeming susceptibility of the measured real equilibrium rate to endogeneity with respect to the actual rate suggests that the Bénassy-Quéré et al. estimates should be taken with a grain of salt. Nonetheless, because they provide one perspective on the extent of currency misalignment, and in part because, at least for several countries, they appear to generate plausible values, the estimates are reported in table 6B.2. In the table, "misalignment" indicates the percent by which the actual number of currency units per dollar exceeds the desired rate (i.e., undervaluation). The table further updates the estimates to end-2004, taking account of actual exchange rates and the excess of national inflation over cumulative US inflation from mid-2003 to end-2004.

Based on the Bénassy-Quéré et al. estimates as updated, at the end of 2004, the euro was approximately at an equilibrium value against the dollar (1.2 percent overvalued), but the yen remained significantly undervalued (by about 22 percent) and had an equilibrium rate of 85 to the dollar. The UK and Australian currencies had already overshot, according to these estimates, and were overvalued by about 8 to 9 percent against the dollar. The Mexican peso was overvalued by about 12 percent and the Turkish lira by about 20 percent.[31]

The authors' estimate of undervaluation of the Chinese renminbi, at 46 percent, was about twice as large as the correction called for by Goldstein (2004). Major undervaluation against the dollar, at about 20 percent, also persisted for other key Asian economies (Korea, India, and Indonesia). As discussed in the main text, the Bénassy-Quéré results are broadly similar to those in this study (except for Argentina, Mexico, and the United Kingdom), despite the completely different methodology.

---

31. Considering that Mexico's current account deficit in 2003 was only 1.5 percent of GDP, it is unclear that the diagnosis of overvaluation of the peso by 12 percent is warranted.

Table 6B.2 Equilibrium exchange rates and misalignment as estimated by Bénassy-Quéré et al. (in currency per dollar, in percent, and in percentage points)

Country	Exchange rate, 2003	Misalignment (percent)	Equilibrium rate, 2003	Exchange rate, end-2004	Differential inflation[a] (percentage points)	Equilibrium rate, end-2004	Misalignment, end-2004
Argentina	2.96	92.5	1.54	2.98	7.5	1.65	80.2
Australia	1.36	–3.5	1.41	1.28	0.2	1.41	–9.2
Brazil	2.93	27.4	2.30	2.66	10.0	2.53	5.3
Canada	1.30	7.8	1.21	1.20	–0.8	1.20	0.5
China	8.29	47.3	5.63	8.29	0.6	5.66	46.4
Euro area	0.81	7.6	0.75	0.73	–0.9	0.74	–1.2
India	45.34	32	34.35	43.73	2.6	35.24	24.1
Indonesia	8,945.82	22.9	7,278.94	9,319.80	5.9	7,708.40	20.9
Japan	108.17	22.1	88.60	103.10	–4.3	84.79	21.6
Korea	1,194.54	37.5	868.76	1,047.50	1.6	882.22	18.7
Mexico	10.81	–13.1	12.43	11.19	2.7	12.76	–12.3
South Africa	7.57	32	5.74	5.67	1.5	5.82	–2.6
Turkey	1.45	0.7	1.44	1.34	20.1	1.73	–22.2
United Kingdom	0.55	–4.4	0.57	0.52	–1.7	0.56	–7.5

a. 18 months.

Sources: Bénassy-Quéré et al. (2004); IMF (2005a).

7

Principal Findings and Policy Implications

The International Debt Cycle

Chapter 1 considers the seeming anomaly of US external deficits and net external debt from the standpoint of the theory of the "international debt cycle." This theory identifies four stages. "Young debtor" countries have net external debt and current account deficits financed by capital inflow in response to high domestic return on capital, which in turn reflects these countries' low endowment of capital. "Mature debtor" countries are beginning to repay debt so they have current account surpluses. "Young creditor" countries have net external assets and run current account surpluses to finance their outflows of capital. "Mature creditor" countries have net assets but are gradually exhausting them by running current account deficits, essentially "clipping their coupons" and consuming out of accumulated external wealth. In principle, as a country develops, it should go in only one direction through this cycle, from young debtor to, eventually, mature creditor.

Fischer and Frenkel (1974) developed a theoretical model that supported this pattern of debt stages. Buiter (1981) suggested a different model in which rich countries with a high rate of "pure time preference" (the "impatience" component of the interest rate) would be chronic debtors and those with a low time preference would be chronic creditors. The United States does not fit the traditional stages, because it falls into the "young debtor" class (external debt, current account deficit) even though it is not a poor, developing country. Moreover, the United States has transited from being a young creditor in the initial postwar decades to being a mature creditor (net creditor but current account deficit) before turning into a young debtor. Although the Buiter proposal might explain the US pattern, the simplest measure of the pure rate of time preference is the real Treasury bill (the only rate at which consumption can be transferred risk-free across time), and this rate has actually been somewhat lower for the United States (1.1 percent average for 1949–2003) than for Germany (2.2 percent) and Japan (1.5 percent).

Chapter 1 develops a dataset on the net international investment position (NIIP) for 45 countries from 1970 through 2003. Where data from the International Monetary Fund (IMF) are not directly available, these estimates are based on cumulating current account balances backward from the earliest year for which the NIIP estimate is available. One important pattern found in the data is that the NIIP, which is the difference between assets and liabilities, is typically much smaller than the underlying gross asset and liability positions. For the United States, gross external liabilities in 2004 were 107 percent of GDP, while gross assets were 85 percent of GDP. The difference amounted to net liabilities of 22 percent of GDP. But the large gross values on both sides mean that moderate proportional changes in the underlying gross amounts (for example, from revaluation effects) can exert a leveraged impact on the net amount. Other countries have even higher gross/net ratios. The 2003 average of external assets and liabilities for Belgium, for example, was 390 percent, while its NIIP was 42 percent of GDP.

Chapter 1 finds that the debt cycle theory is more often contradicted than confirmed by the data for industrial countries, but tends to be more supported by the evidence for developing countries. Only 41 percent of the available country-year observations for industrial countries showed them to be net creditors, whereas 85 percent of the developing-country cases confirmed their net debtor status. Similarly, there was a relatively high (32 percent) incidence of "wrong direction" changes in industrial-country status from one period to the next.

Switzerland (a net creditor at a remarkable 150 percent of GDP), Belgium (42 percent), Japan (38 percent), and Germany (7 percent) have been persistent net creditors (joined only in the 1990s by Norway at 60 percent). But there is a surprisingly large group of industrial countries that have shown a persistent trend of net debtor status, including Australia, Canada, Denmark, Finland, Ireland, New Zealand, Spain, and Sweden. They have been joined as net debtors by another surprisingly large group of countries that have run down earlier net external assets and transited into net external liability positions, including Austria, Greece, the Netherlands, Portugal, the United Kingdom, and the United States (figure 1.4 in chapter 1). The time path of the US NIIP from +11 percent of GDP in 1970–75 to −21 percent in 2000–03 lies essentially in the center of a similarly downward-sloping field of observations for this "creditor-to-debtor" group. Although there is a global discrepancy in which the sum of net liabilities of net debtor countries exceeds the sum of net assets of net creditor countries, even a country-by-country imputed allocation of this discrepancy does not transform any of the industrial-country debtors into creditors. The broad message is that the debt cycle is by no means a heavily dominant pattern for industrial countries, and thus its violation by the United States is by no means unique.

Chapter 1 concludes by presenting evidence for industrial countries that shows a negative correlation between the growth rate and the change in NIIP. Each percentage point of additional average annual growth is associated with a 1.5 percentage point reduction annually in the NIIP as a percent of GDP. Applying the estimated relationship to the United States essentially explains the deterioration of the US NIIP from 1990 to 2002, lending support to the view that higher US growth than in other industrial countries has been a major factor in its eroding net external asset position.

Valuation Effects, Asymmetric Returns, and Economic Net Foreign Assets

Chapter 2 examines structural features of the US NIIP that tend both to make its burden less than might otherwise be expected and to limit the pace of its deterioration to less than might be anticipated from the size of the current account deficit. US external assets tend to be more in equities and its liabilities more in debt. This means that price inflation, which boosts the value of equities but not debt, and dollar depreciation, which revalues foreign equities but not dollar-denominated debt, generally alleviate the net international liability position of the United States. At end-2004, 58 percent of gross US external assets were in direct investment and portfolio equities, compared to 37 percent of foreign assets in the United States. This differential gives rise to a favorable annual drift of an estimated $50 billion annually for the US NIIP from rising equity prices.

An estimated 63 percent of US external assets are in foreign currencies.[1] Taking specific countries' shares in US foreign assets into account, there was a weighted appreciation of foreign currencies against the dollar by 24 percent from end-2001 to end-2003, which would have predicted a favorable valuation change of about $1 trillion. The official US NIIP estimate for net exchange rate valuation effects in this period is instead $647 billion. As a central estimate, each percentage point decline in the dollar against foreign currencies tends to improve the NIIP by about $40 billion, or 0.33 percent of GDP. If there is a small secular downward trend in the real value of the dollar (as suggested by the IMF real exchange rate

---

1. All direct investment and portfolio equity and 30 percent of US residents' holdings of foreign bonds.

index but not the US Federal Reserve's index), then even without major correction of the overvalued dollar, there is an additional contribution to favorable drift in the NIIP from the exchange rate valuation effect. The overall effect of both the price and exchange valuation effects is to curb the pace of decline in the US NIIP, by perhaps 0.5 percent of GDP annually and as much as 1 percent if the "other" statistical "manna from heaven" continues at its average of about $60 billion each year. Unfortunately, this favorable drift is not nearly large enough to outweigh the adverse trend associated with current account deficits on the order of 6 percent of GDP and rising.

The rate of return on US foreign assets has consistently exceeded that on liabilities by about 1.2 percent annually over the past two decades. The theory of portfolio balance might suggest such a pattern, because the United States is a safe market in which foreigners may wish to place the lower-risk, lower-return part of their portfolio, while US residents may seek to place the higher-risk, higher-return portion of their portfolios abroad. Direct investment is the category accounting for higher earnings abroad. From 1992 to 2004, the return on US direct investment abroad averaged 7.1 percent annually, whereas the return on foreign direct investment in the United States averaged only 2.5 percent. The stock of direct investment is $3.3 trillion on the asset side and $2.7 trillion on the liability side. Even if both were equal at $3 trillion, the 4.6 percentage point differential would generate a surplus of about $140 billion annually on the earnings account for direct investment. This is more than enough to offset the deficit in earnings on bonds and loans. However, in this category, foreigners hold about $7.6 trillion whereas US citizens hold only about $3.9 trillion abroad, so each percentage point rise in the interest rate will boost the US earnings deficit on bonds and loans by about $37 billion annually, suggesting some vulnerability as the interest rate cycle returns to more normal rates.

The net result has still been a persistent surplus for the United States in capital income, amounting to $52 billion in 2003 and $36 billion in 2004. This calls into serious question the economic meaning of the US net international liability position of $2.5 trillion at the end of 2004. Economically meaningful debt generates net capital income payments, not net receipts. The data are probably not bad enough to attribute much of the paradox to undercounted foreign assets (though the true value of foreign direct investment in the United States may, in particular, be less than the accounting value). Instead, the structural asymmetry in direct investment returns seems to be the dominant factor. To obtain a better idea of the economic significance of net foreign assets (and especially the economic burden of net foreign liabilities), chapter 2 proposes the metric of capitalized net capital income (CNCI), as opposed to the usual accounting concept (NIIP). It does so by discounting the annual flow of net earnings on capital income by the 10-year bond rate (i.e., treating the year's capital income as a prospectively infinite stream at the same absolute magnitude and obtaining the present value of that stream). The result is a positive rather than negative CNCI amounting to 11.7 percent of GDP in 2003 and 7.2 percent in 2004, but falling to 2 percent in 2005 and -8 percent in 2006 based on the projections of chapter 3. For other industrial countries, in contrast, capital income shows the expected sign given the NIIP, suggesting that the need to make this alternative calculation is primarily important for the United States.

The chapter closes with two additional debt concepts: the present value of net foreign assets (PVNFA), a concept familiar in the context of World Bank estimates for developing countries; and a short-term debt equivalent, the net receivable credit payments within one year (NRCPOY). The PVNFA, which is the concept relevant for the long-term burden of the debt if the principal as well as interest is to be repaid (rather than rolled over as implicitly assumed in the CNCI), shows the end-2004 position at -1.5 percent of GDP, negative and hence a net debtor position, but small. The NRCPOY, the measure most relevant for short-term vulnerability, shows a net debtor position of 1.1 percent of GDP at end-2004, but the size of this net negative position is only one-twentieth that of the more familiar NIIP. The summary implication of these estimates is that in economic and even cash-flow vulnerability terms, the United States is only now entering into meaningful net debtor territory. At the same time, these alternative concepts change the level but not the time trend of the US external asset position. Over the next few years, that trend remains sharply negative.

Forecasting the US Current Account Deficit and Net Foreign Assets

Judging the severity of the problem (if any) posed by prospectively rising net US external liabilities and by the US current account deficit requires having some sense about where they are headed. This in turn requires some framework for forecasting the current account and net foreign assets (both accounting NIIP and economic CNCI). Chapter 3 develops two variants of a forecasting model of the workhorse "elasticities" variety for this purpose. Imports respond to foreign GDP growth (income effect) and to the real exchange rate (price effect). Exports similarly respond to domestic GDP growth and the real exchange rate. Cyclical departures of growth from the trend are also incorporated. In the more conventional version, the income elasticity for US imports is higher than that for US exports, based on the Houthakker-Magee asymmetry (HMA) model typically found in statistical estimates. In the preferred version, however, the arguments of Krugman (1989) and Gagnon (2003) are drawn upon to set the income elasticities as symmetric (the KGS model).[2] The more buoyant trend of past US imports associated with trend income growth is then captured instead by incorporating variables for the rates of growth of capacity of foreign suppliers of US imports and US suppliers of exports. Both models specifically incorporate the initial asset and liabilities stocks of direct investment, portfolio equity, and all credits (bonds and loans). Specific rates of return for each class are then used to calculate capital income.

Simple statistical regressions find that the exchange rate impact on trade takes place as a weighted average of one- and two-year lags. This is important for the projections because it means that there is a "pipeline effect" to be expected for the US trade balance going forward from the dollar depreciations that occurred in 2003 and 2004.

Chapter 3 first tests the models using "backcasts" that compare past trends in the current account against what the models would have predicted. The KGS model is somewhat better in predicting, especially on the side of exports. The models are then used, in conjunction with estimates of the actual current account outcome in 2004, to project the current account, NIIP, and CNCI for 2005–10. The baseline assumptions are that the dollar remains unchanged at its real level in the first five months of 2005; real US growth averages 3.5 percent; and the 10-year bond rate rises from about 4 percent in 2004 to 5.5 percent by 2006. Direct investment flows are projected on the basis of past relationships to GDP, and the current account deficit each year is treated as cumulating into bond debt owed to foreigners.

The two models find that the US current account deficit is likely to rise to a range of 7.3 to 8.1 percent of GDP by 2010, after a temporary slowdown in the pace of its widening in 2005–06 as a result of exchange rate pipeline effects. The NIIP reaches a net liability position of about 52 percent of GDP in both models, and the CNCI moves from +7 percent of GDP in 2004 to net liabilities of about 23 percent by 2010. The chapter discusses the even more pessimistic projections of Mann (2004) and Roubini and Setser (2004), and sets forth the reasons for the differences. One source of moderately more optimistic results here is the explicit inclusion of lagged exchange rate effects. Another crucial difference is that the projections here apply a continued favorable differential in the rate of return on direct investment abroad as opposed to foreign direct investment in the United States. Even though these and other factors soften the projected trends, the results here are similar in qualitative terms to those of the two other studies: The US current account is on a trajectory of ever-widening

---

2. In the HMA model, the income elasticity for US imports is set at 1.7 and that on US exports at 1.0. In the KGS model, both are set at 1.5, and the elasticity for capacity growth is similarly set at 0.75 on both sides.

deficits rather than headed toward correction to a more sustainable deficit of, say, 3 percent of GDP.

The two models are then used to investigate the impact of alternative adjustment scenarios involving varying degrees of further dollar depreciation and changes in assumed foreign and US growth rates. In a favorable adjustment case in which there is a further real appreciation of foreign exchange rates against the dollar by 21 percent above the level of the first five months of 2005, and in which foreign growth accelerates by 0.75 percentage point annually for three years, the current account deficit falls to a range of about 3 percent of GDP in the period 2008–10. Policy parameter measures show the following impacts by the third year: Each percentage point real depreciation of the dollar brings about a 0.14 percent of GDP adjustment in the current account; each year-percentage point rise in foreign growth contributes 0.39 percent of GDP adjustment; each year-percentage point slower US growth, 0.43 percent of GDP; and each percentage point increase in the interest rate on a sustained basis adds 0.43 percent of GDP to the deficit.

The Role of Fiscal Adjustment

Chapter 4 examines the relationship between adjustments of the US fiscal deficit and the external current account deficit. The linkage between the two is based in part on the national income accounts identity, whereby the excess of domestic investment over domestic saving must equal the excess of imports over exports. At the intuitive level, this means that if resources used domestically exceed resources available domestically, supplementary resources from abroad must close the gap. Because the fiscal deficit is dissaving by the government, a wider fiscal deficit means a greater savings gap that needs to be filled by foreign resources, boosting the current account deficit.

When private investment and private saving change, the fiscal deficit will not move in lockstep with the external deficit. A striking paradox of the 1990s was that the current account deficit was widening even as the fiscal accounts were swinging from deficit to surplus. The reason was that the gap created by a surge in investment and a collapse in personal saving more than offset the swing from fiscal dissaving to saving. The breakdown of the "twin deficits" parallel movement in the 1990s does not mean that fiscal accounts can be ignored in seeking external adjustment going forward.

Chapter 4 considers the relationship between the fiscal balance and the strength of the dollar. In the normal or benign region, a wider fiscal deficit tends to push up interest rates and the dollar, so part of a normal external correction involves reducing the fiscal deficit, the interest rate, and the strength of the dollar. However, in a crisis zone in which the fiscal deficit has become so large as to shake confidence, the dollar might collapse rather than strengthen from further widening of the fiscal deficit.

The chapter reviews the sources of the United States' fiscal deterioration from a federal surplus of 2.4 percent of GDP in 2000 to a deficit of 3.6 percent of GDP in 2004. Although the recession of 2001 was initially a significant factor, the dominant influence was the tax cuts adopted in 2001 and 2003. The Organization for Economic Cooperation and Development (OECD 2004b) has estimated that in the absence of the tax cuts, the 2004 fiscal deficit might have been only 1 percent of GDP. The tax cuts thus contributed 2.6 percent of GDP to the fiscal deficit on a cyclically adjusted basis. Tax revenues fell from 20.9 to 16.2 percent of GDP from 2000 to 2004, in part because revenues were exaggerated in 2000 from unusually large capital gains associated with the stock market boom. Spending rose only from 18.4 to 19.9 percent of GDP, although the underlying rise was greater because falling interest rates cut the net interest bill from 2.3 to 1.4 percent of GDP. Falling interest rates had already contributed to deficit reductions in the 1990s, along with the "peace dividend" after the end of the Cold War, which cut defense spending from 5.3 percent of GDP in 1990–91 to 3 percent in 2000–01. Neither a further fall in interest rates nor a further reduction in defense spending can be expected to help narrow the deficit going forward; indeed, rising interest costs can be expected as the interest rate returns to more normal levels from its historic lows.

Chapter 4 also examines the decline in personal saving in recent years. Personal saving fell from 7 percent of disposable income in 1991–92 to about 1 percent by 2004, a decline equivalent to about 4.5 percent of GDP. The ballooning of household wealth in the stock market bubble, and then the offsetting of the fall in stock prices by the surge in housing prices (and the more widespread ownership of homes than stocks) were almost certainly key forces inducing falling saving. Although as a result households may have perceived that they were saving adequately in terms of the changes in their balance sheets, they in fact successively saved less out of current income, which is what matters for the gap between domestic use and availability of resources, and hence for the current account. Although a slowdown in rising asset prices might begin to bring about some revival in personal saving, there is no known public policy remedy capable of doing so.

The baseline projections of the Congressional Budget Office (CBO) show the federal deficit easing to 3 percent of GDP in 2005 (perhaps somewhat less with tax revenue running ahead of expectations) and 1.2 percent by 2010. However, the CBO emphasizes that the ground rules for its projections require the assumption of current law, which does not take account of further revenue losses if the tax cuts are made permanent and the alternative minimum tax is reformed (as the Bush administration seeks).

If in addition discretionary expenses grow at the same rate as GDP rather than only by the rate of inflation, the overall result boosts the CBO's baseline deficit to 3.2 percent by 2010. Gale and Orszag (2004) judge that the most realistic baseline outlook is for the deficit to remain at about 3.5 percent of GDP over 2005–14.

Chapter 4 briefly examines the longer-term fiscal problem. The CBO's central baseline forecast under current policies places the deficit at 14.4 percent of GDP by 2050. The driving force is a widening of Medicare-Medicaid expenditures from the current level of about 4 percent of GDP to about 12 percent, an increase far more important than the widening of the Social Security deficit from 4 to 6 percent of GDP. The chapter estimates that simply freezing the real level of Social Security benefits (by shifting from wage indexing to consumer price indexing) would elimi-nate the 2 percent of GDP increase in the Social Security deficit, and that limiting the "excess cost" growth of medical expenses per beneficiary above GDP growth per capita to 0.5 percent annually instead of the expected 1.7 percent would limit Medicare-Medicaid spending in 2050 to 9 percent of GDP. Together with tax increases by 1 percent of GDP, these two reforms would limit the long-term deficit to 2.5 percent of GDP and hold down federal debt held by the public to 50 percent of GDP instead of the remarkable 185 percent in the CBO long-term baseline.

Appendix 4A develops a formal model linking the fiscal balance to the current account balance in a general equilibrium framework. Its equations include the national accounts identity; the relationship of consumption to disposable income and the interest rate; investment as a function of the interest rate and GDP; the real exchange rate as a function of the interest rate and domestic relative to foreign growth; the interest rate as a function of the size of the fiscal deficit, the excess of GDP over its potential, and the price level; and the price level as a function of the levels of GDP and the real exchange rate. The model captures key feedback effects. These tend to be negative (i.e., undermining initial effects) for exchange rate depreciation. A decline in the dollar boosts net trade and hence GDP and consumption, pushing up the interest rate and thereby pressing the exchange rate upward again even as higher consumption increases imports through the income effect. In contrast, feedback effects from fiscal correction tend to be positive (self-reinforcing). Not only is government dissaving lower, but the induced decline in GDP as well as the decline in the disposable portion of income (if taxes are increased) curtails imports; and the decline in the interest rate from lesser fiscal pressure contributes to a decline in the exchange rate, which helps narrow the trade deficit.

Various simulations with the model show that fiscal adjustment of a given amount tends to yield a trade balance adjustment that is about 40 percent as large; that an exogenous initial decline in the dollar by itself has only a limited effect on the current account; and that the most effective external adjustment occurs when an exchange rate decline is accompanied by a sizable fiscal adjustment. The main thrust of the analysis is to emphasize the crucial role of fiscal adjustment. With the assumed parameters, the model estimates indicate that the size of the fiscal adjustment would need to be 4 percent of GDP, even if accompanied by a 25 percent decline in the dollar, and a modest temporary acceleration in foreign growth, in order to curb the trade deficit from its initial level of 5.2 percent of GDP to 3.1 percent. The model is "comparative static" and does not have specific forecast dates. The model may be unduly pessimistic, in part because normal offsetting influences such as an easing in monetary policy when fiscal policy is tightened (Taylor rule) might not be applied when there is a perceived need to correct the external deficit. Even so, in broad terms, the estimates suggest that it will be necessary to eliminate the fiscal deficit entirely as the fiscal policy role in cutting the US current account deficit to a target of about 3 percent of GDP by 2010. Forceful fiscal adjustment will be required to attain US external adjustment.

Sustainability and Risks of the Current Account Deficit

Chapter 5 examines the vulnerability of the US economy to the large and growing US current account deficit. It first considers potential portfolio satiation for foreigners' demand to accumulate still more US assets. The US current account deficit amounted to 35 percent of the aggregate current account surplus of countries in surplus among the 45 major economies in the early 1990s, and this share rose to over 90 percent by 2001–02. Net US external liabilities rose from 4 percent of global net liabilities of countries in liability positions in 1989 to 54 percent by 2002. Against other benchmarks, however, the relative size of US liabilities is considerably smaller. US net foreign liabilities at end-2002 amounted to only 5.4 percent of US household net wealth (including real estate). This comparison strongly supports the view that any net external debtor difficulties for the United States would be from a liquidity rather than a solvency problem.

Gross US external liabilities rose from an estimated 5.7 percent of rest-of-world gross financial assets (including domestic) in 1992 to 13.2 percent in 2002 and 14.6 percent in 2004. When the baseline projections of chapter 3 are applied against an estimated baseline for rest-of-world assets, this share is projected to rise to about 16 percent by 2010. If one accepts 30 percent as the notional ceiling for holding foreign assets in household portfolios abroad (because of "home bias"), this calculation suggests that the United States is not yet close to bumping up against a ceiling in foreigners' demand for US assets.

Private foreign investors nonetheless appear to have grown more wary of US assets, probably because of the prospects for falling returns after incorporating exchange rate risk, rather than portfolio satiation. As a result, the financing for US deficits has shifted toward the foreign official sector. Official capital inflows—primarily the purchase of US assets (mainly Treasury bonds) for reserves held by foreign central banks—amounted to $278 billion in 2003 and $395 billion in 2004, or about 30 percent of gross capital inflows. By late 2004, there were signs that foreign central banks might diversify away from the dollar, possibly weakening this source of demand going forward.

Chapter 5 examines the traditional thresholds for debt problems in developing countries. These are found to be of limited relevance for the United States for several reasons. First, the CNCI net asset concept is still slightly positive, in contrast to the accounting-based NIIP net asset concept at -22 percent of GDP at end-2004, and hence much further away from the critical net debt threshold of 40 percent of GDP often cited for developing-country debt. Second, empirical studies show no correlation of industrial-country sovereign risk spreads with the ratio of net external debt to GDP, despite a strong negative correlation found for developing countries. Third, the usual ratios with exports as the base tend not to be relevant for the United States because the country's liabilities are in US currency, so the normal key role of exports in generating foreign exchange to service debt denominated in foreign currency is absent. Indeed, the normal developing-country problem from an exchange rate crisis—which balloons the size of foreign debt relative to domestic currency GDP as the exchange rate falls—is turned on its head for the United States. As shown in chapter 2, a fall in the dollar instead balloons the dollar value of equity assets abroad while leaving US external liabilities virtually unchanged in dollar terms, improving rather than worsening the net debtor position.

Short-term risks nonetheless exist. The principal risk is that a loss of confidence in the dollar could precipitate a "hard landing" of the US economy. A major decline in foreign financing of the US current account deficit would place upward pressure on interest rates in the US capital market. If the Federal Reserve thought that a steep fall in the dollar would boost prices through the effect on prices of imports as well as the boost to capacity utilization associated with higher exports and lower import volumes, it might further increase interest rates (or be unprepared to limit their rise in the market). The large presence of financial derivatives also suggests some risk of financial disruption resulting from sharp movement in the dollar or the interest rate. A major rise in the long-term interest rate could push the economy into recession, even if the Federal Reserve did not raise the short-term policy rate (although the resulting combination of a steep yield curve with recession would be unusual). The experience of late 1987 provides some sense of such risks. Concern about the falling dollar at that time, and disagreement between US and German authorities on interest rate policy, contributed to the largest single-day collapse in the stock market in US history in October 1987. On balance, however, a hard landing for the dollar and for the economy is still probably not the most likely outcome, but the chances of this outcome will rise as the US current account deficit continues to rise and the net foreign asset position (whether NIIP or CNCI) erodes further.

More fundamentally, even if foreign investors give the United States an unlimited length of rope by continuing to finance ever-greater buildups in US external liabilities, there is a problem of long-term burden for the US economy as it becomes increasingly indebted abroad. To the extent that the borrowing is primarily directed not toward financing investment but rather toward financing high levels of private consumption and government dissaving, the accumulation of foreign debt amounts to mortgaging the country's economic future. Eventually, there will be a price to pay in the form of a major terms of trade loss as the external debt is serviced. This will reduce the real standard of living of US citizens—many of them of the next generation—from levels otherwise attained as real consumption is eroded through higher import prices. Injudicious, and perhaps inequitable, deferral of the adjustment burden into the distant future is a fundamental reason to address the external deficit even if a sharp break in confidence and a hard landing are considered unlikely.

Illustrative simulations of the long-term problem compare early adjustment with delayed adjustment. Under delay, the baseline current account deficit reaches about 10 percent of GDP and the NIIP reaches -70 percent of GDP by 2015, at which time it is assumed that a severe adjustment will be required involving a large depreciation. For identical NIIP levels of -50 percent of GDP by 2024, more moderate early adjustment involves lesser terms-of-trade loss than later adjustment. The sharper depreciation in the later adjustment accomplishes more of the adjustment in exchange rate valuation gains on foreign assets, however. There is minimal difference between average real consumption under early as opposed to late adjustment, barring a severe recession in the latter case. Instead, the true cost of delay is in distributional inequity between the present and the future. Early adjustment distributes the reduction in consumption from the nonadjustment baseline relatively evenly between the first decade (by 4.6 percent of cumulative GDP) and second decade (by 8.8 percent of GDP, from an unrealistic baseline). In contrast, the delayed adjustment scenario imposes no reduction in consumption from the baseline in the first decade, but sharply higher consumption losses on households in the second decade (12.5 percent of cumulative GDP) as the consequence of postponing reduced consumption.

The views of US policymakers have tended to shift from judging the current account deficit as benign in the late 1990s, when investment was high and fiscal accounts strong, to greater concern by 2004 (Greenspan

2004a, Summers 2004). The debate among economists has placed portfolio optimists (e.g., Richard Cooper, "Two Views on the US Deficit," *Financial Times*, October 31, 2004) against pessimists (Obstfeld and Rogoff 2004), but even Cooper's analysis assumes the US deficit will stabilize at $500 billion annually rather than rising to the $1.2 trillion amount forecast in the baseline for 2010 in chapter 3. Chapter 5 finds the estimates of required exchange rate adjustment in the present study to be more consistent with the Obstfeld-Rogoff results than with more optimistic diagnoses.

Other important recent analyses include Blanchard, Giavazzi, and Sa (2005) and Gourinchas and Rey (2005). The former use a portfolio preference model to show that relatively large ongoing real depreciation of the dollar will be required if the large US current account deficit continues. The reason is that foreigners wish to hold a smaller share of their portfolios in US assets than do US citizens, because of "home bias." Each reduction in US net assets by $1 will induce less than $1 in foreign holdings, unless there is an accompanying decline in the exchange rate that shrinks the proportion that dollar assets would otherwise reach in the foreigners' portfolios. Blanchard, Giavazzi, and Sa suggest that ongoing real depreciation of the dollar in the range of 2.5 to 3 percent annually could be required, even after taking account of favorable exchange rate valuation effects.

Gourinchas and Rey focus on an explanatory model identifying the exchange rate adjustments imposed by market forces in response to variations in the trade balance and capital earnings balance from a long-term downward path. They can statistically explain about 60 percent of exchange rate variation over a three-year horizon. They find that about one-third of adjustment is contributed by exchange rate valuation effects, about the same proportion as found in the present study using a completely different methodology. They argue that the US imbalance is smaller today than it was in the mid-1980s, despite the larger current account deficit relative to GDP, because the larger foreign asset base provides more leverage for the exchange rate valuation effect. However, their analysis nonetheless implies extremely adverse long-term trends in the current account and net foreign liabilities, placing their position closer in qualitative terms to those of Obstfeld and Rogoff and Blanchard, Giavazzi, and Sa than might be inferred at first reading.

Three recent studies associated with the Federal Reserve Board are on the one hand more optimistic, but on the other envision surprisingly little scope for fiscal adjustment to reduce the current account deficit. Croke, Kamin, and Leduc (2005) examine past current account adjustment experiences among industrial countries and find that the "disorderly adjustment" (i.e., hard landing) scenario relating a currency plunge to a recession has not been typical. However, several of their findings imply a relatively painful US adjustment, even if a plunge in the dollar is not the cause. Thus, in distinguishing contractionary from expansionary adjustments, the authors find larger current account deficits (averaging 6 percent of GDP) among the contractionary group (versus 3 percent for the expansionary group). The contractionary group had higher imports relative to exports, and had preadjustment growth above the OECD average. All three of these contractionary-adjustment characteristics are applicable to the United States today.

Erceg, Guerrieri, and Gust (2005) have developed an experimental macroeconomic model with the much-cited result that $1 in fiscal adjustment induces only 20 cents in trade balance adjustment. However, the model contains key assumptions about household behavior ("Ricardian" offsetting increases in consumption that offset one-half of fiscal adjustment) and policy reaction functions (monetary policy offsets and longer-term fiscal policy reversals) that would seem to stack the cards against the efficacy of fiscal policy in curbing the external deficit.

Simulations of the Federal Reserve Board's FRB/Global macroeconomic model provide the basis for the diagnosis by Ferguson (2005) that the large US current account deficit was not caused by fiscal erosion, but is mainly due to acceleration in productivity growth, a downward shock to the household saving rate, a decline in investment abroad, and an increase in global financial integration. However, for technical reasons set forth in chapter 5, considerable caution would seem warranted in relying on these results.

Finally, Bernanke (2005) attributes the widening US current account deficit primarily to the drop in investment in other countries and hence the emergence of a "global saving glut," rather than to a rising US fiscal deficit. His implied policy seems to be to tolerate large current account deficits and wait for investment abroad to revive. However, a close look suggests that this proposition fails key tests. The fair US share of any saving glut from the drop in investment in East Asia and Latin America after the financial crises of 1997–98 would be only about 0.7 percent of US GDP, far too small to explain the widening of the current account deficit. Also, the plunge in the interest rate in the United States after 2001 was in the short-term policy rate (federal funds rate) rather than the long-term rate, but the long-term rate is the market rate that should have fallen if the main influence had been excess saving abroad. Low interest rates were made at home by the Federal Reserve, not abroad. Bernanke would seem to give far too little weight to US fiscal policy as the source of erosion in the US current account. A foreign saving glut certainly did not force the United States to cut taxes for a decade.

Global Impact of US External Imbalance

Chapter 6 examines the impact of the US external imbalance on the rest of the world. For the past decade, the rising US trade deficit has been a major source of demand for the rest-of-world economy. The current account deficit amounted to 2.2 percent of rest-of-world GDP by 2004. The increment to demand has been the highest for developing countries, whose trade balance with the United States rose from 1 percent of their aggregate GDP in 1992 to 4.7 percent in 2002. For Mexico, the upswing amounted to 8 percent of GDP, and for China, 4.9 percent. China's bilateral trade surplus with the United States stood at 8.8 percent of Chinese GDP in 2002. The challenge going forward is for the rest of the world to find domestic sources of demand to replace that from US trade deficits as the United States carries out external adjustment.

The demand placed on global capital markets by the rising US external deficit did not lead to higher global interest rates, an effect that potentially could have undermined the favorable demand effects of the US deficit for the rest of the world. Instead, with the US recession in 2001, US interest rates fell to historically low levels. Moreover, although the rise in the US current account deficit coincided with a decline in capital flows to emerging markets after 1996, the criterion for diagnosing an adverse shock from "crowding out" in world capital markets was not met: International interest rates not only did not rise, they fell sharply. Rising current account surpluses in developing countries by 1999 and thereafter reflected a new phase of export-led growth, fueled in considerable part by exports to the US market.

Moreover, developing countries began to accumulate large reserves in this period. Stiglitz (2003) has criticized this phenomenon as a failure of the global financial system, because low interest earnings on reserves compared with high interest rates on domestic bonds issued to finance reserve accumulation impose costly losses on developing countries. While there was some truth to this argument in the immediate aftermath of the East Asian crisis in 1997–98, the massive reserve holdings by 2003–04 of such countries as China, Korea, Taiwan, and even India far exceeded any prudent levels necessary to protect against external shocks, and instead represented the consequence of export-led growth spurred by increasingly undervalued exchange rates. Indeed, rigidly pegged exchange rates (China, Hong Kong, Malaysia) or de facto quasi-fixed exchange rates (Singapore, Taiwan, Thailand) against the dollar—kept from appreciating through large interventions to purchase reserves—meant that by 2002 and thereafter, the leading developing countries were a source of the problem of international imbalances rather than innocent victims of them. Their exchange rate policies were blocking the full extent of real exchange rate correction needed for the United States to carry out its external adjustment.

When (and if) US external adjustment begins, other countries will need to sustain their growth by shifting toward greater domestic demand. The experience of the 1980s cycle of US imbalances showed that although a hard landing was avoided, there were strong signs of deceleration in growth abroad as the United States curbed its external deficit. As the US current account deficit fell from 3.4 percent of GDP in 1987 to 0.8 percent in 1991–92, growth in the other six large industrial countries fell from 5.3 to 2.2 percent, and growth in the rest of the world fell from 5.2 to 2.5 percent. Even allowing for other influences (Gulf War oil shock, German reunification), that pattern serves as a caution underscoring the importance of boosting demand abroad as the United States adjusts.

Chapter 6 concludes with an analysis of the extent and pattern of further exchange rate realignments likely to be needed to enable the United States to reduce its current account deficit to a sustainable level of 3 to 3.5 percent of GDP. Appendix 6A develops a simple optimization model that minimizes the departure of changes in individual countries' current account balances from a prescribed pattern, subject to the constraint that the resulting weighted-average real exchange rate depreciation for the United States meets a target consistent with this US current account target. The criterion for prescribed current account change is a 40 percent uniform reduction in current account surpluses, which generates the desired global counterpart of the targeted reduction in the US deficit. The appendix gauges the list of "optimal" exchange rate changes against the dollar against the 2002 average, and examines the extent of correction already experienced through March 2005. The finding is that whereas the euro and currencies of several other industrial countries have already appreciated by close to the "optimal" amount, Japan and especially China and other East Asian economies have a long way to go in terms of further appreciation against the dollar. This analysis tends to confirm the notion that to date, the euro has borne a disproportionate share of the international adjustment process. The analysis of exchange rate realignment also shows, however, that if there were to be a generalized move in exchange rates against the dollar, the trade-weighted real appreciations for most countries would tend to be modest, even though their real appreciations against the dollar itself would be large.

The chapter argues that it is strongly in the long-run interests of developing countries to participate in generalized adjustment to permit the United States to achieve its external adjustment. The alternative of prolonged and growing US deficits followed by some form of crisis and hard landing, with high global interest rates and low US growth levels, can only be counterproductive to the growth of developing countries. Moreover, a benefit of appreciation against the dollar for many developing countries would be a reduction in the burden of their external debt, as dollar-denominated debt would become smaller relative to domestic currency GDP levels. The chapter emphasizes, however, that there is a "prisoners' dilemma" of policy coordination, because each country acting in isolation will tend to fear severe loss of competitiveness if it appreciates its currency against the dollar but other countries do not.

Policy Implications

Importance of Adjustment

A central policy conclusion of this study is that it is increasingly important that the United States reduce its external current account deficit. This deficit is no longer benign, as it arguably was in the late 1990s when it was financing high levels of investment instead of high levels of consumption and large government dissaving. Although the true economic burden of net US foreign liabilities is still minimal, that burden will grow substantially. Moreover, the large size of the deficit poses the risk of a hard landing in the event of a loss of confidence, especially because the deficit is likely to continue to rise as a share of GDP. Even if confidence were to be maintained indefinitely, the external deficit would eventually lead to a large burden on future consumers as a consequence of overconsumption today.

Assuming that the deficit is a "problem" cannot be taken for granted—economists have debated whether it is in fact a problem, and if so, how severe are the risks it poses. With the deficit at about 6 percent of GDP and headed to 7½ to 8 percent by 2010, however—far above the range of 4 to 5 percent associated in the past with corrective adjustment in industrial countries—by now, the better part of judgment is almost certainly that reduction of the deficit to a more sustainable level should be a high policy priority.

US Fiscal Adjustment

The first major policy implication of this study is the need for a major correction in the US fiscal deficit. Reasonable baseline estimates show the budget deficit continuing in the range of 3 to 3.5 percent of GDP, taking into account the Bush administration's goal of making the tax cuts permanent. Chapter 4 and the general equilibrium model developed there strongly suggest that the budget deficit should be completely eliminated rather than merely cut in half (as the administration seeks) if the current account deficit is to be cut to the range of 3 percent of GDP. A reasonable target would be to reach a zero federal deficit by 2010. This goal would require reducing the deficit by an average of 0.6 percent of GDP each year between now and then.

Identifying the components of expenditure cuts or tax increases that should be adopted to cut the budget deficit is beyond the scope of this study. However, discretionary spending is so small a part of total spending that it seems likely some role will have to be played by raising taxes (or avoiding making the recent tax cuts permanent). The decline of fiscal revenue from about 20 to 16 percent of GDP has been the driving force in the US swing from fiscal surplus to deficits.

Fiscal adjustment would also ideally be accompanied by at least a partial reversal of the downward trend in personal saving over the past decade. The greater the rebound in personal saving, the smaller the needed fiscal correction. Unfortunately, no policy measures have been shown to have a reliable influence on boosting personal saving, despite myriad tax-advantaged saving mechanisms.

If fiscal correction is not achieved or is only minor (for example, if the fiscal deficit continues at 3 percent of GDP), then the external account is unlikely to adjust by much, even if further real depreciation of the dollar occurs. Under these circumstances, it would be increasingly likely that an eventual external sector adjustment would occur in an undesirable manner, such as a slowdown in growth or even recession. One way this could occur would be if the Federal Reserve were to feel compelled to raise interest rates more than otherwise desirable in order to compensate for the lack of fiscal restraint, in the face of growing inflationary pressure on the economy as it moved beyond potential capacity.

Failure to adjust fiscal policy would also push the US policy mix toward a combination inappropriate from the standpoint of exchange rate correction. A tight monetary policy combined with a loose fiscal policy would boost interest rates and hence, attract foreign capital and keep the dollar from falling as much as would be desirable for external adjustment.

Exchange Rate Realignment

Chapter 6 strongly suggests the need for appreciation against the dollar of the currencies of Japan, China, the other East Asian economies, and also some of the Latin American economies. The massive intervention of central banks to avoid appreciation of the Japanese yen, Chinese renminbi, and other Asian currencies should be discontinued. An objective of international financial and economic policy should be to achieve differentiated further appreciation of currencies against the dollar broadly along the lines identified in chapter 6.

The simplest and perhaps most desirable way to facilitate the necessary exchange rate developments would be for central banks to stop intervening in exchange markets and allow their exchange rates to appreciate. In the key case of China, the mid-July 2005 decision to shift from a fixed rate against the dollar to a managed float against a basket was potentially a major breakthrough. However, its potential for contributing to global adjustment will be frustrated if the authorities intervene heavily to keep the currency only minimally stronger than before. More generally, the "prisoners' dilemma" that inhibits each country from acting alone may necessitate some form of coordinated currency appreciations along the lines of the Smithsonian Agreement of 1971 and the Plaza Accord of 1985.

US policymakers should consider convening an international monetary conference in 2006 in which countries would be expected to set forth their proposed means of participating in the international adjustment that is the necessary counterpart to US external adjustment. For this purpose, the United States would need to have its own house in order by moving ahead with a credible plan to eliminate its fiscal deficit over the next few years. The objective would be a major coordinated appreciation of currencies (especially the yen and East Asian currencies) against the dollar, supported by a commitment to refrain from accumulating reserves until a target range of appreciation against the dollar (such as 20 percent) has occurred.

Domestic Demand Policies

The US current account deficit was about 2½ percent of rest-of-world GDP in 2004 (chapter 6), so cutting the deficit by half (to about 3 percent of US GDP) would withdraw nominal demand equivalent to about 1¼ percent of nominal GDP for the rest of the world. Taking account of terms of trade effects, the withdrawal of real demand would amount to perhaps 1.8 percent of rest-of-world GDP in real terms. Sustained global growth will require increased domestic demand abroad in this order of magnitude as the United States carries out external adjustment. The shift in demand would be phased over time (perhaps four years), but would still represent a substantial and necessary annual increase in domestic demand in the rest of the world. It is useful to consider what policies might contribute to this adjustment.[3]

For Europe and Japan, spurring domestic demand has proven difficult over the past decade. The usual recommendation for Europe is structural change (e.g., liberalization of labor markets). Such reforms could raise demand for investment. However, carrying out structural reforms usually takes several years, and slack demand resulting from US external adjustment is presumably already in the pipeline as a result of the rise of the euro against the dollar from 2002 to 2004, meaning that the demand issue is likely to arise sooner rather than later. Moreover, fiscal policy is not an attractive instrument for boosting European demand, because of difficulties already faced in meeting fiscal targets under the European Union's Stability and Growth Pact. This would suggest that monetary policy will have to be the principal tool for boosting domestic demand to offset falling demand from the United States. The implication is that the European Central Bank should either ease interest rates or at least not increase them if growth picks up.

---

3. See, in particular, Mussa (2005).

Much the same diagnosis applies to Japan's policy options, although the nature of its structural problem has been different (including, in particular, a weak banking system). Japan's public debt stands at 164 percent of GDP on a gross basis and 84 percent on a net basis (deducting what some would consider questionable assets), and it is not in a position to embark on wider fiscal deficits as a means of stimulating demand (OECD 2004c). So again, it is likely to be monetary policy that will be necessary to help assure that Japan's demand remains sufficient as US adjustment takes place. This primarily implies holding the interest rate at very low levels as growth proceeds.

For developing countries, boosting domestic demand to compensate for US external adjustment will likely involve some easing of both fiscal and monetary policy. In countries such as Brazil, where interest rates are extremely high, the reduction of inflationary pressures from an appreciation of the currency against the dollar would provide a favorable environment for reducing interest rates, thereby stimulating investment. Brazil has little scope for fiscal expansion because it already has a relatively high level of public debt. For China, the principal concern in recent years has been that the economy might be overheating, given sustained growth of around 9 to 10 percent. Therefore, an easing in demand associated with US external adjustment might be welcome and at least initially not require any particular policy offset. Even so, because the rising bilateral trade surplus with the United States contributed about 0.5 percent additional annual growth to the Chinese economy over the past decade (as the surplus rose from about 4 to 9 percent of China's GDP), a swing to a declining surplus with the United States could eventually exert enough demand reduction to require offsetting policy measures.

More generally, there should be ample scope for shifting toward domestic demand in developing countries, where the more typical problem is curbing excess demand. Nonetheless, unless conscious policy strategies are adopted, the shift from US to domestic demand could be less than successful, as suggested by the growth slowdown during the previous episode of US external adjustment.

This outline of possible policy approaches warrants an important caveat: The resulting policy mix pattern could hinder the exchange rate adjustment. The ideal policy combination for external adjustment is for the deficit country to undertake fiscal contraction accompanied by unchanged or expansive monetary policy, easing interest rates and bidding down the currency to a more competitive level. The country in surplus does the opposite: It eases fiscal policy to boost demand, and leaves monetary policy unchanged or tightens it so that the potential correction in the exchange rate is not thwarted. But if Europe and Japan cannot apply fiscal stimulus and must resort to monetary stimulus, their policy mix will tend to inhibit the appreciation of their exchange rates. Similarly, if the United

States fails to achieve much fiscal correction and instead applies monetary restraint as a substitute, this will tend to curb the depreciation of the dollar.

Ideally, the most that this policy mix problem would do would be to ensure against a downward overshooting of the dollar. But this consideration does suggest that there may be important limits in the extent to which monetary policy can compensate for constrained fiscal policies in the international adjustment process.

Exchange Rate and Trade Regime Interaction

If a wide array of countries do not allow market forces to bid up their exchange rates against the dollar, and, in particular, if China does not do so, there could be increasing policy attention to retaliatory measures. One approach to keeping any such retaliation as benign as possible for the international trade and financial system might be to apply a countervailing duty against exchange rate subsidization of exports within the framework of the antisubsidy rules of the World Trade Organization (WTO). An official policy accumulating large amounts of reserves to keep a currency undervalued would fit the economic concept of a policy measure that has the effect of subsidizing exports. It can be argued that although the WTO definition of subsidies typically envisions direct payments of public revenue to exporting parties, there are sufficient references to exchange rate practices in the existing WTO antisubsidy rules to encompass remedies against an undervalued exchange rate supported by large intervention.[4]

The IMF, for its part, is supposed to indicate when it believes a country is "manipulating" its exchange rate, and for fixed exchange rates (such as that still maintained by Hong Kong), when the rate should be shifted to a new level because of "fundamental disequilibrium." It is thus plausible that the IMF could be asked (e.g., by the United States) to bring a determination that a country (e.g., China) is engaging in currency manipulation or (in the case of Hong Kong) failing to adjust a fixed exchange rate in fundamental disequilibrium. With such an IMF determination in hand, the United States might find it easier to win a WTO case on countervailing duties against exchange rate subsidization.[5] International blessing for the imposition of a trade penalty would be far preferable to

---

4. For a legal argument along these lines, see China Currency Coalition (2004).

5. Article XV, paragraph 2, of the General Agreement on Tariffs and Trade provides that "contracting parties . . . shall accept the determination of the Fund as to whether action by a contracting party in exchange matters is in accordance with the Articles of Agreement of the International Monetary Fund" (WTO 2005). It also provides (paragraph 4) that "Contracting parties shall not, by exchange action, frustrate the intent of the provisions of this Agreement. . . ." (WTO 2005).

unilateral US action widely perceived to be in violation of US international obligations.

It would be far better if countries were to allow markets to boost exchange rates against the dollar. Any recourse to trade penalties—even ones sanctioned by the IMF and WTO—would be inappropriate until the alternative of suasion had been shown to fail. The alternative of unilateral trade penalties without international approval was applied by the Nixon administration in 1971, when it imposed a 10 percent import surcharge and suspended convertibility of the dollar into gold prior to the exchange rate realignment of the Smithsonian Agreement. A comparable unilateral action today would do serious damage to the fabric of globalization. The alternative of a penalty sanctioned by IMF and WTO rules would likely be seen as much more supportive of the international economic rules of the game.

Withholding Tax on Nonresident Investment Income

Finally, there are grounds for concern that market forces by themselves may not suffice to achieve the extent of real depreciation of the dollar consistent with a more desirable US external balance.[6] If it becomes increasingly clear that the dollar is remaining substantially overvalued (e.g., in comparison with a 20 percent further real appreciation of foreign currencies as quantified in chapters 3 and 6), US policymakers should consider using tax incentives to help moderate foreign capital inflows— the underlying force keeping the dollar overvalued. A withholding tax on nonresident capital income earnings on assets held in the United States would be a market-friendly instrument for this purpose. The size of the tax could be gauged to the degree of diagnosed dollar overvaluation. US authorities presumably would need to secure the cooperation of their foreign counterparts for this purpose, as it would be counterproductive if foreign authorities imposed retaliatory taxes on US earnings abroad. The grounds for such cooperation would be a shared perception that the wide US imbalance poses an ongoing and rising threat to international economic stability.

A withholding tax would reduce the return to foreign investors, thereby curbing capital inflows and hence reducing capital market pressure holding the dollar above levels compatible with long-term targets for the current account deficit and net external debt. One way of thinking about such a tax is as follows. It may well be that the rest of the world considers the US capital market an ideal place to invest, in comparison with their home capital markets. Individual foreign investors, however, might have

---

6. See, in particular, the discussion in chapter 5 on Gourinchas and Rey (2005) and the analysis of the long-term burden of rising external debt.

a collective impact that causes instability for the system by prolonging overvaluation of the dollar to the point where the deficit and net US external debt reach ever more dangerous proportions. A tax would then be a way of internalizing the individual externalities. The tax would also be a means of sharing the rent otherwise going to foreign investors with the future generation of US citizens, who otherwise will bear the sole burden of servicing the debt incurred by excessive consumption of the present generation.

References

Abaroa, Patricia E. 2004. The International Investment Position of the United States at Year-end 2003. *Survey of Current Business* (July): 30–39.

Alexander, Sidney S. 1952. Effects of Devaluation on a Trade Balance. *International Monetary Fund Staff Papers* 2 (April): 263–78.

Allen, Mark, Christoph Rosenberg, Christian Keller, Brad Setser, and Nouriel Roubini. 2002. *A Balance Sheet Approach to Financial Crisis*. IMF Working Paper 02/210. Washington: International Monetary Fund.

Bazdarich, Michael J. 1978. Optimal Growth and Stages in the Balance of Payments. *Journal of International Economics* 8: 425–43.

Barro, Robert J. 1974. Are Government Bonds Net Wealth? *Journal of Political Economy* 82, no. 6: 1095–117.

BEA (Bureau of Economic Analysis). 2004a. *US International Transactions: Second Quarter 2004*. Washington: US Department of Commerce.

BEA (Bureau of Economic Analysis). 2004b. *US Net International Investment Position at Year-end 2003*. Washington: US Department of Commerce.

BEA (Bureau of Economic Analysis). 2004c. *US International Transactions, 1960–Present*. Washington: US Department of Commerce.

BEA (Bureau of Economic Analysis). 2004d. *US Direct Investment Abroad: Balance of Payments and Direct Investment Position Data*. Washington: US Department of Commerce.

BEA (Bureau of Economic Analysis). 2004e. Interactive NIPA Tables. US Department of Commerce, Washington. www.bea.doc.gov (accessed July 10).

BEA (Bureau of Economic Analysis). 2005a. Trade in Goods and Services. US Department of Commerce, Washington. www.bea.doc.gov (accessed July 10).

BEA (Bureau of Economic Analysis). 2005b. *Aggregate Changes in the Net International Investment Position*. Washington: US Department of Commerce.

BEA (Bureau of Economic Analysis). 2005c. US International Transactions Accounts Data. US Department of Commerce, Washington. www.bea.doc.gov (accessed July 10).

BEA (Bureau of Economic Analysis). 2005d. Interactive NIPA Tables. US Department of Commerce, Washington. www.bea.doc.gov (accessed July 10).

BEA (Bureau of Economic Analysis). 2005e. *International Investment Position of the United States at Year-end, 1976–2004.* Washington: US Department of Commerce.

Bénassy-Quéré, Agnès, Pascale Duran-Vigneron, Amina Lahrèche-Révil, and Valérie Mignon. 2004. Burden Sharing and Exchange Rate Misalignments Within the Group of Twenty. In *Dollar Adjustment: How Far? Against What?* eds. C. Fred Bergsten and John Williamson. Washington: Institute for International Economics.

Bergsten, C. Fred, and John Williamson. 1983. Exchange Rates and Trade Policy. In *Trade Policy in the 1980s*, ed. William R. Cline. Washington: Institute for International Economics.

Bernanke, Ben S. 2005. The Global Saving Glut and the US Current Account Deficit. Remarks at the Homer Jones Lecture, St. Louis, April 14. www.federalreserve.gov (accessed July 10).

Bertraut, Carol C., and William L. Griever. 2004. Recent Developments in Cross-Border Investment in Securities. *Federal Reserve Bulletin* (Winter): 19–31.

Birdsall, Nancy, and John Williamson. 2002. *Delivering on Debt Relief: From IMF Gold to a New Aid Architecture.* Washington: Center for Global Development and Institute for International Economics.

Blanchard, Olivier, and Roberto Perotti. 2002. An Empirical Characterization of the Dynamic Effects of Changes in Government Spending and Taxes on Output. *Quarterly Journal of Economics* 117, no. 4 (November): 1329–68.

Blanchard, Olivier, Francesco Giavazzi, and Filipa Sa. 2005. *The US Current Account and the Dollar.* MIT Working Paper 05–02 (May). Cambridge, MA: Massachusetts Institute of Technology Department of Economics.

Bloomberg LP. 2005. www.bloomberg.com (accessed July 12, 2005).

Boskin, Michael J. 2004. Sense and Nonsense about Federal Deficits and Debt. *The Economists' Voice* 1, no. 2.

Buiter, Willem H. 1981. Time Preference and International Lending and Borrowing in an Overlapping-Generations Model. *Journal of Political Economy* 89, no. 4 (August): 769–97.

Calvo, Guillermo A., and Carmen M. Reinhart. 2000. *Fear of Floating.* NBER Working Paper 7993 (November). Cambridge, MA: National Bureau of Economic Research.

Campbell, J. Y., and N. G. Mankiw. 1989. Consumption, Income and Interest Rates: Reinterpreting the Time Series Evidence. In *NBER Macroeconomics Annual*, eds. Olivier Blanchard and Stanley Fischer. Cambridge, MA: MIT Press.

Carlstrom, Charles T., and Timothy S. Fuerst. 2003. *The Taylor Rule: A Guidepost for Monetary Policy?* Economic Commentary (July). Cleveland: Federal Reserve Bank of Cleveland.

CBO (Congressional Budget Office). 2003. *The Long-Term Budget Outlook.* Washington.

CBO (Congressional Budget Office). 2004a. *An Analysis of the President's Budgetary Proposals for Fiscal Year 2005.* Washington.

CBO (Congressional Budget Office). 2004b. *The Budget and Economic Outlook: An Update.* Washington.

CBO (Congressional Budget Office). 2004c. Historical Budget Data. Washington. www.cbo.gov (accessed July 10).

CBO (Congressional Budget Office). 2005a. *The Budget and Economic Outlook: Fiscal Years 2006 to 2015.* Washington.

CBO (Congressional Budget Office). 2005b. Historical Budget Data. Washington. www.cbo.gov (accessed July 10).

CBO (Congressional Budget Office). 2005c. Monthly Budget Review. Washington. www.cbo.gov (accessed July 10).

Central Bank of China, Republic of China (Taiwan). 2004. Statistics. www.cbc.gov.tw/EngHome/statistics.asp.

China Currency Coalition. 2004. Petition for Relief Under Section 301(a) of the Trade Act of 1974, As Amended. Washington. www.chinacurrencycoalition.org/pdfs/petition.pdf (accessed September 9).

Cline, William R. 1976. *International Monetary Reform and the Developing Countries.* Washington: Brookings Institution.

Cline, William R. 1984. *International Debt: Systemic Risk and Policy Response.* Washington: Institute for International Economics.

Cline, William R. 1989. *United States External Adjustment and the World Economy.* Washington: Institute for International Economics.

Cline, William R. 1994. *International Economic Policy in the 1990s.* Cambridge, MA: MIT Press.

Cline, William R. 1995a. *Predicting External Imbalances for the United States and Japan,* POLICY ANALYSES IN INTERNATIONAL ECONOMICS 41. Washington: Institute for International Economics.

Cline, William R. 1995b. *International Debt Reexamined.* Washington: Institute for International Economics.

Cline, William R. 1997. *Trade and Income Distribution.* Washington: Institute for International Economics.

Cline, William R. 2001. Ex-Im, Exports, and Private Capital: Will Financial Markets Squeeze the Bank? In *The Ex-Im Bank in the 21st Century: A New Approach?,* eds. Gary C. Hufbauer and Rita M. Rodriguez. Washington: Institute for International Economics.

Cohen, Daniel. 1997. *Growth and External Debt: A New Perspective on the African and Latin American Tragedies.* CEPR Discussion Papers 1753. Paris: Centre for Economic Policy Research.

Cooper, Richard N. 2001. Is the US Current Account Deficit Sustainable? Will It Be Sustained? *Brookings Papers on Economic Activity* 1. Washington: Brookings Institution.

Council of Economic Advisers. 2004. *Economic Report of the President.* Washington.

Council of Economic Advisers. 2005. *Economic Report of the President.* Washington.

Croke, Hilary, Steven B. Kamin, and Sylvain Leduc. 2005. *Financial Market Developments and Economic Activity During Current Account Adjustments in Industrial Economies.* International Finance Discussion Papers 827 (February). Washington: Federal Reserve Board.

de Rugy, Veronique. 2004. *The Republican Spending Explosion.* Cato Briefing Paper 87. Washington: Cato Institute.

Destler, I. M. 2005. *American Trade Politics, 4th ed.* Washington: Institute for International Economics.

Deutsche Bank. 2004. Deutsche Bank Research, Key Economic Indicators: Korea. Deutsche Bank, Frankfurt. www.dbresearch.com (accessed December 13).

Dooley, Michael, David Folkerts-Landau, and Peter Garber. 2004. *A Map to the Revived Bretton Woods End Game: Direct Investment, Rising Real Wages, and the Absorption of Excess Labor in the Periphery.* New York: Deutsche Bank Global Markets Research.

Erceg, Christopher J., Luca Guerrieri, and Christopher Gust. 2005. *Expansionary Fiscal Shocks and the Trade Deficit.* International Financial Discussion Papers 825 (January). Washington: Federal Reserve Board.

Faust, Jon. 2005. Is Applied Monetary Policy Analysis Hard? Washington: Federal Reserve Board. Photocopy.

Federal Reserve Board. 2005a. Currency Weights: Broad Index of the Foreign Exchange Value of the Dollar. Federal Reserve Statistical Release H.10. www.federalreserve.gov/releases/ (accessed July 10).

Federal Reserve Board. 2005b. Price-Adjusted Broad Dollar Index. www.federalreserve.gov/releases/h10/Summary/indexbc_m.txt (accessed July 10).

Federal Reserve Board. 2005c. Flow of Funds Accounts of the United States. www.federalreserve.gov/releases/ (accessed July 10).

Federal Reserve Board. 2005d. Foreign Exchange Rates (Daily). Statistical Release H.10. www.federalreserve.gov/releases/ (accessed July 10).

Federal Reserve Board. 2005e. Transcript, Federal Open Market Committee Meeting, October 6, 1979. www.federalreserve.gov/FOMC/transcripts/default.htm (accessed July 10).

Feldstein, Martin, and Charles Horioka. 1980. Domestic Saving and International Capital Flows. *The Economic Journal* 90, no. 358 (June): 314–29.

Ferguson, Roger W. 2005. US Current Account Deficit: Causes and Consequences. Remarks at University of North Carolina, April 20. www.federalreserve.gov (accessed July 10).

Fischer, Stanley, and Jacob A. Frenkel. 1974. Economic Growth and Stages of the Balance of Payments: A Theoretical Model. In *Trade, Stability, and Macroeconomics*, eds. George Horwich and Paul A. Samuelson. New York: Academic Press.

Frank, Charles R., Jr., and William R. Cline. 1971. Measurement of Debt-Servicing Capacity: An Application of Discriminant Analysis. *Journal of International Economics* 1 (August): 327–44.

Freund, Caroline L. 2000. *Current Account Adjustment in Industrialized Countries.* International Finance Discussion Papers 692 (December). Washington: Federal Reserve Board of Governors.

Gagnon, Joseph E. 2003. *Long-Run Supply Effects and the Elasticities Approach to Trade.* International Finance Discussion Papers 754 (January). Washington: Federal Reserve Board.

Gagnon, Joseph E. 2004. *Growth-Led Exports: Is Variety the Spice of Life?* International Finance Discussion Papers 822 (November). Washington: Federal Reserve Board.

Gale, William G., and Peter R. Orszag. 2004. The Budget Outlook: Projections and Implications. *The Economists' Voice* 1, no. 2.

Gale, William G., and Samara R. Potter. 2002. An Economic Evaluation of the Economic Growth and Tax Relief Reconciliation Act of 2001. *National Tax Journal* 55, no. 1 (March): 133–86.

Geithner, Timothy F. 2005. Economic Policy and the Sustainability of US Productivity Growth. Remarks at the Puerto Rico Bankers' Association meeting, April 12.

Goldstein, Morris. 2004. China and the Renminbi Exchange Rate. In *Dollar Adjustment: How Much? Against What?* Special Report 17, eds. C. Fred Bergsten and John Williamson. Washington: Institute for International Economics.

Goldstein, Morris, and Philip Turner. 2004. *Controlling Currency Mismatches in Emerging Markets.* Washington: Institute for International Economics.

Goldstein, Morris, Carmen Reinhart, and Graciela Kaminsky. 2000. *Assessing Financial Vulnerability: An Early Warning System for Emerging Markets.* Washington: Institute for International Economics.

Gordon, Robert. 1996. *The Time-Varying NAIRU and Its Implications for Economic Policy.* NBER Working Paper 5735 (August). Cambridge, MA: National Bureau of Economic Research.

Gourinchas, Pierre-Olivier, and Hélène Rey. 2005. *International Financial Adjustment.* CEPR Discussion Paper 4923 (February). London: Centre for Economic Policy Research.

Gramlich, Edward M. 2004. Budget and Trade Deficits: Linked, Both Worrisome in the Long Run, but not Twins. Remarks at Euromoney Bond Investors Congress, London (February).

Greenspan, Alan. 1999. Information, Productivity, and Capital Investment. Remarks to the Business Council, Boca Raton, FL (October 28).

Greenspan, Alan. 2002. The US Economy. Remarks to the Independent Community Bankers of America, Honolulu (March 13).

Greenspan, Alan. 2004a. Euro in Wider Circles. Remarks to the European Banking Congress, Frankfurt (November 19).

Greenspan, Alan. 2004b. Current Account. Remarks to the Economic Club of New York, New York (March 2).

Grubert, Harry. 1997. *Another Look at the Low Taxable Income of Foreign-Controlled Companies in the United States.* Office of Tax Analysis Paper 74 (October). Washington: US Treasury Department.

Helpman, Elhanan, and Paul R. Krugman. 1985. *Market Structure and Foreign Trade: Increasing Returns, Imperfect Competition, and the International Economy.* Cambridge, MA: MIT Press.

Henderson, James E., and Richard E. Quandt. 1971. *Microeconomic Theory: A Mathematical Approach.* New York: McGraw Hill.

Hooper, Peter, and Jaime Marquez. 1995. Exchange Rates, Prices, and External Adjustment. In *Understanding Interdependence: The Macroeconomics of the Open Economy,* ed. Peter B. Kenen. Princeton, NJ: Princeton University Press.

Houthakker, Henry, and Stephen P. Magee. 1969. Income and Price Elasticities in World Trade. *Review of Economics and Statistics* 51: 111–25.

Hufbauer, Gary C., and Yee Wong. 2004. *China Bashing 2004.* International Economic Policy Briefs PB 04-5 (September). Washington: Institute for International Economics.

Hufbauer, Gary C., and Paul L. E. Grieco. 2005. *Reforming the US Corporate Tax.* Washington: Institute for International Economics.

IIF (Institute of International Finance). 1999. *Report of the Working Group on Financial Crises in Emerging Markets.* Washington.

IIF (Institute of International Finance). 2004. Capital Flows to Emerging Market Economies. www.iif.com (accessed October 2).

IMF (International Monetary Fund). 2000. *World Economic Outlook: Asset Prices and the Business Cycle.* Washington.

IMF (International Monetary Fund). 2002. How Worrisome are External Imbalances? In *World Economic Outlook: Trade and Finance.* Washington.

IMF (International Monetary Fund). 2003a. *IMF Committee on Balance of Payments Statistics Annual Report 2002.* Washington.

IMF (International Monetary Fund). 2003b. Transcript of the *World Economic Outlook* Press Conference, September 18. Washington.

IMF (International Monetary Fund). 2004a. How Will the US Budget Deficit Affect the Rest of the World? In *World Economic Outlook.* Washington.

IMF (International Monetary Fund). 2004b. International Financial Statistics. CD-Rom version. Washington.

IMF (International Monetary Fund). 2004c. *World Economic Outlook: The Global Demographic Transition.* Washington.

IMF (International Monetary Fund). 2004d. Direction of Trade Statistics. CD-Rom version. Washington.

IMF (International Monetary Fund). 2004e. *Global Financial Stability Report: Market Developments and Issues.* Washington.

IMF (International Monetary Fund). 2004f. World Economic Outlook Database. Washington. www.imf.org/external/pubs/ft/weo/2004/02/data/index.htm (accessed July 10).

IMF (International Monetary Fund). 2005a. International Financial Statistics. CD-Rom version. Washington.

IMF (International Monetary Fund). 2005b. World Economic Outlook Database. Washington. www.imf.org/external/pubs/ft/weo/2005/01/data/index.htm (accessed July 10).

IMF (International Monetary Fund). 2005c. *World Economic Outlook: Globalization and External Imbalances.* Washington.

IRS (Internal Revenue Service). 2004. Individual Income Tax Returns: Selected Income and Tax Items for Specified Tax Years, 1985-2002. Historical Table. *Statistics of Income Bulletin* (Summer). www.irs.gov/pub/irs-soi/02in01si.xls (accessed July 10).

Jones, Matthew T., and Maurice Obstfeld. 2001. Saving, Investment, and Gold: A Reassessment of Historical Current Account Data. In *Money, Capital Mobility, and Trade: Essays in Honor of Robert Mundell,* eds. Guillermo A. Calvo, Rudi Dornbusch, and Maurice Obstfeld. Cambridge, MA: MIT Press.

Juster, F. Thomas, Joseph P. Lupton, James P. Smith, and Frank Stafford. 2004. *The Decline in Household Saving and the Wealth Effect.* Ann Arbor, MI: University of Michigan.

Kamin, Steven B. 2005. The Revived Bretton Woods System: Does It Explain Developments in Non-China Developing Asia? Paper presented at a conference entitled Revived Bretton Woods System: A New Paradigm for Asian Development? at the Federal Reserve Bank of San Francisco (February 4).

Kindleberger, Charles P. 1958. *International Economics.* Homewood, IL: Richard D. Irwin, Inc.

Kouri, Pentti. 1983. Balance of Payments and the Foreign Exchange Market: A Dynamic Partial Equilibrium Model. In *Economic Interdependence and Flexible Exchange Rates*, eds. J. Bhandari and B. Putnam. Cambridge, MA: MIT Press.

Krugman, Paul. 1989. Differences in Income Elasticities and Trends in Real Exchange Rates. *European Economic Review* 33: 1055–85.

Krugman, Paul. 1991. *Has the Adjustment Process Worked?* POLICY ANALYSES IN INTERNATIONAL ECONOMICS 34. Washington: Institute for International Economics.

Krugman, Paul. 2003. *The Great Unravelling: Losing Our Way in the New Century.* New York: W. W. Norton.

Krugman, Paul, and Lance Taylor. 1978. Contractionary Effects of Devaluation. *Journal of International Economics* 8: 445–56.

Landefeld, J. Steven, Ann M. Lawson, and Douglas B. Weinberg. 1992. Rates of Return on Direct Investment. *Survey of Current Business* 72 (August): 79–86.

Lane, Philip R., and Gian Maria Milesi-Ferretti. 2000. The External Wealth of Nations: Measures of Foreign Assets and Liabilities for Industrial and Developing Countries. International Monetary Fund, Washington. Photocopy (August).

Lane, Philip R., and Gian Maria Milesi-Ferretti. 2001. *Long-Term Capital Movements.* NBER Working Paper 8366 (July). Cambridge, MA: National Bureau of Economic Research.

Leahy, Michael P. 1998. New Summary Measures of the Foreign Exchange Value of the Dollar. *Federal Reserve Bulletin* (October): 811–18.

Levin, Andrew T., John H. Rogers, and Ralph W. Tryon. 1997. *A Guide to FRB/Global.* International Finance Discussion Papers 588 (August). Washington: Federal Reserve Board.

Lewis, Karen K. 1999. Trying to Explain Home Bias in Equities and Consumption. *Journal of Economic Literature* 37, no. 2 (June): 571–608.

Mann, Catherine L. 1999. *Is the U.S. Trade Deficit Sustainable?* Washington: Institute for International Economics.

Mann, Catherine L. 2003. How Long the Strong Dollar? In *Dollar Overvaluation and the World Economy,* Special Report 16, eds. C. Fred Bergsten and John Williamson. Washington: Institute for International Economics.

Mann, Catherine L. 2004. Managing Exchange Rates: Achievement of Global Re-Balancing or Evidence of Global Co-Dependency? *Business Economics* (July): 20–29.

Marazzi, Mario, Nathan Sheets, and Robert Vigfusson. 2005. *Exchange Rate Pass-through to U.S. Import Prices: Some New Evidence.* International Finance Discussion Papers 833 (April). Washington: Federal Reserve Board.

Markowitz, Harry. 1952. Portfolio Selection. *Journal of Finance* 7, no. 1 (March): 77–91.

Marris, Stephen. 1985. *Deficits and the Dollar: The World Economy at Risk.* POLICY ANALYSES IN INTERNATIONAL ECONOMICS 14. Washington: Institute for International Economics.

Mataloni, Raymond J., Jr. 2000. An Examination of the Low Rates of Return of Foreign-Owned U.S. Companies. *Survey of Current Business* (March): 55–73.

McKinnon, Ronald. 2005. Exchange Rates, Wages, and International Adjustment: Japan and China versus the United States. Paper presented at a conference entitled Revived Bretton Woods System: A New Paradigm for Asian Development? at the Federal Reserve Bank of San Francisco, February 4.

Meade, James. 1951. *The Theory of International Economic Policy,* volumes 1 and 2. London: Royal Institute of International Affairs, Oxford University Press.

Meese, Richard, and Kenneth Rogoff. 1983. Empirical Exchange Rate Models of the Seventies: Do They Fit Out-of-Sample? *Journal of International Economics* 14: 3–24.

Moody's Investors Service. 2003. *Sovereign Bond Defaults, Rating Transitions, and Recoveries (1985–2002).* New York: Moody's Investors Service, Global Credit Research.

Mussa, Michael. 2005. Sustaining Global Growth While Reducing External Imbalances. In *The United States and the World Economy: Foreign Economic Policy for the Next Decade,* C.

Fred Bergsten and the Institute for International Economics. Washington: Institute for International Economics.

Net National Disposable Income, Annual National Accounts, Volume 2, 1970–2002 (2003 prov.). Paris. OECD, 2004d.Obstfeld, Maurice, and Kenneth Rogoff. 2000. *The Six Major Puzzles in International Macroeconomics: Is There a Common Cause?* NBER Working Paper 7777 (July). Cambridge, MA: National Bureau of Economic Research.

Obstfeld, Maurice, and Kenneth Rogoff. 2004. *The Unsustainable US Current Account Position Revisited.* NBER Working Paper 10869 (October). Cambridge, MA: National Bureau of Economic Research.

OECD (Organization for Economic Cooperation and Development). 2003. *OECD Economic Outlook* 74 (December). Paris.

OECD (Organization for Economic Cooperation and Development). 2004a. *OECD Economic Outlook* 75 (June). Paris.

OECD (Organization for Economic Cooperation and Development). 2004b. *United States: OECD Economic Surveys.* Paris.

OECD (Organization for Economic Cooperation and Development). 2004c. *OECD Economic Outlook* 76 (December) Paris.

OECD (Organization for Economic Cooperation and Development). 2004d. Net National Disposable Income, Annual National Accounts, volume 2, 1970–2002 (2003 prov.). Paris.

OMB (Office of Management and Budget). 2005a. *Overview of the President's 2006 Budget.* Washington.

OMB (Office of Management and Budget). 2005b. *Historical Tables: Budget of the United States Government, Fiscal Year 2005.* Washington.

Orszag, Peter R. 2002. Macroeconomic Implications of Federal Budget Proposals and the Scoring Process. Testimony before the Subcommittee on Legislative and Budget Process, House Rules Committee (May 2).

Peter, Marcel. 2002. *Estimating Default Probabilities of Emerging Market Sovereigns: A New Look at a Not-So-New Literature.* HEI Working Paper 06/2002. Geneva: Graduate Institute of International Studies.

Peterson, Peter G. 2004. *Running on Empty: How The Democratic and Republican Parties Are Bankrupting Our Future and What Americans Can Do About It.* New York: Farrar, Strauss, and Giroux.

Poterba, James M. 2000. Stock Market Wealth and Consumption. *Journal of Economic Perspectives* 14, no. 2 (Spring): 99–118.

Rajan, Raghuram. 2005. Global Current Account Imbalances: Hard Landing or Soft Landing? Speech to Crédit Suisse First Boston Conference, Hong Kong (March 15). www.imf.org/ external/np/speeches/2005/031505.htm (accessed July 18).

Reinhart, Carmen M., and Kenneth S. Rogoff. 2004. Serial Default and the "Paradox" of Rich-to-Poor Capital Flows. *American Economic Review* 94, no. 2 (May): 53–58.

Reinhart, Carmen M., Kenneth S. Rogoff, and Miguel A. Savastano. 2003. Debt Intolerance. *Brookings Papers on Economic Activity* (Spring) 1: 1–74.

Rivlin, Alice M., and Isabel Sawhill. 2004. *How to Balance the Budget.* Policy Brief 130 (March). Washington: Brookings Institution.

Roubini, Nouriel, and Brad Setser. 2004. The US as a Net Debtor: The Sustainability of the US External Imbalances. New York University. Photocopy (September).

Roubini, Nouriel, and Brad Setser. 2005. Will the Bretton Woods 2 Regime Unravel Soon? The Risk of a Hard Landing in 2005–06. Paper prepared for the conference entitled Revived Bretton Woods System: A New Paradigm for Asian Development? at the San Francisco Federal Reserve Bank, February 4.

Rubin, Robert E., Peter R. Orszag, and Allen Sinai. 2004. Sustained Budget Deficits: Longer-Run US Economic Performance and the Risk of Financial and Fiscal Disarray. Paper presented at the AEA-NAEFA joint session, ASSA Annual Meetings, San Diego, CA, January 4.

Salomon Smith Barney. 2001. Introducing CTERI: A New Guide to Currency Valuation. *Emerging Markets* (January 9). New York: Salomon Smith Barney.

Stiglitz, Joseph. 2003. Dealing with Debt: How to Reform the Global Financial System. *Harvard International Review* (Spring): 54–59.

Summers, Lawrence. 2000a. The Imperative of Balanced Global Economic Growth. Speech at the Institute for International Economics, Washington, January 14.

Summers, Lawrence. 2000b. Statement at the Post-G-7 Press Conference. Press Release LS-346, January 22. Washington: US Treasury Department.

Summers, Lawrence. 2004. The US Current Account Deficit and the Global Economy. Per Jacobsson Lecture, Washington, October 3.

Taiwan Ministry of Economic Affairs. 2005. Economic Indicators. Taipei City: Department of Statistics, Ministry of Economic Affairs. http://2k3dmz2.moea.gov.tw/gnweb/english/e_main.aspx?Page=D (accessed July 10).

Taylor, John B. 1993. *Discretion versus Policy Rules in Practice.* Carnegie Rochester Conference Series on Public Policy 39: 195–214.

Tille, Cedric. 2003. The Impact of Exchange Rate Movements on U.S. Foreign Debt. *Current Issues in Economics and Finance* 9, no. 1 (January), Federal Reserve Bank of New York: 1–7.

Tobin, James. 1958. Liquidity Preference as Behavior Towards Risk. *Review of Economic Studies* 25, no. 67: 65–86.

Truman, Edwin M. 2001. *The International Implications of Paying Down the Debt.* International Economics Policy Briefs PB 01–7 (May). Washington: Institute for International Economics.

Truman, Edwin M. 2004. Budget and External Deficits: Same Family but not Twins. Paper presented at the Federal Reserve Bank of Boston conference entitled The Macroeconomics of Fiscal Policy (June 14–16).

Truman, Edwin M. 2005. The United States and the World Economy. Paper presented at the conference entitled Economic Imbalance: Fiscal and Monetary Policy for Sustainable Growth, at the Levy Economics Institute of Bard College, NY (April 21–22).

UBS. 1998. *Special Report on Social Security.* New York: UBS.

USITC (US International Trade Commission). 2005. United States Interactive Tariff and Trade Dataweb. Washington. www.usitc.gov (accessed July 10).

US Treasury. 2003. *U.S. Holdings of Foreign Securities as of December 31, 2001.* Washington: US Department of the Treasury.

US Treasury. 2004a. *Treasury International Capital System.* US Department of the Treasury, Washington. www.treas.gov/tic (accessed July 10).

US Treasury. 2004b. *The Debt to the Penny and Who Holds It.* Washington: US Department of Treasury Bureau of Public Debt.

US Treasury. 2004c. Final Monthly Treasury Statement of Receipts and Outlays of the United States Government for Fiscal Year 2004 through September 30, 2004. Department of the Treasury, Washington. www.fms.treas.gov.

Van Trotsenberg, Axel, and Alan MacArthur. 1999. *The HIPC Initiative: Delivering Debt Relief to Poor Countries.* Washington: World Bank and International Monetary Fund.

Williamson, John. 1983. The Exchange Rate System. POLICY ANALYSES IN INTERNATIONAL ECONOMICS 5. Washington: Institute for International Economics.

Williamson, John. 2004. Current Account Objectives: Who Should Adjust? In *Dollar Adjustment: How Much? Against What?* Special Report 17, eds. C. Fred Bergsten and John Williamson. Washington: Institute for International Economics.

World Bank. 2002. *World Development Report 2002: Building Institutions for Markets.* Washington.

World Bank. 2004a. World Development Indicators 2004. CD-Rom version. Washington.

World Bank. 2004b. Global Development Finance 2004. CD-Rom version. Washington.

World Bank. 2005. World Development Indicators 2005. CD-Rom version. Washington.

Wren-Lewis, Simon. 2004. The Needed Changes in Bilateral Exchange Rates. In *Dollar Adjustment: How Much? Against What?* Special Report 17, eds. C. Fred Bergsten and John Williamson. Washington: Institute for International Economics.

WTO (World Trade Organization). 2005. *The General Agreement on Tariffs and Trade (GATT 1946).* Geneva. www.wto.org/english/docs_e/legal_e/gatt47_01_e.htm (accessed July 23, 2005).

Index

adjustment, 275
  Blanchard, Giavazzi, and Sa model,
    212–14
  and consumption, 108–109
  external, 131–33
  global, 233–47
  Gourinchas and Rey model, 214–15
  long-run, 216
  Obstfeld and Rogoff model, 211–12
  principal findings, 265–68
  prospects for, 208–209
  scenarios, 90–95
Afghanistan, 124
Africa. *See also specific countries by name*
  current account balance, 253, 254*t*
  debt-export ratio, 168*n*
  saving, investment, current accounts,
    and GDP, 203, 204*t*
alternative minimum tax (AMT), 123
antisubsidy rules, 279
Argentina, 4, 175*n*
  capital supply and current account
    performance, 225
  creditor/debtor status, 17*t*, 25, 25*f*
  current account balance and GDP
    values, 250*t*
  data sources, 31*t*
  equilibrium exchange rates and
    misalignment, 256, 257*t*
  external assets, liabilities, and NIIP, 15*t*

  optimal exchange rate realignment,
    242*t*, 244*n*
  US trade balance, 222, 223*f*
Argentine peso
  real appreciation, 237*t*
  US private external assets, 41*t*
  value against US dollar, 43, 43*t*
ASEAN-4. *See* Association of Southeast
  Asian Nations
Asian currencies, 7. *See also specific*
  countries, currencies by name
assets and liabilities. *See under specific*
  countries by name
Association of Southeast Asian Nations
  (ASEAN-4), 203, 204*t*
Australia
  current account adjustment target, 239
  current account balance, 4, 18, 250*t*
  data sources, 31*t*
  debtor status, 17*t*, 18–19, 20*f*, 260
  equilibrium exchange rate, 255*n*, 256,
    257*t*
  external assets, liabilities, and NIIP, 15*t*
  external debt ratio, 154
  optimal exchange rate realignment,
    242*t*, 244
  rates of return on NIIP, 62, 63*f*
  target changes, 250*t*, 251
  US foreign non-dollar assets in, 93

Chilean peso, 41*t*, 43*t*, 237*t*
China
creditor status, 17*t*, 22, 23*f*
current account balance, 188, 240, 250*t*, 253, 254*t*
data sources, 31*t*
domestic demand policy, 278
equilibrium exchange rates and misalignment, 257*t*
exchange rate rigidity, 187–88, 231–32, 273, 279
investment, 204
optimal exchange rate realignment, 242*t*, 243–44
policy coordination versus laissez-faire, 246–47
purchases of US assets, 155
reserves, 229, 230*f*, 273
trade penalties against, 184
US trade balance, 188, 221, 222*f*, 273
Chinese renminbi (yuan)
real appreciation, 237*t*, 238–39
US private external assets in, 41*t*, 42–43
revaluation of, 184, 188, 256
value against US dollar, 7–8, 43*t*, 231–32, 232*f*, 233
CNCI. *See* capitalized net capital income
Colombia, 242*t*, 250*t*
Colombian peso, 41*t*, 43, 43*t*, 237*t*
Congressional Budget Office (CBO), 110, 122
baseline and alternative fiscal balance projections, 123–24, 123*f*, 266–67
baseline projection of federal revenues and expenditures and fiscal balance, 112, 113*f*
baseline projection of revenues by source, 112–14, 113*f*
discretionary spending projections, 122
consumer prices, 179
consumption
fiscal adjustment and, 108–109
general equilibrium model simulations, 146–49, 147*t*
goods, 11*n*
government spending as, 100*n*
personal, 103–105, 104*t*
US government, 58*n*, 103–105, 104*t*
corporate activity tax, 127*n*
corporate revenues, 112–14, 113*f*
corporate savings, 102, 103*f*
countervailing duties, 279
Cramer's rule, 138*n*

creditor status, 9*n*, 13
crisis
debate, 184–209
indicators, 168–70
risk, 153–217
current account deficit, 1, 2*f*, 5, 18, 103–105, 104*t*, 185–86. *See also specific countries*
backcast outcomes, 79, 79*f*–80*f*
baseline projections, 270
comparison with developing countries, 227, 227*f*
debate about, 184–209
in 1980s, 234–35, 235*f*
under exchange rate adjustment and acceleration of foreign growth, 93–95, 94*t*
forecasting, 263–65
long-term, 180–81, 181*f*
as percent of GDP, 101–102, 102*f*, 250*t*
projections, 69–97, 87*f*–88*f*, 91*f*, 132*n*
relative to rest-of-world GDP, 219–20, 220*f*, 224–25, 224*f*, 273, 277
risks of, 268–72
share in world current account surplus, 155–56, 156*f*
sustainability of, 153–217, 268–72
2004 expected balance and Williamson target, 253, 254*t*
Czech Republic, 17*t*, 25*f*, 31*t*, 237*t*

Danish krone, 42*n*, 237*t*
DAX, 38
debt burden. *See also specific countries*
alternative measures of, 63–66
debt cycle, 10–13, 11*f*, 16–25
and growth performance, 28–29
international, 9–31, 259–61
patterns, 16–18
debtor status, 9*n*, 13
debt ratios, 167–74
defense spending, 115–16, 116*f*
deficit. *See* current account deficit, United States; trade deficit; twin deficits; *specific countries by name*
Deficit Control Act, 122
Denmark
data sources, 31*t*
debtor status, 17*t*, 18, 20*f*, 260
external assets, liabilities, and NIIP, 15*t*
rates of return on NIIP, 62, 63*f*
developed countries, 221*n*, 228*n*. *See also specific countries by name*
GDP growth in, 228, 228*f*

Federal Open Market Committee, 178
Federal Reserve, 40, 46
    Flow of Funds Accounts (FFA),
        117–18, 118*f*
    monetary policy, 179, 234
    policy rate, 206–207
    real broad index, 83*n*
    real exchange rate index, 236–38, 237*t*
    recent analyses, 196–202
Federal Reserve Board Global Model
    (FRB/Global), 129*n*, 207–209, 272
FFA. *See* Flow of Funds Accounts
Finland
    data sources, 31*t*
    debtor status, 17*t*, 18–20, 20*f*, 20*n*, 154,
        260
    external assets, liabilities, and NIIP, 15*t*
    rates of return on NIIP, 62, 63*f*
    sovereign rating, 154*n*
fiscal balance, United States, 99–151, 112*f*
    alternative projections, 123–24, 123*f*
    baseline projections, 112, 113*f*, 122–24,
        123*f*
    general equilibrium model, 134–51
    long-term problem, 125–28
    as percent of GDP, 101–102, 102*f*
Flow of Funds Accounts (FFA), 117–18,
    118*f*
France
    CAC 40, 38
    creditor status, 17*t*, 19*f*
    data sources, 31*t*
    external assets, liabilities, and NIIP, 15*t*
    gross financial assets relative to
        disposable income, 161, 162*f*
    household gross financial assets,
        158–59, 159*f*
    rates of return on NIIP, 62, 63*f*
    rejection of European Union
        constitution, 83*n*, 166–67
FRB/Global model. *See* Federal Reserve
    Board Global model
FTSE 200, 38

general equilibrium model, 129, 267–68
    calibration, 138–46
    framework for, 128–31
    implications, 149–51
    matrix equation, 135*t*
    model, 135–38
    parameters, 129, 145*t*
    relating trade and fiscal balances,
        134–51

simulation results, 146–49, 147*t*
German deutsche mark, 179
Germany
    creditor status, 17*t*, 19*f*
    data sources, 31*t*
    DAX, 38
    dollar policy, 155
    external assets, liabilities, and NIIP, 15*t*
    global equity bubble burst, 159*n*
    household gross financial assets,
        158–59, 159*f*
    Louvre agreement, 179
    rates of return on NIIP, 62, 63*f*
    real Treasury bill rate for, 12–13
Gourinchas and Rey model, 214–15
government consumption, 58*n*, 100*n*,
    103–105, 104*t*
government investment, 103–105, 104*t*
government saving, 101, 103–105, 104*t*
Greece
    current account deficit, 18
    data sources, 31*t*
    debtor status, 17*t*, 18, 20–21, 21*f*, 260
    external assets, liabilities, and NIIP, 15*t*
    rates of return on NIIP, 62, 63*f*
Greenspan, Alan, 185–86
gross domestic product (GDP)
    accounting, 100–101
    debt-to-GDP ratio, 170
    general equilibrium model simulations,
        146–49, 147*t*
    global, 204*t*, 205
    growth in developed and developing
        countries, 228, 228*f*
gross private investment, 103–105, 104*t*
Group of Seven (G-7). *See also specific
    countries*
    global capital stock, 160
    growth in 1980s, 234–35, 235*f*
    household gross financial assets,
        158–59, 159*f*
    Louvre Agreement, 179, 234
growth performance, 28–29, 29*f*
    in 1980s, 234–35, 235*f*

hard-landing scenario, 175–79
health reform, plausible, 127
health spending, 125*n*
Heavily Indebted Poor Countries (HIPC)
    initiative, 64, 169
    enhanced version, 169

gross external liabilities, 22*n*
gross international assets, 22*n*
net international investment position,
    22*n*
rates of return on NIIP, 62, 63*f*
rejection of European Union
    constitution, 83*n*, 166–67
net international investment position
    (NIIP), 260. *See also specific countries*
annual change in, 28–29, 29*f*, 29*n*
baseline projections, 83–85, 84*t*
data sources, 31*t*
estimates of, 13–16, 30, 31*t*
industrial country rates of return on,
    62–63, 63*f*
simple projection model for, 73
net private investment, 102, 103*f*
new economy, 2, 121
newly industrialized economies. *See also
    specific countries, economies by name*
current account adjustment targets, 240
current account balance, 253, 254*t*
saving, investment, current accounts,
    and GDP, 204*t*, 205
New Zealand
current account deficit, 18
data sources, 31*t*
debtor status, 17*t*, 18–19, 20*f*, 260
external assets, liabilities, and NIIP, 15*t*
external debt ratio, 154
rates of return on NIIP, 62, 63*f*
US foreign non-dollar assets in, 93
New Zealand dollar
change against US dollar, 43*t*
real appreciation, 237*t*
US private external assets in, 41*t*, 42
NIIP. *See* net international investment
    position
Nikkei 225, 38
NIPA. *See* national income and product
    accounts
Nixon administration, 279
Nokia, 20*n*
Norway
annual change in NIIP and growth
    rate, 28–29, 29*f*
creditor status, 17*t*, 18–19, 19*f*, 23
data sources, 31*t*
external assets, liabilities, and NIIP, 15*t*
net international investment position,
    23
Norwegian krone
change against US dollar, 43*t*

real appreciation, 237*t*
US private external assets, 41*t*, 42

Obstfeld-Rogoff model, 191–92
key features of, 211–13
Occam's razor, 205
OECD. *See* Organization for Economic
    Cooperation and Development
oil economies, 240. *See also specific
    countries, economies by name*
oil prices, 236, 240*n*
Omnibus Trade and Competitiveness
    Act, 183
OPEC. *See* Organization of Petroleum
    Exporting Countries
Organization for Economic Cooperation
    and Development (OECD), 266
Organization of Petroleum Exporting
    Countries (OPEC), 27, 166*n*

peace dividends, 58, 115, 266
Pebble Beach, 57
personal consumption, 103–105, 104*t*
personal income tax revenues, 114, 114*f*
personal saving(s). *See also specific
    countries*
measures of, 117–18, 118*f*
Peru, 17*t*, 24*f*, 31*t*
Peruvian nsol, 41*t*, 43*t*
Philippine peso
change against US dollar, 43*t*
real appreciation, 237*t*, 239
US private external assets in, 41*t*
Philippines. *See also* Association of
    Southeast Asian Nations
current account adjustment target, 240
current account balance, 188, 250*t*
data sources, 31*t*
debtor status, 17*t*, 24*f*, 25
optimal exchange rate realignment,
    242*t*
Plaza Accord, 3, 179, 234, 247, 276
Poland, 17*t*, 24*f*, 31*t*, 237*t*
policy coordination, 246–47
policy implications, 275–81
portfolio investment stocks, 72
Portugal
annual change in NIIP and growth
    rate, 28–29, 29*f*
current account deficit, 18
data sources, 31*t*
debtor status, 17*t*, 18, 20–21, 21*f*, 260
external assets, liabilities, and NIIP, 15*t*
rates of return on NIIP, 62, 63*f*

subsidies, 279
Summers, Lawrence, 184–86
sustainability benchmarks, 172–74
Sweden
    current account balance and GDP
        values, 250t
    data sources, 31t
    debtor status, 17t, 18, 20f, 260
    external assets, liabilities, and NIIP, 15t
    optimal exchange rate realignment,
        242t
    rates of return on NIIP, 62, 63f
    US foreign non-dollar assets in, 93
Swedish krona
    change against US dollar, 43t
    real appreciation, 237t, 238
    US private external assets in, 41t, 42
Swiss franc
    change against US dollar, 43t
    real appreciation, 237t
    US private external assets, 41t, 42
Switzerland
    annual change in NIIP and growth
        rate, 28–29, 29f
    creditor status, 17t, 18, 19f
    current account balance and GDP
        values, 250t
    data sources, 31t
    external assets, liabilities, and NIIP, 14,
        15t
    optimal exchange rate realignment,
        242t
    rates of return on NIIP, 62, 63f

Taiwan. *See also* newly industrialized
        economies
    creditor status, 17t, 22–23, 23f
    current account balance, 188, 250t, 253
    data sources, 31t
    as developed country, 228n
    as emerging-market economy, 226,
        226n
    exchange rate rigidity, 273
    net capital flows to, 226, 226f
    net international investment position,
        23
    optimal exchange rate realignment,
        242t
    reserves, 229, 230f, 273
Taiwanese dollar
    real appreciation, 237t
    US private external assets, 41t, 42–43
    value against US dollar, 43t, 231, 232f,
        233

tax, withholding, 280–81
tax cuts, 115, 233
tax rate, 146–49, 147t
Taylor rule, 129, 142, 143n, 268
terrorism, war on, 124
Thai baht
    real appreciation, 237t
    US private external assets in, 41t, 43
    value against US dollar, 43t, 231, 232f,
        233
Thailand. *See also* Association of
        Southeast Asian Nations
    creditor status, 25
    current account balance, 188, 250t
    data sources, 31t
    debtor status, 17t, 25f
    exchange rate rigidity, 273
    optimal exchange rate realignment,
        242t
    US trade balance, 222, 223f
trade balance, 134n. *See also specific
        countries*
    baseline projections, 83–85, 84t, 85, 86t
    basic projection equations, 70
    definition of, 1n
    exchange rate interactions, 279–80
    general equilibrium model simulations,
        146–49, 147t
    macro model simulations, 215
trade deficit, 103–105, 104t, 183
trade elasticities, 107
transfers, government spending on, 100n
Treasury bill rates, 12
    real, 260
Treasury bonds, 116
Turkey
    data sources, 31t
    debtor status, 17t, 24f
    equilibrium exchange rates and
        misalignment, 256, 257t
Turkish lira, 237t, 256
twin deficits, 101

Ukraine, 17t, 24f, 31t
United Arab Emirates, 27n
United Kingdom
    current account balance, 18, 250t
    data sources, 31t
    debtor status, 17t, 18, 20–22, 21f, 260
    equilibrium exchange rates and
        misalignment, 256, 257t
    external assets, liabilities, and NIIP, 14,
        15t
    FTSE 200, 38

US Department of Homeland Security, 117
US dollar
defense of, 133
depreciation of, 128n, 166
real appreciation against, 7, 236–38, 237t
real dollars
baseline projections, 83–85, 84t, 85, 86t
under exchange rate adjustment and acceleration of foreign growth, 93–95, 94t
real effective exchange rate, 45–46, 45f
reserves, 166–67, 166n
strong dollar policy, 185, 186
US private external assets in, 40–42, 41t
valuation effects of major adjustments, 46–48

value of other currencies against, 43t, 44, 83n, 166, 179, 231, 232f
Uruguay Round, 184

Venezuela
creditor status, 17t, 22–23, 23f
current account adjustment target, 240
current account balance and GDP values, 250t
data sources, 31t
external debt, 23n
optimal exchange rate realignment, 242t
US trade balance, 222, 222n, 223f
Venezuelan bolivar, 41t, 43t, 237t
Volcker, Paul, 179, 179n, 234

Wallich, Henry, 179n
World Trade Organization (WTO), 184, 279

yen. *See* Japanese yen

Other Publications from the Institute for International Economics

* = out of print

POLICY ANALYSES IN
INTERNATIONAL ECONOMICS Series

1 The Lending Policies of the International
   Monetary Fund*   John Williamson
   August 1982   ISBN 0-88132-000-5
2 "Reciprocity": A New Approach to World
   Trade Policy?*   William R. Cline
   September 1982   ISBN 0-88132-001-3
3 Trade Policy in the 1980s*
   C. Fred Bergsten and William R. Cline
   November 1982   ISBN 0-88132-002-1
4 International Debt and the Stability of the
   World Economy*   William R. Cline
   September 1983   ISBN 0-88132-010-2
5 The Exchange Rate System,* Second Edition
   John Williamson
   Sept. 1983, rev. June 1985   ISBN 0-88132-034-X
6 Economic Sanctions in Support of Foreign
   Policy Goals*
   Gary Clyde Hufbauer and Jeffrey J. Schott
   October 1983   ISBN 0-88132-014-5
7 A New SDR Allocation?*   John Williamson
   March 1984   ISBN 0-88132-028-5
8 An International Standard for Monetary
   Stabilization*   Ronald L. McKinnon
   March 1984   ISBN 0-88132-018-8
9 The Yen/Dollar Agreement: Liberalizing
   Japanese Capital Markets*   Jeffrey A. Frankel
   December 1984   ISBN 0-88132-035-8
10 Bank Lending to Developing Countries: The
   Policy Alternatives*   C. Fred Bergsten,
   William R. Cline, and John Williamson
   April 1985   ISBN 0-88132-032-3
11 Trading for Growth: The Next Round of
   Trade Negotiations*
   Gary Clyde Hufbauer and Jeffrey J. Schott
   September 1985   ISBN 0-88132-033-1
12 Financial Intermediation Beyond the Debt
   Crisis*   Donald R. Lessard, John Williamson
   September 1985   ISBN 0-88132-021-8
13 The United States-Japan Economic Problem*
   C. Fred Bergsten and William R. Cline
   October 1985, 2d ed. January 1987
                              ISBN 0-88132-060-9
14 Deficits and the Dollar: The World Economy
   at Risk*   Stephen Marris
   December 1985, 2d ed. November 1987
                              ISBN 0-88132-067-6
15 Trade Policy for Troubled Industries*
   Gary Clyde Hufbauer and Howard R. Rosen
   March 1986   ISBN 0-88132-020-X

16 The United States and Canada: The Quest for
   Free Trade*   Paul Wonnacott, with an
   appendix by John Williamson
   March 1987   ISBN 0-88132-056-0
17 Adjusting to Success: Balance of Payments
   Policy in the East Asian NICs*
   Bela Balassa and John Williamson
   June 1987, rev. April 1990   ISBN 0-88132-101-X
18 Mobilizing Bank Lending to Debtor
   Countries*   William R. Cline
   June 1987   ISBN 0-88132-062-5
19 Auction Quotas and United States Trade
   Policy*   C. Fred Bergsten, Kimberly Ann
   Elliott, Jeffrey J. Schott, and Wendy E. Takacs
   September 1987   ISBN 0-88132-050-1
20 Agriculture and the GATT: Rewriting the
   Rules*   Dale E. Hathaway
   September 1987   ISBN 0-88132-052-8
21 Anti-Protection: Changing Forces in United
   States Trade Politics*
   I. M. Destler and John S. Odell
   September 1987   ISBN 0-88132-043-9
22 Targets and Indicators: A Blueprint for the
   International Coordination of Economic
   Policy
   John Williamson and Marcus H. Miller
   September 1987   ISBN 0-88132-051-X
23 Capital Flight: The Problem and Policy
   Responses*   Donald R. Lessard and
   John Williamson
   December 1987   ISBN 0-88132-059-5
24 United States-Canada Free Trade: An
   Evaluation of the Agreement*
   Jeffrey J. Schott
   April 1988   ISBN 0-88132-072-2
25 Voluntary Approaches to Debt Relief*
   John Williamson
   Sept.1988, rev. May 1989   ISBN 0-88132-098-6
26 American Trade Adjustment: The Global
   Impact*   William R. Cline
   March 1989   ISBN 0-88132-095-1
27 More Free Trade Areas?*
   Jeffrey J. Schott
   May 1989   ISBN 0-88132-085-4
28 The Progress of Policy Reform in Latin
   America*   John Williamson
   January 1990   ISBN 0-88132-100-1
29 The Global Trade Negotiations: What Can Be
   Achieved?*   Jeffrey J. Schott
   September 1990   ISBN 0-88132-137-0
30 Economic Policy Coordination: Requiem or
   Prologue?*   Wendy Dobson
   April 1991   ISBN 0-88132-102-8

65 The Benefits of Price Convergence:
Speculative Calculations
Gary Clyde Hufbauer, Erika Wada,
and Tony Warren
December 2001   ISBN 0-88132-333-0
66 **Managed Floating Plus**
Morris Goldstein
March 2002   ISBN 0-88132-336-5
67 **Argentina and the Fund: From Triumph
to Tragedy**   Michael Mussa
July 2002   ISBN 0-88132-339-X
68 **East Asian Financial Cooperation**
C. Randall Henning
September 2002   ISBN 0-88132-338-1
69 **Reforming OPIC for the 21st Century**
Theodore H. Moran
May 2003   ISBN 0-88132-342-X
70 **Awakening Monster: The Alien Tort
Statute of 1789**
Gary C. Hufbauer and Nicholas Mitrokostas
July 2003   ISBN 0-88132-366-7
71 **Korea after Kim Jong-il**
Marcus Noland
January 2004   ISBN 0-88132-373-X
72 **Roots of Competitiveness: China's Evolving
Agriculture Interests**   Daniel H. Rosen,
Scott Rozelle, and Jikun Huang
July 2004   ISBN 0-88132-376-4
73 **Prospects for a US-Taiwan FTA**
Nicholas R. Lardy and Daniel H. Rosen
December 2004   ISBN 0-88132-367-5
74 **Anchoring Reform with a US-Egypt
Free Trade Agreement**
Ahmed Galal and Robert Z. Lawrence
April 2005   ISBN 0-88132-368-3
75 **Curbing the Boom-Bust Cycle: Stabilizing
Capital Flows to Emerging Markets**
John Williamson
July 2005   ISBN 08813-330-6

BOOKS

IMF Conditionality* John Williamson, editor
1983   ISBN 0-88132-006-4
Trade Policy in the 1980s* William R. Cline, ed.
1983   ISBN 0-88132-031-5
Subsidies in International Trade*
Gary Clyde Hufbauer and Joanna Shelton Erb
1984   ISBN 0-88132-004-8
**International Debt: Systemic Risk and Policy
Response***   William R. Cline
1984   ISBN 0-88132-015-3
**Trade Protection in the United States: 31 Case
Studies*** Gary Clyde Hufbauer, Diane E. Berliner,
and Kimberly Ann Elliott
1986   ISBN 0-88132-040-4

**Toward Renewed Economic Growth in Latin
America*** Bela Balassa, Gerardo M. Bueno, Pedro-
Pablo Kuczynski, and Mario Henrique Simonsen
1986   ISBN 0-88132-045-5
Capital Flight and Third World Debt*
Donald R. Lessard and John Williamson, editors
1987   ISBN 0-88132-053-6
**The Canada-United States Free Trade Agreement:
The Global Impact***
Jeffrey J. Schott and Murray G. Smith, editors
1988   ISBN 0-88132-073-0
World Agricultural Trade: Building a Consensus*
William M. Miner and Dale E. Hathaway, editors
1988   ISBN 0-88132-071-3
Japan in the World Economy*
Bela Balassa and Marcus Noland
1988   ISBN 0-88132-041-2
**America in the World Economy: A Strategy for
the 1990s***   C. Fred Bergsten
1988   ISBN 0-88132-089-7
**Managing the Dollar: From the Plaza to the
Louvre***   Yoichi Funabashi
1988, 2d. ed. 1989   ISBN 0-88132-097-8
**United States External Adjustment and the World
Economy***   William R. Cline
May 1989   ISBN 0-88132-048-X
Free Trade Areas and U.S. Trade Policy*
Jeffrey J. Schott, editor
May 1989   ISBN 0-88132-094-3
**Dollar Politics: Exchange Rate Policymaking in
the United States***
I. M. Destler and C. Randall Henning
September 1989   ISBN 0-88132-079-X
**Latin American Adjustment: How Much Has
Happened?***   John Williamson, editor
April 1990   ISBN 0-88132-125-7
**The Future of World Trade in Textiles and
Apparel***   William R. Cline
1987, 2d ed. June 1999   ISBN 0-88132-110-9
**Completing the Uruguay Round: A Results-
Oriented Approach to the GATT Trade
Negotiations***   Jeffrey J. Schott, editor
September 1990   ISBN 0-88132-130-3
**Economic Sanctions Reconsidered (2 volumes)
Economic Sanctions Reconsidered:
Supplemental Case Histories**
Gary Clyde Hufbauer, Jeffrey J. Schott, and
Kimberly Ann Elliott
1985, 2d ed. Dec. 1990   ISBN cloth 0-88132-115-X
                          ISBN paper 0-88132-105-2
**Economic Sanctions Reconsidered: History and
Current Policy**   Gary Clyde Hufbauer,
Jeffrey J. Schott, and Kimberly Ann Elliott
December 1990   ISBN cloth 0-88132-140-0
                          ISBN paper 0-88132-136-2
**Pacific Basin Developing Countries: Prospects for
the Future***   Marcus Noland
January 1991   ISBN cloth 0-88132-141-9
                          ISBN paper 0-88132-081-1

Currency Convertibility in Eastern Europe*
John Williamson, editor
October 1991   ISBN 0-88132-128-1
International Adjustment and Financing: The
Lessons of 1985-1991*   C. Fred Bergsten, editor
January 1992   ISBN 0-88132-112-5
North American Free Trade: Issues and
Recommendations*
Gary Clyde Hufbauer and Jeffrey J. Schott
April 1992   ISBN 0-88132-120-6
Narrowing the U.S. Current Account Deficit*
Alan J. Lenz/June 1992   ISBN 0-88132-103-6
The Economics of Global Warming
William R. Cline/June 1992   ISBN 0-88132-132-X
US Taxation of International Income: Blueprint
for Reform*   Gary Clyde Hufbauer,
assisted by Joanna M. van Rooij
October 1992   ISBN 0-88132-134-6
Who's Bashing Whom? Trade Conflict in High-
Technology Industries   Laura D'Andrea Tyson
November 1992   ISBN 0-88132-106-0
Korea in the World Economy*   Il SaKong
January 1993   ISBN 0-88132-183-4
Pacific Dynamism and the International
Economic System*
C. Fred Bergsten and Marcus Noland, editors
May 1993   ISBN 0-88132-196-6
Economic Consequences of Soviet Disintegration*
John Williamson, editor
May 1993   ISBN 0-88132-190-7
Reconcilable Differences? United States-Japan
Economic Conflict*
C. Fred Bergsten and Marcus Noland
June 1993   ISBN 0-88132-129-X
Does Foreign Exchange Intervention Work?
Kathryn M. Dominguez and Jeffrey A. Frankel
September 1993   ISBN 0-88132-104-4
Sizing Up U.S. Export Disincentives*
J. David Richardson
September 1993   ISBN 0-88132-107-9
NAFTA: An Assessment
Gary Clyde Hufbauer and Jeffrey J. Schott/rev. ed.
October 1993   ISBN 0-88132-199-0
Adjusting to Volatile Energy Prices
Philip K. Verleger, Jr.
November 1993   ISBN 0-88132-069-2
The Political Economy of Policy Reform
John Williamson, editor
January 1994   ISBN 0-88132-195-8
Measuring the Costs of Protection
in the United States
Gary Clyde Hufbauer and Kimberly Ann Elliott
January 1994   ISBN 0-88132-108-7
The Dynamics of Korean Economic Development*
Cho Soon/March 1994   ISBN 0-88132-162-1

Reviving the European Union*
C. Randall Henning, Eduard Hochreiter, and
Gary Clyde Hufbauer, editors
April 1994   ISBN 0-88132-208-3
China in the World Economy   Nicholas R. Lardy
April 1994   ISBN 0-88132-200-8
Greening the GATT: Trade, Environment, and
the Future   Daniel C. Esty
July 1994   ISBN 0-88132-205-9
Western Hemisphere Economic Integration*
Gary Clyde Hufbauer and Jeffrey J. Schott
July 1994   ISBN 0-88132-159-1
Currencies and Politics in the United States,
Germany, and Japan   C. Randall Henning
September 1994   ISBN 0-88132-127-3
Estimating Equilibrium Exchange Rates
John Williamson, editor
September 1994   ISBN 0-88132-076-5
Managing the World Economy: Fifty Years after
Bretton Woods   Peter B. Kenen, editor
September 1994   ISBN 0-88132-212-1
Reciprocity and Retaliation in U.S. Trade Policy
Thomas O. Bayard and Kimberly Ann Elliott
September 1994   ISBN 0-88132-084-6
The Uruguay Round: An Assessment*
Jeffrey J. Schott, assisted by Johanna W. Buurman
November 1994   ISBN 0-88132-206-7
Measuring the Costs of Protection in Japan*
Yoko Sazanami, Shujiro Urata, and Hiroki Kawai
January 1995   ISBN 0-88132-211-3
Foreign Direct Investment in the United States,
3d ed., Edward M. Graham and Paul R. Krugman
January 1995   ISBN 0-88132-204-0
The Political Economy of Korea-United States
Cooperation*
C. Fred Bergsten and Il SaKong, editors
February 1995   ISBN 0-88132-213-X
International Debt Reexamined*   William R. Cline
February 1995   ISBN 0-88132-083-8
American Trade Politics, 3d ed., I. M. Destler
April 1995   ISBN 0-88132-215-6
Managing Official Export Credits: The Quest for
a Global Regime*   John E. Ray
July 1995   ISBN 0-88132-207-5
Asia Pacific Fusion: Japan's Role in APEC*
Yoichi Funabashi
October 1995   ISBN 0-88132-224-5
Korea-United States Cooperation in the New
World Order*
C. Fred Bergsten and Il SaKong, editors
February 1996   ISBN 0-88132-226-1
Why Exports Really Matter!*   ISBN 0-88132-221-0
Why Exports Matter More!*   ISBN 0-88132-229-6
J. David Richardson and Karin Rindal
July 1995; February 1996

Fighting the Wrong Enemy: Antiglobal Activists
and Multinational Enterprises Edward M.Graham
September 2000   ISBN 0-88132-272-5
Globalization and the Perceptions of American
Workers
Kenneth F. Scheve and Matthew J. Slaughter
March 2001   ISBN 0-88132-295-4
World Capital Markets: Challenge to the G-10
Wendy Dobson and Gary Clyde Hufbauer,
assisted by Hyun Koo Cho
May 2001   ISBN 0-88132-301-2
Prospects for Free Trade in the Americas
Jeffrey J. Schott/*August 2001* ISBN 0-88132-275-X
Toward a North American Community:
Lessons from the Old World for the New
Robert A. Pastor/*August 2001* ISBN 0-88132-328-4
Measuring the Costs of Protection in Europe:
European Commercial Policy in the 2000s
Patrick A. Messerlin
September 2001   ISBN 0-88132-273-3
Job Loss from Imports: Measuring the Costs
Lori G. Kletzer
September 2001   ISBN 0-88132-296-2
No More Bashing: Building a New Japan–United
States Economic Relationship C. Fred Bergsten,
Takatoshi Ito, and Marcus Noland
October 2001   ISBN 0-88132-286-5
Why Global Commitment Really Matters!
Howard Lewis III and J. David Richardson
October 2001   ISBN 0-88132-298-9
Leadership Selection in the Major Multilaterals
Miles Kahler
November 2001   ISBN 0-88132-335-7
The International Financial Architecture:
What's New? What's Missing?   Peter Kenen
November 2001   ISBN 0-88132-297-0
Delivering on Debt Relief: From IMF Gold to
a New Aid Architecture
John Williamson and Nancy Birdsall,
with Brian Deese
April 2002   ISBN 0-88132-331-4
Imagine There's No Country: Poverty, Inequality,
and Growth in the Era of Globalization
Surjit S. Bhalla
September 2002   ISBN 0-88132-348-9
Reforming Korea's Industrial Conglomerates
Edward M. Graham
January 2003   ISBN 0-88132-337-3
Industrial Policy in an Era of Globalization:
Lessons from Asia
Marcus Noland and Howard Pack
March 2003   ISBN 0-88132-350-0
Reintegrating India with the World Economy
T. N. Srinivasan and Suresh D. Tendulkar
March 2003   ISBN 0-88132-280-6

After the Washington Consensus:
Restarting Growth and Reform
in Latin America   Pedro-Pablo Kuczynski
and John Williamson, editors
March 2003   ISBN 0-88132-347-0
The Decline of US Labor Unions and
the Role of Trade   Robert E. Baldwin
June 2003   ISBN 0-88132-341-1
Can Labor Standards Improve
under Globalization?
Kimberly Ann Elliott and Richard B. Freeman
June 2003   ISBN 0-88132-332-2
Crimes and Punishments? Retaliation
under the WTO   Robert Z. Lawrence
October 2003   ISBN 0-88132-359-4
Inflation Targeting in the World Economy
Edwin M. Truman
October 2003   ISBN 0-88132-345-4
Foreign Direct Investment and Tax
Competition   John H. Mutti
November 2003   ISBN 0-88132-352-7
Has Globalization Gone Far Enough?
The Costs of Fragmented Markets
Scott Bradford and Robert Z. Lawrence
February 2004   ISBN 0-88132-349-7
Food Regulation and Trade:
Toward a Safe and Open Global System
Tim Josling, Donna Roberts, and David Orden
March 2004   ISBN 0-88132-346-2
Controlling Currency Mismatches in
Emerging Markets
Morris Goldstein and Philip Turner
April 2004   ISBN 0-88132-360-8
Free Trade Agreements: US Strategies
and Priorities   Jeffrey J. Schott, editor
April 2004   ISBN 0-88132-361-6
Trade Policy and Global Poverty
William R. Cline
June 2004   ISBN 0-88132-365-9
Bailouts or Bail-ins? Responding
to Financial Crises in Emerging Economies
Nouriel Roubini and Brad Setser
August 2004   ISBN 0-88132-371-3
Transforming the European Economy
Martin Neil Baily and Jacob Kirkegaard
September 2004   ISBN 0-88132-343-8
Chasing Dirty Money: The Fight Against
Money Laundering
Peter Reuter and Edwin M. Truman
November 2004   ISBN 0-88132-370-5
The United States and the World Economy:
Foreign Economic Policy for the Next Decade
C. Fred Bergsten
January 2005   ISBN 0-88132-380-2

Does Foreign Direct Investment Promote
Development? Theodore Moran, Edward
M. Graham, and Magnus Blomström, editors
April 2005 ISBN 0-88132-381-0
American Trade Politics, 4th ed.
I. M. Destler
June 2005 ISBN 0-88132-382-9
Why Does Immigration Divide America?
Public Finance and Political Opposition
to Open Borders
Gordon Hanson
August 2005 ISBN 0-88132-400-0
Reforming the US Corporate Tax
Gary Clyde Hufbauer and Paul L. E. Grieco
September 2005 ISBN 0-88132-384-5
The United States as a Debtor Nation
William R. Cline
September 2005 ISBN 0-88132-399-3

SPECIAL REPORTS

1 **Promoting World Recovery: A Statement**
   on Global Economic Strategy*
   by 26 Economists from Fourteen Countries
   December 1982 ISBN 0-88132-013-7
2 **Prospects for Adjustment in Argentina,**
   Brazil, and Mexico: Responding to the
   Debt Crisis* John Williamson, editor
   June 1983 ISBN 0-88132-016-1
3 **Inflation and Indexation: Argentina, Brazil,**
   and Israel* John Williamson, editor
   March 1985 ISBN 0-88132-037-4
4 **Global Economic Imbalances***
   C. Fred Bergsten, editor
   March 1986 ISBN 0-88132-042-0
5 **African Debt and Financing***
   Carol Lancaster and John Williamson, eds.
   May 1986 ISBN 0-88132-044-7
6 **Resolving the Global Economic Crisis:**
   After Wall Street*
   by Thirty-three Economists from Thirteen
   Countries
   December 1987 ISBN 0-88132-070-6
7 **World Economic Problems***
   Kimberly Ann Elliott/John Williamson, editors
   April 1988 ISBN 0-88132-055-2
   Reforming World Agricultural Trade*
   by Twenty-nine Professionals from Seventeen
   Countries/*1988* ISBN 0-88132-088-9
8 **Economic Relations Between the United**
   States and Korea: Conflict or Cooperation?*
   Thomas O. Bayard and Soogil Young, editors
   January 1989 ISBN 0-88132-068-4

9 **Whither APEC? The Progress to Date and**
   Agenda for the Future* C. Fred Bergsten,
   editor
   October 1997 ISBN 0-88132-248-2
10 **Economic Integration of the Korean**
   Peninsula Marcus Noland, editor
   January 1998 ISBN 0-88132-255-5
11 **Restarting Fast Track*** Jeffrey J. Schott, editor
   April 1998 ISBN 0-88132-259-8
12 **Launching New Global Trade Talks:**
   An Action Agenda Jeffrey J. Schott, editor
   September 1998 ISBN 0-88132-266-0
13 **Japan's Financial Crisis and Its Parallels to**
   US Experience
   Ryoichi Mikitani and Adam S. Posen, eds.
   September 2000 ISBN 0-88132-289-X
14 **The Ex-Im Bank in the 21st Century: A New**
   Approach Gary Clyde Hufbauer
   and Rita M. Rodriguez, editors
   January 2001 ISBN 0-88132-300-4
15 **The Korean Diaspora in the World Economy**
   C. Fred Bergsten and Inbom Choi, eds.
   January 2003 ISBN 0-88132-358-6
16 **Dollar Overvaluation and the World**
   Economy
   C. Fred Bergsten and John Williamson, eds.
   February 2003 ISBN 0-88132-351-9
17 **Dollar Adjustment: How Far? Against What?**
   C. Fred Bergsten and John Williamson, editors
   November 2004 ISBN 0-88132-378-0
18 **The Euro at Five: Ready for a Global Role?**
   Adam S. Posen, editor
   April 2005 ISBN 0-88132-380-2

WORKS IN PROGRESS

NAFTA Revisited: Achievements
and Challenges
Gary Clyde Hufbauer and Jeffrey J. Schott
Making the Rules: Case Studies on
US Trade Negotiation, Vols. 1 and 2
Robert Z. Lawrence, Charan Devereaux,
and Michael Watkins
High Technology and the Globalization
of America
Catherine L. Mann
Germany and the World Economy:
Reform in a Rich Country
Adam S. Posen
Global Forces, American Faces: US Economic
Globalization at the Grass Roots
J. David Richardson
Future of Chinese Exchange Rates
Morris Goldstein and Nicholas R. Lardy

DISTRIBUTORS OUTSIDE THE UNITED STATES

Australia, New Zealand,
and Papua New Guinea
D.A. Information Services
648 Whitehorse Road
Mitcham, Victoria 3132, Australia
tel: 61-3-9210-7777
fax: 61-3-9210-7788
email: service@adadirect.com.au
www.dadirect.com.au

United Kingdom and Europe
(including Russia and Turkey)
The Eurospan Group
3 Henrietta Street, Covent Garden
London WC2E 8LU England
tel: 44-20-7240-0856
fax: 44-20-7379-0609
www.eurospan.co.uk

Japan and the Republic of Korea
United Publishers Services Ltd.
1-32-5, Higashi-shinagawa,
Shinagawa-ku, Tokyo 140-0002 JAPAN
tel: 81-3-5479-7251
fax: 81-3-5479-7307
info@ups.co.jp
For trade accounts only.
Individuals will find IIE books in
leading Tokyo bookstores.

Canada
Renouf Bookstore
5369 Canotek Road, Unit 1
Ottawa, Ontario KlJ 9J3, Canada
tel: 613-745-2665
fax: 613-745-7660
www.renoufbooks.com

India, Bangladesh, Nepal, and Sri Lanka
Viva Books Pvt.
Mr. Vinod Vasishtha
4325/3, Ansari Rd.
Daryaganj, New Delhi-110002
India
tel: 91-11-327-9280
fax: 91-11-326-7224
email: vinod.viva@gndel.globalnet. ems.vsnl.
net.in

Southeast Asia (Brunei, Burma, Cambodia,
Malaysia, Indonesia,
the Philippines, Singapore, Thailand
Taiwan, and Vietnam)
APAC Publishers Services
70 Bedemeer Road #05-03
Hiap Huat House
Singapore 339940
tel: 65-684-47333
fax: 65-674-78916

Visit our Web site at:
www.iie.com
E-mail orders to:
orders@iie.com